Decision Making, edition 1
Copyright © 2017 Giacomo Bonanno, all rights reserved
CreateSpace Independent Publishing Platform; 1st edition (December 7, 2017)
https://www.amazon.com/gp/product/1979856958

ISBN-13: 978-1979856959
ISBN-10: 1979856958

Giacomo Bonanno is Professor of Economics at the
University of California, Davis
http://faculty.econ.ucdavis.edu/faculty/bonanno/

Preface

Two years ago I wrote an open access textbook on Game Theory (http://faculty.econ.ucdavis.edu/faculty/bonanno/GT_Book.html). Encouraged by the many expressions of appreciation from students and scholars around the world, I decided to write a second textbook: this time on Decision Making. I have been teaching an upper-division undergraduate class in Decision Making at the University of California, Davis for many years and was not able to find a suitable textbook. Hopefully this book will fill this gap.

I tried to write the book in such a way that it would be accessible to anybody with minimum knowledge of mathematics (high-school level algebra and some elementary notions of set theory and probability, which are reviewed in the book). The book is appropriate for an upper-division undergraduate class, although some parts of it might be useful also to graduate students.

I have followed the same format as the Game Theory book by concluding each chapter with a collection of exercises that are grouped according to that chapter's sections. Complete and detailed answers for each exercise are given in the last section of each chapter. The book contains a total of 121 fully solved exercises.

I expect that there will be some typos and (hopefully, minor) mistakes. If you come across any typos or mistakes, I would be grateful if you could inform me: I can be reached at gfbonanno@ucdavis.edu. I will maintain an updated version of the book on my web page at

http://www.econ.ucdavis.edu/faculty/bonanno/

I also intend to add, some time in the future, a further collection of exercises with detailed solutions. Details will appear on my web page.

I am very grateful to Elise Tidrick for designing the cover of the book, for meticulously going through each chapter of the book and for suggesting numerous improvements. Her insightful and constructive comments have considerably enhanced this book.

I would like to thank Mathias Legrand for making the latex template used for this book available for free (the template was downloaded from http://www.latextemplates.com/template/the-legrand-orange-book).

Contents

1 Introduction 9

I Decision Problems

2 Outcomes and Preferences 15
2.1 Preference relations **15**
2.2 Rational choice under certainty **19**
2.3 Why completeness and transitivity? **21**
2.4 Exercises **23**
2.4.1 Exercises for Section 2.1: Preference relations 23
2.4.2 Exercises for Section 2.2: Rational choice under certainty 24
2.5 Solutions to Exercises **25**

3 States and Acts 27
3.1 Uncertainty, states, outcomes and acts **27**
3.2 Dominance **29**
3.3 MaxiMin and LexiMin **34**
3.3.1 MaxiMin 34
3.3.2 LexiMin 35
3.4 Regret: a first attempt **36**
3.5 Exercises **38**
3.5.1 Exercises for Section 3.1: Uncertainty, states and acts 38

3.5.2	Exercises for Section 3.2: Dominance	38
3.5.3	Exercises for Section 3.3: MaxiMin and LexiMin	39
3.5.4	Exercises for Section 3.4: Regret: a first attempt	39
3.6	**Solutions to Exercises**	**40**

4 Decision Trees 43

4.1	**Decision trees**	**43**
4.2	**Money lotteries and risk neutrality**	**48**
4.3	**Backward induction**	**49**
4.4	**Beyond money lotteries and risk neutrality**	**60**
4.5	**Exercises**	**61**
4.5.1	Exercises for Section 4.1: Decision Trees	61
4.5.2	Exercises for Section 4.2: Money lotteries and risk neutrality	62
4.5.3	Exercises for Section 4.3: Backward induction	63
4.6	**Solutions to Exercises**	**63**

II Uncertainty and Decision Making

5 Expected Utility Theory 71

5.1	**Money lotteries and attitudes to risk**	**71**
5.2	**Expected utility: theorems**	**73**
5.3	**Expected utility: the axioms**	**81**
5.4	**Exercises**	**89**
5.4.1	Exercises for Section 5.1: Money lotteries and attitudes to risk	89
5.4.2	Exercises for Section 5.2: Expected utility theory	90
5.4.3	Exercises for Section 5.3: Expected utility axioms	92
5.5	**Solutions to Exercises**	**93**

6 Applications of Expected Utility 99

6.1	**States and acts revisited**	**99**
6.2	**Decision trees revisited**	**101**
6.3	**Regret**	**105**
6.4	**The Hurwicz index of pessimism**	**109**
6.5	**Exercises**	**112**
6.5.1	Exercises for Section 6.1: States and acts revisited	112
6.5.2	Exercises for Section 6.2: Decision trees revisited	114
6.5.3	Exercises for Section 6.3: Regret	115
6.5.4	Exercises for Section 6.4: The Hurwicz index of pessimism	116
6.6	**Solutions to Exercises**	**118**

7 Conditional Reasoning 127

7.1 Sets and probability: brief review — 127
7.1.1 Sets 127
7.1.2 Probability 129
7.2 Conditional thinking — 131
7.2.1 The natural frequencies approach 132
7.2.2 Conditional probability 136
7.3 Simpson's paradox — 142
7.4 Exercises — 144
7.4.1 Exercises for Section 7.1: Sets and probability 144
7.4.2 Exercises for Section 7.2: Conditional thinking 145
7.5 Solutions to Exercises — 148

8 Information and Beliefs 155

8.1 Uncertainty and information — 155
8.2 Updating beliefs — 157
8.3 Belief revision — 160
8.4 Information and truth — 163
8.5 Exercises — 165
8.5.1 Exercises for Section 8.1: Uncertainty and information ... 165
8.5.2 Exercises for Section 8.2: Updating beliefs 166
8.5.3 Exercises for Section 8.3: Belief revision 167
8.6 Solutions to Exercises — 168

9 The Value of Information 173

9.1 When is information potentially valuable? — 173
9.2 The value of information when outcomes are sums of money — 179
9.2.1 Perfect information and risk neutrality 179
9.2.2 Perfect information and risk aversion 183
9.2.3 Imperfect information 186
9.3 The general case — 192
9.4 Different sources of information — 197
9.5 Exercises — 203
9.5.1 Exercises for Section 9.1: When is information potentially valuable? .. 203
9.5.2 Exercises for Section 9.2: The value of information when outcomes are sums of money 204
9.5.3 Exercises for Section 9.3: The general case 209
9.5.4 Exercises for Section 9.4: Different sources of information 210
9.6 Solutions to Exercises — 210

III Thinking about Future Selves

10 Intertemporal Choice ... 221
10.1 Introduction — 221
10.2 Present value and discounting — 222
10.3 Exponential discounting — 225
10.3.1 Time consistency — 229
10.4 Hyperbolic discounting — 232
10.4.1 Interpretation of the parameter β — 234
10.5 Dealing with time inconsistency — 236
10.6 Exercises — 240
10.6.1 Exercises for Section 10.2: Present value and discounting — 240
10.6.2 Exercises for Section 10.3: Exponential discounting — 241
10.6.3 Exercises for Section 10.4: Hyperbolic discounting — 241
10.6.4 Exercises for Section 10.5: Dealing with time inconsistency — 242
10.7 Solutions to Exercises — 244

IV Group Decision Making

11 Aggregation of Preferences ... 253
11.1 Social preference functions — 253
11.2 Arrow's Impossibility Theorem — 258
11.3 Illustration of the proof of Arrow's theorem — 266
11.4 Application of Arrow's theorem to individual choice — 273
11.5 Exercises — 275
11.5.1 Exercises for Section 11.1: Social preference functions — 275
11.5.2 Exercises for Section 11.2: Arrow's impossibility theorem — 276
11.5.3 Exercises for Section 11.3: Illustration of the proof of Arrow's theorem — 277
11.5.4 Exercises for Section 11.4: Application of Arrow's theorem to individual choice — 278
11.6 Solutions to Exercises — 278

12 Misrepresentation of Preferences ... 285
12.1 Social choice functions — 285
12.2 Strategic voting — 288
12.3 The Gibbard-Satterthwaite theorem — 296
12.4 Illustration of the proof of the Gibbard-Satterthwaite theorem — 298
12.5 Exercises — 301
12.5.1 Exercises for Section 12.1: Social choice functions — 301
12.5.2 Exercises for Section 12.2: Strategic voting — 302

	12.5.3 Exercises for Section 12.3: The Gibbard-Satterthwaite theorem	306
12.6	**Solutions to Exercises**	**307**

V Biases in Decision Making

13 Biases in Decision Making 315

13.1	Introduction	315
13.2	Incomplete preferences and manipulation of choice	316
13.3	Gains versus losses	318
13.4	Framing	320
13.5	The confirmation bias	323
13.6	The psychology of decision making	325

Index 327

1. Introduction

Life is made up of a never-ending sequence of decisions. Many decisions – such as what to watch on television or what to eat for breakfast – are rather unimportant. Other decisions – such as what career to pursue, whether or not to invest all of one's savings in the purchase of a house – can have a major impact on one's life. This book is concerned with Decision Making, which the Oxford Dictionary defines as "the process of deciding about something important". We will not attempt to address the issue of what decisions are to be considered "important". After all, what one person might consider an unimportant decision may be viewed by another individual as very important. What we are interested in is the process of making decisions and what it means to be a "rational" decision maker.

In the next chapter we define an action a to be *rational* if the outcome that the decision maker (from now on referred to as 'the DM') believes to be associated with a is considered by the DM to be at least as good as the outcome that the DM believes to be associated with any alternative available action. This definition makes it clear that we are focusing on decisions concerning *actions*. Actions produce consequences or *outcomes* and when deciding what action to take, the DM must first try to predict what outcome(s) will be associated with every available action. **Chapter 2** deals with decisions under *certainty*, that is, with situations where the DM has no uncertainty about what the consequences of each action will be. In such situations, choosing among actions is equivalent to choosing among outcomes and the only issue is how to rank outcomes. Chapter 2 discusses the notion of a "rational ranking" of outcomes.

It is rare, however, that one finds himself/herself facing decisions under certainty. Most of the time the outcome of an action is also influenced by external factors that are outside the decision maker's control, such as the side effects of a new drug, or the future price of real estate, or the occurrence of a natural phenomenon (such as a flood or fire or earthquake). We call these external factor *states*. **Chapter 3** and **Chapter 4** deal with the issue of how to represent decision problems under *uncertainty*. In the state-outcome representation (Chapter 3) one associates with every available action a set of outcomes, one for every state. The uncertainty concerns what state will actually materialize. Chapter 3 deals with decision criteria that do not require assigning probabilities to the states. Chapter 4 introduces an alternative representation of decision problems under uncertainty that makes use of *decision trees*.

Chapter 5 and **Chapter 6** deal with situations where the *DM* is able to quantify his/her uncertainty by assigning probabilities to the states. Chapter 5 introduces the theory of *expected utility*, which tries to capture the notion of how to "rationally" rank uncertain prospects and Chapter 6 applies the theory to the state-outcome representation and the decision-tree representation of decision problems under uncertainty.

Chapter 7 and **Chapter 8** are concerned with the issue of information and how to adjust one's beliefs after the receipt of new information. For example, the information could be the result of a blood test or the opinion of an expert or the outcome of an experiment. Chapter 7 deals with conditional reasoning and introduces two equivalent methods: the natural frequencies approach and Bayes' rule. Chapter 8 defines information more precisely and distinguishes between "belief updating" and "belief revision". The former takes place when the information received is not surprising, in the sense that the corresponding event was assigned positive probability in the initial beliefs. The latter is more general and also includes situations where one is faced with information represented by zero-probability events.

Chapter 9 addresses the issue of when information is useful and whether one can assign a value to potential information. For example, how much should one be willing to pay for the opinion of an expert?

The analysis in the first nine chapters deals with decision problems where the outcomes are assumed to take place at a point in time and the *DM*'s current decision has no effect on what options will be available to her in the future. **Chapter 10** addresses the issue of *intertemporal choice* where decisions involve costs and benefits realized at different points in time and thus require comparing one's own welfare at some time (in the present or in the future) with one's own welfare at a later time.

Up to Chapter 10, the focus is on individual decision making. **Chapter 11** and **Chapter 12** turn to *collective decision making*. Groups of individuals, or societies, are also involved in decision making. The group could be the board of directors of a company, or the members of a club, or the residents of a city, or indeed the entire nation (as in the case of general elections). There are two issues that arise in this context. The first is the issue of *preference aggregation*: can the (often conflicting) opinions of the different members of a group be aggregated into a single ranking of the alternatives (to be thought of as "the group's ranking") in a way that does not violate some "natural" requirements? This is the object of Chapter 11. The second issue is whether the decision procedure (or voting rule) employed to arrive at a final choice for society is subject to manipulation, in the sense that the members of the group have an incentive to misrepresent their preferences. This is the issue of *strategic voting* and is the object of Chapter 12.

Chapter 13 closes with a brief overview of biases in decision making and judgment formation. The analysis of the first twelve chapters is based on the notion of rationality: how should a rational decision maker make her decisions or form her judgments? As a matter of fact, individuals often fail to conform to principles of rationality. Psychologists and behavioral economists have uncovered systematic errors that people make in their decision making. Chapter 13 discusses some of these errors and provides a list of references for the reader who is interested in pursuing this topic further.

At the end of each section of each of Chapters 2-12 the reader is invited to test his/her understanding of the concepts introduced in that section by attempting some exercises. In order not to break the flow of the exposition, the exercises are collected in a section at the end of the chapter. Complete and detailed answers for each exercise are given in the last section of each chapter. In total, the book contains 121 fully solved exercises. Attempting to solve the exercises is an integral part of learning the material covered in this book.

The book was written in a way that should be accessible to anyone with minimum knowledge of mathematics: high-school level algebra and some elementary notions of set theory and probability, which are reviewed at the beginning of Chapter 7.

The spacing in this book does not necessarily follow conventional formatting standards. Rather, it is the editor's intention that each step is made plain in order for the student to easily follow along and quickly discover where he/she may grapple with a complete understanding of the material.

Decision Problems

2 Outcomes and Preferences 15
- 2.1 Preference relations
- 2.2 Rational choice under certainty
- 2.3 Why completeness and transitivity?
- 2.4 Exercises
- 2.5 Solutions to Exercises

3 States and Acts 27
- 3.1 Uncertainty, states, outcomes and acts
- 3.2 Dominance
- 3.3 MaxiMin and LexiMin
- 3.4 Regret: a first attempt
- 3.5 Exercises
- 3.6 Solutions to Exercises

4 Decision Trees 43
- 4.1 Decision trees
- 4.2 Money lotteries and risk neutrality
- 4.3 Backward induction
- 4.4 Beyond money lotteries and risk neutrality
- 4.5 Exercises
- 4.6 Solutions to Exercises

2. Outcomes and Preferences

2.1 Preference relations

When we are faced with a decision among alternative courses of action, we need to consider the possible consequences of each action, that is, we need to take into account what the outcome of each action will be. Our objective will then be to choose that action that will bring about an outcome that we consider to be best. Thus, in order to make a "rational choice" of a course of action, we first need to come up with a ranking of the possible outcomes.

Recall the following notation from set theory: $x \in S$ means that x is an element of the set S (usually sets are denoted by capital letters and elements by lower-case letters); $S \subseteq T$ means that S is a *subset* of T, that is, every element of S is also an element of T (for example, if $S = \{a,b,c\}$ and $T = \{a,b,c,d,e\}$, then S is a subset of T).

We will denote by O the set of possible outcomes and assume throughout that it is a finite set: $O = \{o_1, o_2, \ldots, o_m\}$ ($m \geq 1$). $O \times O$ denotes the *Cartesian product* of the set O with itself, that is, the set of *ordered* pairs (o, o') with $o, o' \in O$. Note the importance of the word 'ordered': (o, o') and (o', o) are two *different* pairs.

Definition 2.1.1 A *binary relation* R on a set O is a set of ordered pairs of elements of O, that is, $R \subseteq O \times O$. R is said to be *complete* if, for all $o, o' \in O$ either $(o, o') \in R$ or $(o', o) \in R$ or both. R is *transitive* if for any three elements $o_1, o_2, o_3 \in O$, if it is the case that $(o_1, o_2) \in R$ and $(o_2, o_3) \in R$ then it is also the case that $(o_1, o_3) \in R$.

For example, let $O = \{a, b, c, d, e\}$ and let $R = \{(a,c), (a,d), (c,d), (e,a), (e,c), (e,d)\}$. Then R is *not* complete because neither (a,b) nor (b,a) are in R. On the other hand, R *is* transitive because:

(1) both (a,c) and (c,d) are in R and so is (a,d),
(2) both (e,a) and (a,c) are in R and so is (e,c),
(3) both (e,a) and (a,d) are in R and so is (e,d),
(4) both (e,c) and (c,d) are in R and so is (e,d).

Note that in propositional logic the statement "if p then q" is true if either both p and q are true or p is false (p is called the *antecedent* and q the *consequent*). Thus, in our example, the statement "if $(a,c) \in R$ and $(c,e) \in R$ then $(a,e) \in R$" is true because the antecedent "$(a,c) \in R$ and $(c,e) \in R$" is false (since, while it is true that $(a,c) \in R$, it is false that $(c,e) \in R$ and thus the conjunction of the two statements is false).

> (R) If R is a binary relation on the set O then it is common to express the fact that o is related to o' (according to R) either by writing $(o, o') \in R$ or by writing oRo'.

We use binary relations very often in our daily lives, for example when we rank people according to age ("Ann is older than Bob"), when we compare courses in terms of difficulty ("organic chemistry is more difficult than introductory economics"), when we compare commodities in terms of prices ("a Telsa electric car is more expensive than a Toyota Prius"), etc. Note that, in general, the relation "is older than" is not complete, because it may be that two individuals were born on the same day and at the same time and thus neither of them is older than the other. On the other hand, the relation "is older than or just as old as" is complete (on any set of individuals). Indeed, if one starts with the relation "is older than or just as old as" then one can derive from it the relation "is older than" by defining it as follows: "x is older than y" if (1) "x is older than or just as old as y" and (2) it is not the case that "y is older than or just as old as x". Similarly, from the "is older than or just as old as" relation one can obtain the "is just as old as" relation by defining "x is just as old as y" if (1) "x is older than or just as old as y" and also (2) "y is older than or just as old as x".

> (R) The relations we are interested in are *preference relations* on sets of outcomes. Instead of using the symbol R for such relations we shall use the symbol $\succsim$ and the interpretation of $o \succsim o'$ is that the individual under consideration deems outcome o to be *at least as good as* outcome o', that is, either she thinks that o is better than o' – i.e., she prefers o to o' – or she thinks that o is just as good as o' – i.e., she is indifferent between o and o'.

2.1 Preference relations

Definition 2.1.2 A preference relation $\succsim$ on a set of outcomes O is called *rational* if it is complete and transitive.

Why do we impose completeness and transitivity as requirements for rationality? We postpone a discussion of this issue to Section 2.3.

We shall use the symbol $\succsim$ for "at least as good as", the symbol $\succ$ for "better than" and the symbol $\sim$ for "just as good as". Table 2.1 summarizes the notation.

Notation	Interpretation
$o \succsim o'$	The individual considers outcome o to be *at least as good as o'* (that is, either better than or just as good as)
$o \succ o'$	The individual considers outcome o to be *better than o'* (that is, she prefers o to o')
$o \sim o'$	The individual considers outcome o to be *just as good as o'* (that is, she is indifferent between o and o')

Table 2.1: Notation for preference relations

Definition 2.1.3 We take $\succsim$ to be the basic relation and extract from it the other two relations $\succ$ and $\sim$ as follows:
- $o \succ o'$ if and only if $o \succsim o'$ and $o' \not\succsim o$
 (that is, o is preferred to o' if o is considered to be at least as good as o' but it is not the case that o' is considered to be at least as good as o),
- $o \sim o'$ if and only if $o \succsim o'$ and $o' \succsim o$
 (that is, the individual is indifferent between o and o' if she considers o to be at least as good as o' and she also considers o' to be at least as good as o).

(R) Let $\succsim$ be a complete and transitive "weak preference" relation on a set O. Then the two derived relations $\succ$ (for strict preference) and $\sim$ (for indifference) are also transitive (that is, for any three outcomes o_1, o_2 and o_3, if $o_1 \succ o_2$ and $o_2 \succ o_3$ then $o_1 \succ o_3$ and if $o_1 \sim o_2$ and $o_2 \sim o_3$ then $o_1 \sim o_3$: see Exercises 2.3 and 2.4 in Section 2.4.1).

There are (at least) four ways of representing, or expressing, a complete and transitive preference relation over (or ranking of) a set of outcomes. For example, suppose that $O = \{o_1, o_2, o_3, o_4, o_5\}$ and that we want to represent the following ranking (expressing the preferences of a given individual): o_3 is better than o_5, which is just as good as o_1, o_1 is better than o_4, which, in turn, is better than o_2 (thus, o_3 is the best outcome and o_2 is the worst outcome). We can represent this ranking in one of the following ways.

- As a subset of $O \times O$:

$$\begin{aligned}&\{(o_1,o_1),(o_1,o_2),(o_1,o_4),(o_1,o_5)\\&(o_2,o_2),\\&(o_3,o_1),(o_3,o_2),(o_3,o_3),(o_3,o_4),(o_3,o_5),\\&(o_4,o_2),(o_4,o_4),\\&(o_5,o_1),(o_5,o_2),(o_5,o_4),(o_5,o_5)\}\end{aligned}$$

- By using the notation of Table 2.1: $o_3 \succ o_5 \sim o_1 \succ o_4 \succ o_2$.
- By listing the outcomes in a column, starting with the best at the top and proceeding down to the worst, thus using the convention that if outcome o is listed above outcome o' then o is preferred to o', while if o and o' are written next to each other (on the same row), then they are considered to be just as good:

$$\begin{array}{rl}\text{best} & o_3 \\ & o_1, o_5 \\ & o_4 \\ \text{worst} & o_2\end{array}$$

- By assigning a number to each outcome, with the convention that *if the number assigned to o is greater than the number assigned to o'* then o is preferred to o', and if two outcomes are assigned the same number then they are considered to be just as good. For example, we could choose the following numbers:

$$\begin{array}{ccccc} o_1 & o_2 & o_3 & o_4 & o_5 \\ 6 & 1 & 8 & 2 & 6 \end{array}.$$

Such an assignment of numbers is called a *utility function*. A useful way of thinking of utility is as an "index of satisfaction": the higher the index the better the outcome; however, this suggestion is just to aid memory and should be taken with a grain of salt because a utility function *does not measure anything* and, furthermore, as explained below, the actual numbers used as utility indices are completely arbitrary.[1]

Definition 2.1.4 Given a complete and transitive ranking $\succsim$ of a finite set of outcomes O, a function $U : O \to \mathbb{R}$ (where $\mathbb{R}$ denotes the set of real numbers)[a] is said to be an *ordinal utility function that represents the ranking* $\succsim$ if, for every two outcomes o and o', $U(o) > U(o')$ if and only if $o \succ o'$ and $U(o) = U(o')$ if and only if $o \sim o'$. The number $U(o)$ is called the *utility of outcome o*.[b]

[a] The notation $f : X \to Y$ is used to denote a function which associates with every $x \in X$ an element $y = f(x)$ with $y \in Y$.
[b] Thus, $o \succsim o'$ if and only if $U(o) \geq U(o')$.

---

[1] Note that assigning a utility of 1 to an outcome o does not mean that o is the "first choice". Indeed, in this example a utility of 1 is assigned to the worst outcome: o_2 is the worst outcome because it has the lowest utility (which happens to be 1, in this example).

2.2 Rational choice under certainty

 Note that the statement "for Alice the utility of Mexican food is 10" is in itself a meaningless statement; on the other hand, what would be a meaningful statement is "for Alice the utility of Mexican food is 10 and the utility of Japanese food is 5", because such a statement conveys the information that she prefers Mexican food to Japanese food. However, the two numbers 10 and 5 have no other meaning besides the fact that 10 is greater than 5: for example, we cannot (and should not) infer from these numbers that she considers Mexican food twice as good as Japanese food. The reason for this is that we could have expressed the same fact, namely that she prefers Mexican food to Japanese food, by assigning utility 100 to Mexican food and -25 to Japanese food, or with any other two numbers (as long as the number assigned to Mexican food is larger than the number assigned to Japanese food).

It follows from the above remark that there is an infinite number of utility functions that represent the same ranking. For instance, the following are equivalent ways of representing the ranking $o_3 \succ o_1 \succ o_2 \sim o_4$ (f, g and h are three out of the many possible utility functions):

outcome → utility function ↓	o_1	o_2	o_3	o_4
f	5	2	10	2
g	0.8	0.7	1	0.7
h	27	1	100	1

Utility functions are a particularly convenient way of representing preferences and we shall often make use of them.

> Test your understanding of the concepts introduced in this section, by going through the exercises in Section 2.4.1 at the end of this chapter.

2.2 Rational choice under certainty

By "choice under certainty" we mean a situation where the decision maker – from now on referred to as "the *DM*"– has no doubt as to what outcome will occur after each of the actions that are available to her. In other words, she is certain that if she takes action a_1 then the outcome will be o_1, if she takes action a_2 then the outcome will be o_2, etc. For example, if the *DM* is driving on the freeway and sees a sign that says "Exit 7 to 34th Street in 1 mile, Exit 8 to 59th Street in 2 miles" then the *DM* can be confident that if she takes Exit 7 then she will bring about the outcome where she finds herself on 34th Street and if she takes Exit 8 then she will bring about the outcome where she finds herself on 59th Street.

In our daily lives it is possible – but rare – that we find ourselves operating under conditions of certainty. Most of the time we make decisions under conditions of *un*certainty, where – as far as we know – an available action can lead to several possible outcomes. For example, if we are faced with the decision whether or not to have surgery to remedy an injury, we don't know if the surgery will be successful or not and we don't know if the alternative course of action of not having surgery will lead to spontaneous healing or to a worsening of the pain. The topic of choice under uncertainty is thus more relevant[2] and will be the main focus of the book. In this section we briefly discuss what it means to act rationally under conditions of certainty.

When the *DM* is able to associate a unique outcome to each of the actions available to her, choosing an action is equivalent to choosing an outcome. Assuming that the *DM* has a rational (that is, a complete and transitive) ranking of the outcomes then the following is a natural definition of "rational choice".

Definition 2.2.1 Let A be the set of actions available to the *DM* and let O be the corresponding set of outcomes.[a] We say that action a is a *rational choice* for the *DM* if, letting o be the outcome that the *DM* believes to be associated with a, there is no action $a' \in A$ such that, letting o' be the outcome that the *DM* believes to be associated with a', $o' \succ o$.

[a]That is, $o \in O$ if and only if there is an action $a \in A$ such that o is the outcome that – according to the *DM*'s beliefs – is associated with a.

Thus, an available action a is a rational choice if the outcome that the *DM* believes to be associated with a is considered by the *DM* to be at least as good as the outcome that the *DM* believes to be associated with any alternative available action.

ⓇNote that we have used the expression "the outcome that the *DM believes to be associated* with a" rather than "the outcome *associated* with a" because the *DM* might have erroneous beliefs, that is, she might believe that action a will lead to outcome o, when in fact it will lead to a different outcome o'. In order to assess the rationality of a choice, what matters is what the *DM* believes, not what is actually true.

---

[2]As the French Philosopher Francois-Marie Arouet (1694 - 1778) – more commonly known by his pen name Voltaire – put it, "Doubt is not a pleasant condition, but certainty is an absurd one". The quote appeared in a letter to Frederick II of Prussia in 1767 (see: https://www.causeweb.org/cause/resources/library/r1779/)

2.3 Why completeness and transitivity?

For example, suppose that Ann is about to take a shower and there are two faucets, one labeled 'hot water' and the other 'cold water', and she prefers taking a hot shower to taking a cold shower. Suppose also that the faucets are mislabeled and Ann is unaware of this. Then it would be objectively (or causally) true that "if Ann turns on the faucet labeled 'hot water' she will get cold water"; however, she cannot be judged to be irrational if she holds the belief "if I turn on the faucet labeled 'hot water' I will get hot water" and acts on this belief by turning on the faucet labeled 'hot water'. What matters when judging the rationality of a choice is not what would in fact be the case but what the agent believes would be the case.[3]

> (R) If we represent the *DM*'s preferences by means of a utility function (see Definition 2.1.4) then the expression "choosing a best outcome (that is, an outcome which is at least as good as any other outcome)" can be equivalently stated as "choosing an outcome that has the largest utility". Thus, it is common, in textbooks and scholarly articles, to find the expression "a rational agent makes a choice that maximizes his utility". It should be noted, however, that – while this statement may sound deep to an outsider – it is merely a restatement, using the notion of utility function, of Definition 2.2.1: "maximizing utility" means nothing more (or less) than "choosing a best outcome".

> Test your understanding of the concepts introduced in this section, by going through the exercises in Section 2.4.2 at the end of this chapter.

2.3 Why completeness and transitivity?

In Definition 2.1.2 we imposed completeness and transitivity as requirements of rationality for preferences. Why such requirements?

Let us start with transitivity. Suppose that Don's preferences are not transitive; in particular he prefers coffee (C) to tea (T), tea to orange juice (O) and orange juice to coffee: $C \succ T$, $T \succ O$ and $O \succ C$. Vlad gives Don a cup of tea and tells him "if you wish, you can upgrade to coffee in exchange for a small sum of money"; since Don prefers coffee to tea, he will be willing to pay a small sum, say 10 cents, to exchange tea for coffee. Vlad takes away the tea and brings him coffee and says "if you wish, you can upgrade to orange juice in exchange for a small sum of money"; since Don prefers orange juice to coffee, he will be willing to pay a small sum, say 10 cents, to exchange coffee for orange juice. Vlad takes away the coffee and brings him orange juice and says "if you wish, you can

---

[3] Should we then accept *any* beliefs as "reasonable" or "rational"? For example, consider the following case. In 2011 Harold Camping, president of Family Radio (a California-based Christian radio station), predicted that Rapture (the taking up into heaven of God's elect people) would take place on May 21, 2011. In light of this prediction some of his followers gave up their jobs, sold their homes and spent large sums promoting Camping's claims (http://en.wikipedia.org/wiki/Harold_Camping_Rapture_prediction). Did these people act rationally? According to our Definition 2.2.1 the answer is Yes (presumably, they viewed their proselytizing as "qualifying them for Rapture", undoubtedly an outcome that they preferred to the alternative of enduring the wrath of Judgment Day). Anybody who argues that the above decision was *not* rational must be appealing to a stronger definition of rationality than Definition 2.2.1: one that denies the rationality of holding those beliefs. For our purposes, Definition 2.2.1, although very weak, is sufficient. The issue of rationality of beliefs will be taken up in Chapter 8 when dealing with how to revise one's beliefs when faced with new information.

upgrade to tea in exchange for a small sum of money"; since Don prefers tea to orange juice, he will be willing to pay a small sum, say 10 cents, to exchange orange juice for tea. Now Don is in the situation he started at, namely he has a cup of tea in front of him, but his wealth has been reduced by 30 cents! This cycle can then be repeated indefinitely, leading Don to give up a substantial amount of money. This phenomenon is called a *money pump* and if an individual's preferences are not transitive, he can be subjected to a money pump. Ruling out money pumps is an argument for imposing transitivity of preferences as a requirement of rationality.

In the above example, Don's preferences are complete: given any pair of items from the set $\{C, O, T\}$, Don is able to compare the two items and rank them (however, his ranking fails to be transitive). The lack of completeness of preferences means that there are at least two outcomes o and o' such that the *DM* is unable to rank them: he neither prefers one to the other nor is he indifferent between the two. This means that, if given a choice between o and o', the *DM* is unable to make up his mind. This situation is illustrated in the story of Buridan's ass, where a hungry donkey is placed precisely midway between two stacks of hay; since the ass will always go to ("prefers") whichever is closer, it is unable to choose between the two and dies of hunger.[4] The ability to make a choice between any two outcomes is thus considered to be a minimum requirement of rationality.

While there are good reasons to impose completeness and transitivity as requirements of rationality, it is also easy to understand how these two requirements may come to be violated in practice. Typically, outcomes can be viewed as "bundles of characteristics" and, although it may be straightforward to rank the outcomes in terms of each individual characteristic, it may be difficult to evaluate the overall desirability of one outcome versus another. For example, suppose that Sandra, a successful 30-year old woman, has received marriage proposals from three men: Alex, Brian and Charlie. There are three characteristics that are most important to Sandra in assessing the desirability of a future spouse: intelligence (the more intelligent, the better), physical attractiveness (the more attractive, the better) and annual income (the higher the income, the better). Letting 'H' stand for 'high' (or above average), 'M' for 'medium' (or average) and 'L' for 'low' (or below average), Sandra evaluates the three suitors as follows:

	Intelligence	Attractiveness	Income
Alex	H	L	M
Brian	M	H	L
Charlie	L	M	H

Each suitor is better than the other two in one dimension, but worse than one of the other two in another dimension. If Sandra is unable or unwilling to consider one characteristic as the most important one, she might decide to rank any two suitors as follows: x is better than y if x dominates y in at least two characteristics. According to this criterion, Alex is better than Brian (because he ranks higher in terms of intelligence and income), Brian is better than Charlie (because he ranks higher in terms of intelligence and attractiveness) and Charlie is better than Alex (because he ranks higher in terms of attractiveness and income): Alex $\succ$ Brian, Brian $\succ$ Charlie and Charlie $\succ$ Alex. While this ranking is complete, it fails to satisfy transitivity.

---

[4]The paradox is named after the 14th century French philosopher Jean Buridan; see: https://en.wikipedia.org/wiki/Buridan's_ass.

A similar example can shed light on the reason why sometimes preferences may fail to be complete. Suppose that Ann is considering buying a house and the two most important features are low commuting time (the lower the better) and price (the lower the better). She has seen two houses, H_1 and H_2, which are almost identical in terms of design and square footage. H_1 is at a walking distance from her office, but costs \$500,000, while H_2 costs only \$300,000 but requires a 45-minute commute by car. Unless Ann is willing to either focus on only one characteristic or to attach weights to the two characteristics, she will be unable to rank H_1 versus H_2 (which is not the same as saying that she is indifferent between H_1 and H_2).

2.4 Exercises

The solutions to the following exercises are given in Section 2.5 at the end of this chapter.

2.4.1 Exercises for Section 2.1: Preference relations

Exercise 2.1 Let the set of outcomes be $O = \{o_1, o_2, o_3\}$. Alice says that she is indifferent between o_1 and o_2 and also between o_2 and o_3. Furthermore, she says that she prefers o_1 to o_3. Explain why her preferences are not rational in the sense of Definition 2.1.2. Give a detailed argument, showing each step in the reasoning.

Exercise 2.2 Let the set of outcomes be $O = \{o_1, o_2, o_3\}$. Bob says that he prefers o_1 to o_2 and he prefers o_2 to o_3. He also says that he is indifferent between o_1 and o_3. Explain why Bob's preferences are not rational in the sense of Definition 2.1.2. Give a detailed argument, showing each step in the reasoning.

Exercise 2.3 Prove that if $\succsim$ is a complete and transitive relation on the set O then the derived relation $\succ$ (see Definition 2.1.3) is also transitive.

Exercise 2.4 Prove that if $\succsim$ is a complete and transitive relation on the set O then the derived relation $\sim$ (see Definition 2.1.3) is also transitive.

Exercise 2.5 Let the set of outcomes be $O = \{o_1, o_2, \ldots, o_7\}$. Ann's preference relation over these outcomes is complete and transitive and is as follows:

$$\begin{array}{ll} \text{best} & o_4, o_5 \\ & o_2 \\ & o_1, o_6 \\ & o_7 \\ \text{worst} & o_3 \end{array}$$

For each of the following functions U_1, U_2, U_3 and U_4, determine whether the function is a utility function that represents Ann's preferences.

	o_1	o_2	o_3	o_4	o_5	o_6	o_7
U_1:	5	7	0	10	10	4	2
U_2:	0	3	−10	12	12	0	−5
U_3:	15	18	8	20	20	15	10
U_4:	−7	−4	−12	−1	−1	−7	−9

2.4.2 Exercises for Section 2.2: Rational choice under certainty

Exercise 2.6 Let $O = \{o_1, o_2, \ldots, o_7\}$ be a set of outcomes. Bill has a preference relation on O which is complete and transitive. His preferences have not changed over time and he always chooses rationally. *He also told you that there are only two outcomes that he considers to be just as good as each other* (that is, he is indifferent between them).
  - One time he had to choose from the set $\{o_1, o_2, o_4\}$ and he chose o_2.
  - Another time he had to choose from the set $\{o_4, o_5, o_6\}$ and he chose o_4.
  - A third time he had to choose from the set $\{o_1, o_2, o_3, o_7\}$ and he chose o_1.
  - A fourth time he had to choose from the set $\{o_3, o_4, o_7\}$ and he chose o_4.
  - A fifth time he had to choose from the set $\{o_3, o_5, o_6, o_7\}$ and he chose o_6.
  - A sixth time he had to choose from the set $\{o_5, o_7\}$ and he chose o_7.

(a) Find all the possible preference relations that could represent Bill's preferences (in the sense that his preference relation must be one of the ones in your list).

(b) If Bill had to choose between o_3 and o_5, what would he choose?

2.5 Solutions to Exercises

Solution to Exercise 2.1. According to her statements, $o_1 \sim o_2$, $o_2 \sim o_3$ and $o_1 \succ o_3$. These preferences are clearly complete. Thus, they are not rational if and only if they are not transitive. Indeed, transitivity fails. Since $o_2 \sim o_3$, by definition of $\sim$ we have that $o_3 \succsim o_2$. Similarly, it follows from $o_1 \sim o_2$ that $o_2 \succsim o_1$. From $o_3 \succsim o_2$ and $o_2 \succsim o_1$ it would follow from transitivity that $o_3 \succsim o_1$, but this contradicts Alice's claim that $o_1 \succ o_3$ (since, by definition of $\succ$, $o_1 \succ o_3$ implies that it is **not** the case that $o_3 \succsim o_1$). □

Solution to Exercise 2.2. According to Bob's statements, $o_1 \succ o_2$, $o_2 \succ o_3$ and $o_1 \sim o_3$. These preferences are clearly complete. Thus, they are not rational if and only if they are not transitive. Indeed, transitivity fails. Since $o_1 \sim o_3$, by definition of $\sim$ we have that $o_3 \succsim o_1$. Furthermore, it follows from $o_1 \succ o_2$ that $o_1 \succsim o_2$. From $o_3 \succsim o_1$ and $o_1 \succsim o_2$ it would follow from transitivity that $o_3 \succsim o_2$ but this contradicts Bob's claim that $o_2 \succ o_3$ (since, by definition of $\succ$, $o_2 \succ o_3$ implies that it is **not** the case that $o_3 \succsim o_2$). □

Solution to Exercise 2.3. Let $o_1, o_2, o_3 \in O$ be such that $o_1 \succ o_2$ and $o_2 \succ o_3$. We need to show that $o_1 \succ o_3$. Since $o_1 \succ o_2$, $o_1 \succsim o_2$ and since $o_2 \succ o_3$, $o_2 \succsim o_3$. Thus, by transitivity of $\succsim$, $o_1 \succsim o_3$. It remains to prove that $o_3 \not\succsim o_1$. Suppose that $o_3 \succsim o_1$; then, since $o_1 \succsim o_2$ it would follow from transitivity of $\succsim$ that $o_3 \succsim o_2$, contradicting the hypothesis that $o_2 \succ o_3$. □

Solution to Exercise 2.4. Let $o_1, o_2, o_3 \in O$ be such that $o_1 \sim o_2$ and $o_2 \sim o_3$. We need to show that $o_1 \sim o_3$. Since $o_1 \sim o_2$, $o_1 \succsim o_2$ and since $o_2 \sim o_3$, $o_2 \succsim o_3$; thus, by transitivity of $\succsim$, $o_1 \succsim o_3$. Similarly, since $o_1 \sim o_2$, $o_2 \succsim o_1$ and since $o_2 \sim o_3$, $o_3 \succsim o_2$; thus, by transitivity of $\succsim$, $o_3 \succsim o_1$. It follows from $o_1 \succsim o_3$ and $o_3 \succsim o_1$ that $o_1 \sim o_3$. □

Solution to Exercise 2.5. Recall that Ann's ranking of the outcomes is as follows:

$$
\begin{array}{ll}
\text{best} & o_4, o_5 \\
& o_2 \\
& o_1, o_6 \\
& o_7 \\
\text{worst} & o_3
\end{array}
$$

The candidate utility functions are:

	o_1	o_2	o_3	o_4	o_5	o_6	o_7
U_1:	5	7	0	10	10	4	2
U_2:	0	3	−10	12	12	0	−5
U_3:	15	18	8	20	20	15	10
U_4:	−7	−4	−12	−1	−1	−7	−9

U_1 does not represent Ann's preferences because $o_1 \sim o_6$ (Ann is indifferent between o_1 and o_6) and yet $U_1(o_1) = 5 > U_1(o_6) = 4$. The other three are indeed utility functions that represent Ann's preferences because they all satisfy the property that, for every two outcomes o and o', $U(o) > U(o')$ if and only if $o \succ o'$ and $U(o) = U(o')$ if and only if $o \sim o'$. □

Solution to Exercise 2.6. The information is as follows:
(1) from the set $\{o_1, o_2, o_4\}$ Bill chose o_2; we shall express this more succinctly as follows: $\{o_1, o_2, o_4\} \mapsto o_2$,
(2) $\{o_4, o_5, o_6\} \mapsto o_4$,
(3) $\{o_1, o_2, o_3, o_7\} \mapsto o_1$,
(4) $\{o_3, o_4, o_7\} \mapsto o_4$,
(5) $\{o_3, o_5, o_6, o_7\} \mapsto o_6$,
(6) $\{o_5, o_7\} \mapsto o_7$.

(a) From (1) we deduce that $o_2 \succsim o_1$ and from (3) that $o_1 \succsim o_2$. Thus, it must be that $o_1 \sim o_2$. Since Bill is indifferent only between two outcomes, every other ranking must be strict. From (1) we get $o_1 \succ o_4$, from (2) $o_4 \succ o_5$ and $o_4 \succ o_6$, from (3) $o_1 \succ o_3$ and $o_1 \succ o_7$, from (4) $o_4 \succ o_3$ and $o_4 \succ o_7$, from (5) $o_6 \succ o_3$, $o_6 \succ o_5$ and $o_6 \succ o_7$ and from (6) $o_7 \succ o_5$. Thus, by making use of transitivity, we conclude that there are only three possibilities:

$$\begin{pmatrix} \text{best} & o_1, o_2 \\ & o_4 \\ & o_6 \\ & o_3 \\ & o_7 \\ \text{worst} & o_5 \end{pmatrix}, \quad \begin{pmatrix} \text{best} & o_1, o_2 \\ & o_4 \\ & o_6 \\ & o_7 \\ & o_3 \\ \text{worst} & o_5 \end{pmatrix}, \quad \begin{pmatrix} \text{best} & o_1, o_2 \\ & o_4 \\ & o_6 \\ & o_7 \\ & o_5 \\ \text{worst} & o_3 \end{pmatrix}.$$

(b) We do not have enough information. If his preference relation is one of the first two, then he will choose o_3, but if it is the third one then he will choose o_5. □

3. States and Acts

3.1 Uncertainty, states, outcomes and acts

In the previous chapter we considered the rather unrealistic case where the Decision Maker (*DM*) is certain of what outcome will follow from any of his available actions. In real life we do not enjoy such certainty because the final outcome of any decision that we make is also influenced by external factors over which we have no control. For example, suppose that Ann and Bob are planning their wedding reception. They have a large number of guests and face the choice between two venues: a spacious outdoor area where the guests will be able to roam around or a small indoor area where the guests will feel rather crammed. Ann and Bob want their reception to be a success and their guests to feel comfortable. It seems that the large outdoor area is a better choice; however, there is also an external factor that needs to be taken into account, namely the weather. If it does not rain, then the outdoor area will yield the best outcome but if it does rain then the outdoor area will be a disaster. For Ann and Bob the weather is an external factor over which they have no control (they can try to predict it, but they cannot control it). We shall refer to such external factors as "states of the world" or simply *states* (that is, a state specifies all the external facts that are relevant in determining the outcome associated with any action that is taken).

Definition 3.1.1 A *state* is a complete specification of all the external facts that are relevant to the *DM*. By "external" fact we mean a fact that cannot be controlled by the *DM* (such as the weather).

The presence of alternative states introduces uncertainty. An action, or decision, will typically yield different outcomes, depending on what state actually occurs. At the time of making the decision one can only list, for every action, the set of possible outcomes, one for every state. Instead of using the terms 'action' or 'decision' or 'choice' it is common in the literature to use the term *act*. Thus, a decision problem under uncertainty can be described using a table, where rows correspond to acts (that is, possible decisions) and columns correspond to states (that is, external circumstances over which the *DM* has no control).

Our example for the wedding party can thus be represented as follows ('rec.' stands for 'reception'):

		STATES	
		No rain	Rain
ACTS	choose outdoor venue	successful rec.	disastrous rec.
	choose indoor venue	unremarkable rec.	unremarkable rec.

Note that it is crucial that the states be specified correctly; in particular there should not be a causal link between acts and states. For example, consider a student who reasons as follows:

> There are two states, one where I pass the exam and one where I do not pass the exam. I have two choices: (1) study and forgo going to a party or (2) not study and go to the party. Thus, my decision problem looks as follows:

		STATES	
		Pass exam	Not pass exam
ACTS	study	pass and miss party	fail and miss party
	not study	pass and enjoy party	fail and enjoy party

Hence, the student concludes that he is better off not studying, because – no matter what the actual state turns out to be – he gets a better outcome by not studying as compared to studying. The student's reasoning is fallacious because there is a causal relationship between studying and passing the exam (studying affects the probability of passing the exam). Thus, the student has not reached his decision (not to study) in a rational way.

How should we represent the student's decision problem? We want to acknowledge the causal relationship between studying and passing the exam, while – at the same time – allowing for uncertainty (studying does not guarantee a good grade). We must distinguish between what the student can control (whether or not he studies) and what he cannot control (e.g. the level of difficulty of the exam, which is decided by another person, namely the professor). One possible representation is as follows:

		STATES	
		Difficult exam	Easy exam
ACTS	study	C grade and miss party	A grade and miss party
	not study	F grade but enjoy party	C grade but enjoy party

What is rational for the student to do depends, among other things, on how he ranks the four outcomes.

Definition 3.1.2 Let S be a finite set of states and O a finite set of outcomes. An *act* is a function $a : S \to O$ that associates with every state an outcome.

An act is thus a list of outcomes, one for every state. Hence, a *decision problem under uncertainty* can be represented as a table, where the columns are labeled with states, the rows are labeled with acts and in each cell of the table is listed one outcome. For example if the set of states is $S = \{s_1, s_2, s_3\}$, the set of acts is $A = \{a_1, a_2, a_3, a_4\}$ and the set of outcomes is $O = \{o_1, o_2, \ldots, o_{12}\}$ then the decision problem can be represented by the following table:

state →	s_1	s_2	s_3
act ↓			
a_1	o_1	o_2	o_3
a_2	o_4	o_5	o_6
a_3	o_7	o_8	o_9
a_4	o_{10}	o_{11}	o_{12}

If $a : S \to O$ is an act, we denote by $a(s)$ the outcome that is associated with act a when the state is s. For instance, in the example above we have that $a_3(s_2) = o_8$, that is, the outcome associated with act a_3, when the state is s_2, is o_8.

In the rest of this chapter we turn to the issue of how to make a rational choice in a situation of uncertainty.

> Test your understanding of the concepts introduced in this section, by going through the exercises in Section 3.5.1 at the end of this chapter.

3.2 Dominance

We shall assume throughout that the *DM* has a complete and transitive ranking of the set of outcomes O.

> **Definition 3.2.1** We say that act *a strictly dominates* act b if, for every state s, $a(s) \succ b(s)$, that is, if – for every state s – the outcome associated with act a (in state s) is preferred by the *DM* to the outcome associated with state b (in state s). Equivalently, if we represent the *DM*'s preferences by means of an ordinal utility function $U : O \to \mathbb{R}$, we say that a strictly dominates b if, for every state s, $U(a(s)) > U(b(s))$.

For example, consider the following decision problem:

state →	s_1	s_2	s_3
act ↓			
a_1	o_1	o_2	o_3
a_2	o_4	o_5	o_6
a_3	o_7	o_8	o_9

and suppose that the *DM*'s preferences are as follows:

best	o_3
	o_1, o_8
	o_5
	o_7, o_9
	o_6
	o_4
worst	o_2

Then act a_3 strictly dominates act a_2, since $o_7 \succ o_4$ (state s_1), $o_8 \succ o_5$ (state s_2) and $o_9 \succ o_6$ (state s_3). If we choose the following utility function to represent the *DM*'s preferences

		Utility
best	o_3	6
	o_1, o_8	5
	o_5	4
	o_7, o_9	3
	o_6	2
	o_4	1
worst	o_2	0

then the decision problem can be re-written in terms of utilities as follows:

state $\rightarrow$	s_1	s_2	s_3
act $\downarrow$			
a_1	5	0	6
a_2	1	4	2
a_3	3	5	3

making it easier to see that act a_3 strictly dominates act a_2 ($3 > 1$, $5 > 4$, $3 > 2$). Note that, while a_3 strictly dominates a_2, for any other pair of acts it is not the case that one act strictly dominates the other.

From now on we shall mostly represent decision problems in terms of utilities.

Definition 3.2.2 We say that an act is *strictly dominant* if it strictly dominates every other act.

In the above example there is no strictly dominant act; for instance, a_3 is not strictly dominant because, although it strictly dominates a_2, it does not dominate a_1 (indeed, if the true state is s_1 then a_1 yields a better outcome than the other two acts).

> If there is a strictly dominant act, then (1) it is unique (that is, there is no other strictly dominant act) and (2) it is the obvious rational choice, since it guarantees a better outcome than any other act, no matter what the true state is.

Definition 3.2.3 We say that act a *weakly dominates* act b if, for every state s, $a(s) \succsim b(s)$ and, furthermore, there is at least one state $\hat{s}$ such that $a(\hat{s}) \succ b(\hat{s})$; that is, a weakly dominates b if it yields at least as good an outcome as b in every state and there is at least one state where a yields a better outcome than b. Equivalently, if we represent the *DM*'s preferences by means of an ordinal utility function $U : O \rightarrow \mathbb{R}$, then a weakly dominates b if, for every state s, $U(a(s)) \geq U(b(s))$ and, furthermore, there is at least one state $\hat{s}$ such that $U(a(\hat{s})) > U(b(\hat{s}))$.

3.2 Dominance

■ **Example 3.1** In the following decision problem,

state →	s_1	s_2	s_3
act ↓			
a_1	1	3	1
a_2	0	2	1
a_3	1	3	3
a_4	1	3	3

a_1 weakly dominates a_2, a_3 weakly dominates a_1, a_3 strictly dominates a_2, a_4 weakly dominates a_1 and a_4 strictly dominates a_2. ■

> (R) Note that, according to Definition 3.2.3, in Example 3.1 it is also true that a_3 weakly dominates a_2 (and a_4 weakly dominates a_2), because strict dominance implies weak dominance. In order to be as informative as possible, we will always interpret the expression 'weakly dominates' as 'dominates weakly but not strictly', that is, if we say that act a weakly dominates act b then we imply that there is at least one state s such that $U(a(s)) = U(b(s))$.

> **Definition 3.2.4** Two acts, a and b are *equivalent*, if, for every state s, $a(s) \sim b(s)$. Equivalently, if we represent the *DM*'s preferences by means of an ordinal utility function $U : O \to \mathbb{R}$, acts a and b are equivalent if, for every state s, $U(a(s)) = U(b(s))$.

For instance, in Example 3.1, acts a_3 and a_4 are equivalent.

> **Definition 3.2.5** An act a is *weakly dominant* if, for every other act b, either a dominates (weakly or strictly) b or a and b are equivalent.

In Example 3.1, act a_3 is weakly dominant (it weakly dominates a_1, strictly dominates a_2 and is equivalent to a_4) and so is a_4.

> (R) As noted in the previous remark, since strict dominance implies weak dominance, an act that is strictly dominant also satisfies the definition of weak dominance. Thus, in order to be as informative as possible, we will always interpret the expression 'weakly dominant' as 'weakly, but not strictly, dominant', that is, if we say that act a is weakly dominant then we imply that there is at least one other act b and at least one state s such that $U(a(s)) = U(b(s))$.
> Note also that – while there can be only one strictly dominant act – it is possible that there are several weakly dominant acts (as is the case with a_3 and a_4 in Example 3.1); however, any two weakly dominant acts must be equivalent.

We now illustrate the various notions of dominance (Definitions 3.2.1, 3.2.2, 3.2.3 and 3.2.5) in two examples.

Bill is participating in an auction against one other bidder.

The allowed bids are $10, $20, $30, $40 and $50.

Bill has no control over the opponent's bid and thus we can treat it as a state.

From Bill's point of view, the possible outcomes are of the following type: (1) he does not win the auction and thus pays nothing or (2) he wins the auction and pays $x.

The item is worth $30 to Bill; his ranking of the outcomes is as follows:
- $(win, pay\ \$x) \succ (win, pay\ \$y)$ if and only if $x < y$ (that is, conditional on winning, he prefers to pay less),
- $(win, pay\ \$x) \succ (not\ win)$ if and only if $x < \$30$ (that is, he prefers winning to not winning as long as he pays less than the value of the object to him),
- $(win, pay\ \$30) \sim (not\ win)$ (that is, he is indifferent between not winning and winning and having to pay what the object is worth to him),
- $(not\ win) \succ (win, pay\ \$x)$ if and only if $x > \$30$ (that is, if he has to pay more than the item is worth to him, then he prefers not to win).

The reader should convince himself/herself that the following utility function represents Bill's preferences:

$$U(not\ win) = 0 \text{ and } U(win, pay\ \$x) = 30 - x.$$

We now consider two different auctions.

■ **Example 3.2** (This is an instance of what is known as a "first-price auction"). Bill wins the auction if and only if his bid is greater than, or equal to, the opponent's bid. Furthermore, if Bill wins then he has to pay *his own bid*. We can represent Bill's decision problem as follows (where the numbers are utilities):

opponent's bid (state) →	$10	$20	$30	$40	$50
Bill's bid (act) ↓					
$10	20	0	0	0	0
$20	10	10	0	0	0
$30	0	0	0	0	0
$40	−10	−10	−10	−10	0
$50	−20	−20	−20	−20	−20

It is easy to check that the following are true (instead of writing 'bidding $x' we shall just write '$x'):
- $10 weakly dominates $30 and $40, and strictly dominates $50,
- $20 weakly dominates $30 and $40, and strictly dominates $50,
- $30 weakly dominates $40 and strictly dominates $50,
- $40 strictly dominates $50,
- there is no (weakly or strictly) dominant act.

■

3.2 Dominance

The next example considers a different type of auction.

■ Example 3.3 (This is an instance of what is known as a "second-price auction"). As in Example 3.2, Bill wins the auction if and only if his bid is greater than, or equal to, the opponent's bid; however, in this auction, if Bill wins then he has to pay not his own bid but *the opponent's bid*. We can represent Bill's new decision problem as follows (again, the numbers are utilities):[1]

opponent's bid (state →	$10	$20	$30	$40	$50
Bill's bid (act) ↓					
$10	20	0	0	0	0
$20	20	10	0	0	0
$30	20	10	0	0	0
$40	20	10	0	−10	0
$50	20	10	0	−10	−20

It is easy to check that the following are true (again, instead of writing 'bidding $x' we shall just write '$x'):

- $20 weakly dominates $10, $40 and $50 and is equivalent to $30,
- $30 weakly dominates $10, $40 and $50 and is equivalent to $20,
- $40 weakly dominates $50,
- both $20 and $30 are weakly dominant acts.

Note that for Bill bidding the true value of the object to him, namely $30, is a weakly dominant act. Indeed, it can be proved that in a second-price auction (with any number of bidders), if a bidder's preferences are of the type given above, then it is always a dominant choice to bid one's true value.[2] ■

How do the different notions of dominance relate to rationality? If an act, say a, is strictly dominated by another act, say b, then choosing a is clearly irrational, since switching to b guarantees a better outcome, no matter what the true state is.[3] Thus, a rational *DM* will not choose a strictly dominated act.[4] According to this criterion, in Example 3.2 all we can say is that, if Bill is rational, he will not bid $50 (this is the only strictly dominated act), whereas in Example 2 no bids can be ruled out, since there are no strictly dominated acts.

---

[1] For example, if the opponent's bid is $10 and Bill's bid is $40, then Bill wins the auction and pays not $40 but $10, so that his utility is $30 - 10 = 20$.

[2] For a precise statement of this result and a proof see:
Giacomo Bonanno, *Game Theory: An open access textbook with 165 solved exercises*, http://faculty.econ.ucdavis.edu/faculty/bonanno/GT_Book.html

[3] This does not imply, however, that choosing b is necessarily rational; indeed it may be the case that b itself is strictly dominated by some other act.

[4] It follows that, as remarked above, if there is a strictly dominant act, then it is the obvious and unique rational choice.

What about weak dominance? Can it be rational to choose a weakly dominated act? In the previous chapter we introduced the following definition of rationality (in the context of choice under certainty): an act is rational if, according to the *DM*'s beliefs, it is at least as good as any other act. Consider Example 3.2 and the act of bidding $40. To justify such choice the *DM* could explain that he is convinced that the opponent's bid is $50 and thus bidding $40 is just as good as bidding a lower amount and better than bidding $50. Thus, in order to argue that a bid of $40 is irrational, one would have to question the wisdom of holding the certain belief that the opponent's bid is $50. The choice of a weakly dominated act is irrational *only if the DM is cautious in his beliefs,* in the sense that he does not completely rule out the possibility of any state. It follows that, under cautious beliefs, if there is a weakly dominant act then a rational *DM* should choose it (or any of them, in case there are several); for instance, in Example 3.3 – under cautious beliefs – the only rational bids are $20 and $30.

In later chapters we will consider the case where the *DM* is able to assign (objective or subjective) probabilities to the states (that is, holds probabilistic beliefs) and what notion of rationality is appropriate in that context. In the rest of this chapter we will consider possible decision criteria that apply to situations where the *DM* is *not* able to assign probabilities to the states.

> Test your understanding of the concepts introduced in this section, by going through the exercises in Section 3.5.2 at the end of this chapter.

3.3 MaxiMin and LexiMin

3.3.1 MaxiMin

The MaxiMin criterion reflects extreme pessimism: for each act, the *DM* looks at the worst-case scenario – that is, the worst possible outcome – and then chooses an act which is best in terms of the worst outcome.[5] For example, in the following decision problem (expressed in terms of utilities), for each act we have highlighted (by enclosing it in a box) a worst outcome and the MaxiMin criterion would then select act *b*.

state →	s_1	s_2	s_3	s_4	s_5
act ↓					
a	[0]	1	3	8	5
b	4	3	3	[3]	5
c	7	6	[2]	4	5
d	[1]	2	4	2	5

The MaxiMin criterion can select a unique act, as in the previous example, or a set of acts. For instance, both in Example 3.2 and Example 3.3, the MaxiMin solution is the following set of bids: {$10,$20,$30}.

Note that, if an act is strictly dominated, then it cannot be selected by the MaxiMin criterion.

---

[5] In other words, the *DM* acts as if he was dealing with a demon who chooses the state after observing the *DM*'s choice and whose aim is to make the *DM* as badly off as possible.

3.3 MaxiMin and LexiMin

The MaxiMin criterion can be viewed as too extreme in the underlying pessimism. For example, in the following case (where outcomes are sums of money and the assumption is that *DM* prefers more money to less), it recommends act a, while most people would probably choose act b:

state $\to$	s_1	s_2	s_3
act $\downarrow$			
a	$\boxed{\$1}$	\$1	\$1
b	\$100	\$100	$\boxed{\$0}$

3.3.2 LexiMin

The LexiMin criterion is a refinement of the MaxiMin criterion that applies when the MaxiMin solution consists of two or more acts. Consider the following decision problem:

state $\to$	s_1	s_2	s_3	s_4	s_5
act $\downarrow$					
a	$\boxed{0}$	1	3	1	5
b	4	$\boxed{1}$	3	2	5
c	3	4	4	$\boxed{2}$	5
d	6	3	$\boxed{2}$	3	5

In this case the MaxiMin criterion yields two possible choices: c and d. The LexiMin criterion allows one to narrow down the choice as follows: if the worst outcome is the same, then look at the second-worst outcome and, if necessary, at the third worst outcome, and so on. In the above example, the worst outcome has the same utility, namely 2, for both c and d. Thus, we look at the next worst outcome: utility of 3 in both cases. Hence, we look at the third worst outcome: it has a utility of 4 for c and a utility of 3 for d (there are two outcomes with a utility of 3 under act d; pick one as the second worst and the other as the third worst). Thus, the LexiMin criterion would recommend c. Another way to visualize this is as follows. We need to break the tie between c and d. Write the possible payoffs under c in increasing order and do the same for d:

c	2	3	4	4	5
d	2	3	3	5	6
	worst: same	2nd worst: same	3rd worst: c is better		

hence choose c.

In Example 3.2, the MaxiMin solution is $\{\$10,\$20,\$30\}$ and the LexiMin solution is to bid \$20; in Example 3.3, the MaxiMin solution is $\{\$10,\$20,\$30\}$ and the LexiMin solution is $\{\$20,\$30\}$.

Clearly, the LexiMin criterion – being a refinement of MaxiMin – suffers from the same drawbacks as the latter.

> Test your understanding of the concepts introduced in this section, by going through the exercises in Section 3.5.3 at the end of this chapter.

3.4 Regret: a first attempt

Another criterion that has been suggested has to do with minimizing the maximum regret. For example, consider the following decision problem (where outcomes are sums of money and the assumption is that the *DM* prefers more money to less):

state →	s_1	s_2
act ↓		
a	$20	$40
b	$100	$10

If the *DM* chooses act a then she will be happy if the state turns out to be s_2, but she will regret not having chosen b if the state turns out to be s_1; one could measure the regret experienced by the *DM* in the latter case as the difference between the sum of money she could have obtained ($100) and the sum actually obtained ($20): a regret of $80. On the other hand, if the *DM* chooses b then she will experience regret in the amount of $30 if the state turns out to be s_2 (but she will be happy if the state turns out to be s_1). Thus, it seems that the potential regret is stronger if the *DM* chooses act a ($80) than if she chooses b ($30). The criterion we are considering suggests choosing an act that minimizes the maximum potential regret. According to this criterion, in the above decision problem one should choose b.

The trouble with the MinMaxRegret criterion is that, in general, it is not clear how one should measure regret. In the above example outcomes were expressed as sums of money, but what if they are more general outcomes? For example, consider the following decision problem:

state →	s_1	s_2			
act ↓				best	o_1
a	o_1	o_2	with preferences		o_3
b	o_3	o_4			o_4
				worst	o_2

One could represent these preferences with the following utility function:

		Utility
best	o_1	4
	o_3	3
	o_4	2
worst	o_2	0

and rewrite the decision problem in terms of utilities as

state →	s_1	s_2
act ↓		
a	4	0
b	3	2

Then the maximum regret from choosing act a is 2 units of utility, while the maximum regret from choosing act b is 1 unit of utility; thus, it looks like the MinMaxRegret criterion

3.4 Regret: a first attempt

would recommend choosing b. However, the following is an alternative utility function that represents the same ordinal preferences:

		Utility
best	o_1	8
	o_3	3
	o_4	2
worst	o_2	0

with corresponding decision problem

state →	s_1	s_2
act ↓		
a	8	0
b	3	2

Under this representation, the maximum regret from choosing a is still 2, while the maximum regret from choosing b is now 5, so that the MinMaxRegret criterion would now recommend choosing a. Since the *DM*'s ordinal preferences are the same under the two utility representations, the recommendation should be the same. Hence, we conclude that *the MinMaxRegret criterion is meaningless in a context where the utility function is merely ordinal*.

In order to make sense of the MinMaxRegret criterion one would need to be in a context where the utility function is not ordinal, but cardinal, that is, it incorporates information about the intensity of preferences and not only about the ordinal ranking. Such contexts will be discussed in Chapter 6.

> Test your understanding of the concepts introduced in this section, by going through the exercises in Section 3.5.4 at the end of this chapter.

3.5 Exercises

The solutions to the following exercises are given in Section 3.6 at the end of this chapter.

3.5.1 Exercises for Section 3.1: Uncertainty, states and acts

Exercise 3.1 Consider the following decision problem and preferences:

state →	s_1	s_2	s_3
act ↓			
a_1	o_1	o_2	o_3
a_2	o_4	o_5	o_6
a_3	o_7	o_8	o_9

best	o_1
	o_3, o_8, o_9
	o_5
	o_7
	o_6
	o_4
worst	o_2

Use a utility function with values from the set $\{0, 1, \ldots, 6\}$ to represent these preferences and re-write the decision problem in terms of utilities.

3.5.2 Exercises for Section 3.2: Dominance

Exercise 3.2 In Exercise 3.1, for every pair of acts, state whether one act dominates the other (and, if so, whether it is weak or strict dominance).

Exercise 3.3 Consider the following decision problem where the numbers are utilities:

state →	s_1	s_2	s_3	s_4	s_5
act ↓					
a	0	1	3	1	5
b	0	1	3	2	5
c	1	2	4	2	5
d	1	2	4	2	5

(a) For each pair of acts, state whether one dominates the other and, if so, whether it is weak or strict dominance.
(b) Is there a strictly dominant act?
(c) Is there a weakly dominant act?

3.5 Exercises

Exercise 3.4 You have agreed to participate in a second-price auction against another bidder. The rules are as follows: The possible bids are $10, $20, $30, $40, $50 and $60. The value of the object to you is $30. *In case of ties*, that is, if your bid is equal to the bid of the other bidder, then *the other bidder wins*. If your bid is higher than the bid of the other bidder, you win the object and pay, not your own bid, but the bid submitted by the other bidder (hence the name of "second-price" auction). Your preferences are the same as Bill's preferences in Example 3.3 of Section 3.2.

(a) Represent your decision problem in terms of states, outcomes and acts.

(b) Do you have any acts that are dominant? Are they weakly or strictly dominant?

3.5.3 Exercises for Section 3.3: MaxiMin and LexiMin

Exercise 3.5 Consider the following decision problem where the numbers are utilities:

state →	s_1	s_2	s_3	s_4	s_5	s_6	s_7
act ↓							
a	0	2	3	1	5	4	1
b	0	1	3	2	5	3	6
c	1	2	5	4	5	6	4
d	2	1	3	4	6	4	3
e	3	1	4	6	0	7	0

(a) Find the MaxiMin solution.

(b) Find the LexiMin solution.

3.5.4 Exercises for Section 3.4: Regret: a first attempt

Exercise 3.6 Consider the following decision problem:

state →	s_1	s_2			
act ↓			with preferences	best	o_3
a	o_1	o_2			o_2
b	o_3	o_4			o_1
				worst	o_4

(a) Construct a utility representation with values from the set $\{0, 2, 3, 4\}$ and for each act find the maximum regret (defined as the difference between the maximum utility one could have got and the actual utility one experienced). What act would the MinMaxRegret criterion suggest?

(b) Show that by changing the utility function (while representing the same preferences) you can make the MinMaxRegret criterion select a different act from the one selected in Part (a).

3.6 Solutions to Exercises

Solution to Exercise 3.1. The utility function is as follows

		Utility
best	o_1	6
	o_3, o_8, o_9	5
	o_5	4
	o_7	3
	o_6	2
	o_4	1
worst	o_2	0

with corresponding decision problem

state →	s_1	s_2	s_3
act ↓			
a_1	6	0	5
a_2	1	4	2
a_3	3	5	5

□

Solution to Exercise 3.2. In the decision problem given above (for Exercise 3.1) we have that:
- It is neither the case that a_1 dominates a_2, nor the case that a_2 dominates a_1.
- It is neither the case that a_1 dominates a_3, nor the case that a_3 dominates a_1.
- a_3 strictly dominates a_2.

□

Solution to Exercise 3.3. The decision problem is as follows:

state →	s_1	s_2	s_3	s_4	s_5
act ↓					
a	0	1	3	1	5
b	0	1	3	2	5
c	1	2	4	2	5
d	1	2	4	2	5

(a) b weakly dominates a; c weakly dominates a; d weakly dominates a.
  c weakly dominates b; d weakly dominates b.
  c and d are equivalent.
(b) There is no strictly dominant act.
(c) c is a weakly dominant act and so is d.

□

3.6 Solutions to Exercises

Solution to Exercise 3.4.

(a) We can take the other player's possible bids as the states. Then the decision problem is as follows (in terms of utilities):

States (bids submitted by the other bidder)

		$10	$20	$30	$40	$50	$60
	$10	0	0	0	0	0	0
	$20	20	0	0	0	0	0
Acts	$30	20	10	0	0	0	0
	$40	20	10	0	0	0	0
	$50	20	10	0	−10	0	0
	$60	20	10	0	−10	−20	0

(b) Bidding $30 is equivalent to bidding $40 and both are weakly dominant acts. □

Solution to Exercise 3.5.

(a) Below we highlight, for every act, a worst outcome:

state →	s_1	s_2	s_3	s_4	s_5	s_6	s_7
act ↓							
a	[0]	2	3	1	5	4	1
b	[0]	1	3	2	5	3	6
c	[1]	2	5	4	5	6	4
d	2	[1]	3	4	6	4	3
e	3	1	4	6	[0]	7	0

The MaxiMin solution is $\{c,d\}$.

(b) The LexiMin solution is c (the second worst outcome is the same for both c and d, namely a utility of 2, while the third worst outcome is a utility of 3 for d but 4 for c). □

Solution to Exercise 3.6.

(a) Using the following utility function:

		Utility
best	o_3	4
	o_2	3
	o_1	2
worst	o_4	0

we can rewrite the decision problem as

state →	s_1	s_2
act ↓		
a	2	3
b	4	0

Then the maximum regret from choosing a is 2, while the maximum regret from choosing b is 3. Thus, the MinMaxRegret criterion would recommend choosing a.

(b) The following is an alternative utility function representing the same preferences:

		Utility
best	o_3	7
	o_2	3
	o_1	2
worst	o_4	0

with corresponding decision problem

state →	s_1	s_2
act ↓		
a	2	3
b	7	0

Under this representation, the maximum regret from choosing a is 5, while the maximum regret from choosing b is 3, so that the MinMaxRegret criterion would now recommend choosing b. □

4. Decision Trees

4.1 Decision trees

The representation of decision problems in terms of states and acts is just one possible way of visualizing a decision problem. An alternative representation is in terms of decision trees. In a decision tree we use squares to represent decision points and circles – also called chance nodes – to represent external events, that is, events that the *DM* cannot control. Arrows connect the nodes of the tree (whether they are squares or circles). When an arrow out of a node (square or circle) does not end at another square or circle, then no more decisions need to be made, and no more events take place, and we record the final outcome.

As an illustration, consider the wedding party example of Chapter 3 (Section 3.1), where Ann and Bob are planning their wedding reception and face the choice between two venues: a spacious outdoor area where the guests will be able to roam around or a small indoor area where the guests will feel rather crammed. The weather is also a factor in their decision: if it does not rain, then the outdoor area will yield the best outcome, but if it does rain then the outdoor area will be a disaster. The state-act representation of this decision problem was given in Chapter 3. An alternative representation is given in Figure 4.1 as a decision tree.

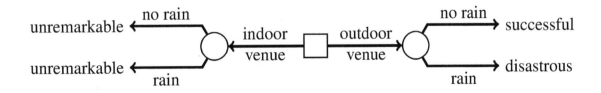

Figure 4.1: The decision tree for the wedding party example

As a further illustration of the notion of decision tree, consider the following example.

■ **Example 4.1** You are a lawyer. The plaintiff, your client, was in an automobile accident, and you are engaged in settlement negotiations with the lawyer for the other party (the defendant). If you go to trial, there will be three possible outcomes:

(1) the judge determines that the defendant was at fault and compensates your client both for the damage to her car, in the amount of $20,000, and for her lost wages, in the amount of $80,000;

(2) the judge determines that the defendant was at fault but compensates your client only for the damage to her car;

(3) the judge determines that your client shared in the fault and awards no compensation.

Going to trial will cost your client $10,000. The defendant has offered $40,000 to settle the case out of court.

Your client's current wealth is W (with $W > 10,000$) and we take the outcome to be the final wealth of your client.

Your client's decision problem is shown as a tree in Figure 4.2. ■

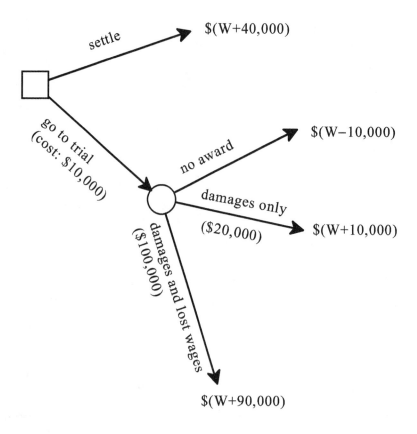

Figure 4.2: The decision tree for Example 4.1

4.1 Decision trees

Of course, the decision problem of Example 4.1 can also be represented in the state-act format, as shown in Figure 4.3 (treating the judge's decision as a state).

		State		
		S_1 damages + lost wages	S_2 damages only	S_3 no award
A c t	settle	$(W+40000)	$(W+40000)	$(W+40000)
	go to trial	$(W+90,000)	$(W+10,000)	$(W−10,000)

Figure 4.3: The state-act representation of Example 4.1

Decision trees provide a simpler and clearer representation than the state-act format in situations where there is a sequential structure to the decision problem. Example 4.2 provides an illustration.

This space added to allow proper alignment of text and figures

■ **Example 4.2** Let us make the decision problem of Example 4.1 more complicated, by adding probabilistic estimates and further options. Your client has asked you (her lawyer) to provide her with probabilities for the possible decisions by the judge. You feel unable to do so, but – based on your past experience – you know that cases similar to hers can be classified into two categories. In the first category – call it category A – are those lawsuits where in the past the judge's decision was to award damages and lost wages in 55% of the cases, damages only in 35% of the cases and nothing in 10% of the cases. In the second category – call it category B – are those lawsuits where the judge's decision was for damages and lost wages in 40% of the cases, for damages only in 45% of the cases and for no award in 15% of the cases. You do not have the expertise to determine to which category your client's case belongs but she can hire an expert to determine that with certainty. Hiring the expert will cost your client C. Of all the past cases similar to the one under consideration, the fraction p were determined to belong to category B and the fraction $(1-p)$ were determined to belong to category A. After hearing the expert's opinion, your client can then decide whether to settle or go to trial. Of course, she can also decide to accept the offered settlement right away or to go to trial without consulting the expert (in which case she saves C). This more complicated decision problem is represented in the decision tree shown in Figure 4.4, where the arrows emanating from circles are now labeled also with probabilities. ■

How would one go about making a decision in complicated situations like the one described in Example 4.2? It turns out that decision trees offer a simple answer to this question, which will be explained in detail in Section 4.3: it is called the "method of backward induction". In order to explain this method, we will first focus on a particularly simple class of decision trees and preferences, namely decision trees where all of the following are true:

1. outcomes are expressed as sums of money,
2. the arrows out of circles are assigned probabilities (the decision tree of Figure 4.4 satisfies these two conditions), and
3. the *DM*'s preferences are characterized by risk neutrality, as explained in the following section.

How to solve more general decision trees will be discussed in Chapter 6, after introducing the theory of Expected Utility in Chapter 5.

> Test your understanding of the concepts introduced in this section, by going through the exercises in Section 4.5.1 at the end of this chapter.

4.1 Decision trees

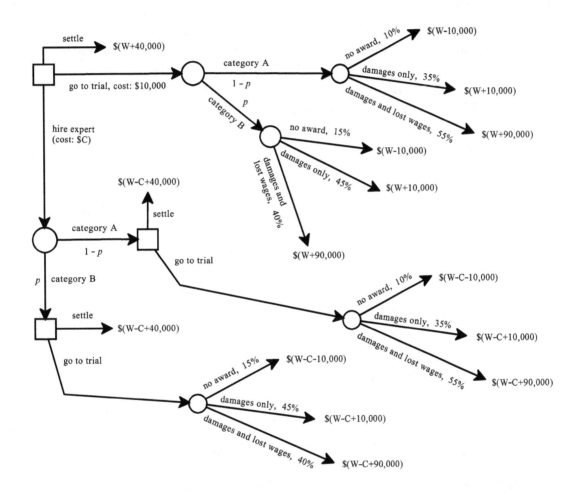

Figure 4.4: The decision tree for Example 4.2

4.2 Money lotteries and risk neutrality

Definition 4.2.1 A *money lottery* is a probability distribution over a list of outcomes, where each outcome consists of a sum of money. Thus, it is an object of the form $\begin{pmatrix} \$x_1 & \$x_2 & ... & \$x_n \\ p_1 & p_2 & ... & p_n \end{pmatrix}$ with $0 \leq p_i \leq 1$ for all $i = 1, 2, ..., n$, and $p_1 + p_2 + ... + p_n = 1$.

We assume that the *DM* is able to rank any two money lotteries and that her ranking is transitive. For example, if asked to choose between getting \$400 for sure – which can be viewed as the degenerate lottery $\begin{pmatrix} \$400 \\ 1 \end{pmatrix}$ – and the lottery[1] $\begin{pmatrix} \$900 & \$0 \\ \frac{1}{2} & \frac{1}{2} \end{pmatrix}$, the *DM* will be able to tell us if she prefers one lottery to the other or she is indifferent between the two. In general, there is no "right answer" to this question, as there is no right answer to the question "do you prefer coffee or tea?": it is a matter of individual taste. In this chapter we will focus on one particular type of preference over money lotteries, known as "risk neutrality". First we need to define the expected value of a money lottery.

Definition 4.2.2 Given a money lottery $\begin{pmatrix} \$x_1 & \$x_2 & ... & \$x_n \\ p_1 & p_2 & ... & p_n \end{pmatrix}$, its *expected value* is the number $(x_1 p_1 + x_2 p_2 + ... + x_n p_n)$.

For example, the expected value of the money lottery $\begin{pmatrix} \$600 & \$180 & \$120 & \$30 \\ \frac{1}{12} & \frac{1}{3} & \frac{5}{12} & \frac{1}{6} \end{pmatrix}$ is

$$\tfrac{1}{12} 600 + \tfrac{1}{3} 180 + \tfrac{5}{12} 120 + \tfrac{1}{6} 30 = 165.$$

Definition 4.2.3 An individual is *risk neutral* if she ranks any two money lotteries on the basis of their expected values, that is, she prefers lottery *A* to lottery *B* if and only if the expected value of *A* is greater than the expected value of *B* and she is indifferent between *A* and *B* if their expected values are the same.

For example, if asked to choose between \$160 for sure – that is, the lottery $A = \begin{pmatrix} \$160 \\ 1 \end{pmatrix}$ – and the lottery $B = \begin{pmatrix} \$600 & \$180 & \$120 & \$30 \\ \frac{1}{12} & \frac{1}{3} & \frac{5}{12} & \frac{1}{6} \end{pmatrix}$, she will choose the latter, since the expected value of *B* is 165, while the expected value of *A* is 160.

Another example: let $C = \begin{pmatrix} \$500 & \$100 & \$75 \\ \frac{1}{5} & \frac{2}{5} & \frac{2}{5} \end{pmatrix}$ and $D = \begin{pmatrix} \$400 & \$180 & \$80 \\ \frac{1}{8} & \frac{1}{2} & \frac{3}{8} \end{pmatrix}$; then a risk neutral individual is indifferent between *C* and *D*, since they have the same expected value: $\tfrac{1}{5} 500 + \tfrac{2}{5} 100 + \tfrac{2}{5} 75 = 170 = \tfrac{1}{8} 400 + \tfrac{1}{2} 180 + \tfrac{3}{8} 80$.

It is important to stress that our focussing on the case of risk neutrality should *not* be taken to imply that a rational individual ought to be risk neutral nor that risk neutrality is empirically particularly relevant. At this stage we assume risk neutrality only because it yields a very simple type of preference over money lotteries and allows us to introduce the notion of backward induction without the heavy machinery of expected utility theory.

---

[1] We can think of this lottery as tossing a fair coin and then giving the *DM* \$900 if it comes up Heads and nothing if it comes up Tails.

4.3 Backward induction

In Chapters 5 and 6 we will develop a more general analysis.

> Test your understanding of the concepts introduced in this section, by going through the exercises in Section 4.5.2 at the end of this chapter.

4.3 Backward induction

Let us go back to the decision tree of Example 4.1 (Figure 4.2) with one addition: you, the lawyer, are able to assign probabilities to the possible decisions of the judge: a 20% chance that there will be no award, a 30% chance that the judge will award damages only and a 50% chance that the judge will award damages and lost wages. Thus, to the tree of Figure 4.2 we add these probabilities. The enriched tree is shown in Figure 4.5.

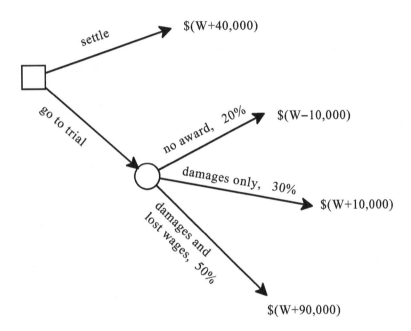

Figure 4.5: The decision tree of Figure 4.2 with the addition of probabilities

We can view the part of the tree that starts at the circle as the money lottery

$$\begin{pmatrix} \$(W+90,000) & \$(W+10,000) & \$(W-10,000) \\ \frac{5}{10} & \frac{3}{10} & \frac{2}{10} \end{pmatrix}.$$

The expected value of this lottery is $(W+90,000)\frac{5}{10} + (W+10,000)\frac{3}{10} + (W-10,000)\frac{2}{10} = W+46,000$. Thus, *if we assume that the client is risk neutral*, then she will consider the lottery to be just as good as getting $\$(W+46,000)$ for sure. Hence, we can simplify the tree by replacing the part that starts at the circle with the outcome $\$(W+46,000)$, as shown in Figure 4.6. It is now clear that the optimal decision is to go to trial: we have indicated this in Figure 4.6 by doubling the corresponding edge.

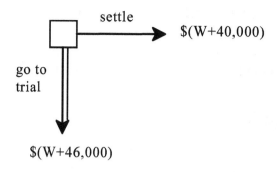

Figure 4.6: The decision tree of Figure 4.5 simplified

This example is a simple illustration of the backward-induction method for solving decision trees, which is defined below.

> **Definition 4.3.1** The backward-induction procedure is as follows.[a]
> 1. Start at a node – square or circle – that is followed only by outcomes and
>   - if the node is a square, choose an optimal action there and reduce the tree by replacing that node, and the arrows that follow that node, with the outcome associated with the chosen action,
>   - if the node is a circle calculate the expected value of the associated money lottery and replace that node, and the arrows that follow that node, with the calculated expected value.
> 2. Repeat Step 1 in the reduced game and iterate the procedure until the decision tree has been reduced to a square followed only by outcomes and then choose an optimal action in that reduced tree.
> 3. Patch together the actions chosen during the procedure to determine an optimal *strategy*.
>
> ---
> [a]Note that, for the moment, the procedure is defined assuming that outcomes are always expressed as sums of money and that the *DM* is risk neutral. The backward-induction procedure for the general case will be defined in Chapter 6.

We now illustrate the backward-induction procedure in two more examples.

Consider first the decision tree of Figure 4.7.

The following steps are illustrated in Figure 4.8.

Step 1: Start at the square numbered 1; there *e* is the optimal action; delete the square numbered 1, together with the arrows after it, and replace it with the outcome $56.

Step 2: In the reduced tree after Step 1, consider the circle numbered 2; it corresponds to the money lottery $\begin{pmatrix} \$90 & \$39 \\ \frac{1}{3} & \frac{2}{3} \end{pmatrix}$ whose expected value is $\frac{1}{3}90 + \frac{2}{3}39 = 56$; replace the circle, together with the arrows that follow it, with the calculated expected value: $56.

Step 3: In the reduced tree after Step 2, consider the square numbered 3; there the optimal action is *b*; replace the square, together with the arrows that follow it, with the outcome 58.

Final step: in the reduced tree after Step 3, *a* is the optimal choice. Hence, *the optimal strategy is as follows: first choose a and then choose b*.

4.3 Backward induction

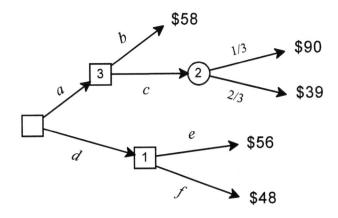

Figure 4.7: A decision tree to illustrate the backward-induction procedure

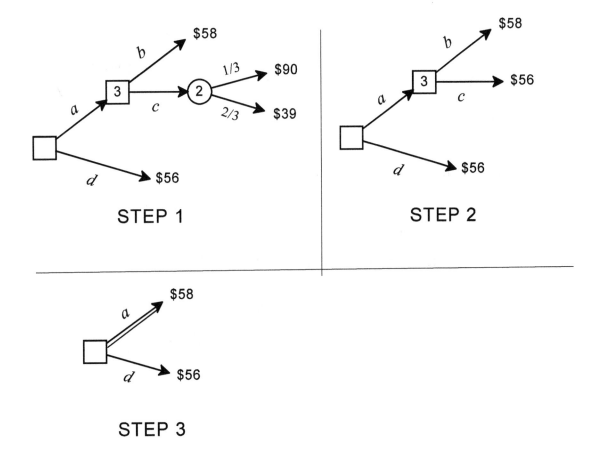

Figure 4.8: The backward-induction steps for the decision tree of Figure 4.7

Now consider the decision tree of Figure 4.4, which is reproduced in Figure 4.9.

Consider the circles (random events) that are followed by outcomes only (the right-most circles). Proceeding from top to bottom we have that:

1. The top circle corresponds to the money lottery

$$\left(\begin{array}{ccc} \$(W-10,000) & \$(W+10,000) & \$(W+90,000) \\ \frac{10}{100} & \frac{35}{100} & \frac{55}{100} \end{array} \right)$$

whose expected value is $(W+52,000)$.

2. The second circle from the top corresponds to the money lottery

$$\left(\begin{array}{ccc} \$(W-10,000) & \$(W+10,000) & \$(W+90,000) \\ \frac{15}{100} & \frac{45}{100} & \frac{40}{100} \end{array} \right)$$

whose expected value is $(W+39,000)$.

3. The third circle from the top corresponds to the money lottery

$$\left(\begin{array}{ccc} \$(W-C-10,000) & \$(W-C+10,000) & \$(W-C+90,000) \\ \frac{10}{100} & \frac{35}{100} & \frac{55}{100} \end{array} \right)$$

whose expected value is $(W-C+52,000)$.

4. The bottom circle corresponds to the money lottery

$$\left(\begin{array}{ccc} \$(W-C-10,000) & \$(W-C+10,000) & \$(W-C+90,000) \\ \frac{15}{100} & \frac{45}{100} & \frac{40}{100} \end{array} \right)$$

whose expected value is $(W-C+39,000)$.

4.3 Backward induction

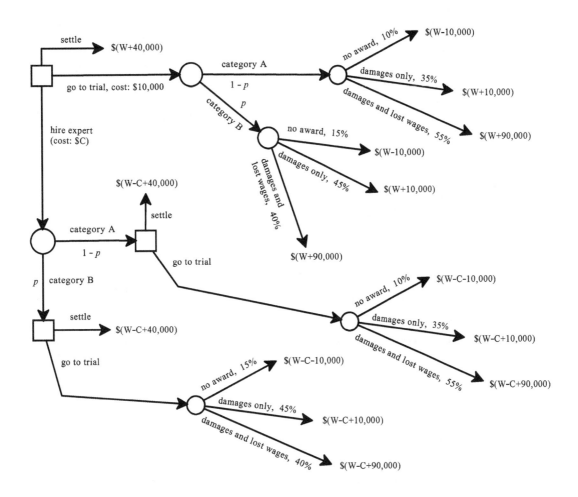

Figure 4.9: Figure 4.4 reproduced

Replacing those circles with the corresponding expected values we get the reduced tree shown in Figure 4.10.

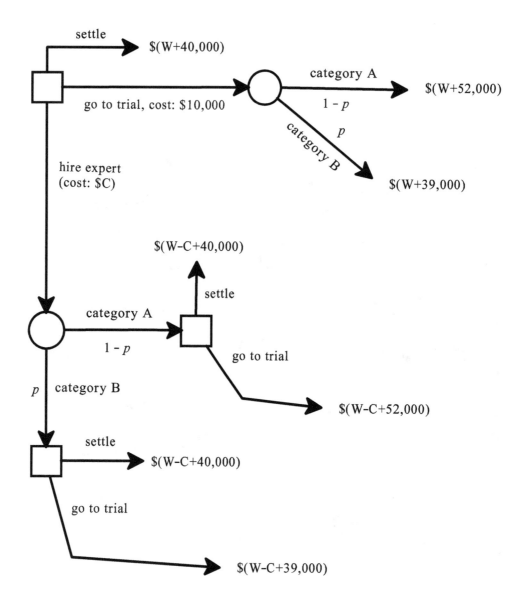

Figure 4.10: The reduced tree of Figure 4.9

4.3 Backward induction

In the reduced tree of Figure 4.10, proceeding from top to bottom we have that:
1. The circle at the top corresponds to the money lottery

$$\begin{pmatrix} \$(W+52,000) & \$(W+39,000) \\ 1-p & p \end{pmatrix}$$

whose expected value is $(W+52,000-13,000p)$.

2. At the square below, the optimal choice is to go to trial.
3. At the bottom square, the optimal choice is to settle.

Replacing those nodes with the corresponding outcomes we obtain the further reduced tree shown in Figure 4.11.

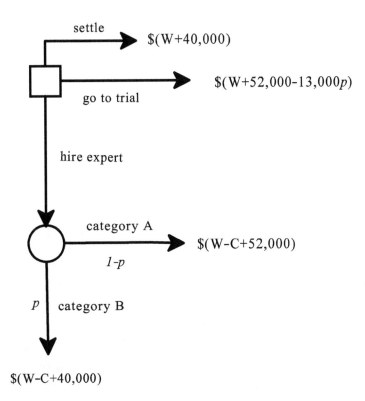

Figure 4.11: The reduced tree of Figure 4.10

In the reduced tree of Figure 4.11, the circle corresponds to the money lottery

$$\begin{pmatrix} \$(W-C+52,000) & \$(W-C+40,000) \\ 1-p & p \end{pmatrix}$$

whose expected value is $(W-C+52,000-12,000p)$.

Replacing the circle with this outcome we get the reduced tree shown in Figure 4.12. The optimal strategy depends on the values of the parameters C and p. First,

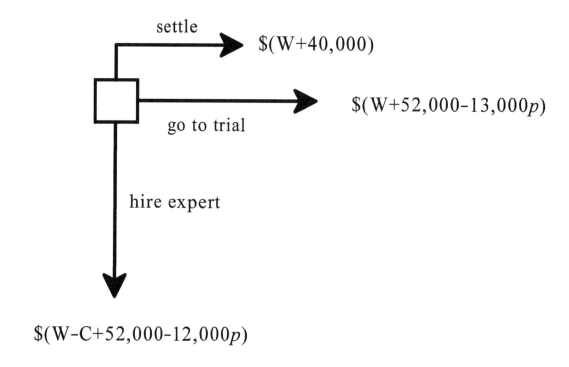

Figure 4.12: The reduced tree of Figure 4.11

let us try a specific pair of values, say $C = 500$ and $p = \frac{4}{5}$. Then going to trial right away yields $\$\left(W + 52,000 - \frac{4}{5}13,000\right) = \$(W + 41,600)$, better than settling right away, which yields $\$(W + 40,000)$. On the other hand, hiring the expert leads to the outcome $\$\left(W + 52,000 - 500 - \frac{4}{5}12,000\right) = \$(W + 41,900)$; hence, hiring the expert is the best option. Thus, when $C = 500$ and $p = \frac{4}{5}$, the optimal strategy is as follows: *hire the expert and then (1) if the expert says that the case belongs to category A then go to trial and (2) if the expert says that the case belongs to category B then settle.*

Now let us find the backward induction solution for all possible values of the parameters C and p. Assuming that $0 < p < 1$, if $C \geq 12,000$ then the option of hiring the expert is strictly worse than the option of settling right away. Thus, we will assume that

$$0 \leq C < 12,000. \tag{4.1}$$

4.3 Backward induction

First let us compare the option of settling right away (from now on denoted by S) with the option of going to trial right away (from now on denoted by T):

$$\begin{cases} \text{if } p < \frac{12}{13} & \begin{array}{l} 52,000 - 13,000p > 40,000, \\ \text{that is, going to trial is strictly better than settling: } T \succ S. \end{array} \\ \text{if } p = \frac{12}{13} & \begin{array}{l} 52,000 - 13,000p = 40,000, \\ \text{that is, going to trial is just as good as settling: } T \sim S. \end{array} \\ \text{if } p > \frac{12}{13} & \begin{array}{l} 52,000 - 13,000p < 40,000, \\ \text{that is, settling is strictly better than going to trial: } S \succ T. \end{array} \end{cases}$$

This is illustrated in Figure 4.13.

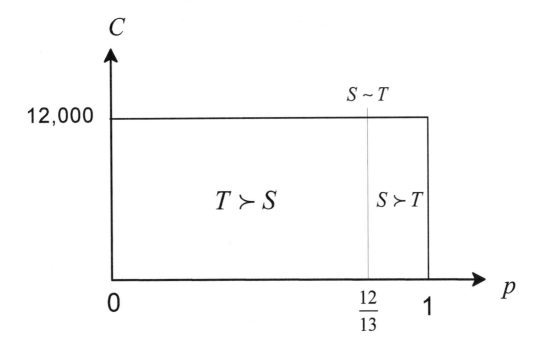

Figure 4.13: Comparison of options S and T

Next let us compare option T and the option of hiring the expert (from now on denoted by H):

$$\begin{cases} \text{if } C < 1,000p, & \text{then } 52,000 - C - 12,000p > 52,000 - 13,000p, \text{ that is, } H \succ T \\ \text{if } C = 1,000p, & \text{then } 52,000 - C - 12,000p = 52,000 - 13,000p, \text{ that is, } H \sim T \\ \text{if } C > 1,000p, & \text{then } 52,000 - C - 12,000p < 52,000 - 13,000p, \text{ that is, } T \succ H \end{cases}$$

This is illustrated in Figure 4.14.

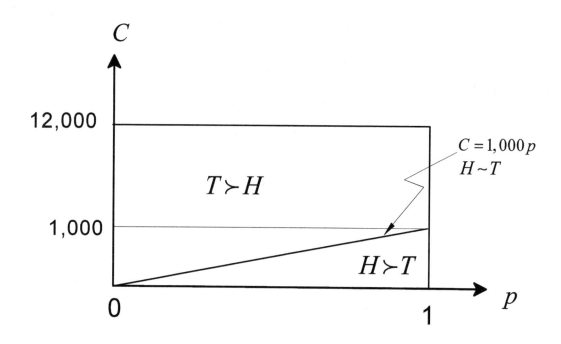

Figure 4.14: Comparison of options H and T

Putting together Figures 4.13 and 4.14 we can identify four regions in the (C,p) parameter space, as shown in Figure 4.15.

1. In the region to the left of the line $p = \frac{12}{13}$ and above the line $C = 1,000p$, $T \succ S$ and $T \succ H$ and thus the optimal decision is T, that is, to go to trial right away.
2. In the region to the left of the line $p = \frac{12}{13}$ and below the line $C = 1,000p$, $H \succ T$ and $T \succ S$ and thus the optimal strategy is H, that is, hire the expert and then (1) if the expert says that the case belongs to category A then go to trial and (2) if the expert says that the case belongs to category B then settle.
3. In the region to the right of the line $p = \frac{12}{13}$ and above the line $C = 1,000p$, $S \succ T$ and $T \succ H$ and thus the optimal decision is S, that is, to settle right away.
4. In the shaded area in Figure 4.15 (the region to the right of the line $p = \frac{12}{13}$ and below the line $C = 1,000p$) we have that $S \succ T$ and $H \succ T$ and thus, in order to determine the optimal decision, we need to compare S and H:

$$\begin{cases} \text{if } C < 12,000(1-p), & \text{then } 52,000 - C - 12,000p > 40,000, \text{ that is, } H \succ S \\ \text{if } C = 12,000(1-p), & \text{then } 52,000 - C - 12,000p = 40,000, \text{ that is, } H \sim S \\ \text{if } C > 12,000(1-p), & \text{then } 52,000 - C - 12,000p < 40,000, \text{ that is, } S \succ H \end{cases}$$

Thus, the shaded area in Figure 4.15 is divided into two subregions:
– in the region to the right of the line $p = \frac{12}{13}$, below the line $C = 1,000p$ and below the line $C = 12,000(1-p)$, the optimal decision is H (that is, the strategy of hiring the expert and then (1) if the expert says that the case belongs to category A then go to trial and (2) if the expert says that the case belongs to category B then settle),
– in the region to the right of the line $p = \frac{12}{13}$, below the line $C = 1,000p$ and above the line $C = 12,000(1-p)$, the optimal decision is S, that is, to settle right away.

4.3 Backward induction

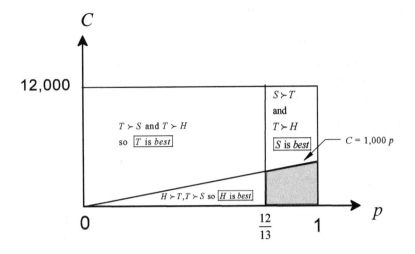

Figure 4.15: Putting together Figures 4.13 and 4.14

Figure 4.16 provides the complete picture.

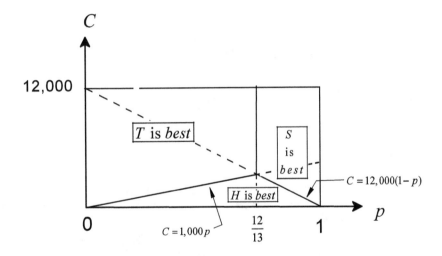

Figure 4.16: The backward-induction solution of the reduced tree of Figure 4.11

Test your understanding of the concepts introduced in this section, by going through the exercises in Section 4.5.3 at the end of this chapter.

4.4 Beyond money lotteries and risk neutrality

So far we have looked at situations where the outcomes consisted of sums of money and the *DM* was assumed to be risk neutral. Typically, however, outcomes may involve something more besides sums of money or they may even be something quite different from sums of money. Consider the following example.

Dave has developed lower back pain and is consulting his doctor on what to do. She tells him that one possibility is to do nothing: just rest and limit his activities and hope that it will heal itself. In her experience, in 40% of the cases the pain subsides spontaneously. Another possibility is to take strong doses of an anti-inflammatory drug for a prolonged period of time. This is an effective and fast way to get rid of the pain. In her experience, it works 80% of the time, without side effects. However, there is a 20% chance that the drug will cause intestinal bleeding, in which case it must be stopped immediately and avoided in the future. Usually this happens within the first week, too soon to have any benefits from the drug in terms of pain reduction. Finally, there is the option of surgery. This type of surgery has been performed many times in the past and it worked in 90% of the patients. For the remaining 10%, however, there was damage to the spine during the procedure which led to permanent numbness in one or both legs, but the pain in the back did go away. We can represent Dave's decision problem using the decision tree shown in Figure 4.17.

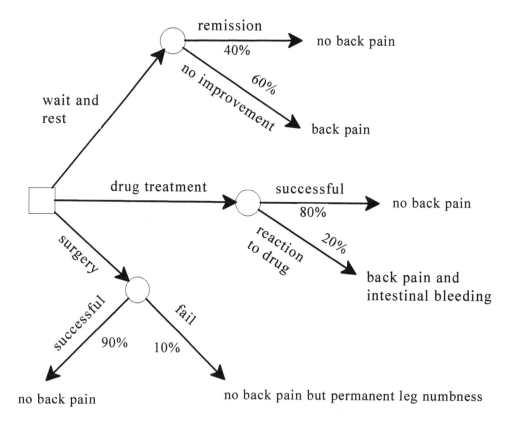

Figure 4.17: A decision tree where the outcomes are not sums of money

The method of backward induction can be used to solve the decision tree of Figure 4.17, but it requires comparing lotteries such as $\left(\begin{array}{cc}\text{no back pain} & \text{back pain} \\ \frac{40}{100} & \frac{60}{100}\end{array}\right)$ and $\left(\begin{array}{cc}\text{no back pain} & \text{back pain and intestinal bleeding} \\ \frac{80}{100} & \frac{20}{100}\end{array}\right)$, which are not money lotteries. The tools we have developed so far do not enable us to do so. We need a more general theory, which is developed in the next chapter.

4.5 Exercises

The solutions to the following exercises are given in Section 4.6 at the end of this chapter.

4.5.1 Exercises for Section 4.1: Decision Trees

Exercise 4.1 You have been offered theft insurance for your new bike, for which you paid $400. The insurance policy will cover you for one year. The premium is $20. You have a deductible of $80, so that – if the bike is stolen – you get a refund of $(400 - 80) = 320. According to actuarial figures for your area, the probability that a bicycle is stolen in any given year is 10%.

Represent your decision problem by means of a decision tree. Express outcomes in terms of your final wealth; your current wealth consists of the value of your bike plus the balance of your checking account which is B. (Clearly, insuring your bike is not a guarantee that it will not be stolen: it is only a guarantee of a refund in case it is stolen.) ∎

Exercise 4.2 You have sued your employer for wrongful termination. They are offering a settlement of $70,000. The alternative is to go to trial, at a cost of $20,000. Your lawyer tells you that there are two possibilities: (1) you win, in which case you can expect an award of $100,000, or (2) you lose, in which case you get nothing. She thinks that there is a 60% chance that you will win. Represent your decision problem by means of a decision tree. Express outcomes in terms of your final wealth; your current wealth consists of $20,000 in your checking account. ∎

Exercise 4.3 You have filed a lawsuit against your employer for sexual harassment. They have offered to settle for $40,000. The alternative is to go to trial, at a cost of $10,000. Your lawyer tells you that there are three possibilities: (1) you win a large amount: $100,000, (2) you win a small amount: $20,000 and (3) you lose and get nothing. She thinks that there is a 50% chance that you will win a large amount, a 30% chance that you will win a small amount and a 20% chance that you will lose. Represent your decision problem by means of a decision tree. Express outcomes in terms of your final wealth (assuming that your current wealth consists of B, with $B > 10,000$). ∎

Exercise 4.4 Your client, who wishes to build a hotel, is trying to decide which of two parcels of land to buy. Parcel A has been offered at a price of $300,000 and Parcel B at a price of $250,000. They seem equally attractive, so your client initially thinks that purchasing the cheaper one, Parcel B, is the better choice. However, in questioning the sellers about the parcels, you learn that Parcel B might have an environmental problem because chemical waste has been dumped on it, whereas no problems are associated with Parcel A. You find that if the waste on Parcel B is hazardous, the law would require your client to clean up the site and that the cost of cleanup would be $200,000. You figure that the odds of Parcel B having this problem are 50%. If she wishes, your client – before making a purchasing decision – can hire an environmental testing firm to determine with certainty whether she would have to clean up Parcel B. Having the environmental firm do the testing would cost her $20,000. Represent this decision problem by means of a decision tree. Express outcomes in terms of the total amount of money that your client would end up paying.

4.5.2 Exercises for Section 4.2: Money lotteries and risk neutrality

Exercise 4.5 Consider the following money lottery:

$$\begin{pmatrix} \$10 & \$15 & \$18 & \$20 & \$25 & \$30 & \$36 \\ \frac{3}{12} & \frac{1}{12} & 0 & \frac{3}{12} & \frac{2}{12} & 0 & \frac{3}{12} \end{pmatrix}$$

(a) What is its expected value?
(b) If a risk-neutral individual is given a choice between the above lottery and $23 for sure, what will she choose?

Exercise 4.6 Consider the following lottery: $\begin{pmatrix} o_1 & o_2 & o_3 \\ \frac{3}{10} & \frac{5}{10} & \frac{2}{10} \end{pmatrix}$ where o_1 is the outcome where you get $100 and an A in the class on Decision Making, o_2 is the outcome where you get a free trip to Disneyland (which would normally cost $500) and a C in the class and o_3 is the outcome where you get a $150 gift certificate at Amazon.com and a B in the class. If you are risk neutral, what sum of money would you consider to be just as good as the lottery?

Exercise 4.7 Given the choice between getting $18 for sure or playing the lottery $\begin{pmatrix} \$10 & \$20 & \$30 \\ \frac{3}{10} & \frac{5}{10} & \frac{2}{10} \end{pmatrix}$, James – who likes money (that is, prefers more money to less) – chooses to get $18 for sure. Is he risk neutral?

4.6 Solutions to Exercises

4.5.3 Exercises for Section 4.3: Backward induction

Exercise 4.8 Assuming that all you care about is your wealth (and prefer more wealth to less) and that you are risk neutral, apply the method of backward induction to the decision tree of Exercise 4.1 to find the optimal decision.

Exercise 4.9 Assuming that all you care about is your wealth (and prefer more wealth to less) and that you are risk neutral, apply the method of backward induction to the decision tree of Exercise 4.2 to find the optimal decision.

Exercise 4.10 Assuming that all you care about is your wealth (and prefer more wealth to less) and that you are risk neutral, apply the method of backward induction to the decision tree of Exercise 4.3 to find the optimal decision.

Exercise 4.11 Assuming that all your client cares about is the total amount he ends up paying (and prefers paying less to paying more) apply the method of backward induction to the decision tree of Exercise 4.4 to find the optimal decision.

4.6 Solutions to Exercises

Solution to Exercise 4.1. The decision tree is shown in Figure 4.18.

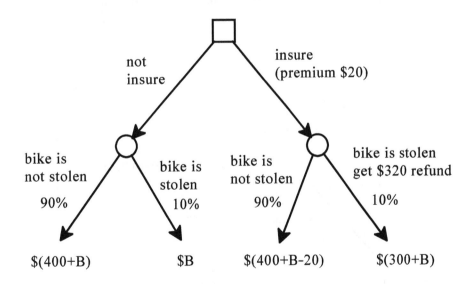

Figure 4.18: The decision tree for Exercise 4.1

Solution to Exercise 4.2. The decision tree is shown in Figure 4.19. □

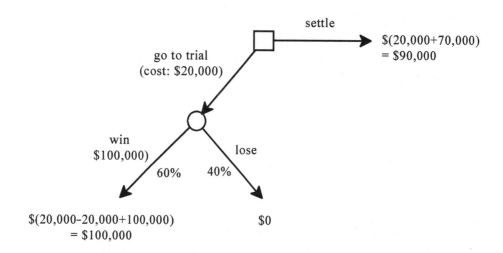

Figure 4.19: The decision tree for Exercise 4.2

Solution to Exercise 4.3. The decision tree is shown in Figure 4.20. □

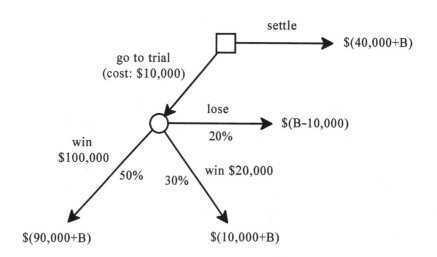

Figure 4.20: The decision tree for Exercise 4.3

4.6 Solutions to Exercises

Solution to Exercise 4.4. The decision tree is shown in Figure 4.21. □

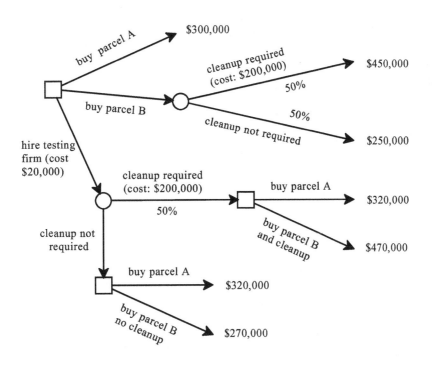

Figure 4.21: The decision tree for Exercise 4.4

Solution to Exercise 4.5.

(a) The expected value is

$$\frac{3}{12}10 + \frac{1}{12}15 + 0\,(18) + \frac{3}{12}20 + \frac{2}{12}25 + (0)\,30 + \frac{3}{12}36 = \frac{263}{12} = \$21.92.$$

(b) A risk-neutral person is indifferent between the lottery and $21.92 for sure. Assuming that she prefers more money to less, she will prefer $23 to $21.92. Thus, since she is indifferent between $21.92 and the lottery, if her preferences are transitive, she will prefer $23 to the lottery. □

Solution to Exercise 4.6. One might be tempted to compute the "expected value" $\frac{3}{10}100 + \frac{5}{10}500 + \frac{2}{10}150 = 310$ and answer: $310. However, this answer would be wrong, because the given lottery is not a money lottery: the outcomes are not just sums of money (they do involve sums of money but also what grade you get in the class). The definition of risk neutrality can only be applied to money lotteries. □

Solution to Exercise 4.7. The expected value of the lottery is $\frac{3}{10}10 + \frac{5}{10}20 + \frac{2}{10}30 = 19$. If James were risk-neutral he would consider the lottery to be just as good as getting $19 for sure and would therefore choose the lottery (since getting $19 is better than getting $18). Hence, he is *not* risk neutral. □

Solution to Exercise 4.8. The decision tree of Exercise 4.1 is reproduced in Figure 4.22.

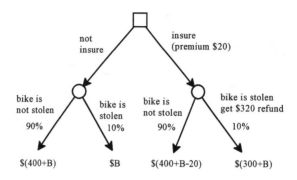

Figure 4.22: Copy of the decision tree of Figure 4.18

The Chance node on the left corresponds to the money lottery $\begin{pmatrix} \$(400+B) & \$B \\ \frac{9}{10} & \frac{1}{10} \end{pmatrix}$ which has an expected value of $\$(360+B)$. The Chance node on the right corresponds to the money lottery $\begin{pmatrix} \$(380+B) & \$(300+B) \\ \frac{9}{10} & \frac{1}{10} \end{pmatrix}$ which has an expected value of $\$(372+B)$. Thus, insuring the bicycle is the better choice. □

Solution to Exercise 4.9. The decision tree of Exercise 4.2 is reproduced in Figure 4.23.

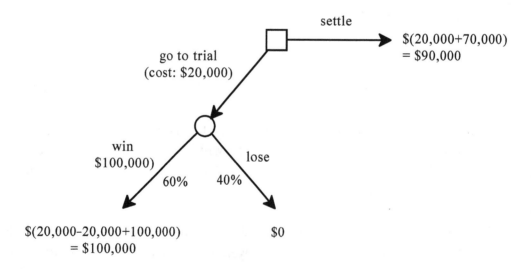

Figure 4.23: Copy of the decision tree of Figure 4.19

The Chance node corresponds to the money lottery $\begin{pmatrix} \$100,000 & \$0 \\ \frac{6}{10} & \frac{4}{10} \end{pmatrix}$ which has an expected value of $\$60,000$. Thus, you will settle. □

4.6 Solutions to Exercises

Solution to Exercise 4.10. The decision tree of Exercise 4.3 is reproduced in Figure 4.24.

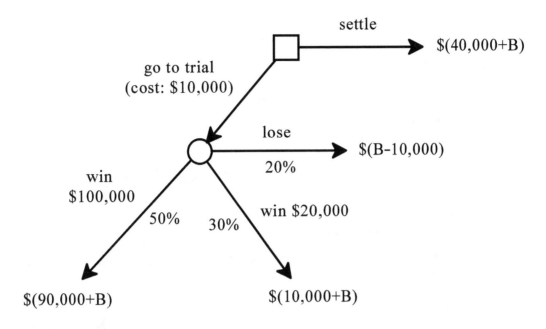

Figure 4.24: Copy of the decision tree of Figure 4.20

The Chance node corresponds to the money lottery

$$\begin{pmatrix} \$(B+90,000) & \$(B+10,000) & \$(B-10,000) \\ \frac{5}{10} & \frac{3}{10} & \frac{2}{10} \end{pmatrix}$$

which has an expected value of $\$(B+46,000)$. Thus, you should go to trial. □

Solution to Exercise 4.11. The decision tree of Exercise 4.4 is reproduced in Figure 4.25.

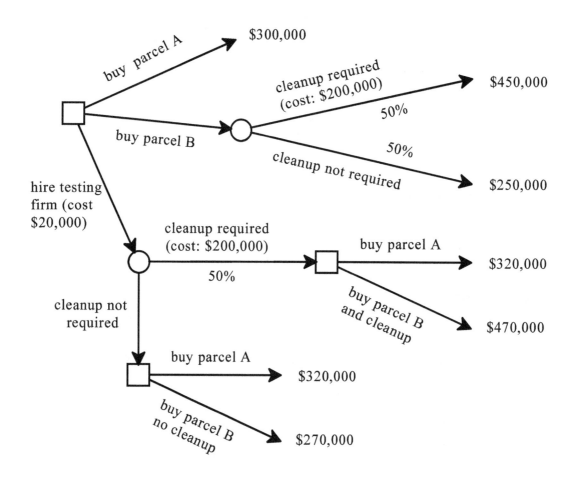

Figure 4.25: Copy of the decision tree of Figure 4.21

At the bottom decision node (square), where cleanup is not required, "Buy B" is the optimal choice and at the right-most one, where cleanup is required, "Buy A" is the optimal choice. Thus, the bottom Chance node corresponds to the lottery $\begin{pmatrix} \$270,000 & \$320,000 \\ \frac{5}{10} & \frac{5}{10} \end{pmatrix}$ whose expected value is $\$295,000$. The top Chance node corresponds to the lottery $\begin{pmatrix} \$450,000 & \$250,000 \\ \frac{5}{10} & \frac{5}{10} \end{pmatrix}$ whose expected value is $\$350,000$. Thus, the optimal strategy is "Hire testing firm and then (1) Buy A if cleanup is required and (2) Buy B if cleanup is not required". □

Uncertainty and Decision Making

5 Expected Utility Theory 71
- 5.1 Money lotteries and attitudes to risk
- 5.2 Expected utility: theorems
- 5.3 Expected utility: the axioms
- 5.4 Exercises
- 5.5 Solutions to Exercises

6 Applications of Expected Utility 99
- 6.1 States and acts revisited
- 6.2 Decision trees revisited
- 6.3 Regret
- 6.4 The Hurwicz index of pessimism
- 6.5 Exercises
- 6.6 Solutions to Exercises

7 Conditional Reasoning 127
- 7.1 Sets and probability: brief review
- 7.2 Conditional thinking
- 7.3 Simpson's paradox
- 7.4 Exercises
- 7.5 Solutions to Exercises

8 Information and Beliefs 155
- 8.1 Uncertainty and information
- 8.2 Updating beliefs
- 8.3 Belief revision
- 8.4 Information and truth
- 8.5 Exercises
- 8.6 Solutions to Exercises

9 The Value of Information 173
- 9.1 When is information potentially valuable?
- 9.2 The value of information when outcomes are sums of money
- 9.3 The general case
- 9.4 Different sources of information
- 9.5 Exercises
- 9.6 Solutions to Exercises

5. Expected Utility Theory

5.1 Money lotteries and attitudes to risk

The introduction of chance moves gives rise to probabilistic outcomes, which we called lotteries. In Chapter 4 we restricted attention to lotteries whose outcomes are sums of money (money lotteries) and to one possible way of ranking such lotteries, based on the notion of risk neutrality. In this section we will continue to focus on money lotteries and define other possible attitudes to risk.[1]

As before, we restrict attention to finite lotteries. Recall that a money lottery is a probability distribution of the form

$$\begin{pmatrix} \$x_1 & \$x_2 & \ldots & \$x_n \\ p_1 & p_2 & \ldots & p_n \end{pmatrix}$$

($0 \leq p_i \leq 1$, for all $i = 1, 2, \ldots, n$, and $p_1 + p_2 + \ldots + p_n = 1$) and that (Definition 4.2.2, Chapter 4) its expected value is the number $(x_1 p_1 + x_2 p_2 + \ldots + x_n p_n)$. If L is a money lottery, we denote by $\mathbb{E}[L]$ the expected value of L. Thus, for example, if

$$L = \begin{pmatrix} \$30 & \$45 & \$90 \\ \frac{1}{3} & \frac{5}{9} & \frac{1}{9} \end{pmatrix} \quad \text{then} \quad \mathbb{E}[L] = \tfrac{1}{3}(30) + \tfrac{5}{9}(45) + \tfrac{1}{9}(90) = 45.$$

Recall also (Definition 4.2.3, Chapter 4) that a person is said to be *risk neutral* if she considers a money lottery to be just as good as its expected value for certain. For example, a risk-neutral person would consider getting $45 with certainty to be just as good as playing lottery $L = \begin{pmatrix} \$30 & \$45 & \$90 \\ \frac{1}{3} & \frac{5}{9} & \frac{1}{9} \end{pmatrix}$. We can now consider different attitudes to risk, besides risk neutrality.

---

[1] In the next section we will consider more general lotteries, where the outcomes need not be sums of money, and introduce the theory of expected utility.

Definition 5.1.1 Let L be a money lottery and consider the choice between L and the degenerate lottery $\begin{pmatrix} \$\mathbb{E}[L] \\ 1 \end{pmatrix}$ (that is, the choice between facing the lottery L or getting the expected value of L with certainty). Then
- An individual who prefers $\$\mathbb{E}[L]$ for certain to L is said to be *risk averse*.
- An individual who is indifferent between $\$\mathbb{E}[L]$ for certain and L is said to be *risk neutral*.
- An individual who prefers L to $\$\mathbb{E}[L]$ for certain is said to be *risk loving*.

Note that if an individual is risk neutral, has transitive preferences over money lotteries and prefers more money to less, then we can tell how that individual ranks any two money lotteries. For example, how would a risk neutral individual rank the two lotteries $L_1 = \begin{pmatrix} \$30 & \$45 & \$90 \\ \frac{1}{3} & \frac{5}{9} & \frac{1}{9} \end{pmatrix}$ and $L_2 = \begin{pmatrix} \$5 & \$100 \\ \frac{3}{5} & \frac{2}{5} \end{pmatrix}$? Since $\mathbb{E}[L_1] = 45$ and the individual is risk neutral, $L_1 \sim \$45$; since $\mathbb{E}[L_2] = 43$ and the individual is risk neutral, $\$43 \sim L_2$; since the individual prefers more money to less, $\$45 \succ \$43$; thus, by transitivity, $L_1 \succ L_2$. On the other hand, knowing that an individual is risk averse, has transitive preferences over money lotteries and prefers more money to less is not sufficient to predict how she will choose between two arbitrary money lotteries. For example, as we will see later (see Exercise 5.11), it is possible that one risk-averse individual will prefer $L_3 = \begin{pmatrix} \$28 \\ 1 \end{pmatrix}$ (whose expected value is 28) to $L_4 = \begin{pmatrix} \$10 & \$50 \\ \frac{1}{2} & \frac{1}{2} \end{pmatrix}$ (whose expected value is 30), while another risk-averse individual will prefer L_4 to L_3. Similarly, knowing that an individual is risk loving, has transitive preferences over money lotteries and prefers more money to less is not sufficient to predict how she will choose between two arbitrary money lotteries.

> **R** Note that "rationality" does not, and should not, dictate whether an individual should be risk neutral, risk averse or risk loving: an individual's attitude to risk is merely a reflection of that individual's preferences. It is a generally accepted principle that *de gustibus non est disputandum* (in matters of taste, there can be no disputes). According to this principle, there is no such thing as an irrational preference and thus there is no such thing as an irrational attitude to risk. From an empirical point of view, however, most people reveal through their choices (e.g. the decision to buy insurance) that they are risk averse, at least when the stakes are high.

As noted above, with the exception of risk-neutral individuals, even if we restrict attention to money lotteries we are not able to say much – in general – about how an individual would choose among lotteries. What we need is a theory of "rational" preferences over lotteries that (1) is general enough to cover lotteries whose outcomes are not necessarily sums of money and (2) is capable of accounting for different attitudes to risk in the case of money lotteries. One such theory is the theory of expected utility, to which we now turn.

> Test your understanding of the concepts introduced in this section, by going through the exercises in Section 5.4.1 at the end of this chapter.

5.2 Expected utility: theorems

The theory of expected utility was developed by the founders of game theory, namely John von Neumann and Oskar Morgenstern, in their 1944 book *Theory of Games and Economic Behavior*. In a rather unconventional way, we shall first (in this section) state the main result of the theory (which we split into two theorems) and then (in the following section) explain the assumptions (or axioms) behind that result. The reader who is not interested in understanding the conceptual foundations of expected utility theory, but wants to understand what the theory says and how it can be used, can study this section and skip the next.

Let O be a set of *basic outcomes*. Note that a basic outcome need not be a sum of money: it could be the state of an individual's health, or whether the individual under consideration receives an award, or whether it will rain on the day of her planned outdoor party, etc. Let $\mathscr{L}(O)$ be the set of *simple lotteries* (or probability distributions) over O. We will assume throughout that O is a finite set: $O = \{o_1, o_2, ..., o_m\}$ ($m \geq 1$). Thus, an element of $\mathscr{L}(O)$ is of the form $\begin{pmatrix} o_1 & o_2 & ... & o_m \\ p_1 & p_2 & ... & p_m \end{pmatrix}$ with $0 \leq p_i \leq 1$, for all $i = 1, 2, ..., m$, and $p_1 + p_2 + ... + p_m = 1$. We will use the symbol L (with or without subscript) to denote an element of $\mathscr{L}(O)$, that is, a simple lottery. Lotteries are used to represent situations of uncertainty. For example, if $m = 4$ and the individual faces the lottery $L = \begin{pmatrix} o_1 & o_2 & o_3 & o_4 \\ \frac{2}{5} & 0 & \frac{1}{5} & \frac{2}{5} \end{pmatrix}$ then she knows that, eventually, the outcome will be one and only one of o_1, o_2, o_3, o_4, but does not know which one; furthermore, she is able to quantify her uncertainty by assigning probabilities to these outcomes. We interpret these probabilities either as objectively obtained from relevant (past) data or as subjective estimates by the individual. For example, an individual who is considering whether or not to insure her bicycle against theft for the following 12 months knows that there are two relevant basic outcomes: either the bicycle will be stolen or it will not be stolen. Furthermore, she can look up data on past bicycle thefts in her area and use the proportion of bicycles that were stolen as an "objective" estimate of the probability that her bicycle will be stolen. Alternatively, she can use a more subjective estimate: for example she might use a lower probability of theft than suggested by the data because she knows herself to be very conscientious and – unlike other people – to always lock her bicycle when left unattended.

The assignment of *zero probability* to a particular basic outcome is taken to be an expression of *belief, not impossibility*: the individual is confident that the outcome will not arise, but she cannot rule out that outcome on logical grounds or by appealing to the laws of nature.

Among the elements of $\mathscr{L}(O)$ there are the degenerate lotteries that assign probability 1 to one basic outcome: for example, if $m=4$ one degenerate lottery is $\begin{pmatrix} o_1 & o_2 & o_3 & o_4 \\ 0 & 0 & 1 & 0 \end{pmatrix}$. To simplify the notation we will often denote degenerate lotteries as basic outcomes, that is, instead of writing $\begin{pmatrix} o_1 & o_2 & o_3 & o_4 \\ 0 & 0 & 1 & 0 \end{pmatrix}$ we will simply write o_3. Thus, in general, the degenerate lottery $\begin{pmatrix} o_1 & ... & o_{i-1} & o_i & o_{i+1} & ... & o_m \\ 0 & 0 & 0 & 1 & 0 & 0 & 0 \end{pmatrix}$ will be denoted by o_i. As another simplification, we will often omit those outcomes that are assigned zero probability. For example, if $m=4$, the lottery $\begin{pmatrix} o_1 & o_2 & o_3 & o_4 \\ \frac{1}{3} & 0 & \frac{2}{3} & 0 \end{pmatrix}$ will be written more simply as $\begin{pmatrix} o_1 & o_3 \\ \frac{1}{3} & \frac{2}{3} \end{pmatrix}$.

As in previous chapters, we shall call the individual under consideration the Decision-Maker, or *DM* for short. The theory of expected utility assumes that the *DM* has a complete and transitive ranking $\succsim$ of the elements of $\mathscr{L}(O)$ (indeed, this is one of the axioms listed in the next section). As in Chapter 2, the interpretation of $L \succsim L'$ is that the *DM* considers L to be at least as good as L'. By completeness, given any two lotteries L and L', either $L \succ L'$ (the *DM* prefers L to L') or $L' \succ L$ (the *DM* prefers L' to L) or $L \sim L'$ (the *DM* is indifferent between L and L'). Furthermore, by transitivity, for any three lotteries L_1, L_2 and L_3, if $L_1 \succsim L_2$ and $L_2 \succsim L_3$, then $L_1 \succsim L_3$. Besides completeness and transitivity, a number of other "rationality" constraints are postulated on the ranking $\succsim$ of the elements of $\mathscr{L}(O)$; these constraints are the so-called Expected Utility Axioms and are discussed in the next section.

Definition 5.2.1 A ranking $\succsim$ of the elements of $\mathscr{L}(O)$ that satisfies the Expected Utility Axioms (listed in the next section) is called a *von Neumann-Morgenstern ranking*.

The following two theorems are the key results in the theory of expected utility.

5.2 Expected utility: theorems

Theorem 5.2.1 [von Neumann-Morgenstern, 1944].
Let $O = \{o_1, o_2, ..., o_m\}$ be a set of basic outcomes and $\mathscr{L}(O)$ the set of simple lotteries over O. If $\succsim$ is a von Neumann-Morgenstern ranking of the elements of $\mathscr{L}(O)$ then there exists a function $U : O \to \mathbb{R}$, called a *von Neumann-Morgenstern utility function*, that assigns a number (called *utility*) to every basic outcome and is such that, for any two lotteries $L = \begin{pmatrix} o_1 & o_2 & ... & o_m \\ p_1 & p_2 & ... & p_m \end{pmatrix}$ and $L' = \begin{pmatrix} o_1 & o_2 & ... & o_m \\ q_1 & q_2 & ... & q_m \end{pmatrix}$,

$$L \succ L' \text{ if and only if } \mathbb{E}[U(L)] > \mathbb{E}[U(L')], \text{ and}$$

$$L \sim L' \text{ if and only if } \mathbb{E}[U(L)] = \mathbb{E}[U(L')]$$

where

$$U(L) = \begin{pmatrix} U(o_1) & U(o_2) & ... & U(o_m) \\ p_1 & p_2 & ... & p_m \end{pmatrix}, \quad U(L') = \begin{pmatrix} U(o_1) & U(o_2) & ... & U(o_m) \\ q_1 & q_2 & ... & q_m \end{pmatrix},$$

$\mathbb{E}[U(L)]$ is the expected value of the lottery $U(L)$ and $\mathbb{E}[U(L')]$ is the expected value of the lottery $U(L')$, that is,

$$\mathbb{E}[U(L)] = p_1 U(o_1) + p_2 U(o_2) + ... + p_m U(o_m), \text{ and}$$

$$\mathbb{E}[U(L')] = q_1 U(o_1) + q_2 U(o_2) + ... + q_m U(o_m).$$

$\mathbb{E}[U(L)]$ is called the *expected utility* of lottery L (and $\mathbb{E}[U(L')]$ the expected utility of lottery L').

We say that any function $U : O \to \mathbb{R}$ that satisfies the property that, for any two lotteries L and L', $L \succsim L'$ if and only if $\mathbb{E}[U(L)] \geq \mathbb{E}[U(L')]$ *represents the preferences* (or ranking) $\succsim$.

Before we comment on Theorem 5.2.1 we give an example of how one can use it. Theorem 5.2.1 sometimes allows us to predict an individual's choice between two lotteries C and D if we know how that individual ranks two different lotteries A and B.

For example, suppose we observe that Susan is faced with the choice between lotteries A and B below and she says that she prefers A to B:

$$A = \begin{pmatrix} o_1 & o_2 & o_3 \\ 0 & 0.25 & 0.75 \end{pmatrix} \qquad B = \begin{pmatrix} o_1 & o_2 & o_3 \\ 0.2 & 0 & 0.8 \end{pmatrix}$$

With this information we can predict which of the following two lotteries C and D she will choose, if she has von Neumann-Morgenstern preferences:

$$C = \begin{pmatrix} o_1 & o_2 & o_3 \\ 0.8 & 0 & 0.2 \end{pmatrix} \qquad D = \begin{pmatrix} o_1 & o_2 & o_3 \\ 0 & 1 & 0 \end{pmatrix} = o_2.$$

Let U be a von Neumann-Morgenstern utility function whose existence is guaranteed by Theorem 5.2.1. Let $U(o_1) = a$, $U(o_2) = b$ and $U(o_3) = c$ (where a, b and c are numbers). Then, since Susan prefers A to B, the expected utility of A must be greater than the expected utility of B: $0.25b + 0.75c > 0.2a + 0.8c$. This inequality is equivalent to $0.25b > 0.2a + 0.05c$ or, dividing both sides by 0.25, $b > 0.8a + 0.2c$. It follows from this and Theorem 5.2.1 that Susan prefers D to C, because the expected utility of D is b and the expected utility of C is $0.8a + 0.2c$. Note that, in this example, we merely used the fact that a von Neumann-Morgenstern utility function *exists*, even though we do not know what the values of this function are.

Theorem 5.2.1 is an example of a "representation theorem" and is a generalization of a similar result for the case of the ranking of a finite set of basic outcomes O. It is not difficult to prove that if $\succsim$ is a complete and transitive ranking of O then there exists a function $U : O \to \mathbb{R}$, called a utility function, such that, for any two basic outcomes $o, o' \in O$, $U(o) \geq U(o')$ if and only if $o \succsim o'$. Now, it is quite possible that an individual has a complete and transitive ranking of O, is fully aware of her ranking and yet she is not able to answer the question "what is your utility function?", perhaps because she has never heard about utility functions. A utility function is a *tool* that we can use to represent her ranking, nothing more than that. The same applies to von Neumann-Morgenstern rankings: Theorem 5.2.1 tells us that if an individual has a von Neumann-Morgenstern ranking of the set of lotteries $\mathscr{L}(O)$ then there exists a von Neumann-Morgenstern utility function that we can use to represent her preferences, but it would not make sense for us to ask the individual "what is your von Neumann-Morgenstern utility function?" (indeed this was a question that could not even be conceived before von Neumann and Morgenstern stated and proved Theorem 5.2.1 in 1944!).

Theorem 5.2.1 tells us that a von Neumann-Morgenstern utility function exists; the next theorem can be used to actually construct such a function, by asking the individual to answer a few questions, formulated in a way that is fully comprehensible to her (that is, without using the word 'utility'). The theorem says that, although there are many utility functions that represent a given von Neumann-Morgenstern ranking, once you know one

5.2 Expected utility: theorems

function you "know them all", in the sense that there is a simple operation that transforms one function into the other.

> **Theorem 5.2.2** [von Neumann-Morgenstern, 1944].
> Let $\succsim$ be a von Neumann-Morgenstern ranking of the set of basic lotteries $\mathscr{L}(O)$, where $O = \{o_1, o_2, ..., o_m\}$. Then the following are true.
>
> **(A)** If $U : O \to \mathbb{R}$ is a von Neumann-Morgenstern utility function that represents $\succsim$, then, for any two real numbers a and b, with $a > 0$, the function $V : O \to \mathbb{R}$ defined by $V(o_i) = aU(o_i) + b$ (for every $i = 1, \ldots, m$) is also a von Neumann-Morgenstern utility function that represents $\succsim$.
>
> **(B)** If $U : O \to \mathbb{R}$ and $V : O \to \mathbb{R}$ are two von Neumann-Morgenstern utility functions that represent $\succsim$, then there exist two real numbers a and b, with $a > 0$, such that $V(o_i) = aU(o_i) + b$ (for every $i = 1, \ldots, m$).

Proof. The proof of Part A of Theorem 5.2.2 is very simple. Let a and b be two numbers, with $a > 0$. The hypothesis is that $U : O \to \mathbb{R}$ is a von Neumann-Morgenstern utility function that represents $\succsim$, that is, that, for any two lotteries $L = \begin{pmatrix} o_1 & \ldots & o_m \\ p_1 & \ldots & p_m \end{pmatrix}$ and $L' = \begin{pmatrix} o_1 & \ldots & o_m \\ q_1 & \ldots & q_m \end{pmatrix}$,

$$L \succsim L' \text{ if and only if } p_1 U(o_1) + \ldots + p_m U(o_m) \geq q_1 U(o_1) + \ldots + q_m U(o_m) \quad (5.1)$$

Multiplying both sides of the inequality (5.1) by $a > 0$ and adding $(p_1 + \cdots + p_m)b$ to the left-hand side and $(q_1 + \cdots + q_m)b$ to the right-hand side[2] we obtain

$$p_1[aU(o_1) + b] + \ldots + p_m[aU(o_m) + b] \geq q_1[aU(o_1) + b] + \ldots + q_m[aU(o_m) + b] \quad (5.2)$$

Defining $V(o_i) = aU(o_i) + b$, it follows from (5.1) and (5.2) that

$$L \succsim L' \text{ if and only if } p_1 V(o_1) + \ldots + p_m V(o_m) \geq q_1 V(o_1) + \ldots + q_m V(o_m),$$

that is, the function V is a von Neumann-Morgenstern utility function that represents the ranking $\succsim$. The proof of Part B will be given later, after introducing more notation and some observations. ∎

---

[2] Note that $(p_1 + \cdots + p_m) = (q_1 + \cdots + q_m) = 1$.

Suppose that the *DM* has a von Neumann-Morgenstern ranking of the set of lotteries $\mathscr{L}(O)$. Since among the lotteries there are the degenerate ones that assign probability 1 to a single basic outcome, it follows that the *DM* has a complete and transitive ranking of the basic outcomes. We shall write o_{best} for a best basic outcome, that is, a basic outcome which is at least as good as any other basic outcome ($o_{best} \succsim o$, for every $o \in O$) and o_{worst} for a worst basic outcome, that is, a basic outcome such that every other outcome is at least as good as it ($o \succsim o_{worst}$, for every $o \in O$). Note that there may be several best outcomes (then the *DM* would be indifferent among them) and several worst outcomes; then o_{best} will denote an arbitrary best outcome and o_{worst} an arbitrary worst outcome. We shall assume throughout that the *DM* is not indifferent among all the outcomes, that is, we shall assume that $o_{best} \succ o_{worst}$.

We now show that, in virtue of Theorem 5.2.2, among the von Neumann-Morgenstern utility functions that represent a given von Neumann-Morgenstern ranking $\succsim$ of $\mathscr{L}(O)$, there is one that assigns the value 1 to the best basic outcome(s) and the value 0 to the worst basic outcome(s). To see this, consider an arbitrary von Neumann-Morgenstern utility function $F: O \to \mathbb{R}$ that represents $\succsim$ and define $G: O \to \mathbb{R}$ as follows: for every $o \in O$, $G(o) = F(o) - F(o_{worst})$. Then, by Theorem 5.2.2 (with $a = 1$ and $b = -F(o_{worst})$), G is also a utility function that represents $\succsim$ and, by construction, $G(o_{worst}) = F(o_{worst}) - F(o_{worst}) = 0$; note also that, since $o_{best} \succ o_{worst}$, it follows that $G(o_{best}) > 0$. Finally, define $U: O \to \mathbb{R}$ as follows: for every $o \in O$, $U(o) = \frac{G(o)}{G(o_{best})}$. Then, by Theorem 5.2.2 (with $a = \frac{1}{G(o_{best})}$ and $b = 0$), U is a utility function that represents $\succsim$ and, by construction, $U(o_{worst}) = 0$ and $U(o_{best}) = 1$. For example, if there are six basic outcomes and the ranking of the basic outcomes is $o_3 \sim o_6 \succ o_1 \succ o_4 \succ o_2 \sim o_5$, then one can take as o_{best} either o_3 or o_6 and as o_{worst} either o_2 or o_5; furthermore, if F is given by

$\begin{pmatrix} o_1 & o_2 & o_3 & o_4 & o_5 & o_6 \\ 2 & -2 & 8 & 0 & -2 & 8 \end{pmatrix}$ then G is the function $\begin{pmatrix} o_1 & o_2 & o_3 & o_4 & o_5 & o_6 \\ 4 & 0 & 10 & 2 & 0 & 10 \end{pmatrix}$ and U is the function $\begin{pmatrix} o_1 & o_2 & o_3 & o_4 & o_5 & o_6 \\ 0.4 & 0 & 1 & 0.2 & 0 & 1 \end{pmatrix}$.

Definition 5.2.2 Let $U: O \to \mathbb{R}$ be a utility function that represents a given von Neumann-Morgenstern ranking $\succsim$ of the set of lotteries $\mathscr{L}(O)$. We say that U is *normalized* if $U(o_{worst}) = 0$ and $U(o_{best}) = 1$.

The transformations described above show how to normalize any given utility function. Armed with the notion of a normalized utility function we can now complete the proof of Theorem 5.2.2.

5.2 Expected utility: theorems

Proof of Part B of Theorem 5.2.2. Let $F: O \to \mathbb{R}$ and $G: O \to \mathbb{R}$ be two von Neumann-Morgenstern utility functions that represent a given von Neumann-Morgenstern ranking of $\mathscr{L}(O)$. Let $U: O \to \mathbb{R}$ be the normalization of F and $V: O \to \mathbb{R}$ be the normalization of G. First we show that it must be that $U = V$, that is, $U(o) = V(o)$ for every $o \in O$. Suppose, by contradiction, that there is an $\hat{o} \in O$ such that $U(\hat{o}) \neq V(\hat{o})$. Without loss of generality we can assume that $U(\hat{o}) > V(\hat{o})$. Construct the following lottery: $L = \begin{pmatrix} o_{best} & o_{worst} \\ \hat{p} & 1-\hat{p} \end{pmatrix}$ with $\hat{p} = U(\hat{o})$ (recall that U is normalized and thus takes on values in the interval from 0 to 1). Then $\mathbb{E}[U(L)] = \mathbb{E}[V(L)] = U(\hat{o})$. Hence, according to U it must be that $\hat{o} \sim L$ (this follows from Theorem 5.2.1), while according to V it must be (again, by Theorem 5.2.1) that $L \succ \hat{o}$ (since $\mathbb{E}[V(L)] = U(\hat{o}) > V(\hat{o})$). Then U and V cannot be two representations of the same ranking. Now let $a_1 = \frac{1}{F(o_{best}) - F(o_{worst})}$ and $b_1 = -\frac{F(o_{worst})}{F(o_{best}) - F(o_{worst})}$. Note that $a_1 > 0$. Then it is easy to verify that, for every $o \in O$, $U(o) = a_1 F(o) + b_1$. Similarly let $a_2 = \frac{1}{G(o_{best}) - G(o_{worst})}$ and $b_2 = -\frac{G(o_{worst})}{G(o_{best}) - G(o_{worst})}$; again, $a_2 > 0$ and, for every $o \in O$, $V(o) = a_2 G(o) + b_2$. We can invert the latter transformation and obtain that, for every $o \in O$, $G(o) = \frac{V(o)}{a_2} - \frac{b_2}{a_2}$. Thus, we can transform F into U, which – as proved above – is the same as V, and then transform V into G thus obtaining the following transformation of F into G:

$$G(o) = aF(o) + b \text{ where } a = \frac{a_1}{a_2} > 0 \text{ and } b = \frac{b_1 - b_2}{a_2}. \qquad \square$$

ⓡ Theorem 5.2.2 is often stated as follows: a utility function that represents a von Neumann-Morgenstern ranking $\succsim$ of $\mathscr{L}(O)$ is *unique up to a positive affine transformation*. An affine transformation is a function $f: \mathbb{R} \to \mathbb{R}$ of the form $f(x) = ax + b$ with $a, b \in \mathbb{R}$. The affine transformation is positive if $a > 0$.

Because of Theorem 5.2.2, a von Neumann-Morgenstern utility function is usually referred to as a *cardinal* utility function.

Theorem 5.2.1 guarantees the existence of a utility function that represents a given von Neumann-Morgenstern ranking $\succsim$ of $\mathscr{L}(O)$ and Theorem 5.2.2 characterizes the set of such functions. Can one actually construct a utility function that represents a given ranking? The answer is affirmative: if there are m basic outcomes one can construct an individual's von Neumann-Morgenstern utility function by asking her at most $(m-1)$ questions. The first question is "what is your ranking of the basic outcomes?". Then we can construct the normalized utility function by first assigning the value 1 to the best outcome(s) and the value 0 to the worst outcome(s). This leaves us with at most $(m-2)$ values to determine. For this we appeal to one of the axioms discussed in the next section, namely the Continuity Axiom, which says that, for every basic outcome o_i there is a probability $p_i \in [0,1]$ such that the *DM* is indifferent between o_i for certain and the lottery that gives a best outcome with probability p_i and a worst outcome with probability $(1-p_i)$:

$$o_i \sim \begin{pmatrix} o_{best} & o_{worst} \\ p_i & 1-p_i \end{pmatrix}.$$

Thus, for each basic outcome o_i for which a utility has not been determined yet, we should ask the individual to tell us the value of p_i such that $o_i \sim \begin{pmatrix} o_{best} & o_{worst} \\ p_i & 1-p_i \end{pmatrix}$; then we can set $U_i(o_i) = p_i$, because the expected utility of the lottery $\begin{pmatrix} o_{best} & o_{worst} \\ p_i & 1-p_i \end{pmatrix}$ is $p_i U_i(o_{best}) + (1-p_i) U_i(o_{worst}) = p_i(1) + (1-p_i)0 = p_i$.

■ **Example 5.1** Suppose that there are five basic outcomes, that is, $O = \{o_1, o_2, o_3, o_4, o_5\}$ and the *DM*, who has von Neumann-Morgenstern preferences, tells us that her ranking of the basic outcomes is as follows: $o_2 \succ o_1 \sim o_5 \succ o_3 \sim o_4$. Then we can begin by assigning utility 1 to the best outcome o_2 and utility 0 to the worst outcomes o_3 and o_4:

$$\begin{pmatrix} \text{outcome:} & o_1 & o_2 & o_3 & o_4 & o_5 \\ \text{utility:} & ? & 1 & 0 & 0 & ? \end{pmatrix}.$$

There is only one value left to be determined, namely the utility of o_1 (which is also the utility of o_5, since $o_1 \sim o_5$). To find this value, we ask the *DM* to tell us what value of p makes her indifferent between the lottery $L = \begin{pmatrix} o_2 & o_3 \\ p & 1-p \end{pmatrix}$ and outcome o_1 with certainty.

Suppose that her answer is: 0.4. Then her normalized von Neumann-Morgenstern utility function is $\begin{pmatrix} \text{outcome:} & o_1 & o_2 & o_3 & o_4 & o_5 \\ \text{utility:} & 0.4 & 1 & 0 & 0 & 0.4 \end{pmatrix}$. Knowing this, we can predict her choice among any set of lotteries over these five basic outcomes. ■

Test your understanding of the concepts introduced in this section, by going through the exercises in Section 5.4.2 at the end of this chapter.

5.3 Expected utility: the axioms

We can now turn to the list of rationality axioms proposed by von Neumann and Morgenstern. This section makes heavy use of mathematical notation and, as mentioned in the previous section, if the reader is not interested in understanding in what sense the theory of expected utility captures the notion of rationality, he/she can skip it without affecting his/her ability to understand the rest of this book.

Let $O = \{o_1, o_2, ..., o_m\}$ be the set of basic outcomes and $\mathscr{L}(O)$ the set of simple lotteries, that is, the set of probability distributions over O. Let $\succsim$ be a binary relation on $\mathscr{L}(O)$. We say that $\succsim$ is a *von Neumann-Morgenstern ranking* of $\mathscr{L}(O)$ if it satisfies the following four axioms or properties.

Axiom 1 [Completeness and transitivity]. $\succsim$ is complete (for every two lotteries L and L' either $L \succsim L'$ or $L' \succsim L$ or both) and transitive (for any three lotteries L_1, L_2 and L_3, if $L_1 \succsim L_2$ and $L_2 \succsim L_3$ then $L_1 \succsim L_3$).

As noted in the previous section, Axiom 1 implies that there is a complete and transitive ranking of the basic outcomes. Recall that o_{best} denotes a best basic outcome and o_{worst} denotes a worst basic outcome and that we are assuming that $o_{best} \succ o_{worst}$, that is, that the *DM* is not indifferent among all the basic outcomes.

Axiom 2 [Monotonicity]. $\begin{pmatrix} o_{best} & o_{worst} \\ p & 1-p \end{pmatrix} \succsim \begin{pmatrix} o_{best} & o_{worst} \\ q & 1-q \end{pmatrix}$ if and only if $p \geq q$.

Axiom 3 [Continuity]. For every basic outcome o_i there is a $p_i \in [0, 1]$ such that
$o_i \sim \begin{pmatrix} o_{best} & o_{worst} \\ p_i & 1-p_i \end{pmatrix}.$

Before we introduce the last axiom we need to define a compound lottery.

Definition 5.3.1 A *compound lottery* is a lottery of the form $\begin{pmatrix} x_1 & x_2 & \cdots & x_r \\ p_1 & p_2 & \cdots & p_r \end{pmatrix}$ where each x_i is either an element of O or an element of $\mathscr{L}(O)$.

For example, let $m = 4$. Then $L = \begin{pmatrix} o_1 & o_2 & o_3 & o_4 \\ \frac{2}{5} & 0 & \frac{1}{5} & \frac{2}{5} \end{pmatrix}$ is a simple lottery (an element of $\mathscr{L}(O)$), while

$$C = \begin{pmatrix} \begin{pmatrix} o_1 & o_2 & o_3 & o_4 \\ \frac{1}{3} & \frac{1}{6} & \frac{1}{3} & \frac{1}{6} \end{pmatrix} & o_1 & \begin{pmatrix} o_1 & o_2 & o_3 & o_4 \\ \frac{1}{5} & 0 & \frac{1}{5} & \frac{3}{5} \end{pmatrix} \\ \frac{1}{2} & \frac{1}{4} & \frac{1}{4} \end{pmatrix}$$

is a compound lottery.[3]

The compound lottery C can be viewed graphically as a tree, as shown in Figure 5.1.

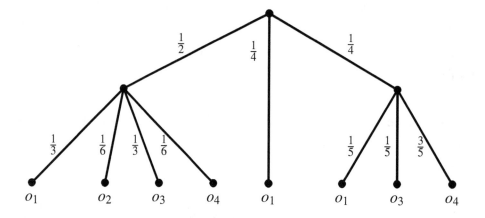

Figure 5.1: A compound lottery

Next we define the simple lottery $L(C)$ corresponding to a compound lottery C. Before introducing the formal definition, we shall explain in an example how to construct such a simple lottery. Continuing with the example of the compound lottery C given above and illustrated in Figure 5.1, first we replace a sequence of edges with a single edge and associate with it the product of the probabilities along the sequence of edges, as shown in Figure 5.2.

---

[3]With $r = 3$, $x_1 = \begin{pmatrix} o_1 & o_2 & o_3 & o_4 \\ \frac{1}{3} & \frac{1}{6} & \frac{1}{3} & \frac{1}{6} \end{pmatrix}$, $x_2 = o_1$, $x_3 = \begin{pmatrix} o_1 & o_2 & o_3 & o_4 \\ \frac{1}{5} & 0 & \frac{1}{5} & \frac{3}{5} \end{pmatrix}$, $p_1 = \frac{1}{2}, p_2 = p_3 = \frac{1}{4}$.

5.3 Expected utility: the axioms

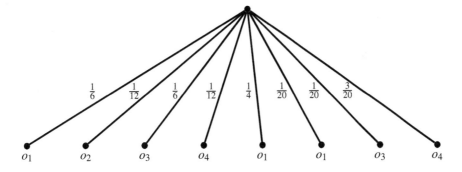

Figure 5.2: Simplification of Figure 5.1 obtained by condensing paths into simple edges and associating with the simple edges the products of the probabilities along the path.

Then we add up the probabilities of each outcome, as shown in Figure 5.3. Thus, the simple lottery $L(C)$ that corresponds to C is $L(C) = \begin{pmatrix} o_1 & o_2 & o_3 & o_4 \\ \frac{28}{60} & \frac{5}{60} & \frac{13}{60} & \frac{14}{60} \end{pmatrix}$, namely the lottery shown in Figure 5.3.

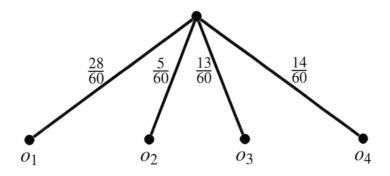

Figure 5.3: Simplification of Figure 5.2 obtained by adding, for each outcome, the probabilities of that outcome.

Definition 5.3.2 Given a compound lottery $C = \begin{pmatrix} x_1 & x_2 & \cdots & x_r \\ p_1 & p_2 & \cdots & p_r \end{pmatrix}$ the *corresponding simple lottery* $L(C) = \begin{pmatrix} o_1 & o_2 & \cdots & o_m \\ q_1 & q_2 & \cdots & q_m \end{pmatrix}$ is defined as follows. First of all, for $i = 1, \ldots, m$ and $j = 1, \ldots, r$, define

$$o_i(x_j) = \begin{cases} 1 & \text{if } x_j = o_i \\ 0 & \text{if } x_j = o_k \text{ with } k \neq i \\ s_i & \text{if } x_j = \begin{pmatrix} o_1 & \cdots & o_{i-1} & o_i & o_{i+1} & \cdots & o_m \\ s_1 & \cdots & s_{i-1} & s_i & s_{i+1} & \cdots & s_m \end{pmatrix} \end{cases}$$

Then $q_i = \sum_{j=1}^{r} p_j o_i(x_j)$.

Continuing the example where

$$C = \begin{pmatrix} \begin{pmatrix} o_1 & o_2 & o_3 & o_4 \\ \frac{1}{3} & \frac{1}{6} & \frac{1}{3} & \frac{1}{6} \end{pmatrix} & o_1 & \begin{pmatrix} o_1 & o_2 & o_3 & o_4 \\ \frac{1}{5} & 0 & \frac{1}{5} & \frac{3}{5} \end{pmatrix} \\ \frac{1}{2} & \frac{1}{4} & \frac{1}{4} \end{pmatrix}$$

we have that

$$r = 3, \quad x_1 = \begin{pmatrix} o_1 & o_2 & o_3 & o_4 \\ \frac{1}{3} & \frac{1}{6} & \frac{1}{3} & \frac{1}{6} \end{pmatrix}, \quad x_2 = o_1 \quad \text{and} \quad x_3 = \begin{pmatrix} o_1 & o_2 & o_3 & o_4 \\ \frac{1}{5} & 0 & \frac{1}{5} & \frac{3}{5} \end{pmatrix},$$

so that

$$o_1(x_1) = \tfrac{1}{3}, \quad o_1(x_2) = 1, \quad \text{and} \quad o_1(x_3) = \tfrac{1}{5}$$

and thus $q_1 = \frac{1}{2}\left(\frac{1}{3}\right) + \frac{1}{4}(1) + \frac{1}{4}\left(\frac{1}{5}\right) = \frac{28}{60}$. Similarly, $q_2 = \frac{1}{2}\left(\frac{1}{6}\right) + \frac{1}{4}(0) + \frac{1}{4}(0) = \frac{1}{12} = \frac{5}{60}$, $q_3 = \frac{1}{2}\left(\frac{1}{3}\right) + \frac{1}{4}(0) + \frac{1}{4}\left(\frac{1}{5}\right) = \frac{13}{60}$ and $q_4 = \frac{1}{2}\left(\frac{1}{6}\right) + \frac{1}{4}(0) + \frac{1}{4}\left(\frac{3}{5}\right) = \frac{14}{60}$.

Axiom 4 [Independence or substitutability]. Consider an arbitrary basic outcome o_i and an arbitrary simple lottery $L = \begin{pmatrix} o_1 & \cdots & o_{i-1} & o_i & o_{i+1} & \cdots & o_m \\ p_1 & \cdots & p_{i-1} & p_i & p_{i+1} & \cdots & p_m \end{pmatrix}$. If $\hat{L}$ is a simple lottery such that $o_i \sim \hat{L}$, then $L \sim M$ where M is the simple lottery corresponding to the compound lottery $C = \begin{pmatrix} o_1 & \cdots & o_{i-1} & \hat{L} & o_{i+1} & \cdots & o_m \\ p_1 & \cdots & p_{i-1} & p_i & p_{i+1} & \cdots & p_m \end{pmatrix}$ obtained by replacing o_i with $\hat{L}$ in L.

We can now prove the first theorem of the previous section.

Proof of Theorem 5.2.1. To simplify the notation, throughout this proof we will assume that we have renumbered the basic outcomes in such a way that $o_{best} = o_1$ and $o_{worst} = o_m$. First of all, for every basic outcome o_i, let $u_i \in [0,1]$ be such that $o_i \sim \begin{pmatrix} o_1 & o_m \\ u_i & 1 - u_i \end{pmatrix}$. The existence of such a value u_i is guaranteed by the Continuity Axiom (Axiom 3); clearly $u_1 = 1$ and $u_m = 0$. Now consider an arbitrary lottery

$$L_1 = \begin{pmatrix} o_1 & \cdots & o_m \\ p_1 & \cdots & p_m \end{pmatrix}.$$

First we show that

$$L_1 \sim \begin{pmatrix} o_1 & o_m \\ \sum\limits_{i=1}^{m} p_i u_i & 1 - \sum\limits_{i=1}^{m} p_i u_i \end{pmatrix} \tag{5.3}$$

5.3 Expected utility: the axioms

This is done through a repeated application of the Independence Axiom (Axiom 4), as follows. Consider the compound lottery

$$\mathscr{C}_2 = \begin{pmatrix} o_1 & \begin{pmatrix} o_1 & o_m \\ u_2 & 1-u_2 \end{pmatrix} & o_3 & \cdots & o_m \\ p_1 & p_2 & p_3 & \cdots & p_m \end{pmatrix}$$

obtained by replacing o_2 in lottery L_1 with the lottery $\begin{pmatrix} o_1 & o_m \\ u_2 & 1-u_2 \end{pmatrix}$ that the DM considers to be just as good as o_2. The simple lottery corresponding to $\mathscr{C}_2$ is

$$L_2 = \begin{pmatrix} o_1 & o_3 & \cdots & o_{m-1} & o_m \\ p_1 + p_2 u_2 & p_3 & \cdots & p_{m-1} & p_m + p_2(1-u_2) \end{pmatrix}.$$

Note that o_2 is assigned probability 0 in L_2 and thus we have omitted it. By Axiom 4, $L_1 \sim L_2$. Now apply the same argument to L_2: let

$$\mathscr{C}_3 = \begin{pmatrix} o_1 & \begin{pmatrix} o_1 & o_m \\ u_3 & 1-u_3 \end{pmatrix} & \cdots & o_{m-1} & o_m \\ p_1 + p_2 u_2 & p_3 & \cdots & p_{m-1} & p_m + p_2(1-u_2) \end{pmatrix}$$

whose corresponding simple lottery is

$$L_3 = \begin{pmatrix} o_1 & \cdots & o_m \\ p_1 + p_2 u_2 + p_3 u_3 & \cdots & p_m + p_2(1-u_2) + p_3(1-u_3) \end{pmatrix}.$$

Note, again, that o_3 is assigned probability zero in L_3. By Axiom 4, $L_2 \sim L_3$; thus, by transitivity (since $L_1 \sim L_2$ and $L_2 \sim L_3$) we have that $L_1 \sim L_3$. Repeating this argument we get that $L_1 \sim L_{m-1}$, where

$$L_{m-1} = \begin{pmatrix} o_1 & o_m \\ p_1 + p_2 u_2 + \ldots + p_{m-1} u_{m-1} & p_m + p_2(1-u_2) + \ldots + p_{m-1}(1-u_{m-1}) \end{pmatrix}.$$

Since $u_1 = 1$ (so that $p_1 u_1 = p_1$) and $u_m = 0$ (so that $p_m u_m = 0$),

$$p_1 + p_2 u_2 + \ldots + p_{m-1} u_{m-1} = \sum_{i=1}^{m} p_i u_i \quad \text{and}$$

$$p_2(1-u_2) + \ldots + p_{m-1}(1-u_{m-1}) + p_m = \sum_{i=2}^{m} p_i - \sum_{i=2}^{m-1} p_i u_i = p_1 + \sum_{i=2}^{m} p_i - \sum_{i=2}^{m-1} p_i u_i - p_1$$

$$= \text{(since } u_1=1 \text{ and } u_m=0\text{)} \sum_{i=1}^{m} p_i - \sum_{i=2}^{m-1} p_i u_i - p_1 u_1 - p_m u_m = \left(\text{since } \sum_{i=1}^{m} p_i = 1\right) 1 - \sum_{i=1}^{m} p_i u_i.$$

Thus, $L_{m-1} = \begin{pmatrix} o_1 & o_m \\ \sum_{i=1}^{m} p_i u_i & 1 - \sum_{i=1}^{m} p_i u_i \end{pmatrix}$, which proves (5.3). Now define the following utility function $U : \{o_1,...,o_m\} \to [0,1]$: $U(o_i) = u_i$, where, as before, for every basic outcome o_i, $u_i \in [0,1]$ is such that $o_i \sim \begin{pmatrix} o_1 & o_m \\ u_i & 1-u_i \end{pmatrix}$. Consider two arbitrary lotteries $L = \begin{pmatrix} o_1 & ... & o_m \\ p_1 & ... & p_m \end{pmatrix}$ and $L' = \begin{pmatrix} o_1 & ... & o_m \\ q_1 & ... & q_m \end{pmatrix}$. We want to show that $L \succsim L'$ if and only if $\mathbb{E}[U(L)] \geq \mathbb{E}[U(L')]$, that is, if and only if $\sum_{i=1}^{m} p_i u_i \geq \sum_{i=1}^{m} q_i u_i$. By (5.3), $L \sim M$, where $M = \begin{pmatrix} o_1 & o_m \\ \sum_{i=1}^{m} p_i u_i & 1 - \sum_{i=1}^{m} p_i u_i \end{pmatrix}$ and also $L' \sim M'$, where $M' = \begin{pmatrix} o_1 & o_m \\ \sum_{i=1}^{m} q_i u_i & 1 - \sum_{i=1}^{m} q_i u_i \end{pmatrix}$.

Thus, by transitivity of $\succsim$, $L \succsim L'$ if and only if $M \succsim M'$; by the Monotonicity Axiom (Axiom 2), $M \succsim M'$ if and only if $\sum_{i=1}^{m} p_i u_i \geq \sum_{i=1}^{m} q_i u_i$. □

The following example, known as the *Allais paradox*, suggests that one should view expected utility theory as a "prescriptive" or "normative" theory (that is, as a theory about how rational people *should* choose) rather than as a descriptive theory (that is, as a theory about the *actual* behavior of individuals). In 1953 the French economist Maurice Allais published a paper regarding a survey he had conducted in 1952 concerning a hypothetical decision problem. Subjects "with good training in and knowledge of the theory of probability, so that they could be considered to behave rationally" were asked to rank the following pairs of lotteries:

$$A = \begin{pmatrix} \$5 \text{ Million} & \$0 \\ \frac{89}{100} & \frac{11}{100} \end{pmatrix} \quad \text{versus} \quad B = \begin{pmatrix} \$1 \text{ Million} & \$0 \\ \frac{90}{100} & \frac{10}{100} \end{pmatrix}$$

and

$$C = \begin{pmatrix} \$5 \text{ Million} & \$1 \text{ Million} & \$0 \\ \frac{89}{100} & \frac{10}{100} & \frac{1}{100} \end{pmatrix} \quad \text{versus} \quad D = \begin{pmatrix} \$1 \text{ Million} \\ 1 \end{pmatrix}.$$

5.3 Expected utility: the axioms

Most subjects reported the following ranking: $A \succ B$ and $D \succ C$. Such ranking violates the axioms of expected utility. To see this, let $O = \{o_1, o_2, o_3\}$ with $o_1 = \$5$ Million, $o_2 = \$1$ Million and $o_3 = \$0$. Let us assume that the individual in question prefers more money to less, so that $o_1 \succ o_2 \succ o_3$ and has a von Neumann-Morgenstern ranking of the lotteries over $\mathscr{L}(O)$. Let $u_2 \in (0,1)$ be such that $D \sim \begin{pmatrix} \$5 \text{ Million} & \$0 \\ u_2 & 1-u_2 \end{pmatrix}$ (the existence of such u_2 is guaranteed by the Continuity Axiom). Then, since $D \succ C$, by transitivity

$$\begin{pmatrix} \$5 \text{ Million} & \$0 \\ u_2 & 1-u_2 \end{pmatrix} \succ C. \tag{5.4}$$

Let C' be the simple lottery corresponding to the compound lottery

$$\begin{pmatrix} \$5 \text{ Million} & \begin{pmatrix} \$5 \text{ Million} & \$0 \\ u_2 & 1-u_2 \end{pmatrix} & \$0 \\ \frac{89}{100} & \frac{10}{100} & \frac{1}{100} \end{pmatrix}.$$

Then $C' = \begin{pmatrix} \$5 \text{ Million} & \$0 \\ \frac{89}{100} + \frac{10}{100}u_2 & 1 - \left(\frac{89}{100} + \frac{10}{100}u_2\right) \end{pmatrix}.$

By the Independence Axiom, $C \sim C'$ and thus, by (5.4) and transitivity,

$$\begin{pmatrix} \$5 \text{ Million} & \$0 \\ u_2 & 1-u_2 \end{pmatrix} \succ \begin{pmatrix} \$5 \text{ Million} & \$0 \\ \frac{89}{100} + \frac{10}{100}u_2 & 1 - \left(\frac{89}{100} + \frac{10}{100}u_2\right) \end{pmatrix}.$$

Hence, by the Monotonicity Axiom, $u_2 > \frac{89}{100} + \frac{10}{100}u_2$, that is,

$$u_2 > \frac{89}{90}. \tag{5.5}$$

Let B' be the simple lottery corresponding to the following compound lottery, constructed from B by replacing the basic outcome '$1 Million' with $\begin{pmatrix} \$5 \text{ Million} & \$0 \\ u_2 & 1-u_2 \end{pmatrix}$:

$$\begin{pmatrix} \begin{pmatrix} \$5 \text{ Million} & \$0 \\ u_2 & 1-u_2 \end{pmatrix} & \$0 \\ \frac{90}{100} & \frac{10}{100} \end{pmatrix}.$$

Then

$$B' = \begin{pmatrix} \$5 \text{ Million} & \$0 \\ \frac{90}{100}u_2 & 1 - \frac{90}{100}u_2 \end{pmatrix}.$$

By the Independence Axiom, $B \sim B'$; thus, since $A \succ B$, by transitivity, $A \succ B'$ and therefore, by the Monotonicity Axiom, $\frac{89}{100} > \frac{90}{100} u_2$, that is, $u_2 < \frac{89}{90}$, contradicting (5.5).

Thus, if one finds the expected utility axioms compelling as axioms of rationality, then one cannot consistently express a preference for A over B and also a preference for D over C.

Another well-known paradox is the *Ellsberg paradox*. Suppose that you are told that an urn contains 30 red balls and 60 more balls that are either blue or yellow. You don't know how many blue or how many yellow balls there are, but the number of blue balls plus the number of yellow ball equals 60 (they could be all blue or all yellow or any combination of the two). The balls are well mixed so that each individual ball is as likely to be drawn as any other. You are given a choice between the bets A and B, where

A = you get \$100 if you pick a red ball and nothing otherwise,

B = you get \$100 if you pick a blue ball and nothing otherwise.

Many subjects in experiments state a strict preference for A over B: $A \succ B$. Consider now the following bets:

C = you get \$100 if you pick a red or yellow ball and nothing otherwise,

D = you get \$100 if you pick a blue or yellow ball and nothing otherwise.

Do the axioms of expected utility constrain your ranking of C and D? Many subjects in experiments state the following ranking: $A \succ B$ and $D \succsim C$. All such people violate the axioms of expected utility. The fraction of red balls in the urn is $\frac{30}{90} = \frac{1}{3}$. Let p_2 be the fraction of blue balls and p_3 the fraction of yellow balls (either of these can be zero: all we know is that $p_2 + p_3 = \frac{60}{90} = \frac{2}{3}$). Then A, B, C and D can be viewed as the following lotteries:

$$A = \begin{pmatrix} \$100 & \$0 \\ \frac{1}{3} & p_2 + p_3 \end{pmatrix}, \quad B = \begin{pmatrix} \$100 & \$0 \\ p_2 & \frac{1}{3} + p_3 \end{pmatrix}$$

$$C = \begin{pmatrix} \$100 & \$0 \\ \frac{1}{3} + p_3 & p_2 \end{pmatrix}, \quad D = \begin{pmatrix} \$100 & \$0 \\ p_2 + p_3 = \frac{2}{3} & \frac{1}{3} \end{pmatrix}$$

Let U be the normalized von Neumann-Morgenstern utility function that represents the individual's ranking; then $U(\$100) = 1$ and $U(0) = 0$. Thus,

$\mathbb{E}[U(A)] = \frac{1}{3}$, $\quad \mathbb{E}[U(B)] = p_2$, $\quad \mathbb{E}[U(C)] = \frac{1}{3} + p_3$, $\quad$ and $\quad \mathbb{E}[U(D)] = p_2 + p_3 = \frac{2}{3}$.

Hence, $A \succ B$ if and only if $\frac{1}{3} > p_2$, which implies that $p_3 > \frac{1}{3}$, so that $\mathbb{E}[U(C)] = \frac{1}{3} + p_3 > \mathbb{E}[U(D)] = \frac{2}{3}$ and thus $C \succ D$ (similarly, $B \succ A$ if and only if $\frac{1}{3} < p_2$, which implies that $\mathbb{E}[U(C)] < \mathbb{E}[U(D)]$ and thus $D \succ C$).

> Test your understanding of the concepts introduced in this section, by going through the exercises in Section 5.4.2 at the end of this chapter.

5.4 Exercises

The solutions to the following exercises are given in Section 5.5 at the end of this chapter.

5.4.1 Exercises for Section 5.1: Money lotteries and attitudes to risk

Exercise 5.1 Find the expected value of the lottery $\begin{pmatrix} 24 & 12 & 48 & 6 \\ \frac{1}{6} & \frac{2}{6} & \frac{1}{6} & \frac{2}{6} \end{pmatrix}$.

Exercise 5.2 Consider the following lottery:

$$\begin{pmatrix} o_1 & o_2 & o_3 \\ \frac{1}{4} & \frac{1}{2} & \frac{1}{4} \end{pmatrix}$$

where

- o_1 = you get an invitation to have dinner at the White House,
- o_2 = you get (for free) a puppy of your choice
- o_3 = you get $600.

What is the expected value of this lottery?

Exercise 5.3 Consider the following money lottery

$$L = \begin{pmatrix} \$10 & \$15 & \$18 & \$20 & \$25 & \$30 & \$36 \\ \frac{3}{12} & \frac{1}{12} & 0 & \frac{3}{12} & \frac{2}{12} & 0 & \frac{3}{12} \end{pmatrix}$$

(a) What is the expected value of the lottery?
(b) Ann prefers more money to less and has transitive preferences. She says that, between getting $20 for certain and playing the above lottery, she would prefer $20 for certain. What is her attitude to risk?
(c) Bob prefers more money to less and has transitive preferences. He says that, given the same choice as Ann, he would prefer playing the lottery. What is his attitude to risk?

Exercise 5.4 Sam has a debilitating illness and has been offered two mutually exclusive courses of action: (1) take some well-known drugs which have been tested for a long time and (2) take a new experimental drug. If he chooses (1) then for certain his pain will be reduced to a bearable level. If he chooses (2) then he has a 50% chance of being completely cured and a 50% chance of no benefits from the drug and possibly some harmful side effects. He chose (1). What is his attitude to risk?

5.4.2 Exercises for Section 5.2: Expected utility theory

Exercise 5.5 Ben is offered a choice between the following two money lotteries:

$$A = \begin{pmatrix} \$4,000 & \$0 \\ 0.8 & 0.2 \end{pmatrix} \quad \text{and} \quad B = \begin{pmatrix} \$3,000 \\ 1 \end{pmatrix}.$$

He says he strictly prefers B to A. Which of the following two lotteries, C and D, will Ben choose if he satisfies the axioms of expected utility and prefers more money to less?

$$C = \begin{pmatrix} \$4,000 & \$0 \\ 0.2 & 0.8 \end{pmatrix}, \quad D = \begin{pmatrix} \$3,000 & \$0 \\ 0.25 & 0.75 \end{pmatrix}.$$

Exercise 5.6 There are three basic outcomes, o_1, o_2 and o_3. Ann satisfies the axioms of expected utility and her preferences over lotteries involving these three outcomes can be represented by the following von Neumann-Morgenstern utility function:

$$V(o_2) = a > V(o_1) = b > V(o_3) = c.$$

Normalize the utility function.

Exercise 5.7 Consider the following lotteries:

$$L_1 = \begin{pmatrix} \$3000 & \$500 \\ \frac{5}{6} & \frac{1}{6} \end{pmatrix}, \quad L_2 = \begin{pmatrix} \$3000 & \$500 \\ \frac{2}{3} & \frac{1}{3} \end{pmatrix},$$

$$L_3 = \begin{pmatrix} \$3000 & \$2000 & \$1000 & \$500 \\ \frac{1}{4} & \frac{1}{4} & \frac{1}{4} & \frac{1}{4} \end{pmatrix}, \quad L_4 = \begin{pmatrix} \$2000 & \$1000 \\ \frac{1}{2} & \frac{1}{2} \end{pmatrix}.$$

Jennifer says that she is indifferent between lottery L_1 and getting \$2,000 for certain. She is also indifferent between lottery L_2 and getting \$1,000 for certain. Finally, she says that between L_3 and L_4 she would chose L_3. Is she rational according to the theory of expected utility? [Assume that she prefers more money to less.]

5.4 Exercises

Exercise 5.8 Consider the following basic outcomes:

- o_1 = a Summer internship at the White House,
- o_2 = a free one-week vacation in Europe,
- o_3 = \$800,
- o_4 = a free ticket to a concert.

Rachel says that her ranking of these outcomes is $o_1 \succ o_2 \succ o_3 \succ o_4$. She also says that

(1) she is indifferent between $\begin{pmatrix} o_2 \\ 1 \end{pmatrix}$ and $\begin{pmatrix} o_1 & o_4 \\ \frac{4}{5} & \frac{1}{5} \end{pmatrix}$ and

(2) she is indifferent between $\begin{pmatrix} o_3 \\ 1 \end{pmatrix}$ and $\begin{pmatrix} o_1 & o_4 \\ \frac{1}{2} & \frac{1}{2} \end{pmatrix}$.

If she satisfies the axioms of expected utility theory, which of the two lotteries
$L_1 = \begin{pmatrix} o_1 & o_2 & o_3 & o_4 \\ \frac{1}{8} & \frac{2}{8} & \frac{3}{8} & \frac{2}{8} \end{pmatrix}$ and $L_2 = \begin{pmatrix} o_1 & o_2 & o_3 \\ \frac{1}{5} & \frac{3}{5} & \frac{1}{5} \end{pmatrix}$ will she choose?

Exercise 5.9 Consider the following lotteries:

$$L_1 = \begin{pmatrix} \$30 & \$28 & \$24 & \$18 & \$8 \\ \frac{2}{10} & \frac{1}{10} & \frac{1}{10} & \frac{2}{10} & \frac{4}{10} \end{pmatrix} \text{ and } L_2 = \begin{pmatrix} \$30 & \$28 & \$8 \\ \frac{1}{10} & \frac{4}{10} & \frac{5}{10} \end{pmatrix}.$$

(a) Which lottery would a risk neutral person choose?

(b) Paul's von Neumann-Morgenstern utility-of-money function is $U(m) = ln(m)$, where ln denotes the natural logarithm. Which lottery would Paul choose?

Exercise 5.10 There are five basic outcomes. Jane has a von Neumann-Morgenstern ranking of the set of lotteries over the set of basic outcomes that can be represented by either of the following utility functions U and V: $\begin{pmatrix} & o_1 & o_2 & o_3 & o_4 & o_5 \\ U: & 44 & 170 & -10 & 26 & 98 \\ V: & 32 & 95 & 5 & 23 & 59 \end{pmatrix}$.

(a) Show how to normalize each of U and V and verify that you get the same normalized utility function.

(b) Show how to transform U into V with a positive affine transformation of the form $x \mapsto ax + b$ with $a, b \in \mathbb{R}$ and $a > 0$.

Exercise 5.11 Consider the following lotteries: $L_3 = \begin{pmatrix} \$28 \\ 1 \end{pmatrix}$, $L_4 = \begin{pmatrix} \$10 & \$50 \\ \frac{1}{2} & \frac{1}{2} \end{pmatrix}$.

(a) Ann has the following von Neumann-Morgenstern utility function: $U_{Ann}(\$m) = \sqrt{m}$. How does she rank the two lotteries?

(b) Bob has the following von Neumann-Morgenstern utility function: $U_{Bob}(\$m) = 2m - \frac{m^4}{100^3}$. How does he rank the two lotteries?

(c) Verify that both Ann and Bob are risk averse, by determining what they would choose between lottery L_4 and its expected value for certain.

5.4.3 Exercises for Section 5.3: Expected utility axioms

Exercise 5.12 Let $O = \{o_1, o_2, o_3, o_4\}$. Find the simple lottery corresponding to the following compound lottery

$$\left(\begin{pmatrix} o_1 & o_2 & o_3 & o_4 \\ \frac{2}{5} & \frac{1}{10} & \frac{3}{10} & \frac{1}{5} \end{pmatrix} \quad o_2 \quad \begin{pmatrix} o_1 & o_3 & o_4 \\ \frac{1}{5} & \frac{1}{5} & \frac{3}{5} \end{pmatrix} \quad \begin{pmatrix} o_2 & o_3 \\ \frac{1}{3} & \frac{2}{3} \end{pmatrix} \right)$$
$$\frac{1}{8} \quad\quad\quad \frac{1}{4} \quad\quad\quad \frac{1}{8} \quad\quad\quad \frac{1}{2}$$

Exercise 5.13 Let $O = \{o_1, o_2, o_3, o_4\}$. Suppose that the *DM* has a von Neumann-Morgenstern ranking of $\mathscr{L}(O)$ and states the following indifference:

$$o_1 \sim \begin{pmatrix} o_2 & o_4 \\ \frac{1}{4} & \frac{3}{4} \end{pmatrix} \quad \text{and} \quad o_2 \sim \begin{pmatrix} o_3 & o_4 \\ \frac{3}{5} & \frac{2}{5} \end{pmatrix}.$$

Find a lottery that the *DM* considers just as good as

$$L = \begin{pmatrix} o_1 & o_2 & o_3 & o_4 \\ \frac{1}{3} & \frac{2}{9} & \frac{1}{9} & \frac{1}{3} \end{pmatrix}.$$

Do not add any information to what is given above (in particular, do not make any assumptions about which outcome is best and which is worst).

5.5 Solutions to Exercises

Exercise 5.14 — More difficult. Would you be willing to pay more in order to reduce the probability of dying within the next hour from one sixth to zero or from four sixths to three sixths? Unfortunately, this is not a hypothetical question: you accidentally entered the office of a mad scientist and have been overpowered and tied to a chair. The mad scientist has put six glasses in front of you, numbered 1 to 6, and tells you that one of them contains a deadly poison and the other five contain a harmless liquid. He says that he is going to roll a die and make you drink from the glass whose number matches the number that shows up from the rolling of the die. You beg to be exempted and he asks you "what is the largest amount of money that you would be willing to pay to replace the glass containing the poison with one containing a harmless liquid?".

Interpret this question as "what sum of money x makes you indifferent between

(1) leaving the poison in whichever glass contains it and rolling the die, and

(2) reducing your wealth by \$$x$ and rolling the die after the poison has been replaced by a harmless liquid". Your answer is: \$$X$.

Then he asks you "suppose that instead of one glass with poison there had been four glasses with poison (and two with a harmless liquid); what is the largest amount of money that you would be willing to pay to replace one glass with poison with a glass containing a harmless liquid (and thus roll the die with 3 glasses with poison and 3 with a harmless liquid)?". Your answer is: \$$Y$.

Show that if $X > Y$ then you do not satisfy the axioms of Expected Utility Theory. [Hint: think about what the basic outcomes are; assume that you do not care about how much money is left in your estate if you die and that, when alive, you prefer more money to less.]

5.5 Solutions to Exercises

Solution to Exercise 5.1 The expected value of the lottery $\begin{pmatrix} 24 & 12 & 48 & 6 \\ \frac{1}{6} & \frac{2}{6} & \frac{1}{6} & \frac{2}{6} \end{pmatrix}$ is

$\frac{1}{6}(24) + \frac{2}{6}(12) + \frac{1}{6}(48) + \frac{2}{6}(6) = 18.$ □

Solution to Exercise 5.2 This was a trick question! There is no expected value because the basic outcomes are not numbers. □

Solution to Exercise 5.3

(a) The expected value of the lottery

$$L = \begin{pmatrix} \$10 & \$15 & \$18 & \$20 & \$25 & \$30 & \$36 \\ \frac{3}{12} & \frac{1}{12} & 0 & \frac{3}{12} & \frac{2}{12} & 0 & \frac{3}{12} \end{pmatrix}$$

is $\mathbb{E}[L] = \frac{3}{12}(10) + \frac{1}{12}(15) + (0)(18) + \frac{3}{12}(20) + \frac{2}{12}(25) + (0)(30) + \frac{3}{12}(36) = \frac{263}{12} = \$21.92$.

(b) Since Ann prefers more money to less, she prefers $21.92 to $20 ($21.92 $\succ$ $20). She said that she prefers $20 to lottery L ($20 $\succ$ L). Thus, since her preferences are transitive, she prefers $21.92 to lottery L ($21.92 $\succ$ L). Hence, she is risk averse.

(c) The answer is: we cannot tell. First of all, since Bob prefers more money to less, he prefers $21.92 to $20 ($21.92 $\succ$ $20). Bob could be risk neutral, because a risk neutral person would be indifferent between L and $21.92 ($L \sim$ $21.92); since Bob prefers $21.92 to $20 and has transitive preferences, if risk neutral he would prefer L to $20. However, Bob could also be risk loving: a risk-loving person prefers L to $21.92 ($L \succ$ $21.92) and we know that he prefers $21.92 to $20; thus, by transitivity, if risk loving, he would prefer L to $20. But Bob could also be risk averse: he could consistently prefer $21.92 to L and L to $20 (for example, he could consider L to be just as good as $20.50). □

Solution to Exercise 5.4 Just like Exercise 5.2, this was a trick question! Here the basic outcomes are not sums of money but states of health. Since the described choice is not one between money lotteries, the definitions of risk aversion/neutrality/love are not applicable. □

Solution to Exercise 5.5 Since Ben prefers B to A, he must prefer D to C.
Proof. Let U be a von Neumann-Morgenstern utility function that represents Ben's preferences. Let $U(\$4,000) = a, U(\$3,000) = b$ and $U(\$0) = c$.
Since Ben prefers more money to less, $a > b > c$. Then $\mathbb{E}[U(A)] = 0.8U(\$4,000) + 0.2U(\$0) = 0.8a + 0.2c$ and $\mathbb{E}[U(B)] = U(\$3,000) = b$.
Since Ben prefers B to A, it must be that $b > 0.8a + 0.2c$.
Let us now compare C and D: $\mathbb{E}[U(C)] = 0.2a + 0.8c$ and $\mathbb{E}[U(D)] = 0.25b + 0.75c$. Since $b > 0.8a + 0.2c$, $0.25b > 0.25(0.8a + 0.2c) = 0.2a + 0.05c$ and thus, adding $0.75c$ to both sides, we get that $0.25b + 0.75c > 0.2a + 0.8c$, that is, $\mathbb{E}[U(D)] > \mathbb{E}[U(C)]$, so that $D \succ C$. Note that the proof would have been somewhat easier if we had taken the normalized utility function, so that $a = 1$ and $c = 0$. □

5.5 Solutions to Exercises

Solution to Exercise 5.6 Define the function U as follows:

$U(x) = \frac{1}{a-c}V(x) - \frac{c}{a-c} = \frac{V(x)-c}{a-c}$ (note that, by hypothesis, $a > c$ and thus $\frac{1}{a-c} > 0$).

Then U represents the same preferences as V.

Then $U(o_2) = \frac{V(o_2)-c}{a-c} = \frac{a-c}{a-c} = 1$, $U(o_1) = \frac{V(o_1)-c}{a-c} = \frac{b-c}{a-c}$, and $U(o_3) = \frac{V(o_3)-c}{a-c} = \frac{c-c}{a-c} = 0$.
Note that, since $a > b > c$, $0 < \frac{b-c}{a-c} < 1$. □

Solution to Exercise 5.7 We can take the set of basic outcomes to be $\{\$3000, \$2000, \$1000, \$500\}$. Suppose that there is a von Neumann-Morgenstern utility function U that represents Jennifer's preferences. We can normalize it so that $U(\$3000) = 1$ and $U(\$500) = 0$.

Since Jennifer is indifferent between L_1 and $\$2000$, $U(\$2000) = \frac{5}{6}$ (since the expected utility of L_1 is $\frac{5}{6}(1) + \frac{1}{6}(0) = \frac{5}{6}$).

Since she is indifferent between L_2 and $\$1000$, $U(\$1000) = \frac{2}{3}$ (since the expected utility of L_2 is $\frac{2}{3}(1) + \frac{1}{3}(0) = \frac{2}{3}$).

Thus, $\mathbb{E}[U(L_3)] = \frac{1}{4}(1) + \frac{1}{4}(\frac{5}{6}) + \frac{1}{4}(\frac{2}{3}) + \frac{1}{4}(0) = \frac{5}{8}$ and $\mathbb{E}[U(L_4)] = \frac{1}{2}(\frac{5}{6}) + \frac{1}{2}(\frac{2}{3}) = \frac{3}{4}$.
Since $\frac{3}{4} > \frac{5}{8}$, Jennifer should prefer L_4 to L_3. Hence, she is not rational according to the theory of expected utility. □

Solution to Exercise 5.8 Normalize her utility function so that $U(o_1) = 1$ and $U(o_4) = 0$.

Since Rachel is indifferent between $\begin{pmatrix} o_2 \\ 1 \end{pmatrix}$ and $\begin{pmatrix} o_1 & o_4 \\ \frac{4}{5} & \frac{1}{5} \end{pmatrix}$, we have that $U(o_2) = \frac{4}{5}$.

Similarly, since she is indifferent between $\begin{pmatrix} o_3 \\ 1 \end{pmatrix}$ and $\begin{pmatrix} o_1 & o_4 \\ \frac{1}{2} & \frac{1}{2} \end{pmatrix}$, $U(o_3) = \frac{1}{2}$. Then

the expected utility of $L_1 = \begin{pmatrix} o_1 & o_2 & o_3 & o_4 \\ \frac{1}{8} & \frac{2}{8} & \frac{3}{8} & \frac{2}{8} \end{pmatrix}$ is $\frac{1}{8}(1) + \frac{2}{8}(\frac{4}{5}) + \frac{3}{8}(\frac{1}{2}) + \frac{2}{8}(0) = \frac{41}{80} =$

0.5125, while the expected utility of $L_2 = \begin{pmatrix} o_1 & o_2 & o_3 \\ \frac{1}{5} & \frac{3}{5} & \frac{1}{5} \end{pmatrix}$ is $\frac{1}{5}(1) + \frac{3}{5}(\frac{4}{5}) + \frac{1}{5}(\frac{1}{2}) =$
$\frac{39}{50} = 0.78$. Hence, she prefers L_2 to L_1. □

Solution to Exercise 5.9

(a) The expected value of L_1 is $\frac{2}{10}(30) + \frac{1}{10}(28) + \frac{1}{10}(24) + \frac{2}{10}(18) + \frac{4}{10}(8) = 18$ and the expected value of L_2 is $\frac{1}{10}(30) + \frac{4}{10}(28) + \frac{5}{10}8 = 18.2$. Hence, a risk-neutral person would prefer L_2 to L_1.

(b) The expected utility of L_1 is

$\frac{1}{5}\ln(30) + \frac{1}{10}\ln(28) + \frac{1}{10}\ln(24) + \frac{1}{5}\ln(18) + \frac{2}{5}\ln(8) = 2.741$

while the expected utility of L_2 is $\frac{1}{10}\ln(30) + \frac{2}{5}\ln(28) + \frac{1}{2}\ln(8) = 2.713$.

Thus, Paul would choose L_1 (since he prefers L_1 to L_2). □

Solution to Exercise 5.10

(a) To normalize U first add 10 to each value and then divide by 180.
Denote the normalization of U by $\bar{U}$. Then

$$\bar{U}: \begin{array}{ccccc} o_1 & o_2 & o_3 & o_4 & o_5 \\ \frac{54}{180}=0.3 & \frac{180}{180}=1 & \frac{0}{180}=0 & \frac{36}{180}=0.2 & \frac{108}{180}=0.6 \end{array}$$

To normalize V first subtract 5 from each value and then divide by 90.
Denote the normalization of V by $\bar{V}$. Then

$$\bar{V}: \begin{array}{ccccc} o_1 & o_2 & o_3 & o_4 & o_5 \\ \frac{27}{90}=0.3 & \frac{90}{90}=1 & \frac{0}{90}=0 & \frac{18}{90}=0.2 & \frac{54}{90}=0.6 \end{array}$$

(b) The transformation is of the form $V(o) = aU(o) + b$. To find the values of a and b plug in two sets of values and solve the system of equations $\begin{cases} 44a+b=32 \\ 170a+b=95 \end{cases}$.

The solution is $a = \frac{1}{2}$, $b = 10$. Thus, $V(o) = \frac{1}{2}U(o) + 10$. □

Solution to Exercise 5.11

(a) Ann prefers L_3 to L_4 ($L_3 \succ_{Ann} L_4$). In fact, $\mathbb{E}[U_{Ann}(L_3)] = \sqrt{28} = 5.2915$ while $\mathbb{E}[U_{Ann}(L_4)] = \frac{1}{2}\sqrt{10} + \frac{1}{2}\sqrt{50} = 5.1167$.

(b) Bob prefers L_4 to L_3 ($L_4 \succ_{Bob} L_3$). In fact, $\mathbb{E}[U_{Bob}(L_3)] = 2(28) - \frac{28^4}{100^3} = 55.3853$ while $\mathbb{E}[U_{Bob}(L_4)] = \frac{1}{2}\left[2(10) - \frac{10^4}{100^3}\right] + \frac{1}{2}\left[2(50) - \frac{50^4}{100^3}\right] = 56.87$.

(c) The expected value of lottery L_4 is $\frac{1}{2}10 + \frac{1}{2}50 = 30$; thus, a risk-averse person would strictly prefer \$30 with certainty to the lottery L_4. We saw in part (a) that for Ann the expected utility of lottery L_4 is 5.1167; the utility of \$30 is $\sqrt{30} = 5.4772$. Thus, Ann would indeed choose \$30 for certain over the lottery L_4.

We saw in part (b) that for Bob the expected utility of lottery L_4 is 56.87; the utility of \$30 is $2(30) - \frac{30^4}{100^3} = 59.19$. Thus, Bob would indeed choose \$30 for certain over the lottery L_4. □

Solution to Exercise 5.12 The simple lottery is $\begin{pmatrix} o_1 & o_2 & o_3 & o_4 \\ \frac{18}{240} & \frac{103}{240} & \frac{95}{240} & \frac{24}{240} \end{pmatrix}$. For example, the probability of o_2 is computed as follows: $\frac{1}{8}\left(\frac{1}{10}\right) + \frac{1}{4}(1) + \frac{1}{8}(0) + \frac{1}{2}\left(\frac{1}{3}\right) = \frac{103}{240}$. □

5.5 Solutions to Exercises

Solution to Exercise 5.13 Using the stated indifference, use lottery L to construct the compound lottery

$$\left(\begin{array}{cccc} \begin{pmatrix} o_2 & o_4 \\ \frac{1}{4} & \frac{3}{4} \end{pmatrix} & \begin{pmatrix} o_3 & o_4 \\ \frac{3}{5} & \frac{2}{5} \end{pmatrix} & o_3 & o_4 \\ \frac{1}{3} & \frac{2}{9} & \frac{1}{9} & \frac{1}{3} \end{array} \right),$$

whose corresponding simple lottery is $L' = \begin{pmatrix} o_1 & o_2 & o_3 & o_4 \\ 0 & \frac{1}{12} & \frac{11}{45} & \frac{121}{180} \end{pmatrix}$.

Then, by the Independence Axiom, $L \sim L'$. □

Solution to Exercise 5.14 Let W be your initial wealth. The basic outcomes are:

1. you do not pay any money, do not die and live to enjoy your wealth W (denote this outcome by A_0),

2. you pay $\$Y$, do not die and live to enjoy your remaining wealth $W - Y$ (call this outcome A_Y),

3. you pay $\$X$, do not die and live to enjoy your remaining wealth $W - X$ (call this outcome A_X),

4. you die (call this outcome D); this could happen because (a) you do not pay any money, roll the die and drink the poison or (b) you pay $\$Y$, roll the die and drink the poison; we assume that you are indifferent between these two outcomes.

Since, by hypothesis, $X > Y$, your ranking of these outcomes must be $A_0 \succ A_Y \succ A_X \succ D$. If you satisfy the von Neumann-Morgenstern axioms, then your preferences can be represented by a von Neumann-Morgenstern utility function U defined on the set of basic outcomes. We can normalize your utility function by setting $U(A_0) = 1$ and $U(D) = 0$. Furthermore, it must be that

$$U(A_Y) > U(A_X). \tag{5.6}$$

The maximum amount $\$P$ that you are willing to pay is that amount that makes you indifferent between (1) rolling the die with the initial number of poisoned glasses and (2) giving up $\$P$ and rolling the die with one less poisoned glass.

Thus – based on your answers – you are indifferent between the two lotteries

$$\begin{pmatrix} D & A_0 \\ \frac{1}{6} & \frac{5}{6} \end{pmatrix} \text{ and } \begin{pmatrix} A_X \\ 1 \end{pmatrix}$$

and you are indifferent between the two lotteries:

$$\begin{pmatrix} D & A_0 \\ \frac{4}{6} & \frac{2}{6} \end{pmatrix} \text{ and } \begin{pmatrix} D & A_Y \\ \frac{3}{6} & \frac{3}{6} \end{pmatrix}.$$

Thus,

$$\underbrace{\tfrac{1}{6}U(D)+\tfrac{5}{6}U(A_0)}_{=\tfrac{1}{6}0+\tfrac{5}{6}1=\tfrac{5}{6}}=U(A_X) \text{ and } \underbrace{\tfrac{4}{6}U(D)+\tfrac{2}{6}U(A_0)}_{=\tfrac{4}{6}0+\tfrac{2}{6}1=\tfrac{2}{6}}=\underbrace{\tfrac{3}{6}U(D)+\tfrac{3}{6}U(A_Y)}_{=\tfrac{3}{6}0+\tfrac{3}{6}U(A_Y)}.$$

Hence, $U(A_X) = \frac{5}{6}$ and $U(A_Y) = \frac{2}{3} = \frac{4}{6}$, so that $U(A_X) > U(A_Y)$, contradicting (5.6). □

6. Applications of Expected Utility

6.1 States and acts revisited

In Chapter 3 we introduced the state-act representation of decision problems and discussed decision criteria that did not depend on the Decision Maker's (*DM*) ability to assign probabilities to the states. If objective probabilities *are* available for the states, or if the *DM* is willing to assign subjective probabilities to them (by quantifying her beliefs), *and* the *DM*'s preferences satisfy the von Neumann-Morgenstern axioms, then each act can be viewed as a lottery and can be evaluated in terms of the expected utility of that lottery. We shall illustrate this with an example.

Alice wants to start a business selling decorative rugs. She has to decide whether to build a small production facility, a medium facility or a large facility. With a small facility she will be committed to producing 1,200 rugs, with a medium facility 1,400 rugs and with a large facility 2,000 rugs. She is uncertain, however, about the demand for rugs. If the economy is stagnant (state s_1) she will only be able to sell 1,200 rugs, if the economy is improving (state s_2) she will be able to sell up to 1,400 rugs and if the economy is experiencing a boom she will be able to sell up to 2,000 rugs. The number of rugs sold will be equal to the number of rugs produced, if demand is at least as large as production, and equal to the number of rugs demanded otherwise. All of this is illustrated in Table (6.1).

state →	s_1	s_2	s_3
act ↓			
small	production: 1,200 demand: 1,200 sale: 1,200	production: 1,200 demand: 1,400 sale: 1,200	production: 1,200 demand: 2,000 sale: 1,200
medium	production: 1,400 demand: 1,200 sale: 1,200	production: 1,400 demand: 1,400 sale: 1,400	production: 1,400 demand: 2,000 sale: 1,400
large	production: 2,000 demand: 1,200 sale: 1,200	production: 2,000 demand: 1,400 sale: 1,400	production: 2,000 demand: 2,000 sale: 2,000

(6.1)

Alice is interested in the profit that she will make. She expects to sell each rug for $102 and the cost of producing each rug is $2. Besides the production cost, there is also the cost of setting up the production facility, which is $50,000 for a small one, $55,000 for a medium one and $60,000 for a large one. Thus, for example, if she chooses a medium facility (cost: $55,000) and thus produces 1,400 rugs (cost: $2,800) and the state turns out to be s_1 (so that she sells only 1,200 rugs) then her profit is: $(1,200(102) - 2,800 - 55,000) = \$64,600$. Table (6.2) shows Alice's decision problem with the outcomes expressed as profits. Suppose that, after consulting an economist who claims to be an expert, Alice assigns the following probabilities to the states:

state	s_1	s_2	s_3
probability	$\frac{1}{4}$	$\frac{2}{4}$	$\frac{1}{4}$

Suppose also that Alice has von Neumann-Morgenstern preferences that are represented by the utility function $U(\$x) = \sqrt{x}$.[1]

state →	s_1	s_2	s_3
act ↓			
small	$70,000	$70,000	$70,000
medium	$64,600	$85,000	$85,000
large	$58,400	$78,800	$140,000

(6.2)

Choosing a small production facility corresponds to the lottery $\begin{pmatrix} \$70,000 \\ 1 \end{pmatrix}$ whose expected utility is $\sqrt{70,000} = 264.575$. Choosing a medium facility corresponds to the lottery

$$\begin{pmatrix} \$64,600 & \$85,000 & \$85,000 \\ \frac{1}{4} & \frac{2}{4} & \frac{1}{4} \end{pmatrix}$$

---

[1] Thus, Alice is risk averse. This can be seen, for example, by comparing the lottery $A = \begin{pmatrix} \$400 \\ 1 \end{pmatrix}$ with the lottery $B = \begin{pmatrix} \$16 & \$784 \\ \frac{1}{2} & \frac{1}{2} \end{pmatrix}$. Since the expected value of B is $\frac{1}{2}16 + \frac{1}{2}784 = 400$, lottery A offers the expected value of B for sure (hence, a risk neutral person would be indifferent between A and B). Alice prefers lottery A to lottery B: in fact, the expected utility of A is $\sqrt{400} = 20$, larger than the expected utility of B, which is $\frac{1}{2}\sqrt{784} + \frac{1}{2}\sqrt{16} = \frac{1}{2}28 + \frac{1}{2}4 = 16$.

whose expected utility is

$$\frac{1}{4}\sqrt{64,600} + \frac{2}{4}\sqrt{85,000} + \frac{1}{4}\sqrt{85,000} = 282.202$$

and choosing a large facility corresponds to the lottery

$$\begin{pmatrix} \$58,400 & \$78,800 & \$140,000 \\ \frac{1}{4} & \frac{2}{4} & \frac{1}{4} \end{pmatrix}$$

whose expected utility is $\frac{1}{4}\sqrt{58,400} + \frac{2}{4}\sqrt{78,800} + \frac{1}{4}\sqrt{140,000} = 294.313$. Thus, Alice will choose a large production facility, since it yields the highest expected utility.[2]

> Test your understanding of the concepts introduced in this section, by going through the exercises in Section 6.5.1 at the end of this chapter.

6.2 Decision trees revisited

In Chapter 4 we introduced the method of backward induction to solve decision trees for the special case where the outcomes are sums of money and the *DM* is risk neutral. Now, armed with the theory of expected utility developed in Chapter 5, we can extend the backward-induction method to the case of general outcomes and/or to attitudes to risk different from risk neutrality.

Let us begin with the example of Section 4.4 (Chapter 4). This example concerns Dave, who has developed lower-back pain and is consulting his doctor on what to do. The doctor tells him that one possibility is to do nothing: just rest and limit his activities and hope that the back will heal itself; in her experience, in 40% of the cases the pain subsides spontaneously. Another possibility is to take strong doses of an anti-inflammatory drug for a prolonged period of time. This is an effective way to get rid of the pain; in her experience, it works 80% of the time, without side effects. However, there is a 20% chance that the drug will cause intestinal bleeding, in which case it must be stopped immediately and avoided in the future. Usually this happens within the first week, too soon to have any benefits from the drug in terms of pain reduction. Finally, there is the option of surgery. This type of surgery has been performed many times in the past and it worked in 90% of the patients. For the remaining 10%, however, there was damage to the spine during the procedure, which led to permanent numbness in one or both legs, but the pain in the back did go away. We represented Dave's decision problem using a decision tree, which is reproduced below in Figure 6.1.

---

[2] On the other hand, the MaxiMin criterion (see Chapter 3, Section 3.3) would prescribe choosing a small production facility.

Chapter 6. Applications of Expected Utility

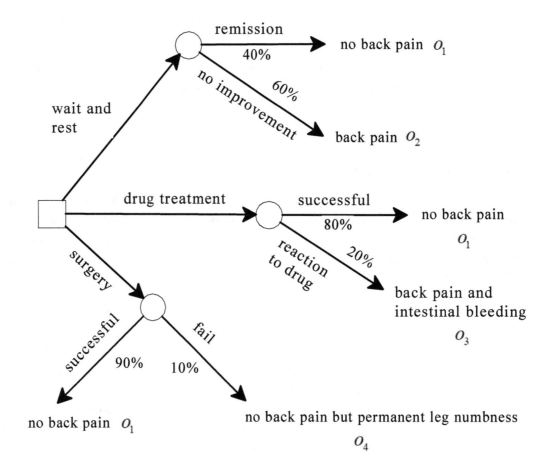

Figure 6.1: Dave's decision tree

6.2 Decision trees revisited

Dave is uncertain as to what to do and, having heard that you are knowledgeable in Decision Making, is asking you to help him. First of all, you explain to him the axioms of expected utility theory. He tells you that he is convinced that they are reasonable axioms and he wants to adhere to them. Then you stipulate that you are going to name the basic outcomes as follows:

outcome	description
o_1	no back pain
o_2	back pain
o_3	back pain and intestinal bleeding
o_4	no back pain but permanent leg numbness

and you ask him to rank them. He informs you that is ranking is:

best	o_1
	o_2
	o_4
worst	o_3

Armed with this information, you decide to construct his normalized von Neumann-Morgenstern utility function. As a first step you assign utility 1 to the best outcome, namely o_1, and utility 0 to the worst outcome, namely o_3. To determine the utility of outcome o_2 you ask him to tell you what value of p would make him indifferent between the lottery $\begin{pmatrix} o_1 & o_3 \\ p & 1-p \end{pmatrix}$ and the lottery $\begin{pmatrix} o_2 \\ 1 \end{pmatrix}$. After giving some consideration to your question, he answers: $p = \frac{3}{4}$. This enables you to assign utility $\frac{3}{4}$ to outcome o_2. You then ask him to tell you what value of p would make him indifferent between the lottery $\begin{pmatrix} o_1 & o_3 \\ p & 1-p \end{pmatrix}$ and the lottery $\begin{pmatrix} o_4 \\ 1 \end{pmatrix}$. His answer is: $p = \frac{1}{8}$. Hence, you assign utility $\frac{1}{8}$ to outcome o_4. Thus, Dave's normalized utility function is

outcome	utility
o_1	1
o_2	$\frac{3}{4}$
o_4	$\frac{1}{8}$
o_3	0

Replacing outcomes with utilities, Dave's decision problem can be re-written as shown in Figure 6.2.

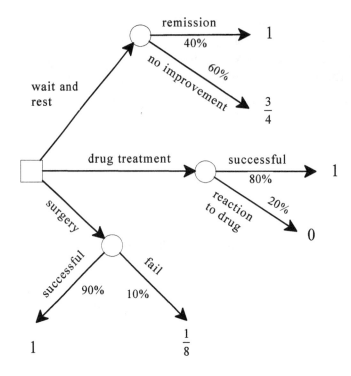

Figure 6.2: Dave's decision tree with outcomes replaced by utilities

Now you apply the method of backward induction to solve the decision tree. The top circle corresponds to a lottery with expected utility $\frac{4}{10}(1) + \frac{6}{10}\left(\frac{3}{4}\right) = 0.85$, the middle circle corresponds to a lottery with expected utility $\frac{8}{10}(1) + \frac{2}{10}(0) = 0.8$ and the bottom circle corresponds to a lottery with expected utility $\frac{9}{10}(1) + \frac{1}{10}\left(\frac{1}{8}\right) = 0.9125$. Thus, the decision tree can be simplified to the one shown in Figure 6.3, showing that Dave's optimal decision is to have surgery.

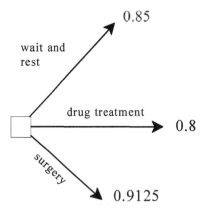

Figure 6.3: The reduced version of the tree of Figure 6.2

Test your understanding of the concepts introduced in this section, by going through the exercises in Section 6.5.2 at the end of this chapter.

6.3 Regret

In Chapter 3 (Section 3.4) we discussed the notion of regret in the context of ordinal rankings of outcomes (using ordinal utility functions) and concluded that the concept of MinMaxRegret was not meaningful in that context. We now re-examine the notion of regret within the context of von Neumann-Morgenstern utility functions.

Suppose that your friend Sue faces the following decision problem represented in terms of states, outcomes and acts:

$$\begin{array}{c|cc} \text{state} \rightarrow & s_1 & s_2 \\ \text{act} \downarrow & & \\ a & o_1 & o_2 \\ b & o_3 & o_4 \end{array} \qquad \text{with preferences} \qquad \begin{array}{cc} \text{best} & o_1 \\ & o_4 \\ & o_3 \\ \text{worst} & o_2 \end{array}$$

Suppose also that Sue satisfies the axioms of expected utility, but is unable to come up with a probability distribution over the set of states $\{s_1, s_2\}$. Yet, she can still contemplate her preferences over all possible hypothetical lotteries on the set of outcomes $\{o_1, o_2, o_3, o_4\}$. She asks you to help her find a von Neumann-Morgenstern utility function that represents her preferences. As explained in Chapter 5, you can – as a first step – assign an arbitrary utility to the best outcome and an arbitrary utility (of course, lower) to the worst outcome. Suppose that you choose the values 100 and 0, respectively.[3] As a second step, you would ask her to tell you what value of p makes her indifferent between the lottery $\begin{pmatrix} o_1 & o_2 \\ p & 1-p \end{pmatrix}$ and getting outcome o_4 for sure. If she satisfies the axioms of expected utility, she must be able to answer this question (indeed, the Continuity Axiom postulates so). Suppose that her answer is: 75%. Then, since the expected utility of the lottery $\begin{pmatrix} o_1 & o_2 \\ 0.75 & 0.25 \end{pmatrix}$ is $0.75(100) + 0.25(0) = 75$, you can assign utility 75 to outcome o_4. As a last step, you would then ask her to tell you what value of p makes her indifferent between the lottery $\begin{pmatrix} o_1 & o_2 \\ p & 1-p \end{pmatrix}$ and getting outcome o_3 for sure. Suppose that her answer is: 50%. Then, since the expected utility of the lottery $\begin{pmatrix} o_1 & o_2 \\ 0.5 & 0.5 \end{pmatrix}$ is $0.5(100) + 0.5(0) = 50$, you can assign utility 50 to outcome o_3. Thus, you have constructed the following von Neumann-Morgenstern utility function:[4]

$$\begin{pmatrix} \text{outcome:} & o_1 & o_2 & o_3 & o_4 \\ \text{utility:} & 100 & 0 & 50 & 75 \end{pmatrix}.$$

Using this utility function we can re-write Sue's decision problem as follows:

$$\begin{array}{c|cc} \text{state} \rightarrow & s_1 & s_2 \\ \text{act} \downarrow & & \\ a & 100 & 0 \\ b & 50 & 75 \end{array} \qquad (6.3)$$

---

[3] If you wanted to construct the normalized utility function you would choose the values 1 and 0, respectively.

[4] The normalized utility function would be $\begin{pmatrix} \text{outcome:} & o_1 & o_2 & o_3 & o_4 \\ \text{utility:} & 1 & 0 & 0.5 & 0.75 \end{pmatrix}.$

Chapter 6. Applications of Expected Utility

After hearing from you the notion of minimizing the maximum regret, Sue decides that she wants to apply that principle in order to decide what to do. You explain to her that, for each state, the potential regret of an act x is the difference between the maximum utility that she could get in that state by choosing the best act for that state and the utility that she gets by choosing act x. Thus, the regret associated with act a in state s_1 is 0 while the regret associated with act a in state s_2 is 75. Hence, the regret table associated with decision problem (6.3) is as follows:

the regret table:

state $\rightarrow$	s_1	s_2
act $\downarrow$		
a	0	75
b	50	0

(6.4)

Since the maximum regret associated with act a is 75 and the maximum regret associated with act b is 50, the principle of minimizing the maximum regret, MinMaxRegret, prescribes choosing act b.

Of course, we need to worry whether the MinMaxRegret principle is meaningful in the context of von Neumann-Morgenster preferences (we know from Chapter 3 that it is *not* meaningful in the context of merely ordinal preferences). Before addressing this issue, we shall give one more example of how to apply the MinMaxRegret principle.

Consider the following decision problem, expressed in terms of von Neumann-Morgenstern utilities:[5]

state $\rightarrow$	s_1	s_2	s_3	s_4
act $\downarrow$				
a	5	80	35	10
b	25	70	30	75
c	60	40	50	45

(6.5)

The corresponding regret table is as follows (with the maximum regret for each act highlighted in a box):

the regret table:

state $\rightarrow$	s_1	s_2	s_3	s_4
act $\downarrow$				
a	55	0	15	$\boxed{65}$
b	$\boxed{35}$	10	20	0
c	0	$\boxed{40}$	0	30

(6.6)

Thus, the MinMaxRegret principle prescribes act b.

---

[5] With the normalized utility function this decision problem would be written as follows (obtained by first subtracting 5 from every utility and then dividing by 75):

state $\rightarrow$	s_1	s_2	s_3	s_4
act $\downarrow$				
a	0	1	$\frac{30}{75}$	$\frac{5}{75}$
b	$\frac{20}{75}$	$\frac{65}{75}$	$\frac{25}{75}$	$\frac{70}{75}$
c	$\frac{55}{75}$	$\frac{35}{75}$	$\frac{45}{75}$	$\frac{40}{75}$

6.3 Regret

Let us now show that, within the context of von Neumann-Morgenstern preferences, the MinMaxRegret principle is indeed meaningful. We need to show that if, with a given von Neumann-Morgenstern utility function, the MinMaxRegret principle prescribes act x then any other von Neumann-Morgenstern utility function that represents the same preferences also prescribes act x. Rather than showing this in general, we will show it for the decision problem considered above in (6.5).

Recall (Theorem 5.2.2, Chapter 5) that if U and V are two alternative von Neumann-Morgenstern utility functions that represent the same preferences, then there are real numbers $\alpha > 0$ and β such that, for every outcome o, $V(o) = \alpha U(o) + \beta$; conversely, if the utility function U is a representation of given von Neumann-Morgenstern preferences then, given arbitrary real numbers $\alpha > 0$ and β, the utility function V defined by $V(o) = \alpha U(o) + \beta$ is also a representation of the same preferences.

Let U be the utility function that appears in decision problem (6.5), which – as shown in the regret table (6.6) – prescribes act b when the MinMaxRegret principle is applied. Choose arbitrary real numbers $\alpha > 0$ and β and define a new utility function V by letting $V(o) = \alpha U(o) + \beta$. Then, using utility function V – which is an alternative representation of the same preferences – the decision problem (6.5) becomes

state →	s_1	s_2	s_3	s_4
act ↓				
a	$5\alpha + \beta$	$80\alpha + \beta$	$35\alpha + \beta$	$10\alpha + \beta$
b	$25\alpha + \beta$	$70\alpha + \beta$	$30\alpha + \beta$	$75\alpha + \beta$
c	$60\alpha + \beta$	$40\alpha + \beta$	$50\alpha + \beta$	$45\alpha + \beta$

(6.7)

Thus, the regret associated with act a in state s_1 is $60\alpha + \beta - (5\alpha + \beta) = 55\alpha$ and similarly for the other states and acts, yielding the following regret table (with the maximum regret for each act highlighted in a box: recall that, by hypothesis, $\alpha > 0$):

the regret table:

state →	s_1	s_2	s_3	s_4
act ↓				
a	55α	0	15α	$\boxed{65\alpha}$
b	$\boxed{35\alpha}$	10α	20α	0
c	0	$\boxed{40\alpha}$	0	30α

(6.8)

It is clear from table (6.8) that the MinMaxRegret principle still prescribes act b (again, recall that $\alpha > 0$), thus confirming the conclusion of table (6.6).

In general, if U is a von Neumann-Morgenstern utility function that represents the DM's preferences and V is an alternative von Neumann-Morgenstern utility function that represents the same preferences, then there exist real numbers $\alpha > 0$ and β such that $V(o) = \alpha U(o) + \beta$, for every basic outcome o. Hence, for every two basic outcomes o and o',

$$V(o') - V(o) = \alpha U(o') + \beta - [\alpha U(o) + \beta] = \alpha U(o') - \alpha U(o) = \alpha \left[U(o') - U(o)\right]$$

so that, by changing the utility function (while representing the same preferences), we merely multiply the regret values by a positive number and thus the act that minimizes the maximum regret remains the same.

We conclude this section by considering what the MinMaxRegret criterion would suggest for the back-pain problem considered in the previous section. Recall that this problem, represented in the decision tree of Figure 6.1, concerns Dave who faces the decision whether to undergo surgery or follow a drug treatment or just wait and rest. The MinMaxRegret principle does not rely on expected utility calculations and thus the probabilities shown in the decision tree are not relevant. Furthermore, before we can apply the notion of regret, we need to recast the decision problem in terms of states and acts.

To start with, we need to clarify what a state is in this case. A state needs to specify all the external facts that are relevant in determining the outcome associated with any action that is taken. There are three such facts.

First of all, there is the issue as to whether the pain would go away with rest. Let us call this fact R; thus, R means that rest would eliminate the pain and $notR$ means that rest would not be effective.

Then there is the issue as to whether Dave's body would tolerate the drug or not. Let us call this fact D; thus, D means drug-tolerance and $notD$ means that the drug would give him intestinal bleeding.

Finally, there is the issue as to whether surgery would be effective in Dave's case. Let us denote this fact by S; thus, S means that surgery would be beneficial and $notS$ that surgery would not be successful.

Each state has to be a full description of the world and thus has to specify which of the above three facts is true. Hence, there are eight states, as shown in Figure 6.4.

Using the normalized utility function calculated in Section 6.2, namely

outcome	utility
o_1	1
o_2	$\frac{3}{4}$
o_4	$\frac{1}{8}$
o_3	0

we obtain the state-act representation shown in Figure 6.4.

		State							
		R,D,S	R,D,notS	R,notD,S	R,notD,notS	notR,D,S	notR,D,notS	notR,notD,S	notR,notD,notS
A	Rest	1	1	1	1	3/4	3/4	3/4	3/4
c	Drug	1	1	0	0	1	1	0	0
t	Surgery	1	1/8	1	1/8	1	1/8	1	1/8

Figure 6.4: The state-act representation of the decision tree of Figure 6.2

6.4 The Hurwicz index of pessimism

The corresponding regret table is shown in Figure 6.5, where the maximum regret for each act is highlighted. Thus, the MinMaxRegret principle prescribes the choice of resting.

		State							
		R,D,S	R,D,notS	R,notD,S	R,notD,notS	notR,D,S	notR,D,notS	notR,notD,S	notR,notD,notS
A	Rest	0	0	0	0	1/4	1/4	1/4	0
c	Drug	0	0	1	1	0	0	1	3/4
t	Surgery	0	7/8	0	7/8	0	7/8	0	5/8

Figure 6.5: The regret table corresponding to Figure 6.4

> Test your understanding of the concepts introduced in this section, by going through the exercises in Section 6.5.3 at the end of this chapter.

6.4 The Hurwicz index of pessimism

In Section 3.3 of Chapter 3 we discussed the MaxiMin principle, within the context of ordinal preferences, and noted that it reflects a notion of extreme pessimism: for each act the *DM* looks at the worst-case scenario – that is, the worst possible outcome – and then chooses an act which is best in terms of the worst outcome. The late economist Leonid Hurwicz, who in 2007 shared the Nobel Memorial Prize in Economic Sciences[6] (with Eric Maskin and Roger Myerson) for work on mechanism design, proposed a more general criterion of choice that incorporates the MaxiMin as a special case. It is a principle that, like the notion of regret, would not be meaningful within the context of merely ordinal utility functions.

Let $\alpha \in [0, 1]$. For each act, the *DM* attaches weight α to the worst outcome associated with that act and weight $(1 - \alpha)$ to the best outcome associated with that act, thus obtaining an index for each act. The *DM* then chooses that act that has the highest index (or one of them, if there are several acts with the highest index). For example, consider the following decision problem, where utilities are von Neumann-Morgenstern utilities:

$$
\begin{array}{c|ccc}
\text{state} \rightarrow & s_1 & s_2 & s_3 \\
\text{act} \downarrow & & & \\
\hline
a_1 & 10 & 2 & 0 \\
a_2 & 8 & 4 & 2 \\
a_3 & 4 & 4 & 4
\end{array}
\tag{6.9}
$$

Then the Hurwicz index associated with each act is calculated as follows:

$$H(a_1; \alpha) = 0\alpha + 10(1-\alpha) = 10 - 10\alpha$$

$$H(a_2; \alpha) = 2\alpha + 8(1-\alpha) = 8 - 6\alpha$$

$$H(a_3; \alpha) = 4\alpha + 4(1-\alpha) = 4$$

---

[6]This is usually referred to as the 'Nobel Prize in Economics'; however, it is in fact the 'Sveriges Riksbank Prize in Economic Sciences in Memory of Alfred Nobel', only given out since 1969.

If $\alpha = \frac{3}{5}$ then we get

$$H(a_1; \tfrac{3}{5}) = 0\tfrac{3}{5} + 10(1 - \tfrac{3}{5}) = 4$$

$$H(a_2; \tfrac{3}{5}) = 2\tfrac{3}{5} + 8(1 - \tfrac{3}{5}) = 4.4$$

$$H(a_3; \tfrac{3}{5}) = 4\tfrac{3}{5} + 4(1 - \tfrac{3}{5}) = 4$$

and thus the *DM* would choose act a_2.

The parameter α is called the *index of pessimism*. If $\alpha = 1$ (extreme pessimism) then the *DM* focuses on the worst outcome and the Hurwicz principle reduces to the MaxiMin principle. If $\alpha = 0$ (complete lack of pessimism, or extreme optimism) then the *DM* simply chooses an act that gives the best outcome in some state. If $0 < \alpha < 1$ then the *DM*'s degree of pessimism is somewhere between these two extremes.

Continuing the example given above in (6.9), we can plot the values $H(a_1; \alpha), H(a_2; \alpha)$ and $H(a_3; \alpha)$ in a diagram where we measure α on the horizontal axis, as shown in Figure 6.6.

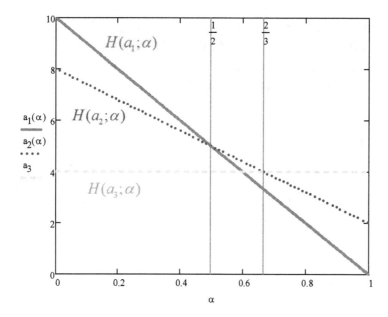

Figure 6.6: The Hurwicz indices for the three acts of decision problem (6.9)

We can see from Figure 6.6 that:
- If $0 \leq \alpha < \tfrac{1}{2}$ then the Hurwicz criterion prescribes act a_1,
- if $\alpha = \tfrac{1}{2}$ then the Hurwicz criterion prescribes either a_1 or a_2,
- if $\tfrac{1}{2} < \alpha < \tfrac{2}{3}$ then the Hurwicz criterion prescribes act a_2,
- if $\alpha = \tfrac{2}{3}$ then the Hurwicz criterion prescribes either a_2 or a_3,
- if $\tfrac{2}{3} < \alpha \leq 1$ then the Hurwicz criterion prescribes act a_3.

6.4 The Hurwicz index of pessimism

		State							
		R,D,S	R,D,notS	R,notD,S	R,notD,notS	notR,D,S	notR,D,notS	notR,notD,S	notR,notD,notS
A	Rest	1	1	1	1	3/4	3/4	3/4	3/4
c	Drug	1	1	0	0	1	1	0	0
t	Surgery	1	1/8	1	1/8	1	1/8	1	1/8

As a final example, let us re-examine, from the point of view of Hurwicz's criterion, Dave's decision problem shown in Figure 6.4, which is reproduced above.

The Hurwicz indices for the three acts are as follows:

$$H(Rest; \alpha) = \tfrac{3}{4}\alpha + 1(1-\alpha) = 1 - \tfrac{1}{4}\alpha.$$
$$H(Drug; \alpha) = (0)\alpha + 1(1-\alpha) = 1 - \alpha.$$
$$H(Surgery; \alpha) = \tfrac{1}{8}\alpha + 1(1-\alpha) = 1 - \tfrac{7}{8}\alpha.$$

For every $\alpha > 0$, $H(Rest; \alpha) > H(Surgery; \alpha) > H(Drug; \alpha)$ and thus, as long as the index of pessimism α is not 0, *Rest* is the unique act prescribed by the Hurwicz criterion (if $\alpha = 0$ then the three acts are equivalent).

As for the case of MinMaxRegret, one needs to show that the Hurwicz criterion is meaningful, in the sense that, if one were to use two different utility functions representing the same von Neumann-Morgenstern preferences, then one would obtain the same answer (using the Hurwicz criterion) for every possible value of the parameter α (which expresses the *DM*'s degree of pessimism). Let us prove this.

Let U be a utility function that represents the *DM*'s von Neumann-Morgenstern preferences. Fix an arbitrary act a and let $\underline{s}(a)$ be a state that yields the lowest utility under act a and $\overline{s}(a)$ be a state that yields the highest utility under act a,[7] that is, letting $o(a,s)$ denote the basic outcome associated with act a and state s,

$$U(o(a,\underline{s}(a))) \leq U(o(a,s)), \text{ for every state } s,$$
$$U(o(a,\overline{s}(a))) \geq U(o(a,s)), \text{ for every state } s. \qquad (6.10)$$

Let V be a different utility function that represents the same preferences. Then, by Theorem 5.2.2 of Chapter 5, there exist two real numbers $c > 0$ and d such that

$$V(o) = cU(o) + d, \text{ for every basic outcome } o. \qquad (6.11)$$

Now, if we multiply both sides of the two inequalities in (6.10) by c and add d to both sides and use (6.11) we obtain

$$V(o(a,\underline{s}(a))) \leq V(o(a,s)), \text{ for every state } s,$$
$$V(o(a,\overline{s}(a))) \geq V(o(a,s)), \text{ for every state } s. \qquad (6.12)$$

It follows from (6.12) that it is still true for utility function V that $\underline{s}(a)$ is a state that yields the lowest utility under act a and $\overline{s}(a)$ is a state that yields the highest utility under act a.

---

[7] For instance, in decision problem (6.9), $\underline{s}(a_1) = s_3$ and $\overline{s}(a_1) = s_1$. The two states $\underline{s}(a)$ and $\overline{s}(a)$ may be different for different acts, that is, they are a function of the act [hence the notation $\underline{s}(a)$ and $\overline{s}(a)$]. If there are several states that yield the lowest utility, then $\underline{s}(a)$ denotes any one of them (and similarly for $\overline{s}(a)$).

Fix a value $\hat{\alpha}$ for the *DM*'s degree of pessimism (with $0 \leq \hat{\alpha} \leq 1$). Under utility function U, the Hurwicz index of act a is

$$H_U(a;\hat{\alpha}) = \hat{\alpha} U(o(a,\underline{s}(a))) + (1-\hat{\alpha})U(o(a,\overline{s}(a))). \tag{6.13}$$

Hence, by (6.12), the Hurwicz index of act a under utility function V is

$$H_V(a,\hat{\alpha}) = \hat{\alpha} V(o(a,\underline{s}(a))) + (1-\hat{\alpha})V(o(a,\overline{s}(a))). \tag{6.14}$$

Let b be an act prescribed by the Hurwicz criterion under utility function U, that is,

$$H_U(b;\hat{\alpha}) \geq H_U(a;\hat{\alpha}), \text{ for every act } a. \tag{6.15}$$

Then it follows from (6.13)-(6.15) that

$$H_V(b;\hat{\alpha}) \geq H_V(a;\hat{\alpha}), \text{ for every act } a. \tag{6.16}$$

Thus, act b is prescribed by the Hurwicz criterion also under utility function V.

> Test your understanding of the concepts introduced in this section, by going through the exercises in Section 6.5.4 at the end of this chapter.

6.5 Exercises

The solutions to the following exercises are given in Section 6.6 at the end of this chapter.

6.5.1 Exercises for Section 6.1: States and acts revisited

Exercise 6.1 Consider the following decision problem and preferences:

state →	s_1	s_2	s_3		best	o_1
act ↓						o_3, o_8, o_9
a_1	o_1	o_2	o_3			o_7
a_2	o_4	o_5	o_6			o_5, o_6
a_3	o_7	o_8	o_9		worst	o_2, o_4

Assume that the *DM* has von Neumann-Morgenstern preferences over the set of lotteries over the set of outcomes $\{o_1, o_2, \ldots, o_9\}$. The *DM* says that she is indifferent between o_8 for sure and a lottery where she gets o_1 with probability 0.7 and o_2 with probability 0.3; she is also indifferent between o_7 for sure and a lottery where she gets o_1 with probability 0.5 and o_4 with probability 0.5; finally, she is indifferent between the following two lotteries: $\begin{pmatrix} o_6 & o_7 & o_9 \\ \frac{1}{3} & \frac{1}{3} & \frac{1}{3} \end{pmatrix}$ and $\begin{pmatrix} o_3 & o_4 \\ \frac{2}{3} & \frac{1}{3} \end{pmatrix}$.

(a) Find the *DM*'s normalized von Neumann-Morgenstern utility function.

(b) Change the utility function so that the lowest value is 0 and the highest value is 100. Use this utility function to re-write the decision problem in terms of utilities.

(c) If the *DM* assigns equal probabilities to all states, what act will she choose?

6.5 Exercises

Exercise 6.2 Consider Alice's decision problem shown below:

state →	s_1	s_2	s_3
act ↓			
small	$70,000	$70,000	$70,000
medium	$64,600	$85,000	$85,000
large	$58,400	$78,800	$140,000

Suppose now that Alice assigns the following probabilities to the states:

state	s_1	s_2	s_3
probability	$\frac{7}{16}$	$\frac{1}{2}$	$\frac{1}{16}$

As before, Alice's von Neumann-Morgenstern utility function is given by $U(\$x) = \sqrt{x}$. What production facility will she choose? ∎

Exercise 6.3 Consider the following decision problem where the numbers are von Neumann-Morgenstern utilities:

state →	s_1	s_2	s_3	s_4	s_5	s_6	s_7
act ↓							
a	0	2	3	1	5	4	1
b	0	1	3	2	5	3	6
c	1	2	5	4	5	6	4
d	2	1	3	4	6	4	3
e	3	1	4	6	0	7	0

The DM assigns the following probabilities to the states:

$$\begin{pmatrix} s_1 & s_2 & s_3 & s_4 & s_5 & s_6 & s_7 \\ \frac{1}{7} & \frac{3}{14} & \frac{2}{7} & \frac{1}{14} & \frac{1}{7} & \frac{1}{14} & \frac{1}{14} \end{pmatrix}.$$

What act will he choose? ∎

Exercise 6.4 Consider the following decision problem:

state →	s_1	s_2		
act ↓			with preferences	best o_3
				o_2
a	o_1	o_2		o_1
b	o_3	o_4		worst o_4

Let U be a von Neumann-Morgenstern utility function that represents the agent's preferences and suppose that $U(o_3) - U(o_2) = U(o_2) - U(o_1) = U(o_1) - U(o_4)$.
  (a) Find the normalized von Neumann-Morgenstern utility function.
  (b) Suppose that the DM learns that state s_1 has a probability 0.2 of occurring. What act will the DM choose?

∎

6.5.2 Exercises for Section 6.2: Decision trees revisited

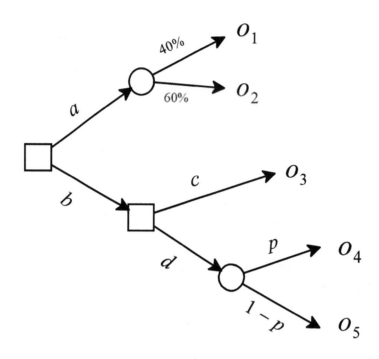

Figure 6.7: A decision tree

Exercise 6.5 Consider the decision tree shown in Figure 6.7. The *DM*'s ranking of the basic outcomes is $o_4 \succ o_1 \succ o_3 \succ o_2 \sim o_5$. The *DM* has von Neumann-Morgenstern preferences over the set of lotteries involving these outcomes. She is indifferent between o_1 for sure and the lottery $\begin{pmatrix} o_2 & o_4 \\ \frac{1}{5} & \frac{4}{5} \end{pmatrix}$ and she is also indifferent between o_3 for sure and the lottery $\begin{pmatrix} o_5 & o_4 \\ \frac{4}{5} & \frac{1}{5} \end{pmatrix}$.

(a) Construct the normalized von Neumann-Morgenstern utility function.
(b) Use the method of backward induction to find the optimal solution for every value of $p \in [0, 1]$.

Exercise 6.6 Jonathan is facing a dilemma. Tomorrow is the last day of the Quarter and his last final exam is in the morning. He has been invited to a party, where Kate is going to be. Jonathan has a crush on Kate. This would be his last chance to see Kate before the next academic year. Jonathan does not know if Kate is interested in him. He has two choices.
- The first choice is to skip the party and study for the final. If he does so, then he expects to get an A if the exam is easy but only a C if the exam is difficult.

6.5 Exercises

- His second choice is to go to the party and approach Kate. Of course, this implies that he will not study for the final, with the consequence that he will get a C if the exam is easy and an F if the exam is difficult. Furthermore, he doesn't know if Kate is interested in him. If he approaches her and she is welcoming then he will have a great time, while if she rejects him then he will feel awful. He is not really interested in the party itself: all he cares about is Kate.

The basic outcomes are thus:

o_1		Stays home, gets A
o_2		Stays home, gets C
o_3	At party, good time with Kate, gets C
o_4	At party, good time with Kate, gets F
o_5		At party, rejected, gets C
o_6		At party, rejected, gets F

Having looked at past exams, Jonathan attaches probability $\frac{3}{4}$ to the exam being easy and probability $\frac{1}{4}$ to the exam being difficult. He has consulted his friend James (who has always had great success with women and professes himself to be an expert on the matter) about the chances that Kate would be welcoming if Jonathan approached her. James's verdict is: probability $\frac{1}{3}$.

(a) Draw a decision tree to represent Jonathan's decision problem.

(b) Jonathan's von Neumann-Morgenstern utility function is as follows:

outcome	o_1	o_2	o_3	o_4	o_5	o_6
utility	4	3	6	5	2	1

Apply the method of backward-induction to solve the decision tree.

6.5.3 Exercises for Section 6.3: Regret

Exercise 6.7 Find the MinMaxRegret solution of the decision problem of Exercise 6.1, reproduced below:

state →	s_1	s_2	s_3
act ↓			
a_1	100	0	70
a_2	0	20	20
a_3	50	70	70

Exercise 6.8 Consider again the decision problem of Exercise 6.3, reproduced below:

state →	s_1	s_2	s_3	s_4	s_5	s_6	s_7
act ↓							
a	0	2	3	1	5	4	1
b	0	1	3	2	5	3	6
c	1	2	5	4	5	6	4
d	2	1	3	4	6	4	3
e	3	1	4	6	0	7	0

(a) Find the MinMaxRegret solution.

(b) Now normalize the utility function (so that the highest value is 1 and the lowest 0) and re-write the decision problem using the new utility function. What is the MinMaxRegret decision solution under the new representation?

Exercise 6.9 Find the MinMaxRegret solution of the decision problem of Exercise 6.4, reproduced below:

state →	s_1	s_2
act ↓		
a	$\frac{1}{3}$	$\frac{2}{3}$
b	1	0

Exercise 6.10 Find the MinMaxRegret solution of the following decision problem (where the numbers are von Neumann-Morgenstern utilities):

state →	s_1	s_2	s_3
act ↓			
a_1	10	2	0
a_2	8	4	2
a_3	4	4	4

6.5.4 Exercises for Section 6.4: The Hurwicz index of pessimism

Exercise 6.11 Consider the following decision problem, where the numbers are von Neumann-Morgenstern utilities:

act/state	s_1	s_2	s_3	s_4
a_1	12	3	6	6
a_2	10	0	10	10
a_3	5	4	5	5
a_4	18	0	4	3

6.5 Exercises

(a) Find the MaxiMin solution.

(b) Find the MinMaxRegret solution.

(c) Suppose that the agent follows the Hurwicz criterion with a pessimism index α.

What will the *DM* choose if $\alpha = 1$?

What will the *DM* choose if $\alpha = 0$?

What will the *DM* choose if $\alpha = \frac{1}{2}$?

For what value of the pessimism index α would the *DM* be indifferent between a_1 and a_2?

Exercise 6.12 Consider the following decision problem, where the numbers are von Neumann-Morgenstern utilities:

state → act ↓	s_1	s_2	s_3
a_1	12	3	2
a_2	8	16	0
a_3	6	4	8

Let α be the *DM*'s index of pessimism.

(a) What act is prescribed by the Hurwicz criterion if $\alpha = \frac{1}{2}$?

(b) For every $\alpha \in [0, 1]$ find the act that is prescribed by the Hurwicz criterion, by plotting the Hurwicz index of each act as a function of α.

Exercise 6.13 Consider again the decision problem of Exercise 6.12, reproduced below:

state → act ↓	s_1	s_2	s_3
a_1	12	3	2
a_2	8	16	0
a_3	6	4	8

Normalize the utility function and show that the act recommended by the Hurwicz criterion under the normalized utility function when $\alpha = \frac{1}{2}$ is the same as the one found in Part (a) of Exercise 6.12.

6.6 Solutions to Exercises

Solution to Exercise 6.1.

(a) First of all, $U(o_1) = 1$ and $U(o_2) = U(o_4) = 0$. Since the agent is indifferent between o_8 for sure and a lottery where she gets o_1 with probability 0.7 and o_2 with probability 0.3, we have that $U(o_3) = U(o_8) = U(o_9) = 0.7$.

Since she is indifferent between o_7 for sure and a lottery where she gets o_1 with probability 0.5 and o_4 with probability 0.5, $U(o_7) = 0.5$. Finally, the expected utility of $\begin{pmatrix} o_6 & o_7 & o_9 \\ \frac{1}{3} & \frac{1}{3} & \frac{1}{3} \end{pmatrix}$ is

$$\tfrac{1}{3}U(o_6) + \tfrac{1}{3}U(o_7) + \tfrac{1}{3}U(o_9) = \tfrac{1}{3}U(o_6) + \tfrac{1}{3}(0.5) + \tfrac{1}{3}(0.7) = \tfrac{1}{3}U(o_6) + 0.4$$

and the expected utility of $\begin{pmatrix} o_3 & o_4 \\ \frac{2}{3} & \frac{1}{3} \end{pmatrix}$ is $\tfrac{2}{3}U(o_3) + \tfrac{1}{3}U(o_4) = \tfrac{2}{3}(0.7) + \tfrac{1}{3}(0) = \tfrac{7}{15}$;

since she is indifferent between those two lotteries, $\tfrac{1}{3}U(o_6) + 0.4 = \tfrac{7}{15}$. Thus, $U(o_6) = \tfrac{1}{5} = 0.2$. Hence, the normalized utility function is:

		Utility
best	o_1	1
	o_3, o_8, o_9	0.7
	o_7	0.5
	o_5, o_6	0.2
worst	o_2, o_4	0

(b) All we need to do is multiply the normalized utility function by 100:

		Utility
best	o_1	100
	o_3, o_8, o_9	70
	o_7	50
	o_5, o_6	20
worst	o_2, o_4	0

Then the decision problem can be written as follows:

state →	s_1	s_2	s_3
act ↓			
a_1	100	0	70
a_2	0	20	20
a_3	50	70	70

(c) We can view act a_1 as a lottery with expected utility $\tfrac{1}{3}100 + \tfrac{1}{3}0 + \tfrac{1}{3}70 = \tfrac{170}{3}$, a_2 as a lottery with expected utility $\tfrac{1}{3}0 + \tfrac{1}{3}20 + \tfrac{1}{3}20 = \tfrac{40}{3}$ and a_3 as a lottery with expected utility $\tfrac{1}{3}50 + \tfrac{1}{3}70 + \tfrac{1}{3}70 = \tfrac{190}{3}$.

Thus, the *DM* would choose a_3. □

6.6 Solutions to Exercises

Solution to Exercise 6.2. Alice's decision problem is reproduced below:

state →	s_1	s_2	s_3
act ↓			
small	$70,000	$70,000	$70,000
medium	$64,600	$85,000	$85,000
large	$58,400	$78,800	$140,000

Choosing a small production facility corresponds to the lottery $\begin{pmatrix} \$70,000 \\ 1 \end{pmatrix}$ whose expected utility is $\sqrt{70,000} = 264.575$.

Choosing a medium facility corresponds to the lottery $\begin{pmatrix} \$64,600 & \$85,000 & \$85,000 \\ \frac{7}{16} & \frac{1}{2} & \frac{1}{16} \end{pmatrix}$ whose expected utility is $\frac{7}{16}\sqrt{64,600} + \frac{1}{2}\sqrt{85,000} + \frac{1}{16}\sqrt{85,000} = 275.193$ and choosing a large facility corresponds to the lottery $\begin{pmatrix} \$58,400 & \$78,800 & \$140,000 \\ \frac{7}{16} & \frac{1}{2} & \frac{1}{16} \end{pmatrix}$ whose expected utility is $\frac{7}{16}\sqrt{58,400} + \frac{1}{2}\sqrt{78,800} + \frac{1}{16}\sqrt{140,000} = 269.469$.

Thus, Alice will choose a medium production facility since it yields the highest expected utility. □

Solution to Exercise 6.3. Act a corresponds to a lottery with expected utility

$$0\left(\tfrac{1}{7}\right) + 2\left(\tfrac{3}{14}\right) + 3\left(\tfrac{2}{7}\right) + 1\left(\tfrac{1}{14}\right) + 5\left(\tfrac{1}{7}\right) + 4\left(\tfrac{1}{14}\right) + 1\left(\tfrac{1}{14}\right) = \tfrac{17}{7}.$$

Act b corresponds to a lottery with expected utility

$$0\left(\tfrac{1}{7}\right) + 1\left(\tfrac{3}{14}\right) + 3\left(\tfrac{2}{7}\right) + 2\left(\tfrac{1}{14}\right) + 5\left(\tfrac{1}{7}\right) + 3\left(\tfrac{1}{14}\right) + 6\left(\tfrac{1}{14}\right) = \tfrac{18}{7}.$$

Act c corresponds to a lottery with expected utility

$$1\left(\tfrac{1}{7}\right) + 2\left(\tfrac{3}{14}\right) + 5\left(\tfrac{2}{7}\right) + 4\left(\tfrac{1}{14}\right) + 5\left(\tfrac{1}{7}\right) + 6\left(\tfrac{1}{14}\right) + 4\left(\tfrac{1}{14}\right) = \tfrac{26}{7}.$$

Act d corresponds to a lottery with expected utility

$$2\left(\tfrac{1}{7}\right) + 1\left(\tfrac{3}{14}\right) + 3\left(\tfrac{2}{7}\right) + 4\left(\tfrac{1}{14}\right) + 6\left(\tfrac{1}{7}\right) + 4\left(\tfrac{1}{14}\right) + 3\left(\tfrac{1}{14}\right) = \tfrac{21}{7}.$$

Act e corresponds to a lottery with expected utility

$$3\left(\tfrac{1}{7}\right) + 1\left(\tfrac{3}{14}\right) + 4\left(\tfrac{2}{7}\right) + 6\left(\tfrac{1}{14}\right) + 0\left(\tfrac{1}{7}\right) + 7\left(\tfrac{1}{14}\right) + 0\left(\tfrac{1}{14}\right) = \tfrac{19}{7}.$$

Thus, the *DM* will choose act c. □

Solution to Exercise 6.4.

(a) First of all, we assign utility 1 to o_3 and utility 0 to o_4.
Let α be the utility of o_2 and β the utility of o_1. Clearly, $\alpha > \beta$. The information we have is that $1 - \alpha = \alpha - \beta$ and $\alpha - \beta = \beta - 0$. From the second equality we get that $\alpha = 2\beta$ and replacing in the first we get that $1 - 2\beta = 2\beta - \beta$, that is, $\beta = \frac{1}{3}$.

Hence, $\alpha = \frac{2}{3}$. Thus, the normalized von Neumann-Morgenstern utility function is:

outcome	o_1	o_2	o_3	o_4
utility	$\frac{1}{3}$	$\frac{2}{3}$	1	0

(b) Using the normalized utility function we can rewrite the decision problem as follows:

state →	s_1	s_2
act ↓		
a	$\frac{1}{3}$	$\frac{2}{3}$
b	1	0

If the probability of state s_1 is $\frac{1}{5}$, act a corresponds to a lottery with expected utility $\frac{1}{5}\left(\frac{1}{3}\right) + \frac{4}{5}\left(\frac{2}{3}\right) = \frac{3}{5} = 0.6$, while b corresponds to a lottery with expected utility $\frac{1}{5}(1) + \frac{4}{5}(0) = \frac{1}{5} = 0.2$. Hence, the *DM* will choose act a. □

Solution to Exercise 6.5.

(a) We can assign utility 1 to the best outcome, namely o_4, and utility 0 to the worst outcomes, namely o_2 and o_5. Hence, from the first indifference we get that the utility of o_1 is $\frac{4}{5}$ and from the second indifference we get that the utility of o_3 is $\frac{1}{5}$.

Thus, the normalized utility function is
outcome	o_1	o_2	o_3	o_4	o_5
utility	$\frac{4}{5}$	0	$\frac{1}{5}$	1	0

(b) The top Chance node corresponds to a lottery with expected utility $\frac{4}{10}\left(\frac{4}{5}\right) + \frac{6}{10}(0) = \frac{8}{25}$ and the bottom Chance node corresponds to a lottery with expected utility $p(1) + (1-p)(0) = p$. Thus,
if $p > \frac{1}{5}$ then at the bottom decision node the optimal decision is d, with a corresponding expected utility of p,
if $p < \frac{1}{5}$ then at the bottom decision node the optimal decision is c, with a corresponding utility of $\frac{1}{5}$ and
if $p = \frac{1}{5}$ then both c and d are optimal and yield a utility of $\frac{1}{5}$. Thus, the maximum utility that can be obtained by choosing b is $max\{p, \frac{1}{5}\}$ (note that $\frac{1}{5} = \frac{5}{25} < \frac{8}{25}$).
Hence, the optimal strategy, as a function of p, is as follows:
(1) if $p < \frac{8}{25}$ then choose a,
(2) if $p > \frac{8}{25}$ then choose first b and then d,
(3) if $p = \frac{8}{25}$ then either choose a or choose first b and then d. □

Solution to Exercise 6.6.

(a) The decision tree is shown in Figure 6.8.

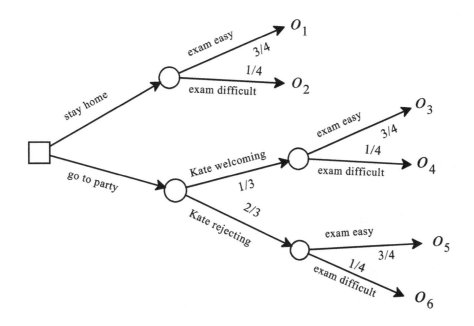

Figure 6.8: The decision tree for Part (a) of Exercise 6.6

(b) The top Chance node corresponds to a lottery with expected utility $\frac{3}{4}(4)+\frac{1}{4}(3)=\frac{15}{4}$, the right-most Chance node below it corresponds to a lottery with expected utility $\frac{3}{4}(6)+\frac{1}{4}(5)=\frac{23}{4}$ and the Chance node below this corresponds to a lottery with expected utility $\frac{3}{4}2+\frac{1}{4}1=\frac{7}{4}$.

Thus, the tree can be reduced to the tree shown in Figure 6.9. The Chance node in this reduced tree corresponds to a lottery with expected utility $\frac{1}{3}\left(\frac{23}{4}\right)+\frac{2}{3}\left(\frac{7}{4}\right)=\frac{37}{12}$. Thus, since $\frac{15}{4}=\frac{45}{12}>\frac{37}{12}$, the optimal decision is to stay at home and study. □

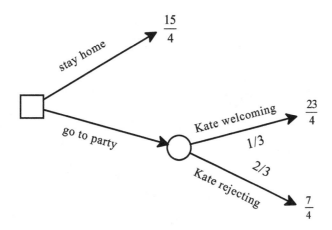

Figure 6.9: The decision tree for Part (b) of Exercise 6.6

Solution to Exercise 6.7. The decision problem is as follows:

state →	s_1	s_2	s_3
act ↓			
a_1	100	0	70
a_2	0	20	20
a_3	50	70	70

The regret table is:

state →	s_1	s_2	s_3
act ↓			
a_1	0	$\boxed{70}$	0
a_2	$\boxed{100}$	50	50
a_3	$\boxed{50}$	0	0

The maximum regrets are thus:

	Maximum regret
a_1	70
a_2	100
a_3	50

Hence, the MinMaxRegret solution is a_3. □

Solution to Exercise 6.8.

(a) The decision problem is:

state →	s_1	s_2	s_3	s_4	s_5	s_6	s_7
act ↓							
a	0	2	3	1	5	4	1
b	0	1	3	2	5	3	6
c	1	2	5	4	5	6	4
d	2	1	3	4	6	4	3
e	3	1	4	6	0	7	0

The corresponding regret table is:

state →	s_1	s_2	s_3	s_4	s_5	s_6	s_7
act ↓							
a	3	0	2	$\boxed{5}$	1	3	5
b	3	1	2	4	1	$\boxed{4}$	0
c	$\boxed{2}$	0	0	2	1	1	2
d	1	1	2	2	0	$\boxed{3}$	3
e	0	1	1	0	$\boxed{6}$	0	6

Thus, the MinMaxRegret solution is c.

6.6 Solutions to Exercises

(b) The MinMaxRegret cannot change if we change the utility function in an admissible way (by multiplying by a positive constant and adding a constant). Let us confirm this for the transformation required by the question (normalization). We need to multiply every utility value by $\frac{1}{7}$, obtaining the following alternative representation of the decision problem:

state →	s_1	s_2	s_3	s_4	s_5	s_6	s_7
act ↓							
a	0	$\frac{2}{7}$	$\frac{3}{7}$	$\frac{1}{7}$	$\frac{5}{7}$	$\frac{4}{7}$	$\frac{1}{7}$
b	0	$\frac{1}{7}$	$\frac{3}{7}$	$\frac{2}{7}$	$\frac{5}{7}$	$\frac{3}{7}$	$\frac{6}{7}$
c	$\frac{1}{7}$	$\frac{2}{7}$	$\frac{5}{7}$	$\frac{4}{7}$	$\frac{5}{7}$	$\frac{6}{7}$	$\frac{4}{7}$
d	$\frac{2}{7}$	$\frac{1}{7}$	$\frac{3}{7}$	$\frac{4}{7}$	$\frac{6}{7}$	$\frac{4}{7}$	$\frac{3}{7}$
e	$\frac{3}{7}$	$\frac{1}{7}$	$\frac{4}{7}$	$\frac{6}{7}$	0	1	0

The regret matrix then becomes:

state →	s_1	s_2	s_3	s_4	s_5	s_6	s_7
act ↓							
a	$\frac{3}{7}$	0	$\frac{2}{7}$	$\boxed{\frac{5}{7}}$	$\frac{1}{7}$	$\frac{3}{7}$	$\frac{5}{7}$
b	$\frac{3}{7}$	$\frac{1}{7}$	$\frac{2}{7}$	$\frac{4}{7}$	$\frac{1}{7}$	$\boxed{\frac{4}{7}}$	0
c	$\boxed{\frac{2}{7}}$	0	0	$\frac{2}{7}$	$\frac{1}{7}$	$\frac{1}{7}$	$\frac{2}{7}$
d	$\frac{1}{7}$	$\frac{1}{7}$	$\frac{2}{7}$	$\frac{2}{7}$	0	$\boxed{\frac{3}{7}}$	$\frac{3}{7}$
e	0	$\frac{1}{7}$	$\frac{1}{7}$	0	$\boxed{\frac{6}{7}}$	0	$\frac{6}{7}$

As before the transformation, the MinMaxRegret solution is c. □

Solution to Exercise 6.9. The decision problem is as follows:

state →	s_1	s_2
act ↓		
a	$\frac{1}{3}$	$\frac{2}{3}$
b	1	0

The regret table is:

state →	s_1	s_2
act ↓		
a	$\frac{2}{3}$	0
b	0	$\frac{2}{3}$

The maximum regret from act a is $\frac{2}{3}$ and the maximum regret from act b is also $\frac{2}{3}$. Thus, the MinMaxRegret solution is $\{a,b\}$. □

Solution to Exercise 6.10. The decision problem is reproduced below, together with the corresponding regret table (with the highest regret highlighted for each act):

decision problem:

state → act ↓	s_1	s_2	s_3
a_1	10	2	0
a_2	8	4	2
a_3	4	4	4

regret table:

	s_1	s_2	s_3
a_1	0	2	[4]
a_2	[2]	0	2
a_3	[6]	0	0

The MinMaxRegret principle prescribes act a_2. □

Solution to Exercise 6.11. The decision problem is as follows:

act/state	s_1	s_2	s_3	s_3
a_1	12	3	6	6
a_2	10	0	10	10
a_3	5	4	5	5
a_4	18	0	4	3

(a) The lowest utility from a_1 is 3, the lowest utility from a_2 is 0, the lowest utility from a_3 is 4, the lowest utility from a_4 is 0. The largest of these values is 4 and thus the MaxiMin solution is a_3.

(b) The regret table is as follows, where the largest value in each row has been highlighted.

act/state	s_1	s_2	s_3	s_3
a_1	[6]	1	4	4
a_2	[8]	4	0	0
a_3	[13]	0	5	5
a_4	0	4	6	[7]

The lowest of the highlighted numbers is 6, thus the MinMaxRegret solution is a_1.

(c) The Hurwicz criterion assigns weight α to the worst outcome and weight $(1 - \alpha)$ to the best outcome. Thus:

$\alpha = 1$ corresponds to the MaxiMin solution and thus the answer is: a_3.

$\alpha = 0$ corresponds to the act that yields the highest utility (in some state) and thus the answer is: a_4.

When $\alpha = \frac{1}{2}$, the Hurwicz indices associated with the acts are:

$a_1 : (3)\frac{1}{2} + (12)\frac{1}{2} = 7.5$
$a_2 : (0)\frac{1}{2} + (10)\frac{1}{2} = 5$
$a_3 : (4)\frac{1}{2} + (5)\frac{1}{2} = 4.5$
$a_4 : (0)\frac{1}{2} + (18)\frac{1}{2} = 9$

The largest value is 9 and thus the Hurwicz criterion prescribes act a_4.

(d) The value of α that would make the *DM* indifferent between a_1 and a_2 would be given by the solution to $3\alpha + 12(1 - \alpha) = 0\alpha + 10(1 - \alpha)$ subject to $0 \leq \alpha \leq 1$, but there is no such solution (the solution to the equation is $\alpha = -2$). Thus, the *DM* would never be indifferent between a_1 and a_2. □

6.6 Solutions to Exercises

Solution to Exercise 6.12. The decision problem is as follows:

state →	s_1	s_2	s_3
act ↓			
a_1	12	3	2
a_2	8	16	0
a_3	6	4	8

(a) When $\alpha = \frac{1}{2}$ the Hurwicz indices of the three acts are:
$H(a_1) = \frac{1}{2}(2) + \frac{1}{2}(12) = 7$,
$H(a_2) = \frac{1}{2}(0) + \frac{1}{2}(16) = 8$,
$H(a_3) = \frac{1}{2}(4) + \frac{1}{2}(8) = 6$.
Thus, when $\alpha = \frac{1}{2}$ the Hurwicz criterion prescribes act a_2.

(b) The Hurwicz indices of the three acts are:
$H(a_1; \alpha) = 2\alpha + 12(1-\alpha) = 12 - 10\alpha$
$H(a_2; \alpha) = 0\alpha + 16(1-\alpha) = 16 - 16\alpha$
$H(a_3; \alpha) = 4\alpha + 8(1-\alpha) = 8 - 4\alpha$.

The plot is shown in Figure 6.10. As is clear from the diagram,

- If $0 \leq \alpha < \frac{2}{3}$ then $H(a_2; \alpha) > H(a_1; \alpha) > H(a_3; \alpha)$ and thus the Hurwicz criterion prescribes act a_2.
- If $\alpha = \frac{2}{3}$ then $H(a_1; \alpha) = H(a_2; \alpha) = H(a_3; \alpha)$ and thus any of the three acts is compatible with the Hurwicz criterion.
- If $\frac{2}{3} < \alpha \leq 1$ then $H(a_3; \alpha) > H(a_1; \alpha) > H(a_2; \alpha)$ and thus the Hurwicz criterion prescribes act a_3. □

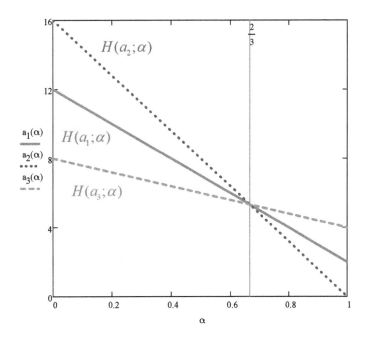

Figure 6.10: The Hurwicz indices for the three acts of Exercise 6.12

Solution to Exercise 6.13. The decision problem is as follows:

state $\rightarrow$	s_1	s_2	s_3
act $\downarrow$			
a_1	12	3	2
a_2	8	16	0
a_3	6	4	8

Since the lowest utility is already 0, in order to normalize the utility function we just need to divide every value by the maximum utility, namely 16:

state $\rightarrow$	s_1	s_2	s_3
act $\downarrow$			
a_1	$\frac{12}{16}$	$\frac{3}{16}$	$\frac{2}{16}$
a_2	$\frac{8}{16}$	1	0
a_3	$\frac{6}{16}$	$\frac{4}{16}$	$\frac{8}{16}$

When $\alpha = \frac{1}{2}$ the Hurwicz indices of the three acts are:

$H(a_1) = \frac{1}{2}\left(\frac{2}{16}\right) + \frac{1}{2}\left(\frac{12}{16}\right) = \frac{7}{16}$,

$H(a_2) = \frac{1}{2}(0) + \frac{1}{2}(1) = \frac{8}{16}$,

$H(a_3) = \frac{1}{2}\left(\frac{4}{16}\right) + \frac{1}{2}\left(\frac{8}{16}\right) = \frac{6}{16}$.

Thus, when $\alpha = \frac{1}{2}$ the Hurwicz criterion prescribes act a_2, confirming what was determined in Part(a) of Exercise 6.12. □

7. Conditional Reasoning

7.1 Sets and probability: brief review

This section is devoted to a very brief review of definitions and concepts from set theory and probability theory.

7.1.1 Sets

We will focus on finite sets, that is, sets that have a finite number of elements. Let U be a finite set. The set of subsets of U is denoted by 2^U. The reason for this notation is that if U contains n elements then there are 2^n subsets of U. For example, if $U = \{a,b,c\}$ then the set of subsets of U is the following collection of $2^3 = 8$ sets:

$$2^U = \{\emptyset, \{a\}, \{b\}, \{c\}, \{a,b\}, \{a,c\}, \{b,c\}, \{a,b,c\}\},$$

where $\emptyset$ denotes the empty set, that is, a set with no elements. The following notation is used to denote membership in a set and to denote that one set is contained in another:

- $x \in A$ means that x is an element of the set A (capital letters are used to denote sets and lower-case letters to denote elements)

- $A \subseteq B$ means that A is a subset of B, that is, every element of A is also an element of B. Note that $A \subseteq B$ allows for the possibility that $A = B$.

- $A \subset B$ denotes the fact that A is a *proper* subset of B (that is, A is a subset of B but there is at least one element of B which is not in A).

Next we review operations that can be performed on sets. These operations are illustrated in Figure 7.1.

- Let $A \in 2^U$. The *complement of A in U*, denoted by $\neg A$, is the set of elements of U that are not in A. When the "universe of discourse" U is clear from the context, one simply refers to $\neg A$ as the *complement of A*. For example, if $U = \{a,b,c,d,e,f\}$ and $A = \{b,d,f\}$ then $\neg A = \{a,c,e\}$. Note that $\neg U = \emptyset$ and $\neg \emptyset = U$.

- Let $A, B \in 2^U$. The *intersection of A and B*, denoted by $A \cap B$, is the set of elements that belong to both A and B. For example, if $U = \{a,b,c,d,e,f\}$, $A = \{b,d,f\}$ and $B = \{a,b,d,e\}$ then $A \cap B = \{b,d\}$. If $A \cap B = \emptyset$ we say that A and B are *disjoint*.

- Let $A, B \in 2^U$. The *union of A and B*, denoted by $A \cup B$, is the set of elements that belong to either A or B (or both). For example, if $U = \{a,b,c,d,e,f\}$, $A = \{b,d,f\}$ and $B = \{a,b,d,e\}$ then $A \cup B = \{a,b,d,e,f\}$.

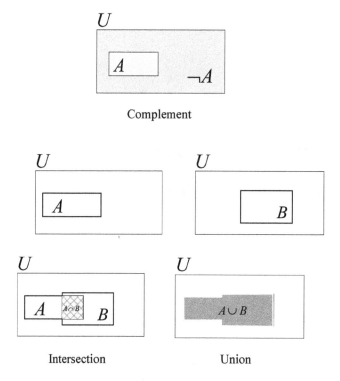

Figure 7.1: Operations on sets

We denote by $A \setminus B$ the set of elements of A that are not in B. Thus, $A \setminus B = A \cap \neg B$. For example, if $A = \{b,d,f\}$ and $B = \{a,b,d,e\}$ then $A \setminus B = \{f\}$ and $B \setminus A = \{a,e\}$.

The following are known as *De Morgan's Laws*:
- $\neg(A \cup B) = \neg A \cap \neg B$
- $\neg(A \cap B) = \neg A \cup \neg B$

Let us verify De Morgan's Laws in the following example:

$U = \{a,b,c,d,e,f,g,h,i,j,k\}$, $A = \{b,d,f,g,h,i\}$ and $B = \{a,b,f,i,k\}$.
$\neg A = \{a,c,e,j,k\}$, $\neg B = \{c,d,e,g,h,j\}$, $A \cup B = \{a,b,d,f,g,h,i,k\}$
$\neg(A \cup B) = \{c,e,j\} = \neg A \cap \neg B$;
$A \cap B = \{b,f,i\}$
thus $\neg(A \cap B) = \{a,c,d,e,g,h,j,k\} = \neg A \cup \neg B$.

7.1.2 Probability

In probability theory the "universal set" U is called the *sample space* and the subsets of U are called *events*. A *probability measure on* U is a function $P : 2^U \to [0,1]$ that assigns to every event $E \in 2^U$ a number greater than or equal to 0 and less than or equal to 1, as shown in Figure 7.2, with the following restrictions:

1. $P(U) = 1$.
2. For every two events $E, F \in 2^U$, if $E \cap F = \emptyset$ then $P(E \cup F) = P(E) + P(F)$.

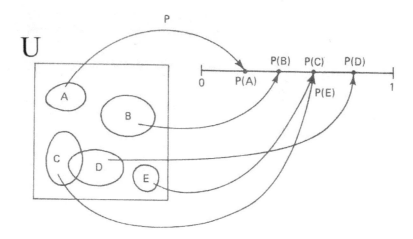

Figure 7.2: A probability measure

From the above two properties one can obtain the following properties (the reader might want to try to prove them using Properties 1 and 2 above):

- $P(\neg E) = 1 - P(E)$, for every event E (this follows from the fact that E and $\neg E$ are disjoint and their union is equal to U).
- $P(\emptyset) = 0$ (this follows from the previous line and the fact that $\emptyset = \neg U$).
- For every two events $E, F \in 2^U$, $P(E \cup F) = P(E) + P(F) - P(E \cap F)$ (see Exercise 7.5).
- For every two events $E, F \in 2^U$, if $E \subseteq F$ then $P(E) \leq P(F)$.
- If $E_1, E_2, ..., E_m \in 2^U$ ($m \geq 2$) is a collection of mutually disjoint sets (that is, for every $i, j = 1, ..., m$ with $i \neq j$, $E_i \cap E_j = \emptyset$) then $P(E_1 \cup E_2 \cup ... \cup E_m) = P(E_1) + P(E_2) + ... + P(E_m)$.

When the set U is finite, a *probability distribution* p on U is a function that assigns to each element $z \in U$ a number $p(z)$, with $0 \leq p(z) \leq 1$, and such that $\sum_{z \in U} p(z) = 1$. Given a probability distribution $p : U \to [0,1]$ on U one can obtain a probability measure $P : 2^U \to [0,1]$ by defining, for every event A, $P(A) = \sum_{z \in A} p(z)$.

Conversely, given a probability measure $P : 2^U \to [0,1]$, one can obtain from it a probability distribution $p : U \to [0,1]$ by defining, for every $z \in U$, $p(z) = P(\{z\})$. Thus, the two notions are equivalent.

Joint and marginal probabilities

Let P be a probability measure on the set U and let A and B be subsets of U. Let the probabilities $P(A \cap B)$, $P(A \cap \neg B)$, $P(\neg A \cap B)$ and $P(\neg A \cap \neg B)$ be given in the form of a table, such as the following table:

	B	$\neg B$
A	0.4	0.2
$\neg A$	0.1	0.3

Thus, $P(A \cap B) = 0.4$, $P(A \cap \neg B) = 0.2$, $P(\neg A \cap B) = 0.1$ and $P(\neg A \cap \neg B) = 0.3$. Notice that these numbers must add up to 1. We call these probabilities *joint probabilities*. From these we can calculate the *marginal probabilities*, namely $P(A)$, $P(\neg A)$, $P(B)$ and $P(\neg B)$. Since $A = (A \cap B) \cup (A \cap \neg B)$ and the two sets $(A \cap B)$ and $(A \cap \neg B)$ are disjoint, $P(A) = P(A \cap B) + P(A \cap \neg B) = 0.4 + 0.2 = 0.6$ and, similarly, $P(\neg A) = 0.1 + 0.3 = 0.4$, $P(B) = 0.4 + 0.1 = 0.5$ and $P(\neg B) = 0.2 + 0.3 = 0.5$.

	B	$\neg B$	Marginal	
A	0.4	0.2	0.6	$P(A)$
$\neg A$	0.1	0.3	0.4	$P(\neg A)$
Marginal	0.5	0.5		
	$P(B)$	$P(\neg B)$		

Let us generalize this. Let $A_1, A_2, ..., A_n$ be a collection of mutually exclusive subsets of U. Note that we don't assume that $A_1 \cup A_2 \cup ... \cup A_n = U$. Let $B_1, B_2, ..., B_m$ be another collection of mutually exclusive subsets of U, but this time we do assume that $B_1 \cup B_2 \cup ... \cup B_m = U$ (that is, $\{B_1, ..., B_m\}$ is a partition of U). Then, given the joint probabilities $p_{ij} = P(A_i \cap B_j)$ we can compute the marginal probabilities $p_i = P(A_i) = \sum_{j=1}^{m} p_{ij} = \sum_{j=1}^{m} P(A_i \cap B_j)$.

Example with $n = 3$ and $m = 4$:

	B_1	B_2	B_3	B_4	Marginal
A_1	0.1	0.2	0	0	$0.3 = P(A_1)$
A_2	0.05	0	0.05	0	$0.1 = P(A_2)$
A_3	0.15	0.1	0	0.2	$0.45 = P(A_3)$

Notice that in this example the marginal probabilities do not add up to 1: $P(A_1) + P(A_2) + P(A_3) = 0.85 < 1$. Hence, we deduce that $A_1 \cup A_2 \cup ... \cup A_n$ is a proper subset of U.

Independence

Two events A and B are said to be *independent* if $P(A \cap B) = P(A) \times P(B)$. For example, let $U = \{a, b, c, d, e, f, g, h, i\}$ and consider the following probability distribution p:

$$\begin{pmatrix} a & b & c & d & e & f & g & h & i \\ \frac{2}{27} & \frac{4}{27} & \frac{7}{27} & \frac{3}{27} & 0 & \frac{5}{27} & 0 & \frac{2}{27} & \frac{4}{27} \end{pmatrix}$$

7.2 Conditional thinking

Let P be the corresponding probability measure. Let $A = \{b,d,f,g,h,i\}$ and $B = \{a,b,e,i\}$. Then $P(A) = p(b) + p(d) + p(f) + p(g) + p(h) + p(i) = \frac{4}{27} + \frac{3}{27} + \frac{5}{27} + 0 + \frac{2}{27} + \frac{4}{27} = \frac{18}{27}$ and $P(B) = p(a) + p(b) + p(e) + p(i) = \frac{2}{27} + \frac{4}{27} + 0 + \frac{4}{27} = \frac{10}{27}$.

Furthermore, $A \cap B = \{b,i\}$ and thus $P(A \cap B) = p(b) + p(i) = \frac{4}{27} + \frac{4}{27} = \frac{8}{27}$.

Since $\frac{8}{27} \neq \frac{18}{27} \times \frac{10}{27}$ ($\frac{8}{27} = 0.296$ and $\frac{18}{27} \times \frac{10}{27} = 0.247$), A and B are *not* independent.

On the other hand, if the probability distribution is as follows:

$$\begin{pmatrix} a & b & c & d & e & f & g & h & i \\ \frac{1}{9} & \frac{1}{9} & \frac{1}{9} & \frac{2}{9} & 0 & \frac{2}{9} & 0 & \frac{1}{9} & \frac{1}{9} \end{pmatrix}$$

then $E = \{a,b,c,e\}$ and $F = \{c,d,e,g\}$ are independent. In fact, $P(E) = \frac{1}{9} + \frac{1}{9} + \frac{1}{9} + 0 = \frac{1}{3}$, $P(F) = \frac{1}{9} + \frac{2}{9} + 0 + 0 = \frac{1}{3}$, $E \cap F = \{c,e\}$ and $P(E \cap F) = \frac{1}{9} + 0 = \frac{1}{9}$, so that $P(E \cap F) = P(E) \times P(F)$.

> Test your understanding of the concepts introduced in this section, by going through the exercises in Section 7.4.1 at the end of this chapter.

7.2 Conditional thinking

Jane, who is 42 years old, has just read an article where it is claimed that it is very important for women in their 40s to be tested for breast cancer by undergoing a mammography. She emails her doctor and asks: what are the chances that I have breast cancer? The doctor replies: there is a 1% probability that you have breast cancer. What does 'probability 1%' mean? One interpretation of probability is in terms of frequencies: '1% probability' means that the frequency of breast cancer in a large population of women in their 40s is 1 out of a 100. Thus, the doctor's answer can be interpreted as meaning 'based on past records of women in your age group, the chances that you belong to the group of women who have breast cancer is 1 in a 100'. This answer motivates Jane to schedule a mammography. A "positive" mammogram suggests the presence of breast cancer, while a "negative" mammogram suggests the absence of cancer. The test, however, is not conclusive. The doctor informs Jane of the following facts:

1. 1% of women whose age is in the range 40-49 have breast cancer.
2. If a woman has breast cancer, the probability that she has a positive mammogram is 90%.
3. If a woman does not have breast cancer, the probability that she has a negative mammogram is 90%.

A week later the doctor gives Jane the bad news that her mammogram was positive. She asks the doctor: in light of the positive mammogram, what are the chances that I have breast cancer? The 1% figure that she was quoted before she decided to have the mammogram was a *prior*, or *unconditional*, probability. What Jane is now seeking is a revised probability *conditional on the information that the test was positive*. What should the doctor's answer be? We shall look at two different, but equivalent, ways of thinking about the problem: the "natural frequencies" approach and the conditional probability approach.

7.2.1 The natural frequencies approach

The "natural frequencies" approach is forcefully promoted by Gerd Gigerenzer in his book *Calculated Risks: How to Know when Numbers Deceive You* (Simon and Schuster, 2002).[1] In the natural frequencies approach one postulates a population size and interprets probabilities as frequencies. The facts listed in Section 7.2 are interpreted as frequencies, as follows:

1. 1 out of 100 women of age 40-49 has breast cancer.
2. Out of 100 women who have breast cancer, 90 give a positive mammography result.
3. Out of 100 women who do not have breast cancer, 90 give a negative mammography result.

To evaluate the chances that a woman with a positive mammogram has breast cancer, choose a reference group size – say 10,000 women in the age range 40-49 – and construct a tree using the above three facts, as shown in Figure 7.3.

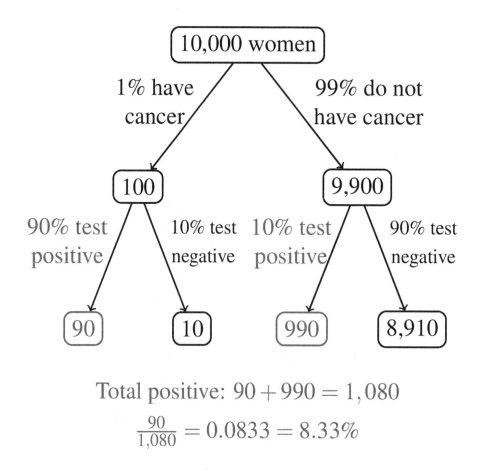

Figure 7.3: A tree constructed using the given facts and a population size of 10,000

---

[1] The example given in Figure 7.3 is based on an example given in Gigerenzer's book. Chapter 5 of the book contains an in-depth analysis of the effectiveness of mammography screening in reducing breast-cancer mortality in women of different age groups.

7.2 Conditional thinking

Using Fact 1, 1% of 10,000 is 100, so that 100 women have breast cancer and 9,900 do not. Using Fact 2, of the 100 women who have breast cancer, 90 give a positive mammogram (a "true" positive) and 10 a negative one (a "false" negative). Using Fact 3, of the 9,900 women who do not have breast cancer 990 (10%) give a positive mammogram (a "false" positive) and the remaining 8,910 (90%) give a negative mammogram (a "true" negative). Thus, the total number of positive test results is $90 + 990 = 1,080$ and of these only 90 have breast cancer; hence, for a woman in her 40s, the chance of having breast cancer when she learns that her mammography result was positive is $\frac{90}{1,080} = 8.33\%$. Similarly, one can compute the probability of *not* having breast cancer upon learning that the mammogram was negative as follows (number of true negatives divided by total number of negatives): $\frac{8,910}{10+8,910} = \frac{8,910}{8,920} = 99.89\%$.

In the medical literature, the true positive rate is called the *sensitivity* of the test and the true negative rate is called the *specificity* of the test.

Is the 8.33% figure obtained in the above example dependent on the population size that we chose, arbitrarily, to be 10,000? If we had chosen a size of 25,000 would the conclusion have been different? The answer is no. Figure 7.4 repeats the calculations, and confirms the conclusion, for any population size n.

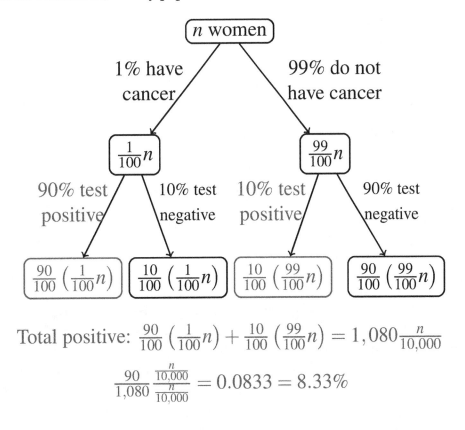

Figure 7.4: A tree similar to Figure 7.3 with a population size of n women

The above example makes it clear that the chances of having a disease, when one tests positive for that disease, depends crucially on *how common the disease is in the population*: this is called the *base rate* of the disease. If the disease is very uncommon then very few people have it and thus – even if the sensitivity of the test (the true positive rate) is very high (close to 100%) – the number at the numerator of the relevant fraction is small and thus the fraction itself is small (as long as the false positive rate is non-negligible), because most of the positive results will be false positive. We shall illustrate this fact in detail below, with reference to HIV.

The HIV test is said to have a true positive rate (or sensitivity) of 99.97% (if you are infected, the blood test will be positive in 99.97% of the cases, while it will be negative – false negative – in 0.03% of the cases, that is, in 3 out of 10,000 cases); furthermore, the false positive rate is 1.5% (15 out of every 1,000 people who are not infected will give a positive result to the blood test).[2]

If this is all you know and you take a blood test and it turns out to be positive, what are the chances that you do have an HIV infection? We want to show that the answer can be any number between 0% and 100%. Let $p \in [0,1]$ be the fraction of the population that is infected with HIV (e.g. if $p = 0.12$ then 12% of the population is infected); p is called the *base rate*.

Let us construct a tree as we did in Figure 7.4: this is shown in Figure 7.5. If n is the size of the relevant population and p is the fraction of the population that is infected with HIV (the base rate), then the total number of infected people is pn and the total number of people who are not infected is $(1-p)n$. Of the pn infected people, 99.97% give a positive blood test result, for a total of $\frac{99.97}{100} pn$ true positive results. Of the $(1-p)n$ who are *not* infected, 1.5% give a positive blood test result, for a total of $\frac{1.5}{100}(1-p)n$ false positive results.

Thus, the total number of positive blood test results is $\frac{99.97}{100} pn + \frac{1.5}{100}(1-p)n = \frac{(98.47p+1.5)n}{100}$, so that the chances of having the HIV virus, *given a positive blood test*, is

$$\frac{\frac{99.97}{100} pn}{\frac{(98.47p+1.5)n}{100}} = \frac{99.97p}{98.47p+1.5}. \quad \text{Let } f(p) = \frac{99.97p}{98.47p+1.5}.$$

The function $f(p)$ is equal to 0 when $p = 0$ and is equal to 1 when $p = 1$ ($f(0) = 0$ and $f(1) = 1$). Figure 7.6 shows the graph of the function for $p \in [0,1]$. Thus, the chances of having the HIV virus, given a positive blood test, can be any number between 0 and 1, depending on the value of the base rate p. In 2015, in the US, 1.2 million people were infected with HIV and the total population was 318.9 million; thus, the fraction of the population infected with HIV was $p = \frac{1.2}{318.9} = 0.003763$.[3] Replacing p with 0.003763 in $f(p) = \frac{99.97p}{98.47p+1.5}$ gives $0.2011 = 20.11\%$.

---

[2]Thus, the true negative rate (or specificity) is $(100-1.5)\% = 98.5\%$.

[3]This figure is not very useful, because it is based on putting all the individuals in the same pool. Different groups of individuals have different probabilities of having HIV. For example, high risk individuals, such as intravenous drug users, have a much higher probability of being infected with HIV than low-risk individuals. Thus, one should use the base rate for the group to which a particular individual belongs.

7.2 Conditional thinking

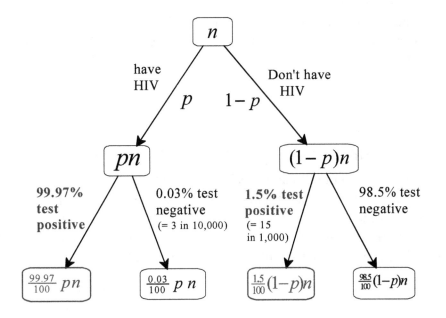

Total positive: $\frac{99.97}{100}pn + \frac{1.5}{100}(1-p)n = \frac{(99.97p + 1.5 - 1.5p)n}{100} = \frac{(98.47p + 1.5)n}{100}$

Chances: $\dfrac{\frac{99.97p}{100}n}{\frac{98.47p+1.5}{100}n} = \dfrac{99.97p}{98.47p+1.5}$

Figure 7.5: The HIV case with a base rate equal to p

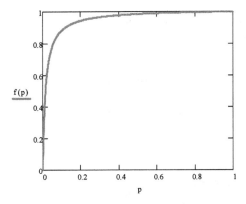

Figure 7.6: The probability of having HIV, given a positive blood test, as a function of the base rate p

7.2.2 Conditional probability

Let $A, B \subseteq U$ be two events (where U is the universal set or sample space) and P a probability measure on U. If $P(B) > 0$, the *conditional probability of A given B*, denoted by $P(A|B)$, is defined as follows:

$$\boxed{P(A|B) = \frac{P(A \cap B)}{P(B)}}. \tag{7.1}$$

For example, if $P(A \cap B) = 0.2$ and $P(B) = 0.6$ then $P(A|B) = \frac{0.2}{0.6} = \frac{1}{3}$.

One way to visualize conditional probability is to think of U as a geometric shape of area 1 (e.g. a square with each side equal to 1 unit of measurement). For a subset A of the unit square, $P(A)$ is the area of A. If B is a non-empty subset of the square then $A \cap B$ is that part of A that lies in B and $P(A|B)$ is the area of $A \cap B$ relative to the area of B, that is, as a fraction of the area of B. This is illustrated in Figure 7.7.

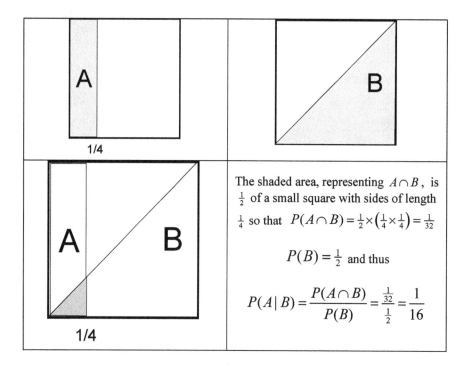

Figure 7.7: Geometric interpretation of the conditional probability $P(A|B)$

Recall that two events A and B are said to be independent if $P(A \cap B) = P(A)\, P(B)$. It follows from this and the definition of conditional probability (7.1) that if A and B are independent then

$$P(A|B) = \frac{P(A \cap B)}{P(B)} = \frac{P(A)\, P(B)}{P(B)} = P(A)$$

and, conversely, if $P(A|B) = P(A)$ then $\frac{P(A \cap B)}{P(B)} = P(A)$ so that $P(A \cap B) = P(A)\, P(B)$. Hence, we can take the following to be an alternative, and equivalent, definition of independence.

7.2 Conditional thinking

Definition 7.2.1 Events A and B are *independent* if $P(A|B) = P(A)$. Note that it follows from this that $P(B|A) = P(B)$.[a]

---
[a] In fact, by (7.1), $P(B|A) = \frac{P(A \cap B)}{P(A)}$ (since $B \cap A = A \cap B$) which becomes equal to $P(B)$ when we replace $P(A \cap B)$ with $P(A)\,P(B)$.

For instance, in the example of Figure 7.7 events A and B are **not** independent, since $P(A|B) = \frac{1}{16} \neq P(A) = \frac{1}{4}$. Hence, it must be that $P(B|A) \neq P(B)$ and, indeed, $P(B|A) = \frac{P(A \cap B)}{P(A)} = \frac{\frac{1}{32}}{\frac{1}{4}} = \frac{1}{8}$, while $P(B) = \frac{1}{2}$.

On the other hand, the two events depicted in Figure 7.8 are independent. In fact, $P(A) = \frac{1}{4}$, $P(B) = \frac{1}{2}$ and $P(A \cap B) = \frac{1}{4}\left(\frac{1}{2}\right) = \frac{1}{8}$, so that $P(A|B) = \frac{P(A \cap B)}{P(B)} = \frac{\frac{1}{8}}{\frac{1}{2}} = \frac{1}{4} = P(A)$.[4]

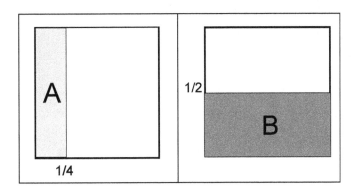

Figure 7.8: Events A and B are independent

Next we derive from the conditional probability formula (7.1) three versions of what is known as *Bayes' rule*.

Let E and F be two events such that $P(E) > 0$ and $P(F) > 0$. Then, using the conditional probability formula (7.1) we get

$$P(E|F) = \frac{P(E \cap F)}{P(F)} \tag{7.2}$$

and

$$P(F|E) = \frac{P(E \cap F)}{P(E)}. \tag{7.3}$$

From (7.3) we get that

$$P(E \cap F) = P(F|E)\,P(E) \tag{7.4}$$

and replacing (7.4) in (7.2) we get

Bayes' formula version 1 : $\boxed{P(E|F) = \dfrac{P(F|E)\,P(E)}{P(F)}}$ (7.5)

---
[4] Similarly, $P(B|A) = \frac{P(A \cap B)}{P(A)} = \frac{\frac{1}{8}}{\frac{1}{4}} = \frac{1}{2} = P(B)$.

As an illustration of how one can use (7.5), consider the following example. You are a doctor examining a middle-aged man who complains of lower back pain. You know that 25% of men in the age group of your patient suffer from lower back pain. There are various causes of lower back pain; one of them is chronic inflammation of the kidneys. This is not a very common disease: it affects only 4% of men in the age group that you are considering. Among those who suffer from chronic inflammation of the kidneys, 85% complain of lower back pain. What is the probability that your patient has chronic inflammation of the kidneys?

Let I denote inflammation of the kidneys and L denote lower back pain. The information you have is that $P(I) = \frac{4}{100}$, $P(L) = \frac{25}{100}$ and $P(L|I) = \frac{85}{100}$. Thus, using (7.5), we get that

$$P(I|L) = \frac{P(L|I)P(I)}{P(L)} = \frac{\frac{85}{100}\left(\frac{4}{100}\right)}{\frac{25}{100}} = 0.136 = 13.6\%.$$

This can also be seen by using natural frequencies. This time we use a table rather than a tree. Let us imagine that there are 2,500 men in the relevant population (men in the age group of your patient). Of these 2,500, 4% (= 100) have inflammation of the kidneys and the remaining 96% (= 2,400) do not (this information is recorded in the column to the right of the table in Figure 7.9). Furthermore, 25% (= 625) have lower-back pain and the remaining 75% (= 1,875) do not (this information is recorded in the row below the table in Figure 7.9). We want to fill in the table shown in Figure 7.9.

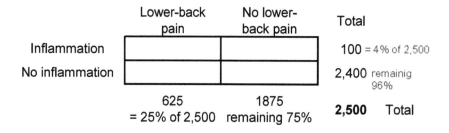

Figure 7.9: Natural frequencies for the lower-back pain example

One last piece of information is that, of the 100 people with inflammation of the kidneys, 85% (= 85) suffer from lower-back pain and thus the remaining 15 do not. This enables us to fill in the top row of the table and to find the probability we were looking for: *among the people who suffer from lower-back pain* (a total of 625) the fraction of those who have inflammation of the kidneys is $\frac{85}{625} = 0.136 = 13.6\%$, confirming the figure obtained above using Bayes' rule. We can also fill the bottom row by (1) subtracting 85 from 625 and (2) by subtracting 15 from 1,875. The complete table is shown in Figure 7.10.

7.2 Conditional thinking

	Lower-back pain	No lower-back pain	Total	
Inflammation	85	15	100	
No inflammation	540	1,860	2,400	
	625	1,875	**2,500**	Total

Figure 7.10: Natural frequencies for the lower-back pain example

We now derive a second version of Bayes' formula. According to Bayes' rule (7.5), $P(E|F) = \frac{P(F|E)P(E)}{P(F)}$. Now, from set theory we have that, given any two sets A and B, $A = (A \cap B) \cup (A \cap \neg B)$ and the two sets $A \cap B$ and $A \cap \neg B$ are disjoint. Thus, $P(A) = P(A \cap B) + P(A \cap \neg B)$.

Hence, in the denominator of Bayes' formula (7.5) we can replace $P(F)$ with $P(F \cap E) + P(F \cap \neg E)$.

Then, using the formula for conditional probability we get that $P(F \cap E) = P(F|E)P(E)$ and $P(F \cap \neg E) = P(F|\neg E)P(\neg E)$.

Thus,

$$P(F) = P(F|E)P(E) + P(F|\neg E)P(\neg E).$$

Replacing this in Bayes' formula (7.5) we get

Bayes' formula version 2 : $\boxed{P(E|F) = \frac{P(F|E)P(E)}{P(F|E)P(E) + P(F|\neg E)P(\neg E)}}$ (7.6)

As an illustration of how one can use (7.6), consider the following example. Enrollment in a Decision Making class is as follows: 60% economics majors (E), 40% other majors ($\neg E$). In the past, 80% of the economics majors passed and 65% of the other majors passed. A student tells you that she passed the class. What is the probability that she is an economics major? Let A stand for "pass the class". Then, using (7.6),

$$P(E|A) = \frac{P(A|E)P(E)}{P(A|E)P(E) + P(A|\neg E)P(\neg E)} = \frac{\frac{80}{100}\left(\frac{60}{100}\right)}{\frac{80}{100}\left(\frac{60}{100}\right) + \frac{65}{100}\left(\frac{40}{100}\right)} = \frac{24}{37} = 64.86\%.$$

One more example: 0.3763% of the population (that is, approximately 4 in 100,000 individuals) is infected with the HIV virus. Let H be the event "a randomly selected individual has the HIV virus". Then $P(H) = 0.003763$ and $P(\neg H) = 0.996237$. A blood test can be used to detect the virus. The blood test, which combines two tests (ELIZA and Western Blot), has a true positive rate (sensitivity) of 99.97% and a true negative rate (specificity) of 98.5%. Thus, (letting '+' denote a positive blood test and '−' a negative blood test) $P(+|H) = 0.9997$, $P(-|H) = 0.0003$, $P(+|\neg H) = 0.015$ and $P(-|\neg H) = 0.985$. Now suppose that you pick an individual at random, administer the blood test and it turns out to be positive. What is the probability that the individual has the HIV virus? That is, what is $P(H|+)$? Using (7.6),

$$P(H|+) = \frac{P(+|H)\, P(H)}{P(+|H)\, P(H) + P(+|\neg H)\, P(\neg H)}$$

$$= \frac{0.9997\,(0.003763)}{0.9997\,(0.003763) + 0.015\,(0.996237)} = 0.201 = 20.1\%$$

which confirms the calculation performed at the end of Section 7.2.1 using the natural frequencies approach.

A generalization of (7.6) is as follows. If $\{E_1, \ldots, E_n\}$ is a partition of the space U,[5]

$$P(F) = P(F|E_1)\, P(E_1) + \cdots + P(F|E_n)\, P(E_n).$$

Thus, using (7.5) we obtain that, for every $i = 1, \ldots, n$,

Bayes' formula version 3 : $\boxed{P(E_i|F) = \dfrac{P(F|E_i)\, P(E_i)}{P(F|E_1)P(E_1) + \ldots + P(F|E_n)P(E_n)}}$ (7.7)

Example: enrollment in a class is restricted to the following majors: economics (E), statistics (S) and math (M). Current enrollment is: 40% E, 35% S and 25% M. Let A be the event "pass the class". According to past data, $P(A|E) = 60\%$, $P(A|S) = 50\%$ and $P(A|M) = 75\%$. A student from this class tells you that she received a passing grade. What is the probability that she is an economics major? Using (7.7),

$$P(E|A) = \frac{P(A|E)\, P(E)}{P(A|E)\, P(E) + P(A|S)\, P(S) + P(A|M)\, P(M)}$$

$$= \frac{\frac{60}{100}\left(\frac{40}{100}\right)}{\frac{60}{100}\left(\frac{40}{100}\right) + \frac{50}{100}\left(\frac{35}{100}\right) + \frac{75}{100}\left(\frac{25}{100}\right)} = \frac{96}{241} = 39.83\%.$$

We conclude with a well-known example, known as the *Monty Hall problem*. You are a contestant in a show. You are shown three doors, numbered 1, 2 and 3. Behind one of them is a new car, which will be yours if you choose to open that door. The door behind which the car was placed was chosen randomly with equal probability (a die was thrown, if it came up 1 or 2 then the car was placed behind Door 1, if it came up 3 or 4 then the car was placed behind Door 2 and if it came up 5 or 6 then the car was placed

---

[5] That is, the sets $E_1, \ldots, E_n$ (1) cover the set U (in the sense that $E_1 \cup \cdots \cup E_n = U$) and (2) are pairwise disjoint (in the sense that, for all $i, j = 1, \ldots, n$ with $i \neq j$, $E_i \cap E_j = \emptyset$).

7.2 Conditional thinking

behind Door 3). You have to choose one door.

Suppose that you have chosen door number 1. Before the door is opened the host tells you that he knows where the car is and, to help you, he will open one of the other two doors, making sure that he opens a door behind which there is no car; if there are two such doors, then he will choose randomly with equal probability. Afterwards he will give you a chance to change your mind and switch to the other closed door, but you will have to pay $20 if you decide to switch. Suppose that initially you chose Door 1 and the host opens Door 3 to show you that the car is not there. Should you switch from Door 1 to Door 2? Assume that, if switching increases the probability of getting the car (relative to not switching), then you find it worthwhile to pay $20 to switch.

We solve this problem using Bayes' formula. For every $n \in \{1,2,3\}$, let D_n denote the event that the car is behind door n and let O_n denote the event that the host opens Door n. The initial probabilities are $P(D_1) = P(D_2) = P(D_3) = \frac{1}{3}$.

We want to compute $P(D_1|O_3)$; if $P(D_1|O_3) \geq \frac{1}{2}$ then you should **not** switch, since there is a cost in switching (recall that Door 1 is your initial choice).

By Bayes' rule, $P(D_1|O_3) = \frac{P(O_3|D_1) P(D_1)}{P(O_3)}$.

We know that $P(D_1) = \frac{1}{3}$ and $P(O_3|D_1) = \frac{1}{2}$ (when the car is behind Door 1 then the host has a choice between opening Door 2 and opening Door 3 and he chooses with equal probability). Thus,

$$P(D_1|O_3) = \frac{\frac{1}{2} \times \frac{1}{3}}{P(O_3)} = \frac{\frac{1}{6}}{P(O_3)}. \tag{7.8}$$

We need to compute $P(O_3)$. Now,

$$P(O_3) = P(O_3|D_1)P(D_1) + P(O_3|D_2)P(D_2) + P(O_3|D_3)P(D_3)$$

$$= P(O_3|D_1)\tfrac{1}{3} + P(O_3|D_2)\tfrac{1}{3} + P(O_3|D_3)\tfrac{1}{3} == \tfrac{1}{2}\left(\tfrac{1}{3}\right) + 1\left(\tfrac{1}{3}\right) + 0\left(\tfrac{1}{3}\right) = \tfrac{1}{6} + \tfrac{1}{3} = \tfrac{1}{2}.$$

because $P(O_3|D_1) = \frac{1}{2}$, $P(O_3|D_2) = 1$ (if the car is behind Door 2 then the host has to open Door 3, since he cannot open the door that you chose, namely Door 1) and $P(O_3|D_3) = 0$ (if the car is behind Door 3 then the host cannot open that door). Substituting $\frac{1}{2}$ for $P(O_3)$ in (7.8) we get that $P(D_1|O_3) = \frac{1}{3}$. Hence, the updated probability that the car is behind the other door (Door 2) is $\frac{2}{3}$ and therefore you should switch.

> Test your understanding of the concepts introduced in this section, by going through the exercises in Section 7.4.2 at the end of this chapter.

7.3 Simpson's paradox

In this section we highlight possible pitfalls of drawing inferences from conditional probabilities. Suppose that there are three events, F, R and T and that we have the following information about some conditional probabilities:

1. $P(R|T \cap F) > P(R|\neg T \cap F)$, and
2. $P(R|T \cap \neg F) > P(R|\neg T \cap \neg F)$.

Since $(T \cap F) \cup (T \cap \neg F) = T$ and $(\neg T \cap F) \cup (\neg T \cap \neg F) = \neg T$, can we infer from the above two pieces of information that $P(R|T) > P(R|\neg T)$?

This seems rather abstract, but consider the following example. A pharmaceutical company has developed a new drug to treat arthritis and is applying to the US Food and Drug Administration (FDA) for permission to market it. The FDA requires the pharmaceutical company to first run some clinical trials. The company gathers 1,200 patients diagnosed with arthritis: 600 women and 600 men. Half of the subjects (600: the treatment group) are given a treatment (in the form of the newly developed drug) and the other half (600: the control group) are given a placebo; none of the subjects knows to which group they belong. At the end of the trial each patient is classified as 'Recovered' or 'Did not recover'. The results are recorded in two tables: one for women and one for men.

The table for **women** is shown in Figure 7.11. R stands for 'Recovered', $\neg R$ for 'Did not recover', T for 'was Treated' (that is, belonged to the group that was administered the drug), $\neg T$ for 'was Not Treated' (that is, belonged to the group that was given a placebo) and 'F' for 'Female'.

FEMALES (F)

		recovered R	did not recover $\neg R$	Total		
treated	T	135	315	450	30% =	$P(R|T \cap F)$
not treated = placebo	$\neg T$	30	120	150	20% =	$P(R|\neg T \cap F)$
	Total	165	435			

Figure 7.11: Data on reaction of women to the new drug

The pharmaceutical company points out to the FDA that the data on women shows that the new drug is effective: it increases the recovery rate by 10% (from $\frac{30}{150} = 20\%$, if not treated, to $\frac{135}{450} = 30\%$, if treated).

The table for **men** is shown in Figure 7.12, where $\neg F$ stands for 'Males' (that is, 'not Females'). Once again, the pharmaceutical company points out to the FDA that the new drug is effective also for men: it increases the recovery rate by 10% (from $\frac{270}{450} = 60\%$, if not treated, to $\frac{105}{150} = 70\%$, if treated).

Hence – concludes the pharmaceutical company – since the drug is effective for women and is also effective for men, it must be effective for everybody and the FDA should approve the drug.

7.3 Simpson's paradox

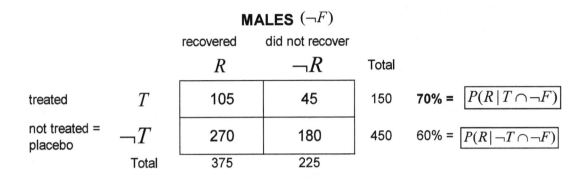

Figure 7.12: Data on reaction of men to the new drug

Is the reasoning of the pharmaceutical company valid?

The FDA reformats the data provided by the pharmaceutical company, by constructing a new table showing the overall data, that is, without separating the subjects into the two categories 'Women' and 'Men'. For example, the entry in the cell (T, R) in the new table is equal to the entry in the cell (T, R) from table table for Women (135) plus the entry in the cell (T, R) from table table for Men (105): $135 + 105 = 240$. The new table, which no longer separates the subjects into the two groups 'Women' and 'Men', is shown in Figure 7.13.

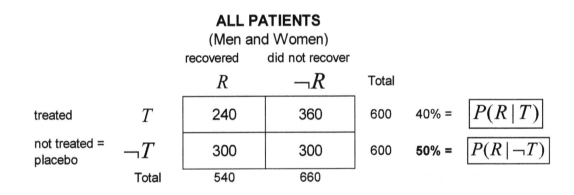

Figure 7.13: Overall data (not separated into Women and Men)

The table in Figure 7.13 shows that, for the entire population of subjects, the drug is **not** effective: on the contrary, it *decreases* the recovery rate by 10% (from $\frac{300}{600} = 50\%$, if not treated, to $\frac{240}{600} = 40\%$, if treated)! Hence, a treatment that appears to be good for women (the first table) and good for men (the second table) is actually bad overall (the last table). This is known as *Simpson's paradox* (named after a UK civil servant who first pointed it out). The paradox says that the overall behavior may be contrary to the behavior in each of a number of subgroups (in the example above female and male).

How can we explain the paradox?

Notice the following facts:

- The disease is more serious for women than for men: focusing on the "$\neg T$" subjects who were administered the placebo (and thus, for these people the disease went untreated), 20% of women recovered (30 out of 150) while 60% of men recovered (270 out of 450).

- In the case of women, 75% (450 out of 600) were administered the drug, while a smaller fraction of men were given the drug: 25% (150 out of 600).

Hence, the drug looked good not because of its intrinsic effectiveness but because it was administered unequally to the sexes: three times as many women (450) – who had a lower chance of spontaneous recovery – were given the drug. Had women and men been handled equally with respect to the administration of the drug (in the sense that the proportion of women receiving the treatment equaled the proportion of men receiving the treatment), then the two separate tables, one for men and one for women, would have exhibited the same 10% reduction in the recovery rate as exhibited in the overall table. In this example, Simpson's paradox arises because the allocation of treatments depended on another variable – gender – that itself had an effect on the recovery rate. This type of dependence is called *confounding* and the two quantities, treatment and gender, are said to be confounded. Because of the confounding, one cannot infer from the apparent effectiveness of the drug in each separate group that the drug is in fact effective. To avoid invalid inferences, what is required is an allocation of treatments to the subjects that is not confounded with any other variable that might have an effect.

7.4 Exercises

The solutions to the following exercises are given in Section 7.5 at the end of this chapter.

7.4.1 Exercises for Section 7.1: Sets and probability

Exercise 7.1 Let U be the universal set (or sample space) and E and F two events. Let the complement of E be denoted by $\neg E$ and the complement of F by $\neg F$. Suppose that $P(E) = \frac{3}{10}$, $P(F) = \frac{3}{5}$ and $P(\neg E \cup \neg F) = \frac{4}{5}$. What is the probability of $E \cup F$?

Exercise 7.2 Consider the following probability distribution:

$$\begin{pmatrix} z_1 & z_2 & z_3 & z_4 & z_5 & z_6 & z_7 \\ \frac{3}{12} & \frac{1}{12} & 0 & \frac{3}{12} & \frac{2}{12} & 0 & \frac{3}{12} \end{pmatrix}.$$

What is the probability of the event $\{z_2, z_3, z_5, z_6, z_7\}$?

7.4 Exercises

Exercise 7.3 Let the universal set be $U = \{z_1, z_2, z_3, z_4, z_5, z_6, z_7, z_8\}$.

Let $A = \{z_2, z_4, z_5, z_7\}$, $B = \{z_3, z_6, z_8\}$, $C = \{z_2, z_6\}$, $D = \{z_3, z_4\}$ and $E = \{z_7, z_8\}$.
You are given the following data: $P(A \cup B) = \frac{21}{24}$, $P(A \cap C) = \frac{5}{24}$, $P(B \cap C) = \frac{3}{24}$, $P(A \cap D) = \frac{2}{24}$, $P(B \cap D) = \frac{3}{24}$, $P(B) = \frac{7}{24}$ and $P(E) = \frac{2}{24}$.

(a) Find the probability $P(z_i)$ for each $i = 1, \ldots, 8$.

(b) Calculate $P((A \cup B) \cap (C \cup D))$.

Exercise 7.4 Let $U = \{a, b, c, d, e, f, g, h, i\}$ and consider the following probability distribution: $\begin{pmatrix} a & b & c & d & e & f & g & h & i \\ \frac{11}{60} & 0 & \frac{7}{60} & \frac{9}{60} & \frac{16}{60} & \frac{5}{60} & \frac{4}{60} & \frac{8}{60} & 0 \end{pmatrix}$.

(a) Let $E = \{a, f, g, h, i\}$. What is the probability of E?

(b) List all the events that have probability 1.

Exercise 7.5 Let P be a probability measure on a finite set U and let A and B be two events (that is, subsets of U). Explain why $P(A \cup B) = P(A) + P(B) - P(A \cap B)$.

Exercise 7.6 You plan to toss a fair coin three times and record the sequence of Heads/Tails.
(a) What is the set of possibilities (or universal set or sample space)?
(b) Let E be the event that you will get at least one Heads. What is E?
(c) What is the probability of event E?
(d) Let F be the event that you will get Tails either in the first toss or in the third toss? [Note: this is *not* an exclusive 'or'.] What is event F?
(e) What is the probability of event F?

7.4.2 Exercises for Section 7.2: Conditional thinking

Exercise 7.7 Recall that, in medical diagnosis, test sensitivity is the ability of a test to correctly identify those *with* the disease (true positive rate), whereas test specificity is the ability of the test to correctly identify those *without* the disease (true negative rate). Consider a test with a sensitivity of 95% and a specificity of 88%. Suppose that there are 6,000 individuals in the relevant population and that 15% of them have a disease called boriosis. Phil takes the test and it turns out to be positive. Draw a tree and use it to calculate the probability that Phil has boriosis.

Exercise 7.8 Use the data given in Exercise 7.7 but replace the base rate of 15% with a variable p.
  (a) Calculate the probability of having boriosis after learning that the blood test was positive. Clearly, it will be an expression involving the variable p.
  (b) For what value of p is the probability of having boriosis, after learning that the blood test was positive, 7.4%?

Exercise 7.9 Consider again the data given in Exercise 7.7. Pamela also took a blood test but, unlike Phil, got a negative result. What is the probability that she has boriosis?

Exercise 7.10 Let A and B be two events such that $P(A) > 0$ and $P(B) > 0$. Prove that $P(A|B) = P(B|A)$ if and only if $P(A) = P(B)$.

Exercise 7.11 Construct an example to show that $P(A|B) = P(B|A)$ does **not** imply that A and B are independent.

Exercise 7.12 There is an urn with 40 balls: 4 red, 16 white, 10 blue and 10 black. You close your eyes and pick a ball at random. Let E be the event "the selected ball is either red or white".
  (a) What is the probability of E?
  (b) Now somebody tells you: "the ball in your hand is not black". How likely is it now that you picked either a red or a white ball?

Exercise 7.13 Suppose there are 3 individuals. It is known that one of them has a virus. A blood test can be performed to test for the virus. If an individual does have the virus, then the result of the test will be positive. However, the test will be positive also for an individual who does not have the virus but has a particular defective gene.

It is known that exactly one of the three individuals has this defective gene: it could be the same person who has the virus or somebody who does not have the virus. A positive test result will come up if and only if either the patient has the virus or the defective gene (or both).

Suppose that Individual 1 takes the blood test and the result is positive. Assuming that all the states are equally likely, what is the probability that he has the virus? [Hint: think of the universal set (or sample space) U as a list of states and each state tells you which individual has the virus and which individual has the defective gene.]

Exercise 7.14 Let A and B be two events such that $P(A) = 0.2, P(B) = 0.5$ and $P(B|A) = 0.1$. Calculate $P(A|B)$.

7.4 Exercises

Exercise 7.15 In a remote rural clinic with limited resources, a patient arrives complaining of low-abdomen pain. Based on all the information available, the doctor thinks that there are only four possible causes: a bacterial infection (b), a viral infection (v), cancer (c), internal bleeding (i). Of the four, only the bacterial infection and internal bleeding are treatable at the clinic. In the past the doctor has seen 600 similar cases and they eventually turned out to be as follows:

b: bacterial infection	v: viral infection	c: cancer	i: internal bleeding
140	110	90	260

The doctor's probabilistic estimates are based on those past cases.

(a) What is the probability that the patient has a treatable disease?

There are two possible ways of gathering more information: a blood test and an ultrasound. A positive blood test will reveal that there is an infection, however it could be either bacterial or viral; a negative blood test rules out an infection and thus leaves cancer and internal bleeding as the only possibilities. The ultrasound, on the other hand, will reveal if there is internal bleeding.

(b) Suppose that the patient gets an ultrasound and it turns out that there is no internal bleeding. What is the probability that he does **not** have a treatable disease? What is the probability that he has cancer?

(c) If instead of getting the ultrasound he had taken the blood test and it had been positive, what would the probability that he had a treatable disease have been?

(d) Now let us go back to the hypothesis that the patient only gets the ultrasound and it turns out that there is no internal bleeding. He then asks the doctor: "if I were to take the blood test too (that is, in addition to the ultrasound), how likely is it that it would be positive?". What should the doctor's answer be?

(e) Finally, suppose that the patient gets both the ultrasound and the blood test and the ultrasound reveals that there is no internal bleeding, while the blood test is positive. How likely is it that he has a treatable disease?

LABEL	number
AE	
AF	
AG	
BE	
BF	
BG	
CE	
CF	
CG	

Figure 7.14: The specimen example

Exercise 7.16 A lab technician was asked to mark some specimens with two letters, the first from the set $\{A,B,C\}$ and the second from the set $\{E,F,G\}$. For example, a specimen could be labeled as AE or BG, etc. He had a total of 220 specimens. He has to file a report to his boss by filling in the table shown in Figure 7.14.

Unfortunately, he does not remember all the figures. He had written some notes to himself, which are reproduced below. Help him fill in the above table with the help of his notes and conditional probabilities. Here are the technician's notes:

(a) Of all the ones that he marked with an E, $\frac{1}{5}$ were also marked with an A and $\frac{1}{5}$ were marked with a B.

(b) He marked 36 specimens with the label CE.

(c) Of all the specimens that he marked with a C, the fraction $\frac{12}{23}$ were marked with a G.

(d) Of all the specimens, the fraction $\frac{23}{55}$ were marked with a C.

(e) The number of specimens marked BG was twice the number of specimens marked BE.

(f) Of all the specimens marked with an A, the fraction $\frac{3}{20}$ were marked with an E.

(g) Of all the specimens marked with an A, $\frac{1}{10}$ were marked with a G.

7.5 Solutions to Exercises

Solution to Exercise 7.1. The general formula is $P(E \cup F) = P(E) + P(F) - P(E \cap F)$.

By The Morgan's Law, $\neg E \cup \neg F = \neg(E \cap F)$.

Thus, since $P(\neg(E \cap F)) = \frac{4}{5}$, we have that $P(E \cap F) = 1 - \frac{4}{5} = \frac{1}{5}$.

Hence, $P(E \cup F) = \frac{3}{10} + \frac{3}{5} - \frac{1}{5} = \frac{7}{10}$. □

Solution to Exercise 7.2.

$$P(\{z_2, z_3, z_5, z_6, z_7\}) = \sum_{i \in \{2,3,5,6,7\}} P(\{z_i\}) = \frac{1}{12} + 0 + \frac{2}{12} + 0 + \frac{3}{12} = \frac{1}{2}.$$

□

Solution to Exercise 7.3.

(a) Since $\{z_1\}$ is the complement of $A \cup B$, $P(z_1) = 1 - \frac{21}{24} = \frac{3}{24}$.

Since $\{z_2\} = A \cap C$, $P(z_2) = \frac{5}{24}$.

Similarly, $P(z_6) = P(B \cap C) = \frac{3}{24}$, $P(z_3) = P(B \cap D) = \frac{3}{24}$ and $P(z_4) = P(A \cap D) = \frac{2}{24}$.

Thus, $P(z_8) = P(B) - P(z_3) - P(z_6) = \frac{7}{24} - \frac{3}{24} - \frac{3}{24} = \frac{1}{24}$.

Hence, $P(z_7) = P(E) - P(z_8) = \frac{2}{24} - \frac{1}{24} = \frac{1}{24}$.

7.5 Solutions to Exercises

Finally, $P(z_5) = 1 - \sum_{i \neq 5} P(z_i) = \frac{6}{24}$. Thus, the probability distribution is:

$$\begin{pmatrix} z_1 & z_2 & z_3 & z_4 & z_5 & z_6 & z_7 & z_8 \\ \frac{3}{24} & \frac{5}{24} & \frac{3}{24} & \frac{2}{24} & \frac{6}{24} & \frac{3}{24} & \frac{1}{24} & \frac{1}{24} \end{pmatrix}$$

(b) $A \cup B = \{z_2, z_3, z_4, z_5, z_6, z_7, z_8\}$, $C \cup D = \{z_2, z_3, z_4, z_6\}$.

Hence, $(A \cup B) \cap (C \cup D) = C \cup D = \{z_2, z_3, z_4, z_6\}$

so $P((A \cup B) \cap (C \cup D)) = P(z_2) + P(z_3) + P(z_4) + P(z_6) = \frac{5}{24} + \frac{3}{24} + \frac{2}{24} + \frac{3}{24} = \frac{13}{24}$. □

Solution to Exercise 7.4. The probability distribution is:

$$\begin{pmatrix} a & b & c & d & e & f & g & h & i \\ \frac{11}{60} & 0 & \frac{7}{60} & \frac{9}{60} & \frac{16}{60} & \frac{5}{60} & \frac{4}{60} & \frac{8}{60} & 0 \end{pmatrix}.$$

(a) Let $E = \{a, f, g, h, i\}$.

Then $P(E) = P(a) + P(f) + P(g) + P(h) + P(i) = \frac{11}{60} + \frac{5}{60} + \frac{4}{60} + \frac{8}{60} + 0 = \frac{28}{60} = \frac{7}{15}$.

(b) The probability-1 events are: $\{a, c, d, e, f, g, h\} = U \setminus \{b, i\}$, $\{a, b, c, d, e, f, g, h\} = U \setminus \{i\}$, $\{a, c, d, e, f, g, h, i\} = U \setminus \{b\}$ and $\{a, b, c, d, e, f, g, h, i\} = U$. □

Solution to Exercise 7.5. Since $P(A) = \sum_{w \in A} P(w)$ and $P(B) = \sum_{w \in B} P(w)$, when adding $P(A)$ to $P(B)$ the elements that belong to both A and B (that is, the elements of $A \cap B$) are added twice and thus we need to subtract $\sum_{w \in A \cap B} P(w)$ from $P(A) + P(B)$ in order to get $\sum_{w \in A \cup B} P(w) = P(A \cup B)$. □

Solution to Exercise 7.6.

(a) There are 8 possibilities: HHH HHT HTH HTT THH THT TTH TTT.

Since the coin is fair, each possibility has the same probability, namely $\frac{1}{8}$.

(b) $E = U \setminus \{TTT\}$, where U is the universal set (the set of 8 possibilities listed above).

(c) $P(E) = P(U) - P(TTT) = 1 - \frac{1}{8} = \frac{7}{8}$.

(d) $F = U \setminus \{HHH, HTH\}$

(e) $P(F) = P(U) - P(\{HHH, HTH\}) = 1 - \frac{1}{8} - \frac{1}{8} = \frac{6}{8} = \frac{3}{4}$. □

Solution to Exercise 7.7. The tree is given in Figure 7.15.

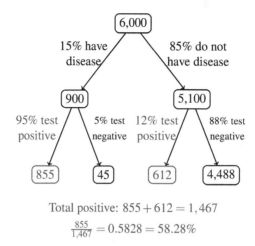

Figure 7.15: The tree for Exercise 7.7

Solution to Exercise 7.8.

(a) The tree is shown in Figure 7.16. The probability of having the disease conditional on a positive blood test is

$$f(p) = \frac{95(6,000)p}{95(6,000)p + 12(6,000)(1-p)} = \frac{95p}{83p+12}.$$

(b) We must solve the equation $\frac{95p}{83p+12} = 0.074$. The solution is $p = 0.01 = 1\%$.

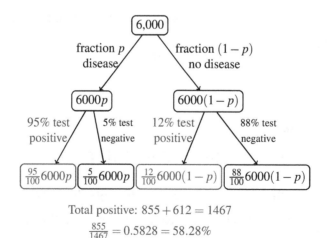

Figure 7.16: The tree for Exercise 7.8

7.5 Solutions to Exercises

Solution to Exercise 7.9. For Pamela the probability of having the disease, given that she had a negative blood test, is (see Figure 7.15): $\frac{45}{45+4,488} = 0.0099 = 0.99\%$ (about 1 in a 1,000). □

Solution to Exercise 7.10. Suppose that $P(A|B) = P(B|A)$.
Since $P(A|B) = \frac{P(A \cap B)}{P(B)}$ and $P(B|A) = \frac{P(A \cap B)}{P(A)}$ it follows that $P(A) = P(B)$.
Conversely, if $P(A) = P(B)$ then $P(A|B) = \frac{P(A \cap B)}{P(B)} = \frac{P(A \cap B)}{P(A)} = P(B|A)$. □

Solution to Exercise 7.11. Example 1. Let $P(A) = \frac{1}{2}$ and let $B = \neg A$.
Then $P(B) = 1 - P(A) = \frac{1}{2}$ and $A \cap B = \emptyset$ so that $P(A \cap B) = 0$ and thus $P(A|B) = \frac{P(A \cap B)}{P(B)} = \frac{0}{\frac{1}{2}} = 0 \neq P(A) = \frac{1}{2}$.
Example 2. $U = \{a,b,c\}, P(a) = P(c) = \frac{2}{5}$ and $P(b) = \frac{1}{5}$. Let $A = \{a,b\}$ and $B = \{b,c\}$.
Then $P(A) = P(B) = \frac{3}{5}$ but $P(A|B) = \frac{P(A \cap B)}{P(B)} = \frac{P(b)}{P(b)+P(c)} = \frac{\frac{1}{5}}{\frac{3}{5}} = \frac{1}{3} \neq P(A) = \frac{3}{5}$. □

Solution to Exercise 7.12.
(a) $P(E) = \frac{4+16}{40} = \frac{1}{2}$.
(b) Let F be the event "the selected ball is not black". Then, initially, $P(F) = \frac{30}{40} = \frac{3}{4}$. Furthermore, $E \cap F = E$. Thus, $P(E|F) = \frac{P(E \cap F)}{P(F)} = \frac{P(E)}{P(F)} = \frac{\frac{1}{2}}{\frac{3}{4}} = \frac{2}{3}$. □

Solution to Exercise 7.13. First we list the possible states. A state is a complete description of the external facts that are relevant: it tells you who has the virus and who has the gene. Let us represent a state as a pair (x,y) interpreted as follows: individual x has the virus and individual y has the defective gene.
Then $U = \{a = (1,1), b = (1,2), c = (1,3), d = (2,1), e = (2,2),$
$f = (2,3), g = (3,1), h = (3,2), i = (3,3)\}$.
Let V_1 be the event "Individual 1 has the virus". Then $V_1 = \{a,b,c\}$.
Let G_1 be the event "Individual 1 has the defective gene". Then $G_1 = \{a,d,g\}$.
Since every state is assumed to have probability $\frac{1}{9}$, $P(V_1) = P(G_1) = \frac{1}{9} + \frac{1}{9} + \frac{1}{9} = \frac{1}{3}$. Let 1_+ be the event that a blood test administered to Individual 1 comes up positive. Then $1_+ = \{a,b,c,d,g\}$ and $P(1_+) = \frac{5}{9}$.
Now we can compute the requested conditional probability as follows (note that $V_1 \cap 1_+ = V_1$):

$$P(V_1|1_+) = \frac{P(V_1 \cap 1_+)}{P(1_+)} = \frac{P(V_1)}{P(1_+)} = \frac{\frac{1}{3}}{\frac{5}{9}} = \frac{3}{5} = 60\%.$$

□

Solution to Exercise 7.14. Using Bayes' rule,

$$P(A|B) = \frac{P(B|A)P(A)}{P(B)} = \frac{(0.1)(0.2)}{0.5} = 0.04 = 4\%.$$

□

Solution to Exercise 7.15. The probabilities are as follows:

$$\begin{array}{c|c|c|c} b & v & c & i \\ \frac{140}{600} = \frac{14}{60} & \frac{110}{600} = \frac{11}{60} & \frac{90}{600} = \frac{9}{60} & \frac{260}{600} = \frac{26}{60} \end{array}$$

(a) The event that the patient has a treatable disease is $\{b,i\}$.
$P(\{b,i\}) = P(b) + P(i) = \frac{14}{60} + \frac{26}{60} = \frac{2}{3}$.

(b) A negative result of the ultrasound is represented by the event $\{b,v,c\}$. A non-treatable disease is the event $\{v,c\}$. Thus,

$$P(\{v,c\}|\{b,v,c\}) = \frac{P(\{v,c\} \cap \{b,v,c\})}{P(\{b,v,c\})} = \frac{P(\{v,c\})}{P(\{b,v,c\})} = \frac{\frac{11}{60} + \frac{9}{60}}{\frac{14}{60} + \frac{11}{60} + \frac{9}{60}} = \frac{10}{17} = 58.82\%.$$

$$P(c|\{b,v,c\}) = \frac{P(c)}{P(\{b,v,c\})} = \frac{\frac{9}{60}}{\frac{14}{60} + \frac{11}{60} + \frac{9}{60}} = \frac{9}{34} = 26.47\%.$$

(c) A positive blood test is represented by the event $\{b,v\}$. A treatable disease is the event $\{b,i\}$. Thus,

$$P(\{b,i\}|\{b,v\}) = \frac{P(\{b,i\} \cap \{b,v\})}{P(\{b,v\})} = \frac{P(b)}{P(\{b,v\})} = \frac{\frac{14}{60}}{\frac{14}{60} + \frac{11}{60}} = \frac{14}{25} = 56\%.$$

(d) Here we want

$$P(\{b,v\}|\{b,v,c\}) = \frac{P(\{b,v\})}{P(\{b,v,c\})} = \frac{\frac{14}{60} + \frac{11}{60}}{\frac{14}{60} + \frac{11}{60} + \frac{9}{60}} = \frac{25}{34} = 73.53\%.$$

(e) We are conditioning on $\{b,v\} \cap \{b,v,c\} = \{b,v\}$; thus, we want $P(\{b,i\}|\{b,v\})$ which was calculated in Part (c) as $\frac{14}{25} = 56\%$. □

Solution to Exercise 7.16. Let $\#xy$ be the *number* of specimens that were marked xy (thus, $x \in \{A,B,C\}$ and $y \in \{D,E,F\}$) and $P(xy) = \frac{\#xy}{220}$ be the *fraction* of specimens that were marked xy; let $\#z$ be the number of specimens whose label contains a $z \in \{A,B,C,D,E,F\}$ and let $P(z) = \frac{\#z}{220}$; finally, let $P(xy|z) = \frac{\#xy}{\#z}$; this is a conditional probability, since

$$\frac{\#xy}{\#z} = \frac{\frac{\#xy}{220}}{\frac{\#z}{220}} = \frac{P(xy)}{P(z)}.$$

With this notation we can re-write the information contained in the technician's notes as follows.

(a) $P(AE|E) = P(BE|E) = \frac{1}{5}$. It follows that the remaining three fifths were marked with a C, that is, $P(CE|E) = \frac{3}{5}$.

7.5 Solutions to Exercises

(b) #$CE = 36$; thus, $P(CE) = \frac{36}{220}$. Since $P(CE|E) = \frac{P(CE)}{P(E)}$,

using (a) we get $\frac{3}{5} = \frac{\frac{36}{220}}{P(E)}$, that is, $P(E) = \frac{36}{220}\left(\frac{5}{3}\right) = \frac{3}{11}$.

Hence, the number of specimens marked with an E is $\frac{3}{11} \cdot 220 = 60$.

Furthermore, since $P(AE|E) = \frac{P(AE)}{P(E)}$, using (a) we get $\frac{1}{5} = \frac{P(AE)}{\frac{3}{11}}$, that is,

$P(AE) = \frac{3}{55}$. Thus, the number of specimens marked AE is $\frac{3}{55} \cdot 220 = 12$.

The calculation for $P(BE|E)$ is identical; thus, the number of specimens marked BE is also 12. So far, we have:

LABEL	number
AE	12
AF	
AG	
BE	12
BF	
BG	
CE	36
CF	
CG	

(c) $P(CG|C) = \frac{12}{23}$. Since $P(CG|C) = \frac{P(CG)}{P(C)}$, it follows that $\frac{12}{23} = \frac{P(CG)}{P(C)}$.

(d) $P(C) = \frac{23}{55}$. Thus, using (c) we get $\frac{12}{23} = \frac{P(CG)}{\frac{23}{55}}$, that is, $P(CG) = \frac{12}{55}$.

Hence, the number of specimens marked CG is $\frac{12}{55} \cdot 220 = 48$.

Since $P(C) = \frac{23}{55}$, the total number of specimens marked with a C is $\frac{23}{55} \cdot 220 = 92$.

Since 36 were marked CE (see the above table) and 48 were marked CG, it follows that the number of specimens marked CF is $92 - 48 - 36 = 8$. Up to this point we have:

LABEL	number
AE	12
AF	
AG	
BE	12
BF	
BG	
CE	36
CF	8
CG	48

(e) The number of BGs is twice the number of BEs. Since the latter is 12 (see the above table), the number of BGs is 24.

(f) $P(AE|A) = \frac{3}{20}$. Since $P(AE|A) = \frac{P(AE)}{P(A)}$ and, from (b), $P(AE) = \frac{3}{55}$, we have that $\frac{3}{20} = \frac{\frac{3}{55}}{P(A)}$. Hence, $P(A) = \frac{3}{55}\left(\frac{20}{3}\right) = \frac{4}{11}$.

Thus, the number of specimens marked with an A is $\frac{4}{11}220 = 80$.

Since $P(A) = \frac{4}{11}$ and, from (d), $P(C) = \frac{23}{55}$, it follows that $P(B) = 1 - \frac{4}{11} - \frac{23}{55} = \frac{12}{55}$.

Thus, the number of specimens marked with a B is $\frac{12}{55} 220 = 48$.

Of these, 12 were marked BE and 24 were marked BG.

Thus, the number of specimens marked BF is $48 - 12 - 24 = 12$.

So far, we have:

LABEL	number
AE	12
AF	
AG	
BE	12
BF	12
BG	24
CE	36
CF	8
CG	48

(g) $P(AG|A) = \frac{1}{10}$. Since $P(AG|A) = \frac{P(AG)}{P(A)}$, and from (f) we have that $P(A) = \frac{4}{11}$ it follows that $\frac{1}{10} = \frac{P(AG)}{\frac{4}{11}}$, that is, $P(AG) = \frac{1}{10}\left(\frac{4}{11}\right) = \frac{4}{110}$.

Thus, the number of specimens marked AG is $\frac{4}{110}220 = 8$.

Since the number marked with an A is $\frac{4}{11}220 = 80$ and the number of those marked AE is 12 and the number of those marked AG is 8, we get that the number of specimens marked AF is $80 - 12 - 8 = 60$.

Thus, we have completed the table:

LABEL	number
AE	12
AF	60
AG	8
BE	12
BF	12
BG	24
CE	36
CF	8
CG	48

□

8. Information and Beliefs

8.1 Uncertainty and information

An individual's state of uncertainty can be represented by a set, listing all the "states of the world" that the individual considers possible. Indeed, this is what we did in Chapter 3 when we represented decision problems in terms of states and acts.

Consider, for example, the state of uncertainty of a doctor who, after listening to her patient's symptoms, reaches the conclusion that there are only five possible causes: (1) a bacterial infection (call this state a), (2) a viral infection (state b), (3) an allergic reaction to a drug (state c), (4) an allergic reaction to food (state d) and (5) environmental factors (state e). Then we can represent the doctor's state of uncertainty by the set $\{a,b,c,d,e\}$, as shown in Figure 8.1.

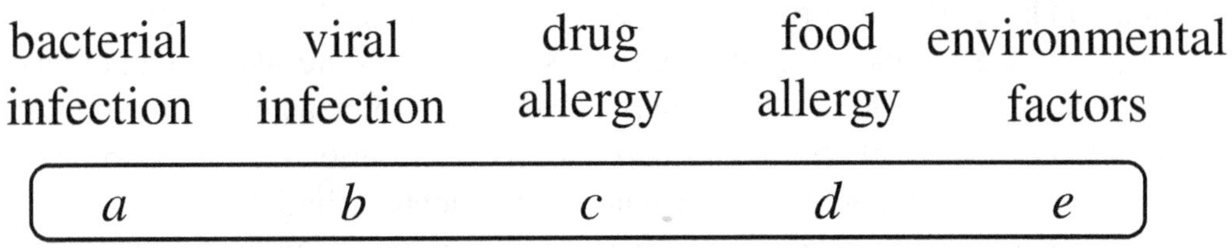

bacterial infection	viral infection	drug allergy	food allergy	environmental factors
a	b	c	d	e

Figure 8.1: The doctor's initial state of uncertainty

Information can be thought of as "reduction of uncertainty". Continuing the above example, suppose that the doctor can order a blood test. A positive blood test will reveal that there is an infection and rule out causes (3)-(5) (that is, states c, d and e); on the other hand, a negative blood test will reveal that there is no infection, thus ruling out causes (1) and (2) (that is, states *a* and *b*). We can represent the information potentially obtained by performing a blood test as a partition of the set of states into two sets: the set $\{a,b\}$, representing the new state of uncertainty after learning that the blood test was positive, and the set $\{c,d,e\}$, representing the new state of uncertainty after learning that the blood test was negative. That is, we can think of the blood test as the partition $\{\{a,b\}, \{c,d,e\}\}$, as shown in Figure 8.2.

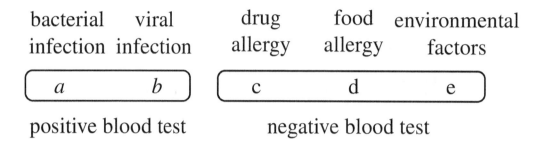

Figure 8.2: The possible states of uncertainty of the doctor after receiving the report on the blood test

> **Definition 8.1.1** A *partition* of a set U is a collection $\{E_1,\ldots,E_n\}$ ($n \geq 1$) of subsets of U such that:
> (1) the sets cover the entire set U, in the sense that $E_1 \cup \cdots \cup E_n = U$ and
> (2) any two different sets are disjoint, that is, if $i \neq j$ then $E_i \cap E_j = \emptyset$.[a]
> When a partition represents information, we call it an *information partition* and we call the elements of the partition *information sets*. We use the expression *perfect information* to refer to the case where the information partition is the finest one, that is, when each information set consists of a single state. For example, if $U = \{a,b,c,d,e\}$, then the perfect information partition is the partition $\{\{a\},\{b\},\{c\},\{d\},\{e\}\}$.
>
> [a]Note that the case $n = 1$ is allowed, so that $\{U\}$ is considered to be a partition of U; we call it the *trivial partition*.

An information set contains all the states that an individual considers possible, that is, the states that the individual cannot rule out, given her information. However, of all the states that are possible, the individual might consider some to be more likely than others and might even dismiss some states as "extremely unlikely" or "implausible". To represent the individual's probabilistic beliefs we use a probability distribution on the information set. To continue the doctor's example described above, the doctor's initial state of uncertainty is represented by the set $\{a,b,c,d,e\}$; however, based perhaps on her past experience with similar cases, she might (1) consider a bacterial infection (state a) to be twice as likely as a viral infection (state b), (2) dismiss a drug allergy (state c) as a plausible explanation and (3) consider a food allergy (state d) to be three times as likely as environmental factors (state e). For example, she might have the following beliefs:

state	a	b	c	d	e
probability	$\frac{4}{10}$	$\frac{2}{10}$	0	$\frac{3}{10}$	$\frac{1}{10}$

Suppose that the doctor orders a blood test and it comes back positive. How should she revise her beliefs in light of this piece of information? This issue is addressed in the next section.

> Test your understanding of the concepts introduced in this section, by going through the exercises in Section 8.5.1 at the end of this chapter.

8.2 Updating beliefs

The issue of how to "rationally" modify one's initial beliefs – expressed as a probability measure P on a set U – after receiving an item of information (represented by a subset F of U) has been studied extensively by philosophers and logicians. Two different situations may arise:

- In one case, the item of information F was not ruled out by the initial beliefs, in the sense that event F was assigned positive probability ($P(F) > 0$). Information might still be somewhat surprising, in case $P(F)$ is small (close to zero), but it is not completely unexpected. We call this case *belief updating*.
- The other case is where the item of information was initially dismissed, in the sense that it was assigned zero probability ($P(F) = 0$). In this case the information received is completely surprising or completely unexpected. We call this case *belief revision*.

In this section we address the issue of belief updating, while the next section deals with belief revision.

It is generally agreed that the rational way to update one's beliefs is by conditioning the initial probability measure on the information received, that is, by using the conditional probability formula (see Chapter 7, Section 7.2).

Definition 8.2.1 We use the expression *belief updating* or *Bayesian updating* to refer to the modification of initial beliefs (expressed by an initial probability distribution P) obtained by applying the conditional probability rule; this assumes that the belief change is prompted by the arrival of new information, represented by an event F such that $P(F) > 0$.

Thus, when receiving a piece of information $F \subseteq U$ such that $P(F) > 0$, one would change one's initial probability measure P into a new probability measure P_{new} by

- reducing the probability of every state in $\neg F$ (the complement of F) to zero (this captures the notion that the information represented by F is trusted to be correct), and
- setting $P_{new}(s) = P(s|F)$ for every state $s \in F$.

Thus, for every state $s \in U$,

$$P_{new}(s) = P(s|F) = \begin{cases} 0 & \text{if } s \notin F \\ \frac{P(s)}{P(F)} & \text{if } s \in F \end{cases} \tag{8.1}$$

(recall the assumption that $P(F) > 0$).
Thus, for every event $E \subseteq U$, $P_{new}(E) = \sum_{s \in E} P_{new}(s) = \sum_{s \in E} P(s|F) = P(E|F)$.

For instance, in the doctor's example, belief updating requires the following. Recall that the doctor's initial beliefs are:

state	a	b	c	d	e
probability	$\frac{4}{10}$	$\frac{2}{10}$	0	$\frac{3}{10}$	$\frac{1}{10}$

Let $+$ be the event that the blood test is positive (that is, $+ = \{a,b\}$ and thus $P(+) = \frac{6}{10}$). Let $-$ be the event that the blood test is negative (that is, $- = \{c,d,e\}$ and thus $P(-) = \frac{4}{10}$). Then

state	a	b	c	d	e
initial beliefs	$\frac{4}{10}$	$\frac{2}{10}$	0	$\frac{3}{10}$	$\frac{1}{10}$
beliefs updated on information $+$	$\frac{4/10}{6/10} = \frac{2}{3}$	$\frac{2/10}{6/10} = \frac{1}{3}$	0	0	0
beliefs updated on information $-$	0	0	$\frac{0}{4/10} = 0$	$\frac{3/10}{4/10} = \frac{3}{4}$	$\frac{1/10}{4/10} = \frac{1}{4}$

As a further example, suppose that there are only three students in a class: Ann, Bob and Carla. The professor tells them that in the last exam one of them got 95 points (out of 100), another 78 and the third 54.

We can think of a state as a triple (a,b,c), where a is Ann's score, b is Bob's score and c is Carla's score. Then, based on the information given by the professor, Ann must consider all of the following states as possible:

$$(95,78,54), (95,54,78), (78,95,54), (78,54,95), (54,95,78) \text{ and } (54,78,95).$$

Suppose, however, that in all the previous exams Ann and Bob always obtained a higher score than Carla and often Ann outperformed Bob. Then Ann might consider states $(95,78,54)$ and $(78,95,54)$ much more likely than $(78,54,95)$ and $(54,78,95)$.

For example, suppose that Ann's beliefs are as follows:

(95,78,54)	(95,54,78)	(78,95,54)	(54,95,78)	(78,54,95)	(54,78,95)
$\frac{16}{32}$	$\frac{8}{32}$	$\frac{4}{32}$	$\frac{2}{32}$	$\frac{1}{32}$	$\frac{1}{32}$

Suppose that, before distributing the exams, the professor says "I was surprised to see that, this time, Ann did not get the highest score". Based on this information, how should Ann revise her beliefs? The information is that Ann did not receive the highest score, which is represented by the event

$$F = \{(78,95,54), (54,95,78), (78,54,95), (54,78,95)\}.$$

Conditioning on this event yields the following updated beliefs:

(95,78,54)	(95,54,78)	(78,95,54)	(54,95,78)	(78,54,95)	(54,78,95)	
0	0	$\frac{4}{8}$	$\frac{2}{8}$	$\frac{1}{8}$	$\frac{1}{8}$	(8.2)

8.2 Updating beliefs

These updated beliefs can be represented more succinctly as follows, by not listing the states that are ruled out by information F (that is, the states in the complement of F, which are zero-probability states in the updated beliefs):

$$\begin{array}{cccc} (78,95,54) & (54,95,78) & (78,54,95) & (54,78,95) \\ \frac{4}{8} & \frac{2}{8} & \frac{1}{8} & \frac{1}{8} \end{array} \qquad (8.3)$$

The belief updating rule can also be applied sequentially if one first receives information F (with $P(F) > 0$) and later receives a further piece of information E (with $E \subseteq F$ and $P(E|F) > 0$). For instance, in the above example, suppose that the professor first informs the students that Ann did not get the highest score and later tells them that Carla received a higher score than Bob. Call F the first piece of information and E the second piece of information. Then, as we saw above, F is the set of states where it is in fact true that Ann did not get the highest score:

$$F = \{(78,95,54), (54,95,78), (78,54,95), (54,78,95)\}.$$

On the other hand, E is the set of states where it is in fact true that Carla received a higher score than Bob:

$$E = \{(95,54,78), (78,54,95), (54,78,95)\}.$$

Ann's updated beliefs after learning information F are given above in (8.2). Updating those beliefs by conditioning on E yields

$$\begin{array}{cccccc} (95,78,54) & (95,54,78) & (78,95,54) & (54,95,78) & (78,54,95) & (54,78,95) \\ 0 & 0 & 0 & 0 & \frac{1}{2} & \frac{1}{2} \end{array}$$

Clearly, this is the same as conditioning the initial beliefs on

$$E \cap F = \{(78,54,95), (54,78,95)\}.$$

Expressing all of this more succinctly, we have that the updated beliefs after learning F are as given in (8.3) above, namely

$$\begin{array}{cccc} (78,95,54) & (54,95,78) & (78,54,95) & (54,78,95) \\ \frac{4}{8} & \frac{2}{8} & \frac{1}{8} & \frac{1}{8} \end{array}$$

and the final beliefs are obtained by conditioning these beliefs on E or, equivalently, by conditioning the initial beliefs on $E \cap F$:

$$\begin{array}{cc} (78,54,95) & (54,78,95) \\ \frac{1}{2} & \frac{1}{2} \end{array}$$

> Test your understanding of the concepts introduced in this section, by going through the exercises in Section 8.5.2 at the end of this chapter.

8.3 Belief revision

How should a rational individual revise her beliefs when receiving information that is completely surprising, that is, when informed of an event E to which her initial beliefs assigned zero probability ($P(E) = 0$)? The best known theory of rational belief revision is the so-called *AGM theory*, which takes its name from its originators: Alchourrón (a legal scholar), Gärdenfors (a philosopher) and Makinson (a computer scientist); their pioneering contribution was published in 1985.[1] Just like the theory of expected utility (Chapter 5), the AGM theory is an axiomatic theory: it provides a list of "rationality" axioms for belief revision and provides a representation theorem.[2] Although the AGM theory was developed within the language of propositional logic, it can be restated in terms of a set of states and a collection of possible items of information represented as events. We first introduce the non-probabilistic version of the theory and then add graded beliefs, that is, probabilities.

Let U be a finite set of states and $\mathscr{E} \subseteq 2^U$ a collection of events (subsets of U) representing possible items of information; we assume that $U \in \mathscr{E}$ and $\emptyset \notin \mathscr{E}$. To represent initial beliefs and revised beliefs we introduce a function $f : \mathscr{E} \to 2^U$, which we call a belief revision function.

Definition 8.3.1 Let U be a finite set of states and $\mathscr{E}$ a collection of events such that $U \in \mathscr{E}$ and $\emptyset \notin \mathscr{E}$. A *belief revision function* is a function $f : \mathscr{E} \to 2^U$ that satisfies the following properties: for every $E \in \mathscr{E}$, (1) $f(E) \subseteq E$ and (2) $f(E) \neq \emptyset$.

The interpretation of a belief revision function is as follows.

- First of all, $f(U)$ represents the initial beliefs, namely the set of states that the individual initially considers possible.[3]
- Secondly, for every $E \in \mathscr{E}$, $f(E)$ is the set of states that the individual would consider possible if informed that the true state belongs to E; thus $f(E)$ represents the individual's *revised beliefs* after receiving information E.[4]

---

[1] Carlos Alchourrón, Peter Gärdenfors and David Makinson, On the logic of theory change: partial meet contraction and revision functions, *Journal of Symbolic Logic*, 1985, Vol. 50, pages 510-530.

[2] We will not list and discuss the axioms here. The interested reader can consult http://plato.stanford.edu/entries/formal-belief/ or, for a discussion which is closer to the approach followed in this section, Giacomo Bonanno, Rational choice and AGM belief revision, *Artificial Intelligence*, 2009, Vol. 88, pages 221-241.

[3] The universal set U can be thought of as representing minimum information: all states are possible. If the initial beliefs were to be expressed probabilistically, by means of a probability distribution P over U, then $f(U)$ would be the support of P, that is, the set of states to which P assigns positive probability. Thus, $f(U)$ would be the smallest event of which the individual would initially be certain (that is, to which she assigns probability 1): she would initially be certain of (assign probability 1 to) any event F such that $f(U) \subseteq F$.

[4] If the revised beliefs after receiving information E were to be expressed probabilistically, by means of a probability distribution P_E over U, then $f(E)$ would be the support of P_E, that is, the set of states to which P_E assigns positive probability. Thus, $f(E)$ would be the smallest event of which the individual would be certain *after having been informed that E*: according to her revised beliefs she would be certain of any event F such that $f(E) \subseteq F$. [Note that, since – by assumption – $f(E) \subseteq E$, the individual is assumed to be certain of the information received (e.g. because she trusts the source of the information).]

8.3 Belief revision

One of the implications of the AGM axioms for belief revision is the following condition, which is known as Arrow's Axiom (proposed by the Nobel laureate Ken Arrow in the context of rational choice, rather than rational belief revision):

$$\text{if } E, F \in \mathcal{E}, \ E \subseteq F \text{ and } E \cap f(F) \neq \emptyset \text{ then } f(E) = E \cap f(F).$$

Arrow's Axiom says that if information E implies information F ($E \subseteq F$) and there are states in E that would be considered possible upon receiving information F ($E \cap f(F) \neq \emptyset$), then the states that the individual would consider possible if informed that E are precisely those that belong to both E and $f(F)$ ($f(E) = E \cap f(F)$).

Although necessary for a belief revision policy that satisfies the AGM axioms, Arrow's Axiom is not sufficient. Before stating the necessary and sufficient conditions for rational belief revision, we remind the reader of the notion of a complete and transitive relation on a set U (Chapter 2, Section 2.1).
In Chapter 2 the relation was denoted by $\succsim$ and was interpreted in terms of preference: $o_1 \succsim o_2$ was interpreted as "the individual considers outcome o_1 to be at least as good as outcome o_2".
In the present context the interpretation is in terms of "plausibility":
$s \succsim s'$ means that the individual considers state s to be *at least as plausible* as state s';
$s \succ s'$ means that s is considered to be *more plausible* than s' and
$s \sim s'$ means that s is considered to be *just as plausible as s'*.

> **Definition 8.3.2** A *plausibility order* on a set of states U is a binary relation $\succsim$ on U that satisfies:
> completeness (for every two states s_1 and s_2, either $s_1 \succsim s_2$ or $s_2 \succsim s_1$, or both) and transitivity (if $s_1 \succsim s_2$ and $s_2 \succsim s_3$ then $s_1 \succsim s_3$).
> We define $s_1 \succ s_2$ as "$s_1 \succsim s_2$ and $s_2 \not\succsim s_1$" and we define $s_1 \sim s_2$ as "$s_1 \succsim s_2$ and $s_2 \succsim s_1$".

The following theorem is based on a result by Adam Grove.[5]

> **Theorem 8.3.1** Let U be a finite set of states, $\mathcal{E}$ a collection of events (representing possible items of information), with $U \in \mathcal{E}$ and $\emptyset \notin \mathcal{E}$, and $f : \mathcal{E} \to 2^U$ a belief revision function (Definition 8.3.1).
> Then the belief revision policy represented by the function f is compatible with the AGM axioms of belief revision if and only if there exists a plausibility order $\succsim$ on U that *rationalizes* f in the sense that, for every $E \in \mathcal{E}$, $f(E)$ is the set of most plausible states in E: $f(E) = \{s \in E : s \succsim s' \text{ for every } s' \in E\}$.

---

[5] Adam Grove, Two modelings for theory change, *Journal of Philosophical Logic*, 1988, Vol. 17, pages 157-170. That result was proved within the context of propositional logic. The version given here is proved in Giacomo Bonanno, Rational choice and AGM belief revision, *Artificial Intelligence*, 2009, Vol. 88, pages 221-241.

Definition 8.3.3 A belief revision function $f : \mathscr{E} \to 2^U$ which is rationalized by a plausibility order is called an *AGM belief revision function*.

An AGM belief revision function satisfies Arrow's Axiom (the reader is asked to prove this in Exercise 8.7). The converse is not true: it is possible for a belief revision function $f : \mathscr{E} \to 2^U$ to satisfy Arrow's Axiom and yet fail to be rationalized by a plausibility order.

Within the context of probabilistic beliefs, let P be the probability distribution on a finite set of states U that represents the initial beliefs and P_E be the probability distribution representing the updated beliefs after receiving information E such that $P(E) > 0$ (thus the information is not surprising).
The *support* of a probability distribution P, denoted by $Supp(P)$, is the set of states to which P assigns positive probability: $Supp(P) = \{s \in U : P(s) > 0\}$.
The rule for *updating* beliefs upon receiving information E (Definition 8.2.1) implies the following:

$$\text{if } E \cap Supp(P) \neq \emptyset \text{ (that is, } P(E) > 0\text{)} \text{ then } Supp(P_E) = E \cap Supp(P). \quad (8.4)$$

We call this the *qualitative belief updating rule* or qualitative Bayes' rule. It is easy to check that the qualitative belief updating rule is implied by Arrow's Axiom (see Exercise 8.8). Thus, by the above remark, an AGM belief revision function has incorporated in it the qualitative belief updating rule. In other words, *belief updating is included in the notion of AGM belief revision*. A belief revision function, however, goes beyond belief updating because it also encodes new beliefs after receipt of surprising information (that is, after being informed of an event E such that $P(E) = 0$).

What is the probabilistic version of AGM belief revision? It turns out that in order to obtain probabilistic beliefs we only need to make a simple addition to an AGM belief revision function $f : \mathscr{E} \to 2^U$.
Let P_0 be any full-support probability distribution on U (that is, P_0 is such that $P_0(s) > 0$, for every $s \in U$).
Then, for every $E \in \mathscr{E}$, let P_E be the probability distribution obtained by conditioning P_0 on $f(E)$ (note: on $f(E)$, not on E):

$$P_E(s) = P_0(s|f(E)) = \begin{cases} \frac{P_0(s)}{\sum_{s' \in f(E)} P_0(s')} & \text{if } s \in f(E) \\ 0 & \text{if } s \notin f(E) \end{cases}$$

Then P_U gives the initial probabilistic beliefs and, for every other $E \in \mathscr{E}$, P_E gives the revised probabilistic beliefs after receiving information E.
The collection $\{P_E\}_{E \in \mathscr{E}}$ of probability distributions on U so obtained gives the individual's *probabilistic* belief revision policy (while the function $f : \mathscr{E} \to 2^U$ gives the individual's *qualitative* belief revision policy).

> **Definition 8.3.4** Let U be a finite set of states and $\mathscr{E}$ a collection of events such that $U \in \mathscr{E}$ and $\emptyset \notin \mathscr{E}$.
>
> A *probabilistic belief revision policy* is a collection $\{P_E\}_{E \in \mathscr{E}}$ of probability distributions on U such that, for every $E \in \mathscr{E}$, $Supp(P_E) \subseteq E$. P_U represents the initial beliefs and, for every other $E \in \mathscr{E}$, P_E represents the revised beliefs after receiving information E.
>
> The collection $\{P_E\}_{E \in \mathscr{E}}$ is called an *AGM probabilistic belief revision policy* if it satisfies the following properties:
> 1. there exists a plausibility order $\succsim$ on U such that, for every $E \in \mathscr{E}$, $Supp(P_E)$ is the set of most plausible states in E, that is, $Supp(P_E) = \{s \in E : s \succsim s' \text{ for every } s' \in E\}$,[a]
> 2. there exists a full-support probability distribution P_0 on U such that, for every $E \in \mathscr{E}$, P_E is the probability distribution obtained by conditioning P_0 on $Supp(P_E)$.
>
> ---
>
> [a]This condition says that if one defines the function $f : \mathscr{E} \to 2^U$ by $f(E) = Supp(P_E)$ then this function is an AGM belief revision function (see Definition 8.3.3).

> Test your understanding of the concepts introduced in this section, by going through the exercises in Section 8.5.3 at the end of this chapter.

8.4 Information and truth

The notion of belief updating and the more general notion of belief revision considered in the previous two sections reflect the assumption that information is trusted to be correct or truthful. That is, if informed that event E has occurred, the *DM* trusts that the true state of the world is in fact an element of E. This presupposes that the source of information is a reputable one.

What constitutes reliable information? Years ago, perhaps, a photograph could be taken as "indisputable evidence". Nowadays, with the advent of sophisticated image-editing software, photographs can be manipulated to misrepresent facts or to create the appearance of an event that did not happen. For example, in March 2004 a political advertisement for George W. Bush, as he was running for president, showed a sea of soldiers at a public event; later the Bush campaign acknowledged that the photo had been doctored, by copying and pasting several soldiers.[6] Videos and voice recordings are, nowadays, also manipulable. What can one trust as a source of reliable information? The testimony of a witness? A newspaper article? A book? A television news report? A claim by the president of the USA? Many of us rely on the internet for information. Can material found on the internet be trusted as accurate? Footnote 6 gives a link to a web page reporting photo tampering throughout history: can one be sure that the information given there is correct? Perhaps if a piece of information is reported by several sources then it can be trusted? Unfortunately, it may simply be the case that an initial piece of incorrect information gets reproduced (in good faith) by different sources and thus becomes "confirmed" information. One is left wondering if, nowadays, there is *any* source of information that is completely reliable.

---

[6] For an interesting account of photo tampering throughout history, see http://www.cs.dartmouth.edu/farid/research/digitaltampering/

Even if one is able to come up with a "safe" list of reliable sources, it can happen that a trustworthy source gives – albeit in good faith – erroneous information. It can also happen that an impostor transmits information in the guise of a trusted source, as illustrated in the following newspaper report:[7]

> Mark J. made a big bet in mid-August [2000] that Emulex shares would decline [...] Instead they soared, leaving him with a paper loss of almost $100,000 in just a week. So J. took matters into his own hands. [...] On the evening of August 24, he sent a fake press release by e-mail to Internet Wire, a Los Angeles service where he had previously worked, warning that Emulex's chief executive had resigned and its earnings were overstated. The next morning, just as financial markets opened, Internet Wire distributed the damaging release to news organizations and Web sites. An hour later, shareholders in Emulex were $2.5 billion poorer. And J. would soon be $240,000 richer. [...] The hoax [...] was revealed within an hour of the first news report and Emulex stock recovered the same day. Still, investors who [believing the fake news release] panicked and sold their shares, or had sell orders automatically executed at present prices, are unlikely to recover their losses.

We will not address the difficult issue of how one should revise one's beliefs in light of new "information" when there is a possibility that the information is erroneous (or even consciously manipulated).

We conclude this section by asking the following question:

> Assuming that information is in fact truthful or correct (in the sense that if it is represented by an event E then the true state of the world is in fact an element of E), does belief updating lead one to get "closer to the truth" than she was before she received the information?

Unfortunately, the answer is: Not necessarily. For example, suppose that the set of states is $U = \{a,b,c,d,e,f,g\}$ and the *DM* has the following initial beliefs:

state	a	b	c	d	e	f	g
probability	$\frac{4}{32}$	$\frac{2}{32}$	$\frac{8}{32}$	$\frac{5}{32}$	$\frac{7}{32}$	$\frac{2}{32}$	$\frac{4}{32}$

For instance, the states could represent diseases that are possible causes of a patient's symptoms and the *DM* is a doctor who is interested in the event that the appropriate treatment for her patient is to administer a drug called Meliorite, which is a common cure for diseases a,c,d and e but would be harmful in the other cases. Thus, the doctor is interested in the event $E = \{a,c,d,e\}$ that the appropriate course of action is to prescribe Meliorite. Initially the doctor attaches the following probability to E being true:

$$P(E) = P(a) + P(c) + P(d) + P(e) = \frac{4}{32} + \frac{8}{32} + \frac{5}{32} + \frac{7}{32} = \frac{24}{32} = \frac{3}{4} = \boxed{75\%}.$$

---

[7]*The Sacramento Bee*, September 1, 2000.

Let us imagine that **the true disease is b** (of course, the doctor does not know this), so that event E is *not* true (that is, Meliorite would actually be harmful to the patient rather than cure him).

Suppose that a test can be performed that can give one of three results: positive (this happens in states a, b and c), negative (this happens in states d, e and f) or neutral (this happens in state g). Thus, we can think of the test as the following partition:

$$\underbrace{a \ b \ c}_{\text{positive result}} \quad \underbrace{d \ e \ f}_{\text{negative result}} \quad \underbrace{g}_{\text{neutral result}}$$

The doctor decides to perform the test and – since we assumed that the true state is b – she is informed that the result is positive. Thus she updates her initial estimate of the probability of E by applying the conditional probability rule (with the information being represented by the event $F = \{a, b, c\}$ that the test result is positive; recall that $E = \{a, c, d, e\}$):

$$P(E|F) = \frac{P(E \cap F)}{P(F)} = \frac{P(\{a,c\})}{P(\{a,b,c\})} = \frac{\frac{4}{32} + \frac{8}{32}}{\frac{4}{32} + \frac{2}{32} + \frac{8}{32}} = \frac{6}{7} = \boxed{86\%}.$$

Thus the truthful information acquired by performing the test induces the doctor to become *more confident of something which is not true*, namely that the drug Meliorite would cure the patient (she increases her probabilistic estimate of the false event E from 75% to 86%).

8.5 Exercises

The solutions to the following exercises are given in Section 8.6 at the end of this chapter.

8.5.1 Exercises for Section 8.1: Uncertainty and information

Exercise 8.1 Suppose that you are doing some research on the effect of the weather on a particular crop in a certain area. You need information on what the weather was like on a certain date in the past. The states that you are interested in are the following and, as far as you know, all of them are possibilities:

s_1	s_2	s_3	s_4	s_5	s_6
sunny	rain	partly cloudy, no rain	snow	cloudy, no rain	hail

(a) What is your initial state of uncertainty?
(b) Somebody offers to give you information on whether or not there was precipitation on that day. Represent the information that is being offered to you as a partition of the set of states.

8.5.2 Exercises for Section 8.2: Updating beliefs

Exercise 8.2 Consider again the example where there are only three students in a class: Ann, Bob and Carla and the professor tells them that in the last exam one of them got 95 points (out of 100), another 78 and the third 54.
Ann's initial beliefs are as follows (where the triple (a,b,c) is interpreted as follows: a is Ann's score, b is Bob's score and c is Carla's score):

$(95,78,54)$	$(95,54,78)$	$(78,95,54)$	$(54,95,78)$	$(78,54,95)$	$(54,78,95)$
$\frac{16}{32}$	$\frac{8}{32}$	$\frac{4}{32}$	$\frac{2}{32}$	$\frac{1}{32}$	$\frac{1}{32}$

(a) Suppose that (before distributing the exams) the professor tells the students that Carla received a lower score than Bob. Let E be the event that represents this information. What is E?

(b) How should Ann update her beliefs in response to information E?

Exercise 8.3 Let the set of states be $U = \{a,b,c,d,e,f,g\}$. Bill's initial beliefs are as follows:

a	b	c	d	e	f	g
$\frac{3}{20}$	$\frac{2}{20}$	$\frac{5}{20}$	$\frac{1}{20}$	$\frac{1}{20}$	$\frac{3}{20}$	$\frac{5}{20}$

(a) Suppose that Bill receives information $E = \{a,c,e,f,g\}$. What are his updated beliefs?

(b) Suppose that, after receiving information E, he later learns a new piece of information, namely $F = \{b,d,e,f,g\}$. What are his final beliefs (that is, after updating first on E and then on F)?

Exercise 8.4 Inspector Gethem has been put in charge of a museum robbery that took place yesterday. Two precious items were stolen: a statuette and a gold tiara, which were displayed in the same room. Surveillance cameras show that only three people visited the room at the time the items disappeared: call them suspect A, suspect B and suspect C. Let a state be a complete specification of who stole what (including the possibility that the same person stole both items).

(a) List all the states.

(b) Inspector Gethem recognizes the suspects and, based on what he knows about them, initially believes that the probability that suspect A stole both items is $\frac{1}{20}$, the probability that suspect B stole both items is $\frac{3}{20}$ and the probability that suspect C stole both items is $\frac{4}{20}$. Furthermore, he assigns the same probability to every other state. What are his initial beliefs?

(c) Suppose now that the inspector receives reliable information that suspect B did not steal the statuette and suspect C did not steal the tiara. What are his beliefs after he updates on this information?

8.5 Exercises

Exercise 8.5 Let the set of states be $U = \{a,b,c,d,e,f,g\}$ and let the individual's initial beliefs be given by the following probability distribution, call it P:

a	b	c	d	e	f	g
$\frac{3}{20}$	0	$\frac{7}{20}$	$\frac{1}{20}$	0	$\frac{4}{20}$	$\frac{5}{20}$

Let $E = \{a,d,e,g\}$.

(a) Calculate $P(E), P(b|E)$ and $P(d|E)$.

(b) Calculate the updated beliefs in response to information E.

Exercise 8.6 The instructor of a class has the following data on enrollment, on average, in the past 10 years:

major	Economics	Mathematics	Philosophy	Psychology	Statistics
enrollment	35%	22%	18%	16%	9%

She believes that the percentages for the current enrollment are the same as in the past.

(a) A student in her class, Jim, tells her that his major is neither Math nor Statistics. What are the instructor's beliefs about Jim's major upon learning this?

(b) After awhile Jim further informs the instructor that he is not an Economics major. What are the instructor's beliefs about Jim's major upon learning this second fact?

(c) Finally, Jim tells the instructor that he is not a Philosophy major. What are the instructor's beliefs about Jim's major upon learning this third fact?

8.5.3 Exercises for Section 8.3: Belief revision

Exercise 8.7 Prove that an AGM belief revision function (Definition 8.3.3) satisfies Arrow's Axiom: if $E, F \in \mathscr{E}$, $E \subseteq F$ and $E \cap f(F) \neq \emptyset$ then $f(E) = E \cap f(F)$.

Exercise 8.8 Prove that the qualitative belief updating rule (8.4) is implied by Arrow's Axiom.

Exercise 8.9 Let $U = \{a,b,c,d,e,g,h,k,m\}$ and let $\succsim$ be the following plausibility order on U (as usual, we use the convention that if the row to which state s belongs is above the row to which state s' belongs then $s \succ s'$, and if s and s' belong to the same row then $s \sim s'$).

$$\begin{array}{rl} \text{most plausible} & b,g \\ & c,k,m \\ & d,h \\ & e \\ \text{least plausible} & a \end{array}$$

Let $\mathscr{E} = \{\{a,e\}, \{d,e,k,m\}, \{b,d,e,k\}, U\}$. Find the belief revision function $f : \mathscr{E} \to 2^U$ that is rationalized by $\succsim$.

Exercise 8.10 As in Exercise 8.9, let $U = \{a,b,c,d,e,g,h,k,m\}$ and

$$\mathcal{E} = \{\underbrace{\{a,e\}}_{E}, \underbrace{\{d,e,k,m\}}_{F}, \underbrace{\{b,d,e,k\}}_{G}, U\}$$

Using the plausibility order of Exercise 8.9, namely

$$\begin{array}{rl} \text{most plausible} & b,g \\ & c,k,m \\ & d,h \\ & e \\ \text{least plausible} & a \end{array}$$

find a collection of probability distributions $\{P_E, P_F, P_G, P_W\}$ that provides an AGM probabilistic belief revision policy (Definition 8.3.4). [There are many; find one.] ■

8.6 Solutions to Exercises

Solution to Exercise 8.1.

(a) Your initial state of uncertainty is represented by the set $\{s_1, s_2, s_3, s_4, s_5, s_6\}$.

(b) The information partition is as follows:

$$\left\{ \underbrace{\{s_2, s_4, s_6\}}_{\text{there was precipitation}} , \underbrace{\{s_1, s_3, s_5\}}_{\text{there was no precipitation}} \right\}$$

□

Solution to Exercise 8.2.

(a) $E = \{(95,78,54), (78,95,54), (54,95,78)\}$. Thus $P(E) = \frac{16}{32} + \frac{4}{32} + \frac{2}{32} = \frac{22}{32}$.

(b) Conditioning on E yields the following beliefs:

$(95,78,54)$	$(95,54,78)$	$(78,95,54)$	$(54,95,78)$	$(78,54,95)$	$(54,78,95)$
$\frac{16/32}{22/32} = \frac{8}{11}$	0	$\frac{4/22}{22/22} = \frac{2}{11}$	$\frac{2/32}{22/32} = \frac{1}{11}$	0	0

□

8.6 Solutions to Exercises

Solution to Exercise 8.3.

(a) Updating on information $E = \{a,c,e,f,g\}$ yields the following beliefs:

a	b	c	d	e	f	g
$\frac{3}{17}$	0	$\frac{5}{17}$	0	$\frac{1}{17}$	$\frac{3}{17}$	$\frac{5}{17}$

(b) Updating the beliefs of Part (a) on information $F = \{b,d,e,f,g\}$ yields the following beliefs:

a	b	c	d	e	f	g
0	0	0	0	$\frac{1}{9}$	$\frac{3}{9}$	$\frac{5}{9}$

□

Solution to Exercise 8.4. Represent a state as a pair (x,y) where x is the suspect who stole the statuette and y is the suspect who stole the tiara.

(a) The set of states is

$$U = \{(A,A),(A,B),(A,C),(B,A),(B,B),(B,C),(C,A),(C,B),(C,C)\}.$$

(b) The inspector's initial beliefs are:

(A,A)	(A,B)	(A,C)	(B,A)	(B,B)	(B,C)	(C,A)	(C,B)	(C,C)
$\frac{1}{20}$	$\frac{2}{20}$	$\frac{2}{20}$	$\frac{2}{20}$	$\frac{3}{20}$	$\frac{2}{20}$	$\frac{2}{20}$	$\frac{2}{20}$	$\frac{4}{20}$

(c) The information is

$$F = \{(A,A),(A,B),(C,A),(C,B)\}.$$

Updating on this information yields the following beliefs:

(A,A)	(A,B)	(A,C)	(B,A)	(B,B)	(B,C)	(C,A)	(C,B)	(C,C)
$\frac{1}{7}$	$\frac{2}{7}$	0	0	0	0	$\frac{2}{7}$	$\frac{2}{7}$	0

□

Solution to Exercise 8.5.

(a) $P(E) = P(a) + P(d) + P(e) + P(g) = \frac{3}{20} + \frac{1}{20} + 0 + \frac{5}{20} = \frac{9}{20}$, $P(b|E) = 0$

and $P(d|E) = \dfrac{\frac{1}{20}}{\frac{9}{20}} = \frac{1}{9}$.

(b) The updated beliefs are as follows:

a	b	c	d	e	f	g
$\frac{3}{9}$	0	0	$\frac{1}{9}$	0	0	$\frac{5}{9}$

□

Solution to Exercise 8.6. The initial beliefs are:

Economics	Mathematics	Philosophy	Psychology	Statistics
$\frac{35}{100}$	$\frac{22}{100}$	$\frac{18}{100}$	$\frac{16}{100}$	$\frac{9}{100}$

(a) Updating on {Economics, Philosophy, Psychology} yields the following beliefs:

Economics	Mathematics	Philosophy	Psychology	Statistics
$\frac{35}{69}$	0	$\frac{18}{69}$	$\frac{16}{69}$	0

(b) Updating the beliefs of Part (a) on {Philosophy, Psychology}[8] yields the following beliefs:

Economics	Mathematics	Philosophy	Psychology	Statistics
0	0	$\frac{18}{34}$	$\frac{16}{34}$	0

(c) Updating the beliefs of Part (b) on {Psychology} yields the following beliefs:

Economics	Mathematics	Philosophy	Psychology	Statistics
0	0	0	1	0

that is, the instructor now knows that the student is a Psychology major. □

---

[8] This is the intersection of the initial piece of information, namely {Economics, Philosophy, Psychology}, and the new piece of information, namely {Mathematics, Philosophy, Psychology, Statistics}. Updating the updated beliefs on {Mathematics, Philosophy, Psychology, Statistics} yields the same result as updating on {Philosophy, Psychology}. Indeed, one would obtain the same result by updating the *initial* beliefs on {Philosophy, Psychology}.

8.6 Solutions to Exercises

Solution to Exercise 8.7. Let $f: \mathcal{E} \to 2^U$ be an AGM belief revision function. Let $E, F \in \mathcal{E}$ be such that $E \subseteq F$ and $E \cap f(F) \neq \emptyset$.
We need to show that $f(E) = E \cap f(F)$.
By definition of AGM belief revision function (Definition 8.3.3), there is a plausibility order $\succsim$ on U such that

$$f(F) = \{s \in F : s \succsim s' \text{ for every } s' \in F\} \tag{8.5}$$

and

$$f(E) = \{s \in E : s \succsim s' \text{ for every } s' \in E\}. \tag{8.6}$$

Choose an arbitrary $s \in E \cap f(F)$.
Then, by (8.5) and the fact that $E \subseteq F$, $s \succsim s'$ for every $s' \in E$ and thus, by (8.6), $s \in f(E)$.
Hence, $E \cap f(F) \subseteq f(E)$. Conversely, choose an arbitrary $s_1 \in f(E)$.

Then, since (by definition of belief revision function: Definition 8.3.1) $f(E) \subseteq E$, $s_1 \in E$. We want to show that $s_1 \in f(F)$ [so that $s_1 \in E \cap f(F)$ and, therefore, $f(E) \subseteq E \cap f(F)$].
Suppose it is not true. Then, by (8.5), there exists an $s_2 \in F$ such that $s_2 \succ s_1$.

Select an $s_3 \in E \cap f(F)$ (recall that, by hypothesis, $E \cap f(F) \neq \emptyset$).

Then, by (8.5) (since $s_2, s_3 \in f(F)$), $s_3 \succsim s_2$, from which it follows (by transitivity of $\succsim$ and the fact that $s_2 \succ s_1$) that $s_3 \succ s_1$.

But then, since $s_3 \in E$, it is not true that $s_1 \succsim s'$ for every $s' \in E$, contradicting - by (8.6) - the hypothesis that $s_1 \in f(E)$. □

Solution to Exercise 8.8. For every event E (representing a possible item of information), let P_E be the probability distribution on E that represents the *revised* beliefs of the individual after receiving information E.
Let P be the probability distribution on U representing the individual's *initial* beliefs.
Define the following belief revision function f : $f(U) = Supp(P)$ and $f(E) = Supp(P_E)$.
Suppose that f satisfies Arrow's Axiom.
Then, for every event E, if $E \cap f(U) \neq \emptyset$ [that is, if $E \cap Supp(P) \neq \emptyset$ or $P(E) > 0$] then $f(E) = E \cap f(U)$ [that is, $Supp(P_E) = E \cap Supp(P)$]. □

Solution to Exercise 8.9. We have that $\mathscr{E} = \{\{a,e\},\{d,e,k,m\},\{b,d,e,k\},U\}$ and $\succsim$ is given by

> most plausible b,g
>
> c,k,m
>
> d,h
>
> e
>
> least plausible a

Then the belief revision function rationalized by this plausibility order is given by: $f(\{a,e\}) = \{e\}$, $f(\{d,e,k,m\}) = \{k,m\}$, $f(\{b,d,e,k\}) = \{b\}$ and $f(U) = \{b,g\}$. $\square$

Solution to Exercise 8.10. From Exercise 8.9 we get that $\{P_E, P_F, P_G, P_U\}$ must be such that $Supp(P_E) = \{e\}$, $Supp(P_F) = \{k,m\}$, $Supp(P_G) = \{b\}$ and $Supp(P_U) = \{b,g\}$. For every full-support probability distribution P_0 on U, there is a corresponding collection $\{P_E, P_F, P_G, P_U\}$. For example, if P_0 is the uniform distribution on U (that assigns probability $\frac{1}{9}$ to every state) then the corresponding $\{P_E, P_F, P_G, P_U\}$ is given by:

state	a	b	c	d	e	g	h	k	m
P_E	0	0	0	0	1	0	0	0	0
P_F	0	0	0	0	0	0	0	$\frac{1}{2}$	$\frac{1}{2}$
P_G	0	1	0	0	0	0	0	0	0
P_U	0	$\frac{1}{2}$	0	0	0	$\frac{1}{2}$	0	0	0

As another example, if P_0 is the following probability distribution

state	a	b	c	d	e	g	h	k	m
P_0	$\frac{1}{50}$	$\frac{3}{50}$	$\frac{11}{50}$	$\frac{4}{50}$	$\frac{8}{50}$	$\frac{9}{50}$	$\frac{5}{50}$	$\frac{2}{50}$	$\frac{7}{50}$

then the corresponding $\{P_E, P_F, P_G, P_U\}$ is given by: P_E and P_G the same as above, and P_F and P_U as follows:

state	a	b	c	d	e	g	h	k	m
P_F	0	0	0	0	0	0	0	$\frac{2}{9}$	$\frac{7}{9}$
P_U	0	$\frac{1}{4}$	0	0	0	$\frac{3}{4}$	0	0	0

$\square$

9. The Value of Information

9.1 When is information potentially valuable?

Since information reduces uncertainty, it should always be valuable, at least in the context of decision making: intuitively, making a decision in a situation of less uncertainty is preferable to making a decision in a situation of greater uncertainty. However, typically the acquisition of information is a costly process and thus one needs to weigh the cost of becoming more informed against the benefit of a more informed decision. In this chapter we discuss how one can quantify the value of potential information.

Are there situations where, no matter how small the cost, one should *not* seek information? The answer is Yes: whenever one can anticipate that *any additional information would not lead to a decision that is different from the decision that would be made in the absence of information*. For example, suppose that a doctor adheres to the following decision rule:

> If a patient's symptoms are consistent with several treatable diseases and one of the possible diseases is more likely than the others to be the cause, then I will prescribe a treatment that targets this most likely cause.

In the late 1980s a study was carried out with a group of doctors to see under what circumstances they would prescribe a costly diagnostic test before making a treatment decision.[1] The doctors were presented with the following decision problem involving fictional diseases:

> A patient's presenting symptoms and history suggest a diagnosis of globoma, with a probability of 0.8. The only other possibilities are popitis and flapemia, each with a probability of 0.1 Each disease has its own treatment which is ineffective against the other two diseases. A test, called ET scan, is available and has the following properties:
> (1) the test will be positive with probability 1 if the patient has popitis,
> (2) the test will be negative with probability 1 if the patient has flapemia and
> (3) the test will be positive with probability 0.5 if the patient has globoma.
> If ET scan were the only test that could be performed and it was somewhat costly, would you prescribe it?

In their answers many doctors said that it would be worthwhile to perform the ET scan, even if it was somewhat costly. The doctors also said that they were inclined to follow the decision rule described above, namely to treat the most likely disease.

First of all, note that, given this decision rule,

- If the ET scan were not performed the doctor would treat the most likely disease, namely globoma.

To see what the doctor should do after learning the result of the ET scan, we need to compute the doctor's updated beliefs after reading the report on the scan. Her original beliefs are:

disease	Globoma (G)	Popitis (P)	Flapemia (F)
probability	0.8	0.1	0.1

Let '+' denote the event that the ET scan is positive and '−' denote the event that the ET scan is negative. The information about the test given above concerns the probability of a positive or negative result conditional on each disease:

$$P(+|G) = 0.5 \quad P(-|G) = 0.5$$
$$P(+|P) = 1 \quad P(-|P) = 0$$
$$P(+|F) = 0 \quad P(-|F) = 1$$

---

[1] Baron, J., Beattie, J. and Hershey, J.C., Heuristics and biases in diagnostic reasoning: II. Congruence, information and certainty, *Organizational Behavior and Human Decision Processes*, 1988, Vol. 42, pages 88-110. See also Jonathan Baron, *Thinking and deciding*, Third Edition, 2000, Cambridge University Press (in particular pages 166-170).

9.1 When is information potentially valuable?

Using Bayes' rule we can compute the doctor's updated beliefs *if she finds out that the ET scan is positive*:

$$P(G|+) = \frac{P(+|G)P(G)}{P(+|G)P(G) + P(+|P)P(P) + P(+|F)P(F)}$$

$$= \frac{(0.5)(0.8)}{(0.5)(0.8) + (1)(0.1) + (0)(0.1)} = 0.8,$$

$$P(P|+) = \frac{P(+|P)P(P)}{P(+|G)P(G) + P(+|P)P(P) + P(+|F)P(F)}$$

$$= \frac{(1)(0.1)}{(0.5)(0.8) + (1)(0.1) + (0)(0.1)} = 0.2$$

and

$$P(F|+) = \frac{P(+|F)P(F)}{P(+|G)P(G) + P(+|P)P(P) + P(+|F)P(F)}$$

$$= \frac{(0)(0.1)}{(0.5)(0.8) + (1)(0.1) + (0)(0.1)} = 0.$$

Thus, the doctor's revised beliefs after learning the the ET scan was positive are:

disease	*Globoma* (G)	*Popitis* (P)	*Flapemia* (F)
probability	0.8	0.2	0

Hence, given her stated decision rule,

- If the ET scan is performed and the result is positive, the doctor will treat globoma (the most likely disease).

Similarly, using Bayes' rule we can compute the doctor's updated beliefs *if she finds out that the ET scan is negative*:

$$P(G|-) = \frac{P(-|G)P(G)}{P(-|G)P(G) + P(-|P)P(P) + P(-|F)P(F)}$$

$$= \frac{(0.5)(0.8)}{(0.5)(0.8) + (0)(0.1) + (1)(0.1)} = 0.8,$$

$$P(P|-) = \frac{P(-|P)P(P)}{P(-|G)P(G) + P(-|P)P(P) + P(-|F)P(F)}$$

$$= \frac{(0)(0.1)}{(0.5)(0.8) + (0)(0.1) + (1)(0.1)} = 0,$$

$$P(F|-) = \frac{P(-|F)P(F)}{P(-|G)P(G) + P(-|P)P(P) + P(-|F)P(F)}$$

$$= \frac{(1)(0.1)}{(0.5)(0.8) + (0)(0.1) + (1)(0.1)} = 0.2.$$

Thus, the doctor's revised beliefs after learning the the ET scan was negative are:

disease	Globoma (G)	Popitis (P)	Flapemia (F)
probability	0.8	0	0.2

Hence, given her stated decision rule,

- If the ET scan is performed and the result is negative, the doctor will treat globoma (the most likely disease).

In conclusion, *the doctor's decision about what disease to treat is the same in all three cases*: no ET scan, ET scan with positive result and ET scan with negative result. Hence, the information provided by the scan is of no use and, since it is costly, it is a waste of resources to perform the scan. As Jonathan Baron notes,[2]

> Sometimes we want information because we are simply curious. [...] Subjects who feel that the tests are worth doing may be pursuing an inappropriate goal (satisfying their curiosity or seeking information for its own sake), which, on reflection, they would decide not to pursue. In fact, when we interviewed and presented this argument to them, all of them admitted that the tests were worthless.

Continuing the example, under what circumstances would the ET scan *possibly* be of value to a doctor whose decision rule is to treat the most likely disease? Let us modify the data by changing the probability of a positive test, given that the patient has globoma. Above we assumed that $P(+|G) = 0.5$ but let us now replace the value 0.5 with a general $p \in (0,1)$. The remaining data is the same as above. Thus:

$$\begin{array}{ll} P(+|G) = p & P(-|G) = 1-p \\ P(+|P) = 1 & P(-|P) = 0 \\ P(+|F) = 0 & P(-|F) = 1 \end{array}$$

Then we can reframe the question as follows:

> What values of p are such that it is *possible* that the ET scan *might* induce the doctor to make a different treatment decision (after learning the result of the scan), relative to the decision that she would make without performing the scan (which is to treat globoma)?

Let us first focus on the case where the result of the scan is *positive*. We saw above that, in this case, the doctor must assign zero probability to the patient having flapemia (since $P(+|F) = 0$ implies that $P(F|+) = 0$). Thus, what we are asking is:

---
[2] Jonathan Baron, *Thinking and deciding*, Third Edition, 2000, Cambridge University Press, page 167.

9.1 When is information potentially valuable?

> What values of p are such that, after learning that the result of the scan was positive, the doctor will consider globoma to be less likely than popitis? That is, what values of p are such that $P(G|+) < P(P|+)$? [3]

Recomputing $P(G|+)$ and $P(P|+)$ by replacing 0.5 with p we get:

$$P(G|+) = \frac{P(+|G)P(G)}{P(+|G)P(G) + P(+|P)P(P) + P(+|F)P(F)}$$

$$= \frac{p(0.8)}{p(0.8) + (1)(0.1) + (0)(0.1)} = \frac{0.8p}{0.8p + 0.1}$$

and

$$P(P|+) = \frac{P(+|P)P(P)}{P(+|G)P(G) + P(+|P)P(P) + P(+|F)P(F)}$$

$$= \frac{(1)(0.1)}{p(0.8) + (1)(0.1) + (0)(0.1)} = \frac{0.1}{0.8p + 0.1}.$$

Thus, what we want is: $\frac{0.8p}{0.8p+0.1} < \frac{0.1}{0.8p+0.1}$ which is equivalent to $p < \frac{1}{8} = 12.5\%$.

On the other hand, in the case where the result of the scan is *negative*, the doctor must assign zero probability to the patient having popitis (since $P(-|P) = 0$ implies that $P(P|-) = 0$). Thus, in this case what we are asking is:

> What values of p are such that, after learning that the result of the scan was negative, the doctor will consider globoma to be less likely than flapemia? That is, what values of p are such that $P(G|-) < P(F|-)$? [4]

Recomputing $P(G|-)$ and $P(F|-)$ by replacing 0.5 with p we get:

$$P(G|-) = \frac{P(-|G)P(G)}{P(-|G)P(G) + P(-|P)P(P) + P(-|F)P(F)}$$

$$= \frac{(1-p)(0.8)}{(1-p)(0.8) + (0)(0.1) + (1)(0.1)} = \frac{0.8(1-p)}{0.8(1-p) + 0.1}$$

and

$$P(F|-) = \frac{P(-|F)P(F)}{P(-|G)P(G) + P(-|P)P(P) + P(-|F)P(F)}$$

$$= \frac{(1)(0.1)}{(1-p)(0.8) + (0)(0.1) + (1)(0.1)} = \frac{0.1}{0.8(1-p) + 0.1}.$$

---

[3] Since – when the result of the scan is positive – there are only two possibilities, namely globoma and popitis, it would be equivalent to ask "what values of p are such that $P(G|+) < \frac{1}{2}$"?

[4] Again, since – when the result of the scan is negative – there are only two possibilities, namely globoma and flapemia, it would be equivalent to ask "what values of p are such that $P(G|-) < \frac{1}{2}$"?

Thus, what we want is: $\frac{0.8(1-p)}{0.8(1-p)+0.1} < \frac{0.1}{0.8(1-p)+0.1}$ which is equivalent to $p > \frac{7}{8} = 87.5\%$.

In conclusion, the answer to the question

> What values of $p = P(+|G)$ are such that it is *possible* that the ET scan *might* induce the doctor to make a different treatment decision (after learning the result of the scan), relative to the decision that she would make without performing the scan (which is to treat globoma)?

is

$$\text{either } P(+|G) < \tfrac{1}{8} \text{ or } P(+|G) > \tfrac{7}{8}. \tag{9.1}$$

If $P(+|G) < \frac{1}{8}$ then there is the possibility that the ET scan will induce the doctor not to treat globoma: this happens if the result of the test is positive, in which case the doctor will prescribe a treatment for popitis (on the other hand, if the result is negative then the doctor will treat globoma, as she would in the absence of a scan: see Exercise 9.1a); similarly, if $P(+|G) > \frac{7}{8}$, then the doctor will react to a negative scan result by prescribing a treatment for flapemia (while, if the result is positive, she will treat globoma: see Exercise 9.1b).

If $P(+|G)$ satisfies one of the conditions in (9.1) then the ET scan is *potentially valuable*, in the sense that there is at least one possible item of information that would induce the doctor to take a different action than the one she would take without information. Should the doctor then prescribe the test in such cases? The answer to this question depends on how the cost of the test compares to the potential benefit of choosing what is judged to be the best treatment.

Typically, the cost of a test is easy to measure: it can be quantified as a sum of money. How can one quantify the potential benefit of the test? In other words, how can one measure the value of information? The rest of this chapter will examine this issue.

> Test your understanding of the concepts introduced in this section, by going through the exercises in Section 9.5.1 at the end of this chapter.

9.2 The value of information when outcomes are sums of money

When the possible outcomes are sums of money, it is relative easy to compute the value of information. We shall look at several situations.

9.2.1 Perfect information and risk neutrality

There is one situation where computing the value of information is particularly easy: when the decision maker (*DM*) is risk neutral and information is perfect. Thus, we shall start with this case.

Suppose that you are risk neutral and that you have two investment opportunities: A and B which will yield the following changes in your wealth (gains/losses):

probability	$\frac{2}{10}$	$\frac{5}{10}$	$\frac{3}{10}$
state →	s_1	s_2	s_3
act ↓			
A	(-20)	$100	$10
B	$200	$10	$20

Your initial wealth is $100. First of all, *in the absence of further information, you will choose B*. This can be seen by either framing the problem in terms of total wealth or in terms of changes in wealth (note that we are computing expected values, since your are risk neutral):

- **In terms of total wealth.** $\mathbb{E}[A] = \frac{2}{10}(100-20) + \frac{5}{10}(100+100) + \frac{3}{10}(100+10) = \$149$ and $\mathbb{E}(B) = \frac{2}{10}(100+200) + \frac{5}{10}(100+10) + \frac{3}{10}(100+20) = \boxed{\$151}$.

- **In terms of changes in wealth.** $\mathbb{E}[A] = \frac{2}{10}(-20) + \frac{5}{10}(100) + \frac{3}{10}(10) = \$49$ and $\mathbb{E}[B] = \frac{2}{10}(200) + \frac{5}{10}(10) + \frac{3}{10}(20) = \boxed{\$51}$.

When the DM is risk neutral the two methods (total wealth and changes in wealth) are equivalent; in other words, *the initial wealth is irrelevant*. We will thus perform calculations in terms of changes in wealth.

Suppose now that, *before making your investment decision*, you have the opportunity to consult an expert. In exchange for an up-front fee of $x the expert will correctly tell you what the true state is. Thus, the information offered by the expert can be viewed as the finest partition of the set of states $\{s_1, s_2, s_3\}$, namely $\{\{s_1\}, \{s_2\}, \{s_3\}\}$. That is, we are in the case of perfect information (see Definition 8.1 in Chapter 8). If you choose to hire the expert, then you can wait for the expert to tell you what the state is and make your investment decision accordingly. The fee of $x has to be paid before the expert provides you with information about the state. *What is the largest amount $x that you would be willing to pay for consulting the expert?*

You can think ahead and see what investment decision you would make, *conditional on the information provided by the expert*.

- If the expert tells you that the true state is s_1 then you will choose investment B and make a profit of $200.
- If the expert tells you that the true state is s_2 then you will choose investment A and make a profit of $100.

- If the expert tells you that the true state is s_3 then you will choose investment B and make a profit of $20.

Of course, you don't know now what the expert will tell you later! However, *according to your initial beliefs*, the probability that the true state is s_1 – and thus that the expert will tell you so – is $\frac{2}{10}$; similarly, you assign probability $\frac{5}{10}$ to the expert telling you that the state is s_2 and probability $\frac{3}{10}$ to the expert telling you that the true state is s_3. Hence, you can compute your *expected net profit* from consulting the expert for a fee of $\$x$ as follows:[5]

$$\tfrac{2}{10}(200-x) + \tfrac{5}{10}(100-x) + \tfrac{3}{10}(20-x) = \boxed{96-x}.$$

Since the profit you expect if you act without consulting the expert (and thus making your optimal decision, which – as shown above – is to select investment B) is $\$51$,

- if $96 - x > 51$, that is, if $x < 45$, then it pays to consult the expert,
- if $96 - x < 51$, that is, if $x > 45$, then you are better off not consulting the expert,
- if $96 - x = 51$, that is, if $x = 45$, then you are indifferent between consulting and not consulting the expert.

Thus, we can conclude that *the maximum amount that you are willing to pay for the information provided by the expert is $\$45$*.[6] In other words, *the value of the information provided by the expert is $\$45$*.

The reasoning above can be seen as an instance of *backward induction* (see Chapter 4). To make this more transparent, we will now analyse a second example by constructing a decision tree.

Ann, who is risk neutral, faces the following decision problem (as before, the sums of money are changes in wealth):

	probability	$\frac{2}{8}$	$\frac{4}{8}$	$\frac{2}{8}$
	state →	s_1	s_2	s_3
act ↓				
A		$4	$36	$49
B		$64	$81	$9
C		$25	$100	$16

Ann can either make her decision now or consult an expert, who will provide her with perfect information about the state. If she decides to consult the expert, then she will be able to condition her choice of action on what she learned from the expert. The expert charges an up-front fee of $\$x$. For what values of x is it in her interest to consult the expert?

---

[5] This calculation is carried out in terms of changes in wealth. The calculation in terms of total wealth is: $\tfrac{2}{10}(100+200-x) + \tfrac{5}{10}(100+100-x) + \tfrac{3}{10}(100+20-x) = 196-x$.
[6] In terms of total wealth one would compare $\$(196-x)$ (see Footnote 5) with $\$151$ and obtain the same conclusion.

9.2 The value of information when outcomes are sums of money

We can represent Ann's decision problem as a decision tree as shown in Figure 9.1, where the double edges represent the optimal decisions conditional on the information received.

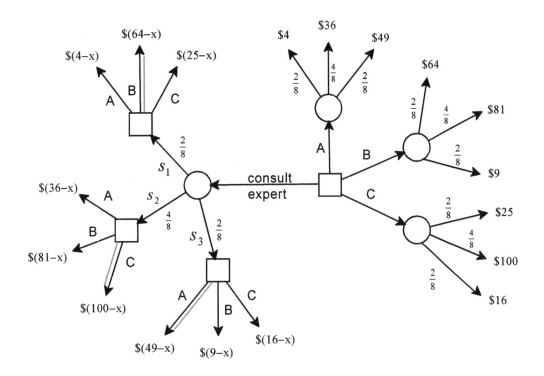

Figure 9.1: Ann's decision problem

Using backward induction, we can

- replace the lottery corresponding to taking action A (without consulting the expert), namely $\begin{pmatrix} \$4 & \$36 & \$49 \\ \frac{2}{8} & \frac{4}{8} & \frac{2}{8} \end{pmatrix}$ with its expected value (recall that Ann is risk neutral):

$$\tfrac{2}{8}(4) + \tfrac{4}{8}(36) + \tfrac{2}{8}(49) = 31.25,$$

- replace the lottery corresponding to taking action B (without consulting the expert), namely $\begin{pmatrix} \$64 & \$81 & \$9 \\ \frac{2}{8} & \frac{4}{8} & \frac{2}{8} \end{pmatrix}$ with its expected value: $\tfrac{2}{8}(64) + \tfrac{4}{8}(81) + \tfrac{2}{8}(9) = 58.75$,

- replace the lottery corresponding to taking action C (without consulting the expert), namely $\begin{pmatrix} \$25 & \$100 & \$16 \\ \frac{2}{8} & \frac{4}{8} & \frac{2}{8} \end{pmatrix}$ with its expected value: $\frac{2}{8}(25) + \frac{4}{8}(100) + \frac{2}{8}(16) = 60.25$,

- replace the decision nodes following each piece of information provided by the expert with the corresponding optimal decision (B if s_1, C if s_2 and A if s_3) and thus reduce the decision to consult the expert to the lottery

$$\begin{pmatrix} \$(64-x) & \$(100-x) & \$(49-x) \\ \frac{2}{8} & \frac{4}{8} & \frac{2}{8} \end{pmatrix}$$

and then replace the lottery with its expected value, namely $78.25 - x$.

Thus, the initial decision tree can be reduced to the tree shown in Figure 9.2 on the following page.

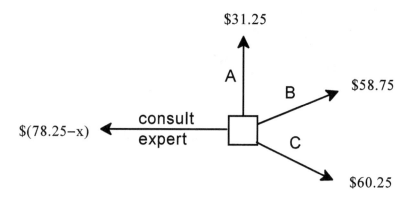

Figure 9.2: The simplified tree of Figure 9.1

It is clear from Figure 9.2 that
- if $78.25 - x < 60.25$, that is, if $x > 18$, then it is best for Ann not to consult the expert (and take action C),
- if $78.25 - x > 60.25$, that is, if $x < 18$, then it is in Ann's interest to consult the expert (and then take the action appropriate for the information provided by the expert: B if s_1, C if s_2 and A if s_3),
- if $78.25 - x = 60.25$, that is, if $x = 18$, then Ann is indifferent between consulting and not consulting the expert.

Thus, the maximum amount that Ann would be willing to pay for the expert's services is $18.

9.2 The value of information when outcomes are sums of money

9.2.2 Perfect information and risk aversion

In this section we continue to assume that outcomes are sums of money and there is perfect information but we drop the assumption of risk neutrality. We shall re-examine the two examples of Section 9.2.1 under the hypothesis that the *DM* is risk averse; more precisely, we assume that the *DM* satisfies the axioms of Expected Utility Theory and that her von Neuman-Morgenstern utility-of-money function is $U(\$x) = \sqrt{x}$.

In the first example, the *DM* is facing two investment opportunities: *A* and *B* which will yield the following changes in her wealth (gains/losses):

probability	$\frac{2}{10}$	$\frac{5}{10}$	$\frac{3}{10}$
state →	s_1	s_2	s_3
act ↓			
A	(-20)	$100	$10
B	$200	$10	$20

When the *DM* is not risk neutral it is no longer valid to perform calculations in terms of changes in wealth.[7] Thus, we will consider total wealth, assuming that the *DM*'s initial wealth is $100. First we determine the optimal decision in the absence of information (that is, if the *DM* does not consult the expert).

- The expected utility of choosing investment *A* is
$$\mathbb{E}[U(A)] = \tfrac{2}{10}\sqrt{100-20} + \tfrac{5}{10}\sqrt{100+100} + \tfrac{3}{10}\sqrt{100+10} = \boxed{12.0063}.$$

- The expected utility of choosing investment *B* is
$$\mathbb{E}[U(B)] = \tfrac{2}{10}\sqrt{100+200} + \tfrac{5}{10}\sqrt{100+10} + \tfrac{3}{10}\sqrt{100+20} = 11.9945.$$

Thus, in the absence of information, the *DM* would choose investment *A*.[8]

Suppose now that the *DM* can pay $x up front to obtain perfect information. Then it is clear that if informed that the state is s_1 she will choose *B*, if informed that the state is s_2 she will choose *A* and if informed that the state is s_3 she will choose *B*. Thus,

- the *DM*'s expected utility from availing herself of perfect information is

$$\tfrac{2}{10}\sqrt{100+200-x} + \tfrac{5}{10}\sqrt{100+100-x} + \tfrac{3}{10}\sqrt{100+20-x}$$
$$= \frac{2\sqrt{300-x} + 5\sqrt{200-x} + 3\sqrt{120-x}}{10}.$$

Call the above expression $f(x)$:

$$f(x) = \frac{2\sqrt{300-x} + 5\sqrt{200-x} + 3\sqrt{120-x}}{10}.$$

The maximum amount that the *DM* is willing to pay for perfect information is that value of x that solves the equation $f(x) = 12.0063$ (12.0063 is the utility that she gets if she does not consult the expert and takes the corresponding optimal action, which is *A*). This is not an easy equation to solve. However, we can try two significant values of the function $f(x)$.

---

[7]Furthermore, if one were to try to compute the utility of the outcome that occurs if the *DM* takes action *A* and the state is s_1 one would have to take the square root of a negative number!

[8]This is in contrast to what a risk-neutral person would do, which – as determined in Section 9.2.1 – is to choose investment *B*.

First of all, if we set $x = 0$ then we get that $f(0) = 13.8215$, showing that – if information is free – then the *DM* will definitely want it (without information her expected utility is 12.0063, with free information her expected utility is 13.8215). The other interesting value is $x = 45$, because \$45 is the maximum amount that a risk-neutral person would be willing to pay for perfect information (as shown in Section 9.2.1). Now, $f(45) = 12.0168$ implying that the *DM* is *strictly better off* paying \$45 for perfect information: $12.0168 > 12.0063$. Thus, the solution to the equation $f(x) = 12.0063$ is a number *greater than* 45.[9] Thus, our risk-averse person is willing to pay more for perfect information than the risk-neutral person.

Let us now revisit the second example of Section 9.2.1 where the decision problem was as follows (as before, the sums of money represent changes in wealth):

probability	$\frac{2}{8}$	$\frac{4}{8}$	$\frac{2}{8}$
state →	s_1	s_2	s_3
act ↓			
A	\$4	\$36	\$49
B	\$64	\$81	\$9
C	\$25	\$100	\$16

We represented this decision problem as a tree in Figure 9.1. In Section 9.2.1 we focused on the case of risk-neutrality. Here we want to continue looking at the case of a risk-averse *DM* whose von Neumann-Morgenstern utility-of-money function is $U(\$x) = \sqrt{x}$. To make calculations easy, let us assume that *the DM's initial wealth is zero*, so that changes in wealth and total wealth coincide (in Exercise 9.6 the reader is asked to look at a case with positive initial wealth). We can re-draw Figure 9.1 by replacing monetary outcomes with the corresponding utilities (for example, outcome \$64 is replaced with a utility of $\sqrt{64} = 8$). The re-drawn tree is shown in Figure 9.3.

Let us now consider a particular value of x (which is the fee charged by the expert). Let us take the value $x = 20$. We know from Section 9.2.1 that the maximum amount that a risk-neutral person would be willing to pay for perfect information is \$18, so that if $x = 20$ a risk-neutral *DM* would choose *not* to hire the expert. What about our risk-averse *DM*? Using backward induction we can replace the lotteries corresponding to taking (with no information) actions *A*, *B* and *C*, respectively, with their expected utilities which are:

- For A: $\frac{2}{8}(2) + \frac{4}{8}(6) + \frac{2}{8}(7) = 5.25$,
- for B: $\frac{2}{8}(8) + \frac{4}{8}(9) + \frac{2}{8}(3) = 7.25$,
- for C: $\frac{2}{8}(5) + \frac{4}{8}(10) + \frac{2}{8}(4) = 7.25$,

so that, in the absence of information, the *DM* would choose either action *B* or action *C* and get an expected utility of 7.25.

---

[9]This footnote is for the mathematically sophisticated reader. First one can show that the function $f(x)$ is strictly decreasing in x by calculating the first derivative: $\frac{d}{dx}\left(\frac{2\sqrt{300-x}+5\sqrt{200-x}+3\sqrt{120-x}}{10}\right) = -\frac{1}{10\sqrt{300-x}} - \frac{1}{4\sqrt{200-x}} - \frac{3}{20\sqrt{120-x}}$, which is negative for every meaningful value of x (that is, for $x \leq 120$). Hence, since $f(45) > 12.0063$, the solution to the equation $f(x) = 12.0063$ is greater than 45. Indeed, the solution is $x = 45.2397$.

9.2 The value of information when outcomes are sums of money

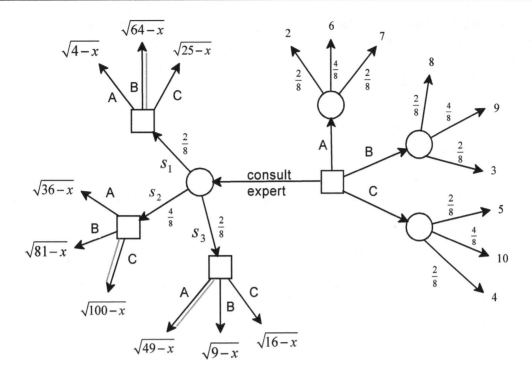

Figure 9.3: The tree of Figure 9.1 with utilities instead of sums of money

On the other hand, the expected utility of paying $20 for perfect information is

- $\frac{2}{8}\sqrt{64-20} + \frac{4}{8}\sqrt{100-20} + \frac{2}{8}\sqrt{49-20} = 7.4767$.

The reduced tree is shown in Figure 9.4.

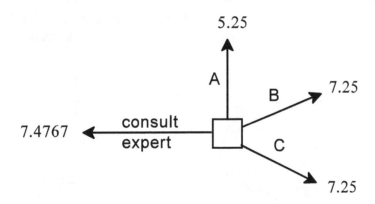

Figure 9.4: The reduced tree of Figure 9.3

Thus, *DM* would be willing to pay $20 for perfect information. Indeed, the maximum amount that our *DM* would be willing to pay for perfect information must be greater than $20 (while a risk-neutral person would not go beyond $18).[10]

---

[10]The maximum amount that the *DM* would be willing to pay for perfect information is $23.18. In fact, $\frac{2}{8}\sqrt{64-23.18} + \frac{4}{8}\sqrt{100-23.18} + \frac{2}{8}\sqrt{49-23.18} = 7.25$.

In Section 9.5.1 we considered the case of perfect information and risk neutrality and in this section the case of perfect information and risk aversion. What about the case of risk loving? We shall not discuss the case of risk loving because the logic is exactly the same as in the case of risk aversion: all that changes is the utility function. In Exercise 9.9 the reader is asked to analyze a case of perfect information where the *DM* is risk loving.

9.2.3 Imperfect information

So far we have considered the value of perfect information. In this section, while continuing to assume that outcomes are sums of money, we turn to the case of imperfect information, which arises when the partition that represents the possible items of information has at least one element containing two or more states.

Consider the following decision problem, where the amounts are changes in wealth (gains/losses):

probability	$\frac{1}{3}$	$\frac{1}{12}$	$\frac{1}{6}$	$\frac{1}{4}$	$\frac{1}{6}$
state →	s_1	s_2	s_3	s_4	s_5
act ↓					
a	$56	$376	$64	$36	$284
b	$89	$200	$100	$241	$25
c	$124	$161	$(-4)	$25	$376

Consider first the case where the *DM* is risk neutral. Then, as we saw above, the *DM*'s initial wealth is irrelevant and we can carry out the analysis in terms of changes in wealth. First of all, let us determine what the *DM* would do in the absence of further information. The expected values of the lotteries associated with the three actions are:

$$\mathbb{E}[a] = \tfrac{1}{3}56 + \tfrac{1}{12}376 + \tfrac{1}{6}64 + \tfrac{1}{4}36 + \tfrac{1}{6}284 = 117,$$

$$\mathbb{E}[b] = \tfrac{1}{3}89 + \tfrac{1}{12}200 + \tfrac{1}{6}100 + \tfrac{1}{4}241 + \tfrac{1}{6}25 = \boxed{127.4167},$$

$$\mathbb{E}[c] = \tfrac{1}{3}124 + \tfrac{1}{12}161 + \tfrac{1}{6}(-4) + \tfrac{1}{4}25 + \tfrac{1}{6}376 = 123.$$

Thus, in the absence of information, the DM would choose action b.

9.2 The value of information when outcomes are sums of money

Suppose that the *DM* has the opportunity to pay $\$x$ now to have an expert give her some information about the state later (so that the *DM* will be able to make a more informed decision about what action to take). The expert will not be able to give the *DM* perfect information: he will only be able to let her know whether the state is (1) either s_1 or s_2 (one piece of information) or (2) neither s_1 nor s_2 (the other possible piece of information).

Thus, the information that the expert is offering the *DM* is represented by the partition $\{\{s_1, s_2\}, \{s_3, s_4, s_5\}\}$. The *DM* can look ahead and figure out what she would do after receiving each piece of information.

- If given information $\{s_1, s_2\}$ the *DM* would, first of all, have to update her beliefs. Using Bayes' rule her updated beliefs would be $\begin{smallmatrix} s_1 & s_2 & s_3 & s_4 & s_5 \\ \frac{4}{5} & \frac{1}{5} & 0 & 0 & 0 \end{smallmatrix}$ or, written more succinctly, $\begin{smallmatrix} s_1 & s_2 \\ \frac{4}{5} & \frac{1}{5} \end{smallmatrix}$. Given these updated beliefs, the decision problem would become

probability	$\frac{4}{5}$	$\frac{1}{5}$
state →	s_1	s_2
act ↓		
a	$\$(56-x)$	$\$(376-x)$
b	$\$(89-x)$	$\$(200-x)$
c	$\$(124-x)$	$\$(161-x)$

so that

$$\mathbb{E}[a] = \tfrac{4}{5}(56-x) + \tfrac{1}{5}(376-x) = 120 - x,$$

$$\mathbb{E}[b] = \tfrac{4}{5}(89-x) + \tfrac{1}{5}(200-x) = 111.2 - x,$$

$$\mathbb{E}[c] = \tfrac{4}{5}(124-x) + \tfrac{1}{5}(161-x) = \boxed{131.4 - x}.$$

Thus, if informed that $\{s_1, s_2\}$ the DM would choose action c.

- If given information $\{s_3, s_4, s_5\}$ the *DM* would, first of all, have to update her beliefs. Using Bayes' rule her updated beliefs would be $\begin{smallmatrix} s_3 & s_4 & s_5 \\ \frac{2}{7} & \frac{3}{7} & \frac{2}{7} \end{smallmatrix}$. Given these updated beliefs, the decision problem would become

probability	$\frac{2}{7}$	$\frac{3}{7}$	$\frac{2}{7}$
state →	s_3	s_4	s_5
act ↓			
a	$\$(64-x)$	$\$(36-x)$	$\$(284-x)$
b	$\$(100-x)$	$\$(241-x)$	$\$(25-x)$
c	$\$(-4-x)$	$\$(25-x)$	$\$(376-x)$

so that

$$\mathbb{E}[a] = \tfrac{2}{7}(64-x) + \tfrac{3}{7}(36-x) + \tfrac{2}{7}(284-x) = 114.8571 - x,$$

$$\mathbb{E}[b] = \tfrac{2}{7}(100-x) + \tfrac{3}{7}(241-x) + \tfrac{2}{7}(25-x) = \boxed{139-x},$$

$$\mathbb{E}[c] = \tfrac{2}{7}(-4-x) + \tfrac{3}{7}(25-x) + \tfrac{2}{7}(376-x) = 117 - x.$$

Thus, if informed that $\{s_3, s_4, s_5\}$ the DM would choose action b.

What is the *DM*'s expected utility of availing herself of the offered information? Given her initial beliefs, the probability that she will be informed that $\{s_1, s_2\}$ is $\tfrac{1}{3} + \tfrac{1}{12} = \tfrac{5}{12}$ and the probability that she will be informed that $\{s_3, s_4, s_5\}$ is $\tfrac{1}{6} + \tfrac{1}{4} + \tfrac{1}{6} = \tfrac{7}{12}$. Thus, she can compute her expected utility from paying x for the information as follows:

$$\frac{5}{12} \underbrace{(131.4-x)}_{\text{utility from taking action } c} + \frac{7}{12} \underbrace{(139-x)}_{\text{utility from taking action } b} = 135.8333 - x$$

Thus, since the maximum expected utility that the *DM* gets without information is 127.4167 (by taking action b),

- If $135.8333 - x > 127.42$, that is, if $x < 8.413$, then the *DM* is better off hiring the expert,
- if $135.8333 - x < 127.42$, that is, if $x > 8.413$, then the *DM* is better off not hiring the expert,
- if $135.8333 - x = 127.42$, that is, if $x = 8.413$, then the *DM* is indifferent between hiring and not hiring the expert.

Thus, the maximum price that the *DM* is willing to pay for information

$$\{\{s_1, s_2\}, \{s_3, s_4, s_5\}\}$$

is \$8.41.

It should be clear that, once again, what we have done is to apply the method of backward induction. To make this more transparent, we can represent the decision problem as a tree, as shown in Figure 9.5. Applying backward induction with the calculations shown in Figure 9.5, we can reduce the tree as shown in Figure 9.6.

9.2 The value of information when outcomes are sums of money

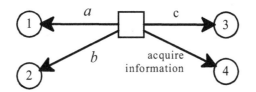

With the following modules:

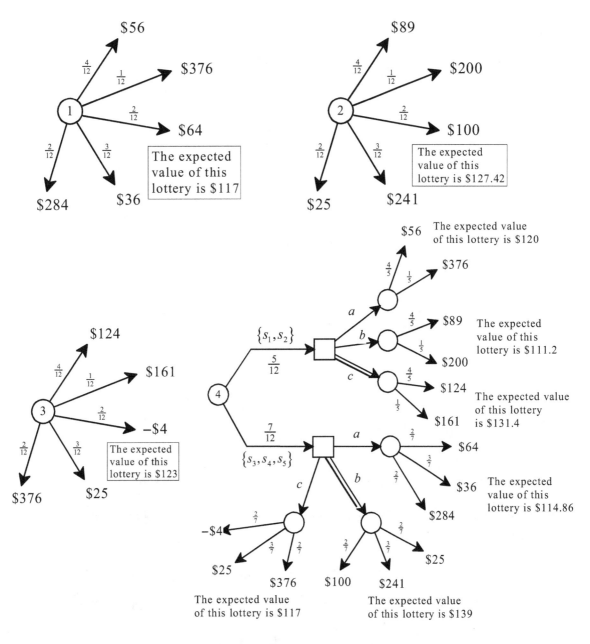

Figure 9.5: The decision problem represented as a tree

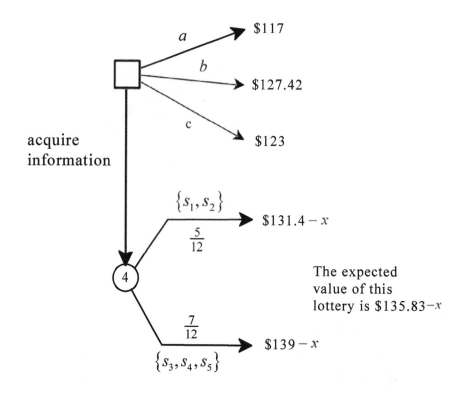

Figure 9.6: The reduced version of the tree of Figure 9.5

Let us now analyze the above decision problem from the point of view of a risk-averse *DM* whose von Neumann-Morgenstern utility-of-money function is $U(\$x) = \sqrt{x}$ and whose initial wealth is \$200. The decision problem expressed in terms of changes in wealth (gains/losses) is as before, namely:

probability	$\frac{4}{12}$	$\frac{1}{12}$	$\frac{2}{12}$	$\frac{3}{12}$	$\frac{2}{12}$
state →	s_1	s_2	s_3	s_4	s_5
act ↓					
a	\$56	\$376	\$64	\$36	\$284
b	\$89	\$200	\$100	\$241	\$25
c	\$124	\$161	−\$4	\$25	\$376

In the absence of information, the expected utility of the lottery associated with each action is (recall that the *DM*'s initial wealth is \$200):

$$\mathbb{E}[U(a)] = \tfrac{4}{12}\sqrt{256} + \tfrac{1}{12}\sqrt{576} + \tfrac{2}{12}\sqrt{264} + \tfrac{3}{12}\sqrt{236} + \tfrac{2}{12}\sqrt{484} = 17.55,$$

$$\mathbb{E}[U(b)] = \tfrac{4}{12}\sqrt{289} + \tfrac{1}{12}\sqrt{400} + \tfrac{2}{12}\sqrt{300} + \tfrac{3}{12}\sqrt{441} + \tfrac{2}{12}\sqrt{225} = \boxed{17.97},$$

$$\mathbb{E}[U(c)] = \tfrac{4}{12}\sqrt{324} + \tfrac{1}{12}\sqrt{361} + \tfrac{2}{12}\sqrt{196} + \tfrac{3}{12}\sqrt{225} + \tfrac{2}{12}\sqrt{576} = 17.67.$$

Thus, in the absence of information the DM would choose b.

9.2 The value of information when outcomes are sums of money

As before, suppose that the *DM* is offered information represented by the partition $\{\{s_1,s_2\},\{s_3,s_4,s_5\}\}$. Let the up-front fee charged by the expert be $8.50 (an amount that, as we saw above, a risk neutral person would *not* be willing to pay). If the *DM* decides to hire the expert, then her choice of action will depend on what piece of information she gets from the expert.

- If given information $\{s_1,s_2\}$ the *DM*'s updated beliefs are $\begin{array}{cc} s_1 & s_2 \\ \frac{4}{5} & \frac{1}{5} \end{array}$. Given these updated beliefs, the decision problem becomes

probability	$\frac{4}{5}$	$\frac{1}{5}$
state →	s_1	s_2
act ↓		
a	$(256 − 8.5)	$(576 − 8.5)
b	$(289 − 8.5)	$(400 − 8.5)
c	$(324 − 8.5)	$(361 − 8.5)

so that

$$\mathbb{E}[U(a)] = \tfrac{4}{5}\sqrt{256-8.5} + \tfrac{1}{5}\sqrt{576-8.5} = 17.3502,$$

$$\mathbb{E}[U(b)] = \tfrac{4}{5}\sqrt{289-8.5} + \tfrac{1}{5}\sqrt{400-8.5} = 17.3558,$$

$$\mathbb{E}[U(c)] = \tfrac{4}{5}\sqrt{324-8.5} + \tfrac{1}{5}\sqrt{361-8.5} = \boxed{17.9649}.$$

Thus, if informed that $\{s_1,s_2\}$ the DM would choose action c.

- If given information $\{s_3,s_4,s_5\}$ the *DM*'s updated beliefs are $\begin{array}{ccc} s_3 & s_4 & s_5 \\ \frac{2}{7} & \frac{3}{7} & \frac{2}{7} \end{array}$. Given these updated beliefs, the decision problem becomes

probability	$\frac{2}{7}$	$\frac{3}{7}$	$\frac{2}{7}$
state →	s_3	s_4	s_5
act ↓			
a	$(264 − 8.5)	$(236 − 8.5)	$(484 − 8.5)
b	$(300 − 8.5)	$(441 − 8.5)	$(225 − 8.5)
c	$(196 − 8.5)	$(225 − 8.5)	$(576 − 8.5)

so that

$$\mathbb{E}[U(a)] = \tfrac{2}{7}\sqrt{264-8.5} + \tfrac{3}{7}\sqrt{236-8.5} + \tfrac{2}{7}\sqrt{484-8.5} = 17.2614,$$

$$\mathbb{E}[U(b)] = \tfrac{2}{7}\sqrt{300-8.5} + \tfrac{3}{7}\sqrt{441-8.5} + \tfrac{2}{7}\sqrt{225-8.5} = \boxed{17.9949},$$

$$\mathbb{E}[U(c)] = \tfrac{2}{7}\sqrt{196-8.5} + \tfrac{3}{7}\sqrt{225-8.5} + \tfrac{2}{7}\sqrt{576-8.5}) = 17.0246.$$

Thus, if informed that $\{s_3,s_4,s_5\}$ the DM would choose action b.

Given the *DM*'s initial beliefs, the probability that she will be informed that $\{s_1,s_2\}$ is $\frac{5}{12}$ and the probability that she will be informed that $\{s_3,s_4,s_5\}$ is $\frac{7}{12}$. Thus, she can compute her expected utility from paying $8.5 for the information as

$$\frac{5}{12}\underbrace{17.9649}_{\text{utility from taking action } c} + \frac{7}{12}\underbrace{17.9949}_{\text{utility from taking action } b} = 17.9824$$

which is greater than 17.97 (the maximum expected utility that the *DM* gets without information, by taking action *b*). Hence, the *DM* is better off hiring the expert.

Also in this section we restricted attention to risk neutrality and risk aversion. What about the case of risk loving? Since the logic is exactly the same as in the case of risk aversion (one just uses a different utility function), we shall not discuss risk loving. In Exercise 9.10 the reader is asked to analyze a case of imperfect information where the *DM* is risk loving.

> Test your understanding of the concepts introduced in this section, by going through the exercises in Section 9.5.2 at the end of this chapter.

9.3 The general case

In the general case, where outcomes are not sums of money, it may be more difficult to calculate the value of information. However, it is relatively simple to compare the option of not availing oneself of information to the option of acquiring information *at a specified cost*. In this section we show how one would go about doing so.

Let us go back to the example of the fictional diseases considered in Section 9.1. The patient is informed that there are three possible causes of his symptoms: globoma, popitis and flapemia, and that past data suggests that the probabilities are as follows:

disease	Globoma (G)	Popitis (P)	Flapemia (F)
probability	0.8	0.1	0.1

The patient is also told that he can treat only one disease and that a drug targeted to one disease is ineffective against the other two. If the chosen drug matches the actual disease, the patient will be cured, otherwise all his symptoms will remain. To make things simple, let us assume that, after a failed attempt to treat a disease, it would be too dangerous for the patient to try another drug, targeted to a different disease. Finally, the patient is told that he can undergo an ET scan, for which he will have to pay K. The result of the scan can be positive (+) or negative (−) and the conditional probabilities are as follows:[11]

$$P(+|G) = 0.1 \quad P(-|G) = 0.9$$
$$P(+|P) = 1 \quad P(-|P) = 0$$
$$P(+|F) = 0 \quad P(-|F) = 1$$

The patient's initial wealth is W (with $W > K$). Let us represent the patient's decision problem in terms of states, acts and outcomes. We can think of a state as a pair (x, y) where x is the disease that the patient has (thus, x is either G or P or F) and y is the result of the scan if it were to be taken (thus, y is either + or −). For example, $(G, -)$ is the state where the patient has disease G *and* if he takes the scan then the result will be negative. Using the doctor's initial assessment and the given conditional probabilities we can compute the probabilities of all the states. By the conditional probability rule, $P(+|G) = \frac{P(G,+)}{P(G)}$ so that $P(G,+) = P(+|G) \times P(G) = 0.1 \times 0.8 = 0.08$. Similarly, $P(G,-) = 0.9 \times 0.8 = 0.72$, etc. Thus, the probabilities are as follows:

state:	(G,+)	(G,−)	(P,+)	(P,−)	(F,+)	(F,−)
probability:	0.08	0.72	0.1	0	0	0.1

---
[11] Note that $P(+|G) < \frac{1}{8}$ and thus the scan is potentially valuable, as shown in Section 9.1.

9.3 The general case

We will ignore the two states that have zero probability and thus let the set of states be $\{(G,+),(G,-),(P,+),(F,-)\}$:

state:	$(G,+)$	$(G,-)$	$(P,+)$	$(F,-)$
probability:	0.08	0.72	0.1	0.1

There are many possible plans of action for the patient, but some of them do not make sense. For example, the plan to take the scan and then treat F if the scan is positive and treat P if the scan is negative is doomed to failure: there is no state where the plan manages to treat the patient's actual disease. However, for completeness, we will list all the possible plans of action; we will then show that half of them should be dropped because they are dominated. There are twelve possible plans of action ($\neg S$ means 'do not take the scan', S means 'take the scan', G means 'treat disease G', etc.):

$(\neg S, G)$:	Do not take the scan and treat disease G
$(\neg S, P)$:	Do not take the scan and treat disease P
$(\neg S, F)$:	Do not take the scan and treat disease F
(S, G) :	Scan and treat G no matter whether the scan is + or −
(S, P) :	Scan and treat P no matter whether the scan is + or −
(S, F) :	Scan and treat F no matter whether the scan is + or −
$(S, G+, P-)$:	Scan and treat G if scan is + and P if scan is −
$(S, G+, F-)$:	Scan and treat G if scan is + and F if scan is −
$(S, P+, G-)$:	Scan and treat P if scan is + and G if scan is −
$(S, P+, F-)$:	Scan and treat P if scan is + and F if scan is −
$(S, F+, G-)$:	Scan and treat F if scan is + and G if scan is −
$(S, F+, P-)$:	Scan and treat F if scan is + and P if scan is −

To complete the representation of the decision problem we need to specify what a possible outcome is. We can represent an outcome as a pair (x,y) where x is either c for 'cured' or $\neg c$ for 'not cured' and y is the level of the patient's wealth, which is $\$W$ if he does not take the scan and $\$(W-K)$ if he takes the scan. It is natural to assume that the patient values both his health and his wealth. That is,

- conditional on the same level of wealth, he prefers to be cured than to remain sick:

$$(c, W) \succ (\neg c, W) \quad \text{and} \quad (c, W-K) \succ (\neg c, W-K) \tag{9.2}$$

- conditional on the same state of health, he prefers more money to less:

$$(c, W) \succ (c, W-K) \quad \text{and} \quad (\neg c, W) \succ (\neg c, W-K). \tag{9.3}$$

This is not a full specification of the patient's preferences, but it is sufficient to show that six plans of action are dominated. Consider the following reduced representation of the decision problem, where we have written only some of the acts (or plans of action):

state → act ↓	$(G,+)$	$(G,-)$	$(P,+)$	$(F,-)$
$(\neg S, G)$	(c, W)	(c, W)	$(\neg c, W)$	$(\neg c, W)$
$(\neg S, P)$	$(\neg c, W)$	$(\neg c, W)$	(c, W)	$(\neg c, W)$
$(\neg S, F)$	$(\neg c, W)$	$(\neg c, W)$	$(\neg c, W)$	(c, W)
(S, G)	$(c, W-K)$	$(c, W-K)$	$(\neg c, W-K)$	$(\neg c, W-K)$
(S, P)	$(\neg c, W-K)$	$(\neg c, W-K)$	$(c, W-K)$	$(\neg c, W-K)$
(S, F)	$(\neg c, W-K)$	$(\neg c, W-K)$	$(\neg c, W-K)$	$(c, W-K)$

It is clear that, by (9.2) and (9.3),

- (S, G) is strictly dominated by $(\neg S, G)$ (same health outcome but less wealth in each state),
- (S, P) is strictly dominated by $(\neg S, P)$ (same health outcome but less wealth in each state),
- (S, F) is strictly dominated by $(\neg S, F)$ (same health outcome but less wealth in each state).

Thus, we can drop three acts $((S, G), (S, P)$ and $(S, F))$ from consideration. Now consider the following subset of acts:

state $\rightarrow$	$(G, +)$	$(G, -)$	$(P, +)$	$(F, -)$
act $\downarrow$				
$(S, G+, P-)$	$(c, W-K)$	$(\neg c, W-K)$	$(\neg c, W-K)$	$(\neg c, W-K)$
$(S, G+, F-)$	$(c, W-K)$	$(\neg c, W-K)$	$(\neg c, W-K)$	$(c, W-K)$
$(S, P+, G-)$	$(\neg c, W-K)$	$(c, W-K)$	$(c, W-K)$	$(\neg c, W-K)$
$(S, F+, G-)$	$(\neg c, W-K)$	$(c, W-K)$	$(\neg c, W-K)$	$(\neg c, W-K)$
$(S, F+, P-)$	$(\neg c, W-K)$	$(\neg c, W-K)$	$(\neg c, W-K)$	$(\neg c, W-K)$.

It is clear that, by (9.2) and (9.3),

- $(S, G+, P-)$ is weakly dominated by $(S, G+, F-)$,[12]
- $(S, F+, G-)$ is weakly dominated by $(S, P+, G-)$,
- $(S, F+, P-)$ is weakly dominated by $(S, P+, G-)$.

Thus, we can drop three more acts $((S, G+, P-), (S, F+, G-)$ and $(S, F+, P-))$ from consideration.[13] Hence, we are left with the following reduced decision problem:

probability:	0.08	0.72	0.1	0.1
state $\rightarrow$	$(G, +)$	$(G, -)$	$(P, +)$	$(F, -)$
act $\downarrow$				
$(\neg S, G)$	(c, W)	(c, W)	$(\neg c, W)$	$(\neg c, W)$
$(\neg S, P)$	$(\neg c, W)$	$(\neg c, W)$	(c, W)	$(\neg c, W)$
$(\neg S, F)$	$(\neg c, W)$	$(\neg c, W)$	$(\neg c, W)$	(c, W)
$(S, G+, F-)$	$(c, W-K)$	$(\neg c, W-K)$	$(\neg c, W-K)$	$(c, W-K)$
$(S, P+, F-)$	$(\neg c, W-K)$	$(\neg c, W-K)$	$(c, W-K)$	$(c, W-K)$
$(S, P+, G-)$	$(\neg c, W-K)$	$(c, W-K)$	$(c, W-K)$	$(\neg c, W-K)$

---

[12]$(S, G+, F-)$ yields a better outcome than $(S, G+, P-)$ in state $(F, -)$ and the same outcome in every other state.

[13]Note that if act A is weakly dominated by act B and all the states under consideration have positive probability, then the expected utility of act A is strictly less than the expected utility of act B.

9.3 The general case

In order to proceed, we need to know more about the patient's preferences, in particular, how he ranks the two outcomes $(\neg c, W)$ and $(c, W - K)$: if the patient were guaranteed that an expenditure of \$K$ would lead to his recovery, would he be willing to spend that sum of money? If the answer is No, that is, if $(\neg c, W) \succ (c, W - K)$, then $(S, G+, F-)$ would be strictly dominated by $(\neg S, G)$, $(S, P+, F-)$ would be strictly dominated by $(\neg S, P)$ and $(S, P+, G-)$ would be strictly dominated by $(\neg S, P)$ so that the patient will decide not to take the scan (in which case, as shown below, the best choice is to treat G). Thus, we will assume that $(c, W - K) \succ (\neg c, W)$, that is, the patient would be willing to pay \$K$ to be cured with certainty. Hence, the patient's ranking of the outcomes is:

	outcome
best	(c, W)
	$(c, W - K)$
	$(\neg c, W)$
worst	$(\neg c, W - K)$

If we assume that the patient satisfies the axioms of Expected Utility Theory, we can focus on his normalized von Neumann-Morgenstern utility function, which assigns value 1 to the best outcome and 0 to the worst outcome. We don't have enough information about the other two values, so let us call them p and q, where $p = U(c, W - K)$ and $q = U(\neg c, W)$. Thus, we have that

	outcome	utility	
best	(c, W)	1	
	$(c, W - K)$	p	with $0 < q < p < 1$.
	$(\neg c, W)$	q	
worst	$(\neg c, W - K)$	0	

Then we can rewrite the reduced decision problem in terms of utilities:

probability:	0.08	0.72	0.1	0.1
state →	$(G,+)$	$(G,-)$	$(P,+)$	$(F,-)$
act ↓				
$(\neg S, G)$	1	1	q	q
$(\neg S, P)$	q	q	1	q
$(\neg S, F)$	q	q	q	1
$(S, G+, F-)$	p	0	0	p
$(S, P+, F-)$	0	0	p	p
$(S, P+, G-)$	0	p	p	0

The reader should convince herself/himself that no act is weakly or strictly dominated.[14]

What is the optimal choice for the patient? Let us analyze the decision problem in two steps. First of all, *if* the patient decided to *not* have the scan, what treatment should he choose? We need to compute the following expected utilities:

---

[14]For example, $(S, G+, F-)$ is not dominated because in state $(F, -)$ it is better than $(\neg S, G)$ (since $p > q$) and in state $(G, +)$ it is better than every other act (other than $(\neg S, G)$), since $p > q > 0$.

- $\mathbb{E}[U(\neg S, G)] = 0.8 + 0.2q$,
- $\mathbb{E}[U(\neg S, P)] = 0.1 + 0.9q$,
- $\mathbb{E}[U(\neg S, F)] = 0.1 + 0.9q$.

Since $q < 1$, we have that $0.8 + 0.2q > 0.1 + 0.9q$ and thus – conditional on not taking the scan – the patient should treat G (which makes sense, since – according to the initial beliefs – G is the most likely disease). As a second step, let us see what the patient should do *conditional on taking the scan*. We need to compute the following expected utilities:

- $\mathbb{E}[U(S, G+, F-)] = 0.18p$,
- $\mathbb{E}[U(S, P+, F-)] = 0.2p$,
- $\mathbb{E}[U(S, P+, G-)] = 0.82p$.

Thus, conditional on taking the scan, the best policy is to treat P if the scan is positive and G if the scan is negative. Indeed, as we saw in Section 9.1, the patient's beliefs, updated on the information that the scan is positive, are such that P is the most likely disease and the beliefs updated on the information that the scan is negative are such that G is the most likely disease. Thus, the final step consists in comparing $(\neg S, G)$ and $(S, P+, G-)$. Recall that the expected utilities are:

- $\mathbb{E}[U(\neg S, G)] = 0.8 + 0.2q$,
- $\mathbb{E}[U(S, P+, G-)] = 0.82p$.

Hence, the optimal decision is as follows:

- if $0.8 + 0.2q > 0.82p$, that is, if $p < 0.9756 + 0.2439q$, then the best plan is to not take the scan and treat G,
- if $0.8 + 0.2q < 0.82p$, that is, if $p > 0.9756 + 0.2439q$, then the best plan is to take the scan and then treat P if the scan is positive and treat G if the scan is negative.
- if $0.8 + 0.2q = 0.82p$, that is, if $p = 0.9756 + 0.2439q$, then either of the above two plans is optimal.

To summarize, in order to make his decision, the patient needs to ask himself the following two questions:

1. What value of $r \in (0,1)$ would make me indifferent between the following two lotteries: $\begin{pmatrix} (c,W) & (\neg c, W-K) \\ r & 1-r \end{pmatrix}$ and $\begin{pmatrix} (c, W-K) \\ 1 \end{pmatrix}$? The answer to this question gives the value of p.

2. What value of $s \in (0,1)$ would make me indifferent between the following two lotteries: $\begin{pmatrix} (c,W) & (\neg c, W-K) \\ s & 1-s \end{pmatrix}$ and $\begin{pmatrix} (\neg c, W) \\ 1 \end{pmatrix}$? The answer to this question gives the value of q.

9.4 Different sources of information

If the answer to the second question is a value grater than or equal to 0.1 (so that $q \geq 0.1$) then it is not possible for p to be less than 1 and also greater than $0.9756 + 0.2439\,q$ (since $q \geq 0.1$ implies that $0.9756 + 0.2439\,q \geq 1$) and thus the optimal decision is to not take the scan and treat G: $(\neg S, G)$. If, on the other hand, the answer to the second question is a value less than 0.1 then the optimal decision depends on the answer to the first question.

For example, if the answer to the second question is 0.05 (so that $q = 0.05$) and the answer to the first question is 0.99 (so that $p = 0.99$) then the optimal decision is $(S, P+, G-)$ (take the scan and treat P if positive and G if negative), because $0.99 > 0.9756 + (0.2439)(0.05) = 0.9878$; if the answer to the second question is 0.05 (so that $q = 0.05$) and the answer to the first question is 0.9 (so that $p = 0.9$) then the optimal decision is $(\neg S, G)$ (not take the scan and treat G).

> Test your understanding of the concepts introduced in this section, by going through the exercises in Section 9.5.3 at the end of this chapter.

9.4 Different sources of information

As a way of summarizing the topics considered in this chapter, in this section we will go through an example where the *DM* is faced with two possible sources of information.

A risk-neutral investor faces two alternative investment opportunities. Investment 1 will yield a profit of $\$8,000,000$ if the market conditions are Good (G) and nothing if the market conditions are Bad (B). Investment 2 yields a profit of $\$12,000,000$ if G and a loss of $\$8,000,000$ if B. The probabilities of G and B are p and $(1-p)$, respectively:

	p	$1-p$
	G	B
Investment 1	$\$8M$	0
Investment 2	$\$12M$	$\$(-8M)$

The expected return from Investment 1 is $8p + 0(1-p) = 8p$ and the expected return from Investment 2 is $12p - 8(1-p) = 20p - 8$. Note that, $8p > 20p - 8$ if and only if $p < \frac{2}{3}$. Thus, in the absence of further information, the *DM* will:

- choose Investment 1 if $p < \frac{2}{3}$,
- choose Investment 2 if $p > \frac{2}{3}$,
- choose either one if $p = \frac{2}{3}$.

198   Chapter 9. The Value of Information

Suppose now that, before the investment takes place, the investor can consult one of two experts. One is Expert A, who always correctly forecasts G but is as reliable as a coin toss when it comes to B (that is, she gets it right 50% of the time). That is, letting A_G stand for "Expert A forecasts G" and A_B stand for "Expert A forecasts B",

$$P(A_G|G) = 1, \quad P(A_B|G) = 0, \quad P(A_G|B) = P(A_B|B) = \tfrac{1}{2}. \tag{9.4}$$

The other is Expert Z, who always correctly forecasts B but is as reliable as a coin toss when it comes to G. That is, letting Z_G stand for "Expert Z forecasts G" and Z_B stand for "Expert Z forecasts B",

$$P(Z_G|G) = P(Z_B|G) = \tfrac{1}{2}, \quad P(Z_G|B) = 0, \quad P(Z_B|B) = 1. \tag{9.5}$$

Let us first compute the probability that Expert A will forecast G. This can be done using the rules of probability,[15] but we can also see it graphically as shown in Figure 9.7.

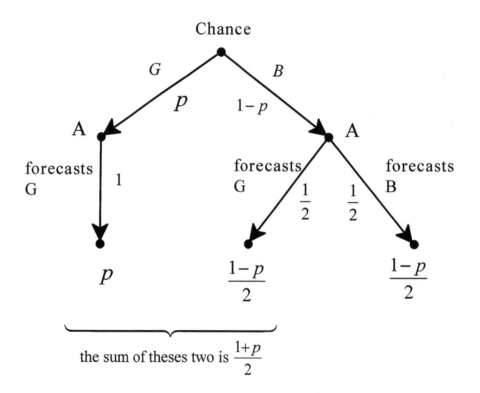

Figure 9.7: Expert A's forecast

---

[15] $P(A_G) = P(A_G|G) \times P(G) + P(A_G|B) \times P(B) = 1 \times p + \tfrac{1}{2} \times (1-p) = \tfrac{1+p}{2}$.

9.4 Different sources of information

Similarly, we can compute the probability that Expert Z forecasts B as shown in Figure 9.8.[16]

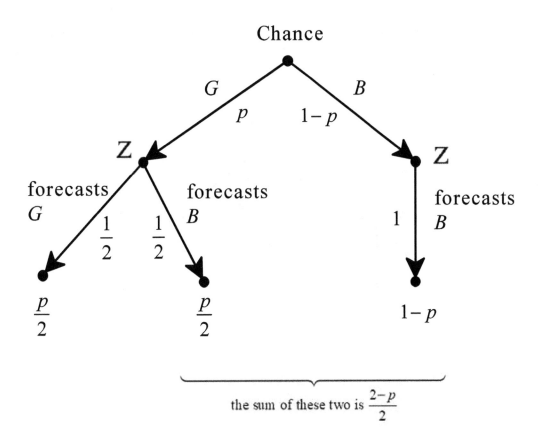

Figure 9.8: Expert Z's forecast

In what follows we will assume that

$$\boxed{p = \frac{3}{4}}$$

so that, in the absence of consultation with an expert, the *DM* will choose Investment 2, whose expected value is $7M$ (while the expected value of Investment 1 is $6M$).

---

[16]Or, using the rules of probability: $P(Z_B) = P(Z_B|G) \times P(G) + P(Z_B|B) \times P(B) = \frac{1}{2} \times p + 1 \times (1-p) = \frac{2-p}{2}$.

We now want to calculate the value of consulting Expert A and the value of consulting Expert Z.

Let us begin with Expert A. Suppose that Expert A has been consulted and her forecast is G. What is the probability that G is in fact true? We can compute this probability using Bayes' rule[17] or graphically as shown in Figure 9.9 (where the blue number on the left of each node is that node's prior probability and the red number on the right is the posterior, or updated, probability and the rounded rectangles represent information).[18]

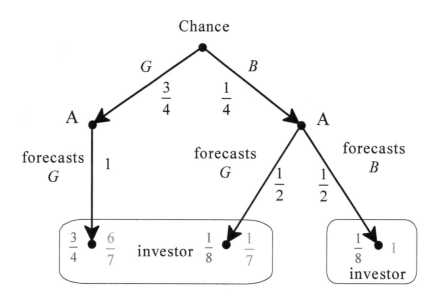

Figure 9.9: Expert A

Thus, if Expert A reports that the state is B then the *DM* will attach probability 1 to B and choose Investment 1 (with zero expected return) while if Expert A reports that the state is G then the *DM* will attach probability $\frac{6}{7}$ to G and probability $\frac{1}{7}$ to B and choose Investment 2 (since the expected return from Investment 1 is $\frac{6}{7}(8) + \frac{1}{7}(0) = \frac{48}{7}$ while the expected return from Investment 2 is $\frac{6}{7}12 + \frac{1}{7}(-8) = \frac{64}{7}$). Thus, the expected return from consulting Expert A is (recall that $P(A_G) = \frac{7}{8}$: see Footnote 17):

$$P(A_G) \times \tfrac{64}{7} + P(A_B) \times 0 = \tfrac{7}{8} \times \tfrac{64}{7} + \tfrac{1}{8} \times 0 = \boxed{8}. \tag{9.6}$$

---

[17] Recall that $P(A_G) = \frac{1+p}{2} = \frac{1+\frac{3}{4}}{2} = \frac{7}{8}$. Then, by Bayes' rule, $P(G|A_G) = \frac{P(A_G|G) \times P(G)}{P(A_G)} = \frac{1 \times \frac{3}{4}}{\frac{7}{8}} = \frac{6}{7}$.

[18] The colors show in the pdf version of the book, not in the print version.

9.4 Different sources of information

Let us now consider Expert Z. Suppose that Expert Z has been consulted and his forecast is B. What is the probability that B is in fact true? We can compute this probability using Bayes' rule[19] or graphically as shown in Figure 9.10 (where, as before, the blue number on the left of each node is that node's prior probability and the red number on the right is the posterior probability and the rounded rectangles represent information).

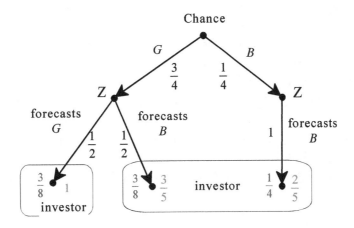

Figure 9.10: Expert Z

Thus, if Expert Z reports that the state is G then the DM will attach probability 1 to G and choose Investment 2 (with an expected return of $12M$) while if Expert Z reports that the state is B then the DM will attach probability $\frac{3}{5}$ to G and probability $\frac{2}{5}$ to B and choose Investment 1 (since the expected return from Investment 1 is $\frac{3}{5}(8) + \frac{2}{5}(0) = \frac{24}{5}$ while the expected return from Investment 2 is $\frac{3}{5}(12) + \frac{2}{5}(-8) = \frac{20}{5}$). Thus, the expected return from consulting Expert Z is (recall that $P(Z_B) = \frac{5}{8}$: see Footnote 19):

$$P(Z_G) \times 12 + P(Z_B) \times \tfrac{24}{5} = \tfrac{3}{8} \times 12 + \tfrac{5}{8} \times \tfrac{24}{5} = \boxed{7.5}. \tag{9.7}$$

Comparing (9.6) and (9.7) we see that Expert A is more valuable than Expert Z. Whether the investor will decide to consult an expert, or make her investment decision without consultation, will depend on how much it costs to consult an expert. Relative to no consultation, the *gain* from consulting Expert A is $8 - 7 = 1$ (recall that the maximum expected utility from not consulting an expert is 7, obtained by choosing Investment 2) and the *gain* from consulting Expert Z is $8 - 7.5 = 0.5$. Let x_A be the fee charged by Expert A and x_B the fee charged by Expert Z. Then:

- if $x_A < 1$ and $1 - x_A > 0.5 - x_B$, that is, if $x_A < \min\{1, 0.5 + x_B\}$ then the optimal decision is to consult Expert A and then choose Investment 1 if Expert A reports B and Investment 2 if Expert A reports G,
- if $x_A > \min\{1, 0.5 + x_B\}$ and $x_B < 0.5$ then the optimal decision is to consult Expert Z and then choose Investment 1 if Expert Z reports B and Investment 2 if Expert Z reports G,

---

[19] Recall that $P(Z_B) = \frac{2-p}{2} = \frac{2-\frac{3}{4}}{2} = \frac{5}{8}$. Then, by Bayes' rule, $P(B|Z_B) = \frac{P(Z_B|B) \times P(B)}{P(Z_B)} = \frac{1 \times \frac{1}{4}}{\frac{5}{8}} = \frac{2}{5}$.

- in every other case it is optimal to choose Investment 2 without consulting an expert.[20]

Suppose that consulting the experts is **free** ($x_A = x_B = 0$). Then the *DM* would certainly benefit from consulting an expert and, having to choose between them, she will choose Expert A. But why limit herself to one consultation? Would it pay to consult *both* experts? As before, we need to compute the probabilities of *G* and *B* conditional on the information acquired from the two experts, which can be one of three: (1) both experts claim that the state is *G* (A_G and Z_G), (2) both experts claim that the state is *B* (A_B and Z_B) and (3) Expert A claims that the state is *G* and Expert Z claims that the state is *B* (A_G and Z_B). We will assume that the opinions of the experts are independent, so that, for example, $P(A_G Z_B | G) = P(A_G | G) \times P(Z_B | G)$. We can compute these conditional probabilities using Bayes' rule (see Exercise 9.12) or graphically as shown in Figure 9.11 (as before, the blue number on the left of a node is the prior, or unconditional, probability of that node, while the red number on the right of the node is the probability conditional on the information represented by the rounded rectangle that encloses that node).

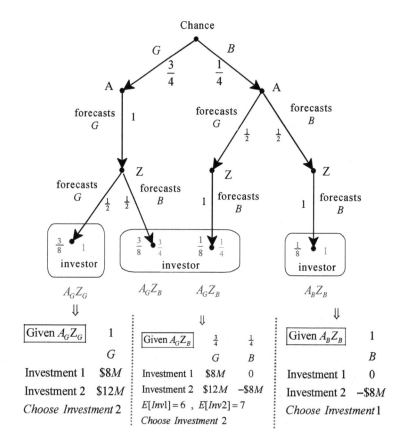

Figure 9.11: Consulting both experts

---

[20]Not necessarily *uniquely* optimal: it may be that not consulting an expert is just as good as consulting an expert. This would be true, for example, if $x_A = 1$ and $x_B > 0.5$, in which case the investor would be indifferent between no consultation and consulting Expert A.

Thus,

- if both experts report G then the investor will attach probability 1 to G and choose Investment 2, expecting a return of 12,
- if both experts report B then the investor will attach probability 1 to B and choose Investment 1, expecting a return of 0,
- if Expert A reports G and Expert Z reports B then the investor will attach probability $\frac{3}{4}$ to G and probability $\frac{1}{4}$ to B and will thus choose Investment 2, expecting a return of 7.[21]

Thus, the expected return from consulting both experts is:

$$P(A_G Z_G) \times 12 + P(A_B Z_B) \times 0 + P(A_G Z_B) \times 7$$
$$= \tfrac{3}{8} \times 12 + \tfrac{1}{8} \times 0 + \left(\tfrac{3}{8} + \tfrac{1}{8}\right) \times 7 = \tfrac{64}{8} = 8.$$

Hence, the expected return from consulting both experts is the same as the expected return from consulting only Expert A. In other words, consulting Expert Z has no additional value once Expert A has been consulted.

> Test your understanding of the concepts introduced in this section, by going through the exercises in Section 9.5.4 at the end of this chapter.

9.5 Exercises

The solutions to the following exercises are given in Section 9.6 at the end of this chapter.

9.5.1 Exercises for Section 9.1: When is information potentially valuable?

> **Exercise 9.1** Consider again the case of the three diseases (flapemia, globoma and popitis) discussed in Section 9.1. Let the conditional probabilities of a positive and a negative scan be
>
> | $P(+\mid G) = p$ | $P(-\mid G) = 1-p$ |
> |---|---|
> | $P(+\mid P) = 1$ | $P(-\mid P) = 0$ |
> | $P(+\mid F) = 0$ | $P(-\mid F) = 1$ |
>
> **(a)** Show that if $p < \tfrac{7}{8}$ and the result of the scan is negative, then globoma is the most likely disease.
>
> **(b)** Show that if $p > \tfrac{1}{8}$ and the result of the scan is positive, then globoma is the most likely disease.

---

[21] The expected value of Investment 1 is $\tfrac{3}{4}(8) + \tfrac{1}{4}(0) = 6$ while the expected value of Investment 2 is $\tfrac{3}{4}(12) + \tfrac{1}{4}(-8) = 7$.

Exercise 9.2 Consider again the case of the three diseases (flapemia, globoma and popitis) discussed in Section 9.1. Let us now change the data of the problem. The doctor's initial beliefs are as follows:

disease	Globoma (G)	Popitis (P)	Flapemia (F)
probability	0.3	0.5	0.2

Let the conditional probabilities of a positive and a negative scan be

$$P(+|G) = 0.9 \quad P(-|G) = 0.1$$
$$P(+|P) = 0.7 \quad P(-|P) = 0.3$$
$$P(+|F) = 0.2 \quad P(-|F) = 0.8$$

As before, assume that the doctor's decision rule is to treat the disease that she considers most likely.

(a) What disease will the doctor treat if she does not perform a scan?
(b) What disease will the doctor treat if she performs the scan and the result is positive?
(c) What disease will the doctor treat if she performs the scan and the result is negative?

9.5.2 Exercises for Section 9.2: The value of information when outcomes are sums of money

Exercise 9.3 David faces the following investment opportunities, where the amounts of money represent changes in his wealth. His initial wealth is $30. David is risk neutral.

	probability	$\frac{1}{2}$	$\frac{1}{2}$
	state $\rightarrow$	s_1	s_2
act $\downarrow$			
A		$70	$19
B		$24	$53

(a) Which investment opportunity will he choose? Perform the relevant calculations in terms of changes in wealth and also in terms of total wealth.
(b) An expert offers to provide David with perfect information concerning the state. What is the maximum amount that David is willing to pay the expert for his services (assuming that the payment is to be made before the information is revealed)? Again, perform the relevant calculations in terms of changes in wealth and also in terms of total wealth.

9.5 Exercises

Exercise 9.4 As in Exercise 9.3, David faces the following investment opportunities, where the amounts of money represent changes in his wealth. His initial wealth is $30. This time assume that David is not risk neutral: his von Neumann-Morgenstern utility-of-money function is $U(\$x) = \sqrt{x}$.

probability	$\frac{1}{2}$	$\frac{1}{2}$
state →	s_1	s_2
act ↓		
A	$70	$19
B	$24	$53

(a) Which investment opportunity will he choose?
(b) An expert offers to provide David with perfect information concerning the state. Write an equation whose solution gives the maximum amount that David is willing to pay the expert for his services (assuming that the payment is to be made before the information is revealed).
(c) Would David be willing to pay $18 for perfect information?

Exercise 9.5 Both Bill and Carla face two investment opportunities: A and B which will yield the following changes in wealth (gains/losses):

probability	$\frac{2}{10}$	$\frac{5}{10}$	$\frac{3}{10}$
state →	s_1	s_2	s_3
act ↓			
A	$(−20)	$100	$10
B	$200	$10	$20

Both Bill and Carla have an initial wealth of $500. Bill is risk-neutral, while Carla has the following von Neumann-Morgenstern utility-of-money function: $U(\$x) = \sqrt{x}$.
(a) Which of A and B will Bill choose?
(b) Which of A and B will Carla choose?
(c) Does Carla's choice depend on her initial wealth (that is, could her choice be different with different levels of initial wealth)?
(d) Suppose that an expert offers to provide perfect information (that is, to reveal what the true state is) for a fee of $42.50. Bill has to pay the expert *before* the information is revealed. Will Bill accept the offer?
(e) Suppose that an expert offers to provide perfect information (that is, to reveal what the true state is) for a fee of $42.50. Carla has to pay the expert *before* the information is revealed. Will Carla accept the offer?

Exercise 9.6 Let us revisit the second example of Section 9.2.2 where the decision problem was as follows (the sums of money represent changes in wealth):

probability	$\frac{2}{8}$	$\frac{4}{8}$	$\frac{2}{8}$
state →	s_1	s_2	s_3
act ↓			
A	$4	$36	$49
B	$64	$81	$9
C	$25	$100	$16

The *DM*'s initial wealth is $300 and her von Neumann-Morgenstern utility-of-money function is $U(\$x) = \sqrt{x}$.
  (a) What action will the *DM* choose?
  (b) Suppose that an expert offers to provide the *DM* with perfect information for a fee of $46 (to be paid before the information is revealed). Will the *DM* accept the offer?
  (c) Write an equation whose solution gives the maximum amount of money that the *DM* is willing to pay for perfect information.

Exercise 9.7 Once again, consider the following decision problem, where the sums of money represent changes in wealth:

probability	$\frac{2}{8}$	$\frac{4}{8}$	$\frac{2}{8}$
state →	s_1	s_2	s_3
act ↓			
A	$4	$36	$49
B	$64	$81	$9
C	$25	$100	$16

Assume now that the expert is no longer able to provide perfect information: the information that he is offering is represented by the partition $\{\{s_1\}, \{s_2, s_3\}\}$. In this exercise we focus on the case where the *DM* is risk neutral and in the following exercise we will consider the case of a risk-averse *DM*.
  (a) What would the *DM* do if she decided *not* to consult the expert?
  (b) If the expert charges $x for providing the information, for what values of x would the *DM* hire the expert (by paying $x before the information is revealed)?

9.5 Exercises

Exercise 9.8 Consider a *DM* whose initial wealth is $400 and whose von Neuman-Morgenstern utility-of-money function is $U(\$x) = \sqrt{x}$. As in the previous exercise, consider the following decision problem (where the sums of money represent changes in wealth):

probability	$\frac{2}{8}$	$\frac{4}{8}$	$\frac{2}{8}$
state →	s_1	s_2	s_3
act ↓			
A	$4	$36	$49
B	$64	$81	$9
C	$25	$100	$16

Assume, again, that the information that the expert is offering is represented by the partition $\{\{s_1\},\{s_2,s_3\}\}$.

(a) What would the *DM* do if she decided *not* to consult the expert?

(b) If the expert charges $4 for providing the information, would the *DM* hire the expert (by paying $4 before the information is revealed)?

■

Exercise 9.9 As in Exercise 9.4, David faces the following investment opportunities, where the amounts of money represent changes in his wealth. His initial wealth is $30. This time assume that David is risk loving: his von Neumann-Morgenstern utility-of-money function is $U(\$x) = x^2$.

probability	$\frac{1}{2}$	$\frac{1}{2}$
state →	s_1	s_2
act ↓		
A	$70	$19
B	$24	$53

(a) Which investment opportunity will he choose?

(b) An expert offers to provide David with perfect information concerning the state. Write an equation whose solution gives the maximum amount that David is willing to pay the expert for his services (assuming that the payment is to be made before the information is revealed).

(c) Would David be willing to pay $18 for perfect information?

■

Exercise 9.10 Amy faces the following investment opportunities, where the amounts of money represent changes in her wealth. Her initial wealth is $40. Amy is risk loving: her von Neumann-Morgenstern utility-of-money function is $U(\$x) = x^2$.

probability	$\frac{1}{8}$	$\frac{3}{8}$	$\frac{1}{8}$	$\frac{3}{8}$
state →	s_1	s_2	s_3	s_4
act ↓				
A	(-10)	$10	$20	$30
B	$35	$(-5)	$25	$15

(a) Which investment opportunity will she choose?

(b) An expert offers to provide Amy with information represented by the partition $\{\{s_1, s_2\}, \{s_3, s_4\}\}$ for a price of $4. Should Amy accept?

9.5.3 Exercises for Section 9.3: The general case

Exercise 9.11 Andrea is seeing her doctor for persistent debilitating symptoms. The doctor tells her that her symptoms are consistent with two diseases: Anxiomatitis (A) and Boredomitis (B). Based on his past experience, the doctor thinks that Andrea has disease A with probability 60% and disease B with probability 40%. An expensive test, which is not covered by Andrea's insurance, could give some information about her disease. The test costs $250 and can give a positive (+) or a negative (−) result. The conditional probabilities are as follows:

$$\begin{array}{ll} P(+|A) = 80\% & P(-|A) = 20\% \\ P(+|B) = 10\% & P(-|B) = 90\% \end{array} \qquad (9.8)$$

Andrea's initial wealth is $900. If she takes the test she will have to pay for it herself. There is a treatment for disease A which will not be effective against disease B and there is a treatment for disease B which will not be effective against disease A. Pursuing one treatment precludes pursuing the other treatment later on. Andrea is asked to choose between the following six options:

$(\neg T, A)$:	Not take the test and treat disease A
$(\neg T, B)$:	Not take the test and treat disease B
(T, A) :	Test and treat disease A no matter whether the test is + or −
(T, B) :	Test and treat disease B no matter whether the test is + or −
$(T, A+, B-)$:	Test and treat disease A if test is + and disease B if test is −
$(T, B+, A-)$:	Test and treat disease B if test is + and disease A if test is −

An outcome can be thought of as a pair (x, y) where x is either c for 'cured' or $\neg c$ for 'not cured' and y is the level of Andrea's wealth (which is $900 if she does not take the test and $650 if she takes the test). Andrea ranks the outcomes as follows:

	outcome
best	$(c, \$900)$
	$(c, \$650)$
	$(\neg c, \$900)$
worst	$(\neg c, \$650)$

Think of a state as a pair (x, y) where x is the disease that Andrea has (thus, x is either A or B) and y is the result of the test if it were to be taken (thus, y is either + or −). For example, $(A, -)$ is the state where Andrea has disease A *and* if she takes the test then the result will be negative.

(a) Using the doctor's initial assessment (A with probability 60% and B with probability 40%) and the conditional probabilities given in (9.8), compute the probabilities of the four states.

(b) Write Andrea's decision problem in terms of acts, states and *outcomes*.

(c) Assuming that Andrea satisfies the axioms of Expected Utility Theory, and using her normalized von Neumann-Morgenstern utility function (use variables p and q for the values that you don't know), re-write Andrea's decision problem in terms of acts, states and *utilities*.

(d) Which acts are strictly dominated?

(e) If Andrea were to decide not to take the test, which disease would she want to be treated?

(f) If Andrea were to decide to take the test, what treatment policy (that is, treatment decision conditional on the outcome of the test) would she want to implement?

(g) What restrictions on $U(c,\$650)$ and $U(\neg c,\$900)$ would guarantee that Andrea would choose to take the test?

(h) If $U(c,\$650) = 0.86$ and $U(\neg c,\$900) = 0.3$, will Andrea decide to take the test?

9.5.4 Exercises for Section 9.4: Different sources of information

Exercise 9.12 Consider the two-expert example at the end of Section 9.4: there are two states, G with probability p and B with probability $(1-p)$ and two experts, A and Z, who independently give their opinions on which state has occurred, with the following conditional probabilities (where A_G means that Expert A reports that the state is G, etc.):

$$P(A_G|G) = 1, \quad P(A_B|G) = 0, \quad P(A_G|B) = P(A_B|B) = \tfrac{1}{2}.$$

$$P(Z_B|B) = 1, \quad P(Z_G|B) = 0, \quad P(Z_G|G) = P(Z_B|G) = \tfrac{1}{2}.$$

Use Bayes' rule to compute the probabilities $P(G|A_GZ_G), P(G|A_GZ_B), P(G|A_BZ_B)$.

9.6 Solutions to Exercises

Solution to Exercise 9.1.

(a) We saw in Section 9.1 that

$$P(G|-) = \frac{0.8(1-p)}{0.8(1-p)+0.1}, \quad P(P|-) = 0 \text{ and } P(F|-) = \frac{0.1}{0.8(1-p)+0.1}.$$

Thus, globoma is the most likely disease, conditional on a negative scan, if and only if $\frac{0.8(1-p)}{0.8(1-p)+0.1} > \frac{0.1}{0.8(1-p)+0.1}$, which is true if and only if $0.8(1-p) > 0.1$, that is, if and only if $p < \tfrac{7}{8}$.

Thus, if $p < \tfrac{7}{8}$ then it is indeed the case that, conditional on a negative scan, globoma is the most likely disease.

(b) We saw in Section 9.1 that $P(G|+) = \frac{0.8p}{0.8p+0.1}, P(P|+) = \frac{0.1}{0.8p+0.1}$ and $P(F|+) = 0$. Thus, globoma is the most likely disease, conditional on a positive scan, if and only if $\frac{0.8p}{0.8p+0.1} > \frac{0.1}{0.8p+0.1}$ which is true if and only if $0.8p > 0.1$, that is, if and only if $p > \tfrac{1}{8}$. Thus, if $p > \tfrac{1}{8}$ then it is indeed the case that, conditional on a positive scan, globoma is the most likely disease.

9.6 Solutions to Exercises

Solution to Exercise 9.2. The data is:

disease	Globoma (G)	Popitis (P)	Flapemia (F)
probability	0.3	0.5	0.2

$$P(+|G) = 0.9 \quad P(-|G) = 0.1$$
$$P(+|P) = 0.7 \quad P(-|P) = 0.3$$
$$P(+|F) = 0.2 \quad P(-|F) = 0.8$$

(a) Without a scan the doctor will treat popitis, since it is more likely than the other two diseases.

(b) We need to compute the conditional probabilities:

$$P(G|+) = \frac{P(+|G)P(G)}{P(+|G)P(G) + P(+|P)P(P) + P(+|F)P(F)}$$

$$= \frac{0.9\,(0.3)}{0.9\,(0.3) + 0.7\,(0.5) + 0.2(0.2)} = 40.91\%,$$

$$P(P|+) = \frac{P(+|P)P(P)}{P(+|G)P(G) + P(+|P)P(P) + P(+|F)P(F)}$$

$$= \frac{0.7\,(0.5)}{0.9\,(0.3) + 0.7\,(0.5) + 0.2(0.2)} = 53.03\%,$$

$$P(F|+) = \frac{P(+|F)P(F)}{P(+|G)P(G) + P(+|P)P(P) + P(+|F)P(F)}$$

$$= \frac{0.2\,(0.2)}{0.9\,(0.3) + 0.7\,(0.5) + 0.2(0.2)} = 6.06\%.$$

Thus, after a positive scan, the doctor would treat popitis.

(c) We need to compute the conditional probabilities:

$$P(G|-) = \frac{P(-|G)P(G)}{P(-|G)P(G) + P(-|P)P(P) + P(-|F)P(F)}$$

$$= \frac{0.1\,(0.3)}{0.1\,(0.3) + 0.3\,(0.5) + 0.8(0.2)} = 8.82\%,$$

$$P(P|-) = \frac{P(-|P)P(P)}{P(-|G)P(G) + P(-|P)P(P) + P(-|F)P(F)}$$

$$= \frac{0.3\,(0.5)}{0.1\,(0.3) + 0.3\,(0.5) + 0.8(0.2)} = 44.12\%,$$

$$P(F|-) = \frac{P(-|F)P(F)}{P(-|G)P(G) + P(-|P)P(P) + P(-|F)P(F)}$$

$$= \frac{0.8\,(0.2)}{0.1\,(0.3) + 0.3\,(0.5) + 0.8(0.2)} = 47.06\%$$

Thus, after a positive scan, the doctor would treat flapemia. □

Solution to Exercise 9.3.

(a) In terms of changes in wealth: $\mathbb{E}[A] = \frac{1}{2}70 + \frac{1}{2}19 = \boxed{44.5}$ and $\mathbb{E}[B] = \frac{1}{2}24 + \frac{1}{2}53 = 38.5$; thus, he would choose A.
In terms of total wealth: $\mathbb{E}[A] = \frac{1}{2}(30+70) + \frac{1}{2}(30+19) = \boxed{74.5}$ and $\mathbb{E}[B] = \frac{1}{2}(30+24) + \frac{1}{2}(30+53) = 68.5$; thus, he would choose A.

(b) If informed that the state is s_1, David will choose A and if informed that the state is s_2, he will choose B.

Let x be the fee requested by the expert. Then the value of perfect information is given as follows.

In terms of changes in wealth: $\frac{1}{2}(70-x) + \frac{1}{2}(53-x) = 61.5 - x$; thus, the maximum amount he is willing to pay for perfect information is the solution to the equation $61.5 - x = 44.5$ which is $17.

In terms of total wealth: $\frac{1}{2}(30+70-x) + \frac{1}{2}(30+53-x) = 91.5 - x$; thus, the maximum amount he is willing to pay for perfect information is the solution to the equation $91.5 - x = 74.5$ which is $17. □

Solution to Exercise 9.4.

(a) $\mathbb{E}[U(A)] = \frac{1}{2}\sqrt{30+70} + \frac{1}{2}\sqrt{30+19} = \boxed{8.5}$ and $\mathbb{E}[U(B)] = \frac{1}{2}\sqrt{30+24} + \frac{1}{2}\sqrt{30+53} = 8.2295$. Thus, he would choose A.

(b) If informed that the state is s_1, David will choose A and if informed that the state is s_2, he will choose B.

Let x be the fee requested by the expert. Then the expected utility from perfect information is: $\frac{1}{2}\sqrt{30+70-x} + \frac{1}{2}\sqrt{30+53-x}$.

Thus, the maximum amount he is willing to pay for perfect information is the solution to the equation $\frac{1}{2}\sqrt{30+70-x} + \frac{1}{2}\sqrt{30+53-x} = 8.5$ (which is $19).

(c) Yes, because $\frac{1}{2}\sqrt{30+70-18} + \frac{1}{2}\sqrt{30+53-18} = 8.5588 > 8.5$. □

9.6 Solutions to Exercises

Solution to Exercise 9.5.

(a) Since – when a *DM* is risk neutral – the initial wealth is irrelevant, the calculations done in Section 9.2.1 remain valid and thus Bill would choose *B*.

(b) For Carla the expected utility of choosing investment *A* is

$$\mathbb{E}[U(A)] = \frac{2}{10}\sqrt{500-20} + \frac{5}{10}\sqrt{500+100} + \frac{3}{10}\sqrt{500+10} = 23.4042.$$

and the expected utility of choosing investment *B* is

$$\mathbb{E}[U(B)] = \frac{2}{10}\sqrt{500+200} + \frac{5}{10}\sqrt{500+10} + \frac{3}{10}\sqrt{500+20} = \boxed{23.4241}.$$

Thus, Carla would choose *B*.

(c) We saw in Section 9.2.2 that with an initial wealth of $100 Carla would choose *A*; thus, her decision *does* depend on her initial wealth.

(d) Once again, since for a risk-neutral person the initial wealth is irrelevant, the conclusion reached in Section 9.2.1 – namely that the maximum amount that Bill would be willing to pay for perfect information is $45 – remains valid.

(e) It is clear that if informed that the state is s_1, Carla will choose *B*, if informed that the state is s_2, she will choose *A* and if informed that the state is s_3, she will choose *B*. Thus, her expected utility from availing herself of perfect information by paying $x is $\frac{2}{10}\sqrt{500+200-x} + \frac{5}{10}\sqrt{500+100-x} + \frac{3}{10}\sqrt{500+20-x} = \frac{2\sqrt{700-x} + 5\sqrt{600-x} + 3\sqrt{520-x}}{10}$.

Call this expression $f(x)$. Since $f(42.5) = 23.4896$ is greater than the maximum utility she can get without information (namely, 23.4241 by taking action *B*), Carla (unlike Bill) would indeed be willing to pay $42.5 for perfect information. □

Solution to Exercise 9.6.

(a) Expected utilities are as follows: $\mathbb{E}[U(A)] = \frac{2}{8}\sqrt{304} + \frac{4}{8}\sqrt{336} + \frac{2}{8}\sqrt{349} = 18.1944$, $\mathbb{E}[U(B)] = \frac{2}{8}\sqrt{364} + \frac{4}{8}\sqrt{381} + \frac{2}{8}\sqrt{309} = 18.9239$ and $\mathbb{E}[U(C)] = \frac{2}{8}\sqrt{325} + \frac{4}{8}\sqrt{400} + \frac{2}{8}\sqrt{316} = \boxed{18.951}$. Thus, the *DM* would choose *C*.

(b) If informed that s_1, the *DM* would choose *B*, if informed that s_2, she would choose *C* and if informed that s_3, she would choose *A*. Thus, the expected utility of availing herself of perfect information for a fee of $46 is: $\frac{2}{8}\sqrt{364-46} + \frac{4}{8}\sqrt{400-46} + \frac{2}{8}\sqrt{349-46} = 18.2173$; since this is less than 18.951 the *DM* would not be willing to pay $46 for perfect information.

(c) The equation is $\frac{2}{8}\sqrt{364-x} + \frac{4}{8}\sqrt{400-x} + \frac{2}{8}\sqrt{349-x} = 18.951$ (the solution is 18.758). □

Solution to Exercise 9.7.

(a) If the *DM* takes action *A*, then she faces the lottery $\begin{pmatrix} \$4 & \$36 & \$49 \\ \frac{2}{8} & \frac{4}{8} & \frac{2}{8} \end{pmatrix}$, whose expected value is $\frac{2}{8}(4) + \frac{4}{8}(36) + \frac{2}{8}(49) = 31.25$.

If she takes action *B*, then she faces the lottery $\begin{pmatrix} \$64 & \$81 & \$9 \\ \frac{2}{8} & \frac{4}{8} & \frac{2}{8} \end{pmatrix}$, whose expected value is $\frac{2}{8}(64) + \frac{4}{8}(81) + \frac{2}{8}(9) = 58.75$.

If she takes action *C*, then she faces the lottery $\begin{pmatrix} \$25 & \$100 & \$16 \\ \frac{2}{8} & \frac{4}{8} & \frac{2}{8} \end{pmatrix}$, whose expected value is $\frac{2}{8}(25) + \frac{4}{8}(100) + \frac{2}{8}(16) = \boxed{60.25}$.

Thus, her optimal choice, if she does not consult the expert, is action *C*. Indeed we did all theses calculations in Section 9.2.1!

(b) If the *DM* hires the expert, then the expert will either tell her that the true state is s_1, in which case it would be optimal for her to take action *B*, or the expert would tell her that the true state is either s_2 or s_3, in which case what should the *DM* do? She should first update her beliefs based on the information $\{s_2, s_3\}$. Using Bayes' rule, her updated beliefs are $\begin{matrix} s_1 & s_2 & s_3 \\ 0 & \frac{2}{3} & \frac{1}{3} \end{matrix}$. Using these updated beliefs she can compute the expected utility of each action.

If she takes action *A*, her expected utility is $\frac{2}{3}(36-x) + \frac{1}{3}(49-x) = 40.33 - x$.
If she takes action *B*, her expected utility is $\frac{2}{3}(81-x) + \frac{1}{3}(9-x) = 57 - x$.
If she takes action *C*, her expected utility is $\frac{2}{3}(100-x) + \frac{1}{3}(16-x) = 72 - x$.

Thus, she would take action *C*, because it yields a higher expected utility than the other two actions.

Is it worth consulting the expert? The *DM*'s expected utility when she does not consult the expert is $\boxed{60.25}$ (the expected utility of taking action *C*, which is the best action when no further information is available, as shown above). The expected utility of paying $x to the expert for information $\{\{s_1\}, \{s_2, s_3\}\}$ is computed as follows. According to the *DM*'s initial beliefs, with probability $\frac{2}{8}$ the expert will tell her that the state is s_1, in which case she will take action *B* and get a utility of $(64-x)$; with probability $\frac{4}{8} + \frac{2}{8} = \frac{6}{8}$ she will be given information $\{s_2, s_3\}$, in which case, as shown above, she will take action *C* and get an expected utility of $(72-x)$. Thus, the *DM*'s expected utility, if she consults the expert for a fee of $x, is: $\frac{2}{8}(64-x) + \frac{6}{8}(72-x) = \boxed{70-x}$. Thus, it is in her interest to hire the expert and pay his fee of $x if and only if $70 - x > 60.25$, that is, if $x < 9.75$ (if $x = 9.75$ then she is indifferent between hiring and not hiring the expert). Thus, if $x < 9.75$ the *DM* will hire the expert and then act as follows: if told s_1, then she will take action *B* and if told $\{s_2, s_3\}$, she will take action *C*. □

9.6 Solutions to Exercises

Solution to Exercise 9.8.

(a) If the *DM* takes action *A*, then she faces the lottery $\begin{pmatrix} \$404 & \$436 & \$449 \\ \frac{2}{8} & \frac{4}{8} & \frac{2}{8} \end{pmatrix}$ (where the sums of money represent her total wealth), whose expected utility is $\frac{2}{8}\sqrt{404} + \frac{4}{8}\sqrt{436} + \frac{2}{8}\sqrt{449} = 20.7626$.

If she takes action *B*, then she faces the lottery $\begin{pmatrix} \$464 & \$481 & \$409 \\ \frac{2}{8} & \frac{4}{8} & \frac{2}{8} \end{pmatrix}$, whose expected utility is $\frac{2}{8}\sqrt{464} + \frac{4}{8}\sqrt{481} + \frac{2}{8}\sqrt{409} = 21.407$.

If she takes action *C*, then she faces the lottery $\begin{pmatrix} \$425 & \$500 & \$416 \\ \frac{2}{8} & \frac{4}{8} & \frac{2}{8} \end{pmatrix}$, whose expected utility is $\frac{2}{8}\sqrt{425} + \frac{4}{8}\sqrt{500} + \frac{2}{8}\sqrt{416} = \boxed{21.4332}$.

Thus, her optimal decision, if she does not consult the expert, is to take action C.

(b) If the *DM* hires the expert, then the expert will either tell her that the true state is s_1, *in which case it would be optimal for her to take action B*, or the expert would tell her that the true state is either s_2 or s_3, in which case what should the *DM* do? She should first update her beliefs based on the information $\{s_2, s_3\}$. Using Bayes' rule, her updated beliefs are $\begin{array}{ccc} s_1 & s_2 & s_3 \\ 0 & \frac{2}{3} & \frac{1}{3} \end{array}$. Using these updated beliefs she can compute the expected utility of each action.

If she takes action *A*, her expected utility is $\frac{2}{3}\sqrt{436-4} + \frac{1}{3}\sqrt{449-4} = 20.8881$.
If she takes action *B*, her expected utility is $\frac{2}{3}\sqrt{481-4} + \frac{1}{3}\sqrt{409-4} = 21.2684$.
If she takes action *C*, her expected utility is $\frac{2}{3}\sqrt{500-4} + \frac{1}{3}\sqrt{416-4} = \boxed{21.6133}$.

Thus, she would take action C, because it yields a higher expected utility than the other two actions.

Is it worth consulting the expert? The *DM*'s expected utility when she does not consult the expert is $\boxed{21.4332}$ (the expected utility of taking action *C*, which is the best action when no further information is available, as shown above).

The expected utility of paying \$4 to the expert for information $\{\{s_1\}, \{s_2, s_3\}\}$ is computed as follows. According to the *DM*'s initial beliefs, with probability $\frac{2}{8}$ the expert will tell her that the state is s_1, in which case she will take action *B* and get a utility of $\sqrt{464-4} = 21.4476$; with probability $\frac{4}{8} + \frac{2}{8} = \frac{6}{8}$ she will be given information $\{s_2, s_3\}$, in which case, as shown above, she will take action *C* and get an expected utility of 21.6133.

Thus, the *DM*'s expected utility, if she consults the expert for a fee of \$4, is: $\frac{2}{8}21.4476 + \frac{6}{8}21.6133 = \boxed{21.5719}$. Thus, it is indeed in her interest to hire the expert and pay his fee of \$4; she will then act as follows: if told s_1, she will take action *B* and if told $\{s_2, s_3\}$, she will take action *C*. □

Solution to Exercise 9.9.

(a) $\mathbb{E}[U(A)] = \frac{1}{2}(30+70)^2 + \frac{1}{2}(30+19)^2 = \boxed{6,200.5}$ and
$\mathbb{E}[U(B)] = \frac{1}{2}(30+24)^2 + \frac{1}{2}(30+53)^2 = 4,902.5$. Thus, he would choose A.

(b) If informed that the state is s_1, David will choose A and if informed that the state is s_2, he will choose B.

Let x be the fee requested by the expert. Then the value of perfect information is given as follows: $\frac{1}{2}(30+70-x)^2 + \frac{1}{2}(30+53-x)^2 = x^2 - 183x + \frac{16,889}{2}$; thus, the maximum amount he is willing to pay for perfect information is the solution to the equation $x^2 - 183x + \frac{16,889}{2} = 6,200.5$ (which is \$13.21686).

(c) No, because $\frac{1}{2}(30+70-18)^2 + \frac{1}{2}(30+53-18)^2 = 5,474.5 < 6,200.5$. □

Solution to Exercise 9.10.

(a) $\mathbb{E}[U(A)] = \frac{1}{8}(40-10)^2 + \frac{3}{8}(40+10)^2 + \frac{1}{8}(40+20)^2 + \frac{3}{8}(40+30)^2 = \boxed{3,337.5}$ and
$\mathbb{E}[U(B)] = \frac{1}{8}(40+35)^2 + \frac{3}{8}(40-5)^2 + \frac{1}{8}(40+25)^2 + \frac{3}{8}(40+15)^2 = 2,825$. Thus, the DM would choose action A.

(b) If informed that the state belongs to $\{s_1, s_2\}$, Amy should update her beliefs to

$\begin{array}{cc} s_1 & s_2 \\ \frac{1}{4} & \frac{3}{4} \end{array}$ so that

$\mathbb{E}[U(A)] = \frac{1}{4}(40-10-4)^2 + \frac{3}{4}(40+10-4)^2 = 1,756$ and
$\mathbb{E}[U(B)] = \frac{1}{4}(40+35-4)^2 + \frac{3}{4}(40-5-4)^2 = \boxed{1,981}$.

Thus, in this case she would choose B.

On the other hand, if informed that the state belongs to $\{s_3, s_4\}$, Amy should update her beliefs to $\begin{array}{cc} s_3 & s_4 \\ \frac{1}{4} & \frac{3}{4} \end{array}$ so that

$\mathbb{E}[U(A)] = \frac{1}{4}(40+20-4)^2 + \frac{3}{4}(40+30-4)^2 = \boxed{4,051}$ and
$\mathbb{E}[U(B)] = \frac{1}{4}(40+25-4)^2 + \frac{3}{4}(40+15-4)^2 = 2,881$.

Thus, in this case she would choose A.

Hence, her expected utility from hiring the expert is $\frac{4}{8}(1,981) + \frac{4}{8}(4,051) = 3,016$. Since this is less than $3,337.5$, Amy is better off without hiring the expert. □

9.6 Solutions to Exercises

Solution to Exercise 9.11.

(a) By the conditional probability rule, $P(+|A) = \frac{P(A,+)}{P(A)}$; hence,
$P(A,+) = P(+|A) \times P(A) = 0.8 \times 0.6 = 0.48$.
Similarly, $P(A,-) = 0.2 \times 0.6 = 0.12$, $P(B,+) = 0.1 \times 0.4 = 0.04$ and $P(B,-) = 0.9 \times 0.4 = 0.36$.
Thus, the probabilities are as follows:

state:	$(A,+)$	$(A,-)$	$(B,+)$	$(B,-)$
probability:	0.48	0.12	0.04	0.36

(b) The decision problem is as follows:

probability	0.48	0.12	0.04	0.36
state →	$(A,+)$	$(A,-)$	$(B,+)$	$(B,-)$
act ↓				
$(\neg T, A)$	$(c, \$900)$	$(c, \$900)$	$(\neg c, \$900)$	$(\neg c, \$900)$
$(\neg T, B)$	$(\neg c, \$900)$	$(\neg c, \$900)$	$(c, \$900)$	$(c, \$900)$
(T, A)	$(c, \$650)$	$(c, \$650)$	$(\neg c, \$650)$	$(\neg c, \$650)$
(T, B)	$(\neg c, \$650)$	$(\neg c, \$650)$	$(c, \$650)$	$(c, \$650)$
$(T, A+, B-)$	$(c, \$650)$	$(\neg c, \$650)$	$(\neg c, \$650)$	$(c, \$650)$
$(T, B+, A-)$	$(\neg c, \$650)$	$(c, \$650)$	$(c, \$650)$	$(\neg c, \$650)$

(c) The normalized utility function is as follows, with $0 < q < p < 1$:

	outcome	utility
best	$(c, \$900)$	1
	$(c, \$650)$	p
	$(\neg c, \$900)$	q
worst	$(\neg c, \$650)$	0

Thus, in terms of utilities, the decision problem is as follows:

probability	0.48	0.12	0.04	0.36
state →	$(A,+)$	$(A,-)$	$(B,+)$	$(B,-)$
act ↓				
$(\neg T, A)$	1	1	q	q
$(\neg T, B)$	q	q	1	1
(T, A)	p	p	0	0
(T, B)	0	0	p	p
$(T, A+, B-)$	p	0	0	p
$(T, B+, A-)$	0	p	p	0

(d) (T, A) is strictly dominated by $(\neg T, A)$ and (T, B) is strictly dominated by $(\neg T, B)$.

(e) The expected utility of $(\neg T, A)$ is $0.6 + 0.4q$ while the expected utility of $(\neg T, B)$ is $0.6q + 0.4$. The former is greater than the latter if and only if $6 + 4q > 6q + 4$ if and only if $2 > 2q$, which is true, since $q < 1$. Thus, if Andrea decided *not* to take the test then she would treat disease A.

(f) Since (T,A) and (T,B) are strictly dominated, Andrea will not consider them. Thus, we only need to compare $(T,A+,B-)$ and $(T,B+,A-)$. The expected utility of $(T,A+,B-)$ is $0.84p$, while the expected utility of $(T,B+,A-)$ is $0.16p$. Thus, if she decided to take the test, Andrea would want to treat A if the test is positive and B if the test is negative.

(g) We are looking for the conditions under which the expected utility from $(T,A+,B-)$ exceeds the expected utility from $(\neg T, A)$, that is, $0.84p > 0.6 + 0.4q$. This is true if and only if $p > 0.7143 + 0.4762q$.

(h) Yes, because $0.86 > 0.7143 + 0.4762 \times 0.3 = 0.8572$. □

Solution to Exercise 9.12.

By Bayes' rule,

$$P(G|A_G Z_G) = \frac{P(A_G Z_G|G) \times P(G)}{P(A_G Z_G|G) \times P(G) + P(A_G Z_G|B) \times P(B)}$$

By independence, $P(A_G Z_G|G) = P(A_G|G) \times P(Z_G|G) = 1 \times \frac{1}{2} = \frac{1}{2}$ and $P(A_G Z_G|B) = P(A_G|B) \times P(Z_G|B) = \frac{1}{2} \times 0 = 0$. Thus,

$$P(G|A_G Z_G) = \frac{\frac{1}{2} \times p}{\frac{1}{2} \times p + 0 \times (1-p)} = 1.$$

Similarly,

$$P(G|A_G Z_B) = \frac{P(A_G Z_B|G) \times P(G)}{P(A_G Z_B|G) \times P(G) + P(A_G Z_B|B) \times P(B)}$$

By independence, $P(A_G Z_B|G) = P(A_G|G) \times P(Z_B|G) = 1 \times \frac{1}{2} = \frac{1}{2}$ and $P(A_G Z_B|B) = P(A_G|B) \times P(Z_B|B) = \frac{1}{2} \times 1 = \frac{1}{2}$. Thus,

$$P(G|A_G Z_B) = \frac{\frac{1}{2} \times p}{\frac{1}{2} \times p + \frac{1}{2} \times (1-p)} = p.$$

Finally,

$$P(G|A_B Z_B) = \frac{P(A_B Z_B|G) \times P(G)}{P(A_B Z_B|G) \times P(G) + P(A_B Z_B|B) \times P(B)}$$

By independence, $P(A_B Z_B|G) = P(A_B|G) \times P(Z_B|G) = 0 \times \frac{1}{2} = 0$ and $P(A_B Z_B|B) = P(A_B|B) \times P(Z_B|B) = \frac{1}{2} \times 1 = \frac{1}{2}$. Thus,

$$P(G|A_B Z_B) = \frac{0 \times p}{0 \times p + \frac{1}{2} \times (1-p)} = 0.$$

□

III Thinking about Future Selves

10 Intertemporal Choice 221
    10.1   Introduction
    10.2   Present value and discounting
    10.3   Exponential discounting
    10.4   Hyperbolic discounting
    10.5   Dealing with time inconsistency
    10.6   Exercises
    10.7   Solutions to Exercises

10. Intertemporal Choice

10.1 Introduction

So far we have considered decision problems where the outcomes were implicitly assumed to take place at a point in time and the *DM*'s current decision had no effect on what options would be available to her in the future. For many decisions – such as decisions about borrowing and saving, exercise, nutrition, education, etc. – costs are incurred and benefits obtained at different points in time and thus require comparing one's own welfare at some time t with one's own welfare at some later time $t' > t$. Furthermore, a decision today might affect the options that will be available at a later date. We call such such situations *intertemporal choice problems*.

For example, suppose that every month John sets aside $200 to be used for entertainment expenses during the weekends. If, on the first weekend, John spends the entire $200 to try to impress his new date by taking her to a posh restaurant, then he will not have any money left for entertainment for the rest of the month. He has to weigh the potential benefit of this decision (a suitably impressed date) against the future "cost" of not being able to, for example, join his friends at the movie theater or at a restaurant. Another example of an intertemporal choice problem is the decision of how much of one's income to set aside for retirement: in this case the tradeoff is between consumption when young and consumption when old.

A common trait of human beings is a tendency to favor present rewards relative to later ones. In the 1960s the psychologist Walter Mischel ran a number of experiments at Stanford university on delayed gratification involving children, mostly around the ages of 4 and 5. In these experiments, each child was offered a choice between a small reward (one marshmallow) available immediately or a larger reward (two marshmallows) available with a delay of approximately 15 minutes; during this short period of time the child was left alone, without distractions, and facing the temptation of eating the one marshmallow lying in front of him/her. This became known as the "Marshmallow test". A video of this experiment can be found on youtube.com.[1] As the video shows, some children are unable to resist the temptation to eat the single marshmallow before 15 minutes elapse (thus forgoing the larger later reward), while others muster enough self control to delay gratification and enjoy two marshmallows at the end of the 15-minute period. Follow-up studies showed that those children who were able to delay gratification, tended in later life to have higher SAT scores than their counterparts, lower levels of substance abuse, and were reported by their parents to be more competent.

This chapter discusses how to think about intertemporal decision problems and how to represent different attitudes concerning the trade-off between earlier rewards/costs and later rewards/costs.

10.2 Present value and discounting

Suppose I promise to give you $100 and ask you to decide whether I should give it to you today or a year from today. What would you choose? Most people would choose to get $100 today. There are a number of reasons why. One reason is *uncertainty*. The future is necessarily clouded in uncertainty: you know you are alive now and can enjoy $100 now, but you cannot be certain that you will be alive a year from now; you do not know if I will be around next year to give you the promised $100; you do not know if I would keep my promise next year, etc. Another reason is *impatience*: usually people tend to favor current enjoyments/rewards/pleasures over future ones.

What if the choice were between $100 today and more than $100 a year from today, say $110. What would you choose? The same considerations apply in this case: uncertainty, impatience, etc. might induce you to choose the smaller sum of money today. What about $100 versus $500 a year from today? The difficulty in making such choices is that we are comparing two very different objects: a sum of money available today is not directly comparable to a (possibly different) sum of money available in the future. We could, however, force them to be comparable by modifying the choice problem as follows. What would/should you choose between:

- $B a year from today, and
- $A today with the constraint that you cannot spend this money until a year has passed?

When the choice problem is framed this way, then the considerations raised above concerning uncertainty, impatience, etc., no longer apply, because we have made the two options directly comparable: we are comparing two sums of money available for use a year from now. In such a case, your choice is no longer a matter of preference: there is now a *rational* way of choosing that everybody should conform to. If you take $A today and cannot spend it until next year, your best course of action is to deposit it into an interest-bearing account. Let the yearly interest rate be r. Then after one year the initial deposit of $100 (the principal) will have increased by an interest payment of $100r$, so that the balance of your account will be $(100 + 100r) = \$100(1+r)$. We call this the *future value of* $100 *today*: more precisely, the value, one year from today, of $100 today. Then the answer to the above question is clear:

- choose $A today if $A(1+r) > B$ and choose $B a year from today if $A(1+r) < B$ (and you would be indifferent between the two if $A(1+r) = B$).

---

[1] https://www.youtube.com/watch?v=QX_oy9614HQ

10.2 Present value and discounting

An alternative, but equivalent, approach is to consider the *present value* of $B a year from today instead of the future value of $A today. The present value of $B available one year from today is that sum of money x that – if available today and deposited in an account that yields interest at the yearly rate r – would become $B after one year; that is, it is the solution to the equation

$$x(1+r) = B.$$

Hence, the present value of $B available one year from today is

$$B\left(\frac{1}{1+r}\right).$$

While r is called the *interest rate* or *discount rate*, $\left(\frac{1}{1+r}\right)$ is called the *discount factor* and is usually denoted by δ:

$$\delta = \frac{1}{1+r}.$$

Hence, we can write the present value of $B available one year from today as $B\delta$. The above decision rule can also be written in terms of present values as:

- choose $A today if $A > B\delta$ and choose $B a year from today if $A < B\delta$ (and you would be indifferent between the two if $A = B\delta$).

The comparison in terms of present values is preferable to the comparison in terms of future values when different future sums of money are considered. For example, suppose that you are turning 25 today and a relative of yours, who recently passed away, left the following provision in his will: on each of your 26th, 27th, 28th, 29th and 30th birthdays you will receive $12,000. What is the present value of this sequence of future payments?

- The present value of $12,000 paid to you on your 26th birthday is, as explained above,

$$\$\left[12,000\left(\frac{1}{1+r}\right)\right] = \$(12,000\delta).$$

- The present value of $12,000 paid to you on your 27th birthday is that sum of money x that – if available today and deposited in an account that yields interest at the yearly rate r – would become $12,000 after two years, that is, it is the solution to the equation[2] $x(1+r)^2 = 12,000$, which is

$$\$\left[12,000\left(\frac{1}{(1+r)^2}\right)\right] = \$\left[12,000\left(\frac{1}{1+r}\right)^2\right] = \$(12,000\delta^2).$$

- The present value of $12,000 paid to you on your 28th birthday is

$$\$\left[12,000\left(\frac{1}{1+r}\right)^3\right] = \$(12,000\delta^3).$$

---

[2] Why this equation? If you deposit $x into an account that pays interest at the yearly rate r, then – after one year – the balance of your account will be $y, where $y = x(1+r)$ and this will become the new principal on which interest is calculated from that time onwards, so that – after one more year – you account balance will be $y(1+r) = [x(1+r)](1+r) = x(1+r)^2$.

- Similarly for the remaining sums of money: the present value of $12,000 paid to you t years from now is $(12,000\, \delta^t)$.

Thus, the present value of the above sequence of payments is

$$12,000\delta + 12,000\delta^2 + 12,000\delta^3 + 12,000\delta^4 + 12,000\delta^5 = 12,000 \sum_{n=1}^{5} \delta^n.$$

For example, if $r = 8\%$ then $\delta = \frac{1}{1.08} = 0.9259$ and the present value of the above sequence of payments is

$$12,000 \left(0.9259 + 0.9259^2 + 0.9259^3 + 0.9259^4 + 0.9259^5\right) = 47,912.52.$$

Thus, getting $47,912.52 today is equivalent to getting $12,000 on each birthday from the 26th to the 30th. In what sense is it equivalent? In the precise sense that with $47,912.52 today you can *exactly* replicate that sequence. To see this, imagine that you get $47,912.52 today and put this entire amount in an account that yields interest at the yearly rate of 8%. Then,

- After one year (on your 26th birthday) you will have $[47,912.52(1.08)] = $51,745.52 in your account. Withdraw $12,000 from the account (thus making this sum available to yourself on your 26th birthday) and leave the remaining $(51,745.52 - 12,000) = $39,745.52 in the account.

- After one more year (on your 27th birthday) you will have $[39,745.52(1.08)] = $42,925.16 in you account. Withdraw $12,000 from the account (thus making this sum available to yourself on your 27th birthday) and leave the remaining $(42,925.16 - 12,000) = $30,925.16 in the account.

- After one more year (on your 28th birthday) you will have $[30,925.16(1.08)] = $33,399.17 in you account. Withdraw $12,000 from the account (thus making this sum available to yourself on your 28th birthday) and leave the remaining $(33,399.17 - 12,000) = $21,399.17 in the account.

- After one more year (on your 29th birthday) you will have $[21,399.17(1.08)] = $23,111.11 in you account. Withdraw $12,000 from the account (thus making this sum available to yourself on your 29th birthday) and leave the remaining $(23,111.11 - 12,000) = $11,111.11 in the account.

- After one more year (on your 30th birthday) you will find $11,111.11(1.08) = $12,000 in your account, available to you on your 30th birthday.

To sum up, if

- (1) we call today date 0,
- (2) date t is t periods into the future,
- (3) r is the rate of interest per period, and
- (4) $\delta = \frac{1}{1+r}$,

then

★ The present value (that is, the value at date 0) of $B available at date t is[3]

$$B\delta^t.$$

★ The present value of the sequence $\langle \$B_0, \$B_1, \ldots, \$B_n \rangle$ (where, for every $t = 0, 1, \ldots, n$, $\$B_t$ is a sum of money available at date t) is

$$B_0\delta^0 + B_1\delta^1 + \cdots + B_n\delta^n.$$

> Test your understanding of the concepts introduced in this section, by going through the exercises in Section 10.6.1 at the end of this chapter.

10.3 Exponential discounting

The notion of discounting explains why, as long as the rate of interest is positive, $B today is preferable to $B at a later date. It is important to understand, however, that *the notion of present value has nothing to do with impatience*. The rationale for preferring $100 today to $100 a year from now is *not* that you don't have to wait one year to spend $100: the idea is that if you get $100 now and put it in an interest-bearing account *and wait one year*, then you will have more than $100 to spend a year from now. However, if one is truly faced with the choice between, say, $1,000 today *with no restrictions* (that is, being free to spend this money any time) and, say, $1,500 a year from now, then the notion or present value becomes irrelevant. It can be perfectly rational to prefer $1,000 today even if the rate of interest is less than 50%;[4] indeed, even if the rate of interest is zero. You might need $1,000 now to pay an overdue bill, or you might be in poor health and not be sure that you will be alive a year from now or, less dramatically, you might just prefer to spend $1,000 today instead of waiting one year to spend the larger sum of $1,500. Furthermore, it may be that the options that you are considering are not sums of money. For example, suppose that you employer wants to reward your performance and offers a choice between an all-expenses-paid 3-day vacation in Hawaii starting today or an all-expenses-paid 7-day vacation in Hawaii three months from now. In this case one cannot even compute the present value of a 7-day vacation in Hawaii three months from now! It is clear that, in principle, a 7-day vacation is better than a 3-day vacation, but what makes the choice difficult is that the latter can be enjoyed immediately, while one has to wait three months to enjoy the former. Intuitively, somebody who chooses the shorter, but earlier, vacation displays more impatience that somebody who chooses the longer, later, vacation. How can we model impatience? A common approach in economics is to model impatience with a formula that is mathematically similar to present-value discounting, but conceptually quite different.

Before we go into the details, it is worth noting that the approach is very general and applies not only to rewards but also to costs, such as the unpleasantness associated with an onerous activity. For example, if you need to submit an essay for a class tomorrow by noon and face the decision between working on it now or working on it tomorrow morning, then

---

[3] Recall that, for every number x, $x^0 = 1$ and thus $B\delta^0 = B(1) = B$, so that the present value (at date 0) of $B available at date 0 is $B, as it should be!

[4] 50% is the value of r that makes the present value of $1,500 a year from now equal to $1,000. Thus, if $r < 50\%$ then the present value of $1,500 a year from now is greater than $1,000.

– if you are like many students – you prefer to postpone the task. Wanting to experience a reward earlier or wanting to avoid spoiling your present moment with an unpleasant activity, by postponing it, are both manifestations of *favoring the present over the future*.

In what follows we will not restrict ourselves to outcomes that are sums of money, but rather we will consider general outcomes.

Let Z be a set of outcomes[5] and $T = \{0, 1, \ldots, n\}$ be a set of dates, where $t = 0$ is interpreted as now, $t = 1$ is interpreted as one period from now, etc. Depending on the context, a period could be a year or a month or a week, etc.

The Cartesian product $Z \times T$ is the set of *dated outcomes*: $(z,t) \in Z \times T$ means that outcome z is to be experienced at date t.

We consider an individual who, at date 0, has a complete and transitive preference relation $\succsim_0$ on $Z \times T$. The interpretation of $(z,t) \succsim_0 (z',s)$ is that – at date 0 (the subscript of $\succsim$) – the individual considers outcome z experienced at time t to be at least as good as outcome z' experienced at time s, with $t \geq 0$ and $s \geq 0$.[6] As usual, strict preference is denoted by $\succ$ and indifference is denoted by $\sim$.

For example, let z be "a 3-day trip to Disneyland" and z' be "a 5-day trip to Chicago" and take a period to be a week. Then $(z,4) \succ_0 (z',1)$ means that today (date 0: the subscript of $\succ$) the individual prefers a 3-day trip to Disneyland four weeks from now to a 5-day trip to Chicago next week.

Note that if we restrict attention to pairs of the form $(z,0)$, then we have a ranking of the outcomes for date 0: this would correspond to the preference relation for static choice that we considered in Chapter 2. But we want to go beyond this, by expressing also how the individual ranks the pairs (z,t) for t possibly greater than 0.

Furthermore, we also want to consider the individual's preferences at any date t, expressed by the preference relation $\succsim_t$. In this case, if we write $(z,\hat{t}) \succ_t (z',\bar{t})$ then we assume that $\hat{t} \geq t$ and $\bar{t} \geq t$ (otherwise we would be capturing wishful thinking: see Footnote 6). Continuing the previous example of the 3-day trip to Disneyland (outcome z) versus the 5-day trip to Chicago (outcome z'), it is possible that today the individual prefers waiting four weeks for a 3-day trip to Disneyland relative to waiting one week for a 5-day trip to Chicago: $(z,4) \succ_0 (z',1)$ but after one week he reverses his preferences: $(z',1) \succ_1 (z,4)$ (that is, after one week he prefers going to Chicago right away rather than waiting three more weeks to go to Disneyland).

The ranking $\succsim_t$ at time t restricted to pairs of the form (z,t) is called the *instantaneous ranking at date t*. Let $u_t : Z \to \mathbb{R}$ (where $\mathbb{R}$ denotes the set of real numbers) be a utility function that represents this instantaneous ranking, in the sense that $u_t(z) \geq u_t(z')$ if and only if $(z,t) \succsim_t (z',t)$.

---

[5] In previous chapters we denoted an outcome with the letter 'o', but in this chapter we will use the letter 'z' to avoid potential confusion between the letter o and the number 0, which will be used to denote the present.

[6] We allow for $t \neq s$. The reason for restricting t and s to be greater than, or equal to, 0 is that we want to model decisions that affect the present or the future. There is nothing wrong, from a conceptual point of view, with stating preferences about the past. For example, if yesterday you wasted two hours watching a mediocre movie, then you can express the following preferences: (not watch, -1) $\succ_0$ (watch, -1), that is, today (date 0) you prefer if yesterday (date -1) you had not watched the movie, that is, you regret watching the movie. However, the past cannot be changed and current decisions can only affect the present or the future. There is no point in analyzing preferences over past outcomes, since they merely represent wishful thinking.

10.3 Exponential discounting

The *exponential utility* (or *discounted utility*) model assumes that at date 0 the ranking $\succsim_0$ of $Z \times T$ can be represented by the utility function $U_0 : Z \times T \to \mathbb{R}$ given by

$$\boxed{U_0(z,t) = \delta^t u_t(z)} \tag{10.1}$$

where δ is called the *discount factor* and is such that $0 < \delta \leq 1$. By analogy to the notion of present value, we let $\delta = \frac{1}{1+\rho}$ and call $\rho \geq 0$ the *discount rate*. Thus,

$$(z,t) \succsim_0 (z',s) \text{ if and only if } U_0(z,t) \geq U_0(z',s), \text{ that is, } \delta^t u_t(z) \geq \delta^s u_s(z'). \tag{10.2}$$

■ **Example 10.1** Let z denote "going to the movies" and z' denote "going to dinner at a restaurant". Today (date 0) Ann is indifferent between $(z,0)$ and $(z',2)$, that is, she is indifferent between going to the movies today and going to the restaurant the day after tomorrow (periods are measured in days): $(z,0) \sim_0 (z',2)$.

Suppose also that Ann's preferences can be represented by a utility function of the form (10.1) above and $u_0(z) = 3$ and $u_2(z') = 5$. What is Ann's discount factor? What is her discount rate?

Since $(z,0) \sim_0 (z',2)$, $U_0(z,0) = U_0(z',2)$, that is, $\delta^0 u_0(z) = \delta^2 u_2(z')$;[7] thus, $3 = 5\delta^2$ so that $\delta = \sqrt{\frac{3}{5}} = \sqrt{0.6} = 0.775$.

Furthermore, since $\delta = \frac{1}{1+\rho}$, to find the discount rate we have to solve the equation $\frac{1}{1+\rho} = 0.775$. The solution is $\rho = 0.29$.

Continuing the example, suppose that – before she makes her decision between going to the movies today or to dinner the day after tomorrow – Ann learns that an option she thought she did not have, namely going to a dance performance (outcome z'') tomorrow, is now available and $u_1(z'') = 4$. What decision will she make? We saw above that $U_0(z,0) = U_0(z',2) = 3$; on the other hand, $U_0(z'',1) = \delta u_1(z'') = (0.775)(4) = 3.1$. Hence, she will choose to go to the dance performance tomorrow (her preferences today are: $(z'',1) \succ_0 (z,0) \sim_0 (z',2)$). ■

One special case is where instantaneous utility is always the same, that is, $u_t(z) = u(z)$, for every $t \in T$ (and for every $z \in Z$). Thus, the instantaneous utility of, say, spending a day at Disneyland is the same, no matter whether you go today or tomorrow or 10 days from now. Then, if you have a choice between outcome z today and outcome z tomorrow, what will you choose? We have to distinguish two cases. First of all, let us normalize the instantaneous utility function so that the utility of the *status quo* is 0.

Case 1: $u(z) > 0$. This means that outcome z is better than the *status quo*. For example, z might be a pleasurable activity, like watching a movie, playing a video game, etc. Then $U_0(z,0) = \delta^0 u(z) = u(z)$ and $U_0(z,1) = \delta^1 u(z) = \delta u(z)$. If $\delta < 1$ (and $u(z) > 0$), then $\delta u(z) < u(z)$ and thus you prefer experiencing z today to experiencing it tomorrow. Thus, $\delta < 1$ captures the notion of impatience (that is, favoring the present over the future): you would rather do something pleasurable today than do it later.

---

[7] Recall that, for every number x, $x^0 = 1$.

Case 2: $u(z) < 0$. This means that outcome z is worse than the *status quo*. For example, z might be an unpleasant activity, like washing the dishes, doing homework, etc. Also in this case $U_0(z,0) = \delta^0 u(z) = u(z)$ and $U_0(z,1) = \delta^1 u(z) = \delta u(z)$. If $\delta < 1$ (and $u(z) < 0$), then $\delta u(z) > u(z)$ and thus you will want to delay experiencing z. Once again, $\delta < 1$ captures the notion of favoring the present over the future: you would rather postpone something unpleasant to a later date.

A more general situation is one where we do not simply compare one outcome at date t with another outcome at date s but a series of outcomes at dates $t_1, t_2, \ldots$ with a different series of outcomes at those same dates. For example, let m denote "watching a movie" and h "doing homework" and suppose that instantaneous utility is the same at every date, with $u_t(m) = u(m) = 2$ and $u_t(h) = u(h) = 1$, for every $t \in T$. Suppose also that the discount factor is $\delta = 0.9$. Imagine that you have two choices:

	Today date 0	Tomorrow date 1
Plan A:	m	h
Plan B:	h	m

Thus, Plan A is to watch a movie today and do the homework tomorrow, while Plan B is to reverse the order of these two activities. Let us rewrite the above table in terms of instantaneous utilities:

	Today date 0	Tomorrow date 1
Plan A:	2	1
Plan B:	1	2

How do you rank these two plans? What is the utility of Plan A? And the utility of Plan B? A commonly used extension of the utility representation (10.1) is the following additive representation:

$$U_0(\text{Plan A}) = \delta^0 u(m) + \delta^1 u(h) = 2 + (0.9)(1) = 2.9,$$

$$U_0(\text{Plan B}) = \delta^0 u(h) + \delta^1 u(m) = 1 + (0.9)(2) = 2.8.$$

Thus, you will choose to watch the movie now and do the homework tomorrow. Does it seem familiar?

As a further example, suppose that Bob has to decide between the following two plans:

date:	0	1	2
Plan A:	x	y	z
Plan B:	y	z	x

Assume that his preferences have an exponential utility representation, so that

$$U_0(\text{Plan A}) = \delta^0 u_0(x) + \delta^1 u_1(y) + \delta^2 u_2(z) = u_0(x) + \delta u_1(y) + \delta^2 u_2(z)$$

and $U_0(\text{Plan B}) = u_0(y) + \delta u_1(z) + \delta^2 u_2(x).$

10.3 Exponential discounting

If $u_0(x) = 1, u_1(y) = 4, u_2(z) = 3, u_0(y) = 4, u_1(z) = 2, u_2(x) = 0$, we can re-write the decision problem in terms of utilities as follows:

date:	0	1	2
Plan A:	1	4	3
Plan B:	4	2	0

For what value of the discount factor δ will Bob choose Plan A? $U_0(\text{Plan A}) = 1 + 4\delta + 3\delta^2$ and $U_0(\text{Plan B}) = 4 + 2\delta + 0\delta^2$; hence, Bob will choose Plan A if $1 + 4\delta + 3\delta^2 > 4 + 2\delta$, that is, if $\delta > 0.7208$ (and will choose Plan B if $\delta < 0.7208$ and will be indifferent between the two plans if $\delta = 0.7208$).

10.3.1 Time consistency

Suppose that you make a plan today involving future activities or outcomes. For example, suppose that today is Monday and you have to submit your homework on Thursday morning. Let z denote the activity/outcome of doing the homework. You can do it today (option $(z, Monday)$) or tomorrow (option $(z, Tuesday)$) or on Wednesday (option $(z, Wednesday)$). Suppose that your ranking today (Monday: the subscript of $\succ$) is

$$(z, Tuesday) \succ_{Monday} (z, Wednesday) \succ_{Monday} (z, Monday)$$

that is, doing the homework today is your least preferred option, but you prefer to do it with a day to spare (on Tuesday) rather than at the last moment (on Wednesday). Thus, you decide to postpone doing the homework. However, there is no way today of forcing your "Tuesday-self" to do the homework on Tuesday. All you can do is decide whether or not to do the homework today (Monday) and – if you decide to postpone – then the decision of when to do the homework will be made by your future self. So today you decide to postpone and plan to do the homework tomorrow. You wake up on Tuesday and have to decide when to do the homework. Obviously, the option $(z, Monday)$ is no longer available, but the other two options are. On this new day (Tuesday) you have preferences over these two options. We must distinguish two cases.

Case 1: your Tuesday preference are

$$(z, Tuesday) \succ_{Tuesday} (z, Wednesday),$$

as they were on Monday. Then you will decide to do the homework today (Tuesday). In this case we say that your preferences are *time-consistent*: if at an earlier date (e.g. Monday) you make some plans for a future date (e.g. Tuesday), then when that future date comes along your plans do not change.

Case 2: your Tuesday preference are

$$(z, Wednesday) \succ_{Tuesday} (z, Tuesday),$$

a reversal of what they were on Monday. Then you will decide, once again, to postpone doing the homework. In this case we say that your preferences are *time-inconsistent*: if at an earlier date you make some plans for a future date, then when that future date comes along you no longer want to carry out those plans.

Let us consider another example. Today is Monday and you have to decide on some activities, call them x, y and z, for Friday, Saturday and Sunday. You can ask yourself how you rank alternative plans (for Friday, Saturday and Sunday) today but you can also ask yourself how you will rank those alternative plans (for Friday, Saturday and Sunday) on, say, Thursday. Suppose that you are thinking about two plans in particular, shown in Figure 10.1.

	Monday (today, date 0)	Tuesday (date 1)	Wesdesday (date 2)	Thursday (date 3)	Friday (date 4)	Saturday (date 5)	Sunday (date 6)
Plan A					x	y	z
Plan B					y	z	x

Figure 10.1: Two possible week-end plans

At time 0 (on Monday) the utilities are as follows:

$$U_0(\text{Plan A}) = \delta^4 u_4(x) + \delta^5 u_5(y) + \delta^6 u_6(z)$$

$$U_0(\text{Plan B}) = \delta^4 u_4(y) + \delta^5 u_5(z) + \delta^6 u_6(x).$$

What are the utilities on Thursday (= date 3)? The dominant approach is to assume that the structure of the preferences does not change so that

$$U_3(\text{Plan A}) = \delta^{(4-3)} u_4(x) + \delta^{(5-3)} u_5(y) + \delta^{(6-3)} u_6(z) = \delta u_4(x) + \delta^2 u_5(y) + \delta^3 u_6(z)$$

$$U_3(\text{Plan B}) = \delta^{(4-3)} u_4(y) + \delta^{(5-3)} u_5(z) + \delta^{(6-3)} u_6(x) = \delta u_4(y) + \delta^2 u_5(z) + \delta^3 u_6(x).$$

In other words, the utility at time t of outcome w occurring at time $t+s$ is

$$\boxed{U_t(w, t+s) = \delta^s u_{t+s}(w)}.\qquad(10.3)$$

Continuing the example, suppose that your daily discount factor is $\delta = 0.95$ and

$u_4(x) = 4, u_5(y) = 1, u_6(z) = 5$
$u_4(y) = 2, u_5(z) = 3, u_6(x) = 6.$

Then we can rewrite the problem in terms of instantaneous utilities as shown in Figure 10.2.

	Monday (today, date 0)	Tuesday (date 1)	Wesdesday (date 2)	Thursday (date 3)	Friday (date 4)	Saturday (date 5)	Sunday (date 6)
Plan A					4	1	5
Plan B					2	3	6

Figure 10.2: The decision problem in terms of utilities

How do you rank the two plans at date 0?

$$U_0(\text{Plan A}) = \delta^4 u(x) + \delta^5 u(y) + \delta^6 u(z) = (0.95)^4(4) + (0.95)^5(1) + (0.95)^6(5) = 7.71$$

10.3 Exponential discounting

$$U_0(\text{Plan B}) = \delta^4 u(y) + \delta^5 u(z) + \delta^6 u(x) = (0.95)^4(2) + (0.95)^5(3) + (0.95)^6(6) = 8.36.$$

Hence, on Monday (date 0) you prefer Plan B to Plan A:

Plan B $\succ_0$ *Plan A.*

How will you feel about these two plans on Thursday (date 3)?

$$U_3(\text{Plan A}) = \delta u(x) + \delta^2 u(y) + \delta^3 u(z) = (0.95)(4) + (0.95)^2(1) + (0.95)^3(5) = 8.99$$

$$U_3(\text{Plan B}) = \delta u(y) + \delta^2 u(z) + \delta^3 u(x) = (0.95)(2) + (0.95)^2(3) + (0.95)^3(6) = 9.75$$

thus, on Thursday you also prefer Plan B to Plan A:

Plan B $\succ_3$ *Plan A.*

How will you feel about these two plans on Friday (date 4)?

$$U_4(\text{Plan A}) = u(x) + \delta u(y) + \delta^2 u(z) = 4 + (0.95)(1) + (0.95)^2(5) = 9.46$$

$$U_4(\text{Plan B}) = u(y) + \delta u(z) + \delta^2 u(x) = 2 + (0.95)(3) + (0.95)^2(6) = 10.27$$

thus, on Friday you also prefer Plan B to Plan A:

Plan B $\succ_4$ *Plan A.*

Since your ranking does not change over time, your preferences are time consistent.

It is an important feature of *exponential discounting* that it *implies time consistency*. The proof is quite simple. We illustrate the proof for the case where at date t you compare two plans involving dates $t+4, t+5, \ldots, t+10$:

date:	$t+4$	$t+5$	...	$t+10$
Plan A:	x_4	x_5	...	x_{10}
Plan B:	y_4	y_5	...	y_{10}

Then

$$U_t(\text{Plan A}) = \delta^4 u_{t+4}(x_4) + \delta^5 u_{t+5}(x_5) + \ldots + \delta^{10} u_{t+10}(x_{10}),$$

and

$$U_t(\text{Plan B}) = \delta^4 u_{t+4}(y_4) + \delta^5 u_{t+5}(y_5) + \ldots + \delta^{10} u_{t+10}(y_{10}).$$

Suppose that you prefer Plan A: $U_t(\text{Plan A}) > U_t(\text{Plan B})$, that is,

$$\delta^4 u_{t+4}(x_4) + \delta^5 u_{t+5}(x_5) + \ldots + \delta^{10} u_{t+10}(x_{10}) > \delta^4 u_{t+4}(y_4) + \delta^5 u_{t+5}(y_5) + \ldots + \delta^{10} u_{t+10}(y_{10}).$$
(10.4)

Now date t + 4 comes along and your utility becomes

$$U_{t+4}(Plan\,A) = \delta^0 u_{t+4}(x_4) + \delta^1 u_{t+5}(x_5) + ... + \delta^6 u_{t+10}(x_{10}),$$

and

$$U_{t+4}(Plan\,B) = \delta^0 u_{t+4}(y_4) + \delta^1 u_{t+5}(y_5) + ... + \delta^6 u_{t+10}(y_{10}).$$

Divide both sides of (10.4) by δ^4 (note that, since $\delta > 0$, $\delta^4 > 0$) to get

$$\delta^0 u_{t+4}(x_4) + \delta^1 u_{t+5}(x_5) + ... + \delta^6 u_{t+10}(x_{10}) > \delta^0 u_{t+4}(y_4) + \delta^1 u_{t+5}(y_5) + ... + \delta^6 u_{t+10}(y_{10})$$

that is,

$$U_{t+4}(Plan\,A) > U_{t+4}(Plan\,B).$$

> Test your understanding of the concepts introduced in this section, by going through the exercises in Section 10.6.2 at the end of this chapter.

10.4 Hyperbolic discounting

On January 1, 2017 Roy was asked whether he would rather get $1,000 nine months later (i.e. on October 1, 2017) or $1,500 fifteen months later (i.e. on April 1, 2018). His answer was "$1,500 in 15 months". On October 1, 2017 (9 months after the first interview) he was offered to reconsider the initial choice: "would you rather get $1,000 today (October 1, 2017) or $1,500 in 6 months (i.e. on April 1, 2018)?" His answer was "I would rather get $1,000 today", thus displaying time inconsistency. This example illustrates a commonly observed phenomenon: many individuals prefer an immediate, smaller reward to a later, larger reward, but prefer the latter to the former when both alternatives are equally delayed. Such people are said to exhibit *diminishing impatience* (or *present bias*). Numerous experimental studies have shown that this is a robust characteristic of many people's preferences. Then we must conclude that the preferences of such people cannot be represented by the exponential utility model described in the previous section, since – as shown in the previous section – exponential utility implies time consistency.

A somewhat similar model to the exponential utility model that is capable of capturing the type of time inconsistency illustrated above is the *hyperbolic discounting* model. With hyperbolic discounting a higher discount rate or, equivalently, a lower discount factor (implying a higher degree of impatience) is used between the present and the near future, and a lower discount rate or higher discount factor (that is, a lower degree of impatience) between the near future and the more distant future. The simplest version of hyperbolic discounting is the so-called (β, δ) *model*. This model can be seen as a small departure from the exponential discounting model. With exponential discounting the utility now (= date 0) of outcome z at date $t \geq 0$ is $U_0(z,t) = \delta^t u_t(z)$. This applies to both $t = 0$ and $t > 0$. We can write exponential discounting as follows:

$$U_0(z,t) = \begin{cases} \delta^0 u_0(z) = u_0(z) & \text{if } t = 0 \\ \delta^t u_t(z) & \text{if } t > 0. \end{cases}$$

10.4 Hyperbolic discounting

More generally, if $s \geq t$:

$$U_t(z,s) = \begin{cases} u_t(z) & \text{if } s = t \\ \delta^{s-t} u_s(z) & \text{if } s > t. \end{cases}$$

With hyperbolic discounting the utility now (= date 0) of outcome z at date $t \geq 0$ is

$$U_0(z,t) = \begin{cases} \delta^0 u_0(z) = u_0(z) & \text{if } t = 0 \\ \beta \delta^t u_t(z) & \text{if } t > 0 \end{cases}$$

with $0 < \beta < 1$ (if $\beta = 1$ then we are back to the case of exponential discounting). More generally,

$$\boxed{U_t(z,s) = \begin{cases} u_t(z) & \text{if } s = t \\ \beta \delta^{s-t} u_s(z) & \text{if } s > t. \end{cases}} \quad (s \geq t).$$

■ **Example 10.2** Suppose that you are a hyperbolic discounter with monthly discount factor $\delta = 0.95$ and parameter $\beta = 0.8$ and your instantaneous utility of money is $u_t(\$m) = \sqrt{m}$ for every t (thus the same at every date).

You are given the following choice: (A) $100 twelve months from now or (B) $160 sixteen months from now. Then

$$U_0(\$100, 12) = \beta \delta^{12} \sqrt{100} = (0.8)(0.95)^{12} 10 = 4.32 \quad \text{and}$$
$$U_0(\$160, 16) = \beta \delta^{16} \sqrt{160} = (0.8)(0.95)^{16} (12.65) = 4.45.$$

Thus, you choose Option B: $160 sixteen months from now. Twelve months later you are given a chance to reconsider. Thus, at that time your choice is between (A) $100 now or (B) $160 four months from now. Then

$$U_{12}(\$100, 12) = \delta^0 \sqrt{100} = 10 \quad \text{and}$$
$$U_{12}(\$160, 16) = \beta \delta^4 \sqrt{160} = (0.8)(0.95)^4 (12.65) = 8.24;$$

hence, you change your mind and switch to Option A, displaying time inconsistency. ■

■ **Example 10.3** Today is Friday and you are planning your weekend. Let x denote "go on a trip", y "clean the house without help", w "clean the house with help" and z "go to a party". You have two options: (A) go on a trip (outcome x) tomorrow and clean the house without help (outcome y) on Sunday, or (B) clean the house with help (outcome w) tomorrow and go to a party (outcome z) on Sunday:

	Friday (date 0)	Saturday (date 1)	Sunday (date 2)
Plan A		x	y
Plan B		w	z

Suppose that $u_1(x) = 4, u_2(y) = 0, u_1(w) = 1$ and $u_2(z) = 6$. Thus, in utility terms we have:

	Friday (date 0)	Saturday (date 1)	Sunday (date 2)
Plan A		4	0
Plan B		1	6

Suppose that $\delta = \frac{7}{10}$ and $\beta = \frac{2}{3}$. What plan will you choose on Friday?

$$U_0(\text{Plan } A) = 4\beta\delta + 0\beta\delta^2 = 4\left(\frac{2}{3}\right)\left(\frac{7}{10}\right) = \frac{28}{15} = 1.867$$

and

$$U_0(\text{Plan } B) = 1\beta\delta + 6\beta\delta^2 = \left(\frac{2}{3}\right)\left(\frac{7}{10}\right) + 6\left(\frac{2}{3}\right)\left(\frac{7}{10}\right)^2 = \frac{182}{75} = 2.427.$$

Thus, you decide that you will follow Plan B: do the cleaning on Saturday with help and go to the party on Sunday:

$$\boxed{\text{Plan } B \succ_{\text{Friday}} \text{Plan } A}.$$

Now it is Saturday morning and, as you wake up, you think about what to do this week-end. You remember "choosing" Plan B yesterday. Do you want to stick with this choice?

$$U_1(\text{Plan } A) = 4 + 0\beta\delta = 4$$

and

$$U_1(\text{Plan } B) = 1 + 6\beta\delta = 1 + 6\left(\frac{2}{3}\right)\left(\frac{7}{10}\right) = \frac{19}{5} = 3.8.$$

Thus, you will change your plans and switch to Plan A: go on the trip today and clean the house without help on Sunday:

$$\boxed{\text{Plan } A \succ_{\text{Saturday}} \text{Plan } B}.$$

∎

10.4.1 Interpretation of the parameter β

What does the parameter β capture? To answer this question, let us first consider the case of exponential discounting. The general formula for exponential discounting is
$U_0(z,t) = \begin{cases} u_0(z) & \text{if } t = 0 \\ \delta^t u_t(z) & \text{if } t > 0 \end{cases}$ when evaluation takes place at date 0 and $t \geq 0$ is the date at which outcome z is experienced. To simplify the exposition, let us focus on the case where $u_t(z) = u(z)$ for all t (that is, the instantaneous utility of z is the same at every date). Then,

$$\text{with exponential discounting:} \quad U_0(z,t) = \begin{cases} u(z) & \text{if } t = 0 \\ \delta^t u(z) & \text{if } t > 0. \end{cases}$$

We assume that $u(z) > 0$.

Consider first the *utility cost of delaying z by one period from date 1 to date 2*. $U_0(z,1) = \delta u(z)$ and $U_0(z,2) = \delta^2 u(z) = \delta(\delta u(z)) = \delta U_0(z,1)$ so that

$$U_0(z,2) = \delta U_0(z,1) \quad \text{or} \quad \frac{U_0(z,2)}{U_0(z,1)} = \frac{\delta U_0(z,1)}{U_0(z,1)} = \delta.$$

10.4 Hyperbolic discounting

Assuming that $0 < \delta < 1$ (and $u(z) > 0$ so that $U_0(z,1) = \delta u(z) > 0$), $U_0(z,2) = \delta U_0(z,1) < U_0(z,1)$, that is, the delay reduces time-0 utility by a factor of δ (the utility cost of delaying is $(1-\delta)u(z)$).

Consider now the *utility cost of delaying z by one period from date 0 to date 1*: $U_0(z,0) = u(z)$ and $U_0(z,1) = \delta u(z) = \delta U_0(z,0)$. Thus,

$$U_0(z,1) = \delta U_0(z,0) \quad \text{or} \quad \frac{U_0(z,1)}{U_0(z,0)} = \frac{\delta U_0(z,0)}{U_0(z,0)} = \delta.$$

Hence, *with exponential discounting the utility cost of delaying z by one period is the same, no matter whether the delay is from date 0 to date 1 or from date 1 to date 2.*

Now consider the case of hyperbolic discounting. The general formula for hyperbolic discounting is $U_0(z,t) = \begin{cases} u_0(z) & \text{if } t = 0 \\ \beta \delta^t u_t(z) & \text{if } t > 0 \end{cases}$ (with $0 < \beta < 1$ and $0 < \delta \leq 1$) when evaluation takes place at date 0 and $t \geq 0$ is the date at which outcome z is experienced. Again, let us focus on the case where $u_t(z) = u(z) > 0$ for all t (that is, the instantaneous utility of z is the same at every date). Then

$$\text{with hyperbolic discounting:} \quad U_0(z,t) = \begin{cases} u(z) & \text{if } t = 0 \\ \beta \delta^t u(z) & \text{if } t > 0. \end{cases}$$

Consider first the *utility cost of delaying z by one period from date 1 to date 2*. $U_0(z,1) = \beta \delta u(z)$ and $U_0(z,2) = \beta \delta^2 u(z) = \delta(\beta \delta u(z)) = \delta U_0(z,1)$. So

$$U_0(z,2) = \delta U_0(z,1) \quad \text{or} \quad \frac{U_0(z,2)}{U_0(z,1)} = \frac{\delta U_0(z,1)}{U_0(z,1)} = \delta.$$

Assuming, as before, that $0 < \delta < 1$ (and $u(z) > 0$), $U_0(z,2) = \delta U_0(z,1) < U_0(z,1)$, that is, the delay reduces time-0 utility by a factor of δ (the utility cost of delaying is $(1-\delta)u(z)$). Consider now the utility *cost of delaying z by one period from date 0 to date 1*. $U_0(z,0) = u(z)$ and $U_0(z,1) = \beta \delta u(z) = \beta \delta U_0(z,0)$. So

$$U_0(z,1) = \beta \delta U_0(z,0) \quad \text{or} \quad \frac{U_0(z,1)}{U_0(z,0)} = \frac{\beta \delta U_0(z,0)}{U_0(z,0)} = \beta \delta.$$

Assuming that $0 < \beta < 1$, it follows that the delay reduces time-0 utility by a factor of $\beta \delta < \delta$ (the utility cost of delaying is $(1 - \beta \delta)u(z) > (1-\delta)u(z)$). Thus, *there is a larger drop in utility in delaying from now to tomorrow than in delaying from tomorrow to the day after tomorrow*. Hence, β *is a measure of the bias towards the present*: the lower β the more important the present becomes relative to one period ahead.

If your preferences are represented by the hyperbolic discounting model and you are sufficiently introspective, then you will realize that any plans that you make today might be overruled by your future self. Then it seems that there is no point in making any plans at all! What can a sophisticated decision maker do to protect himself from his future self? This is the topic of the next section.

> Test your understanding of the concepts introduced in this section, by going through the exercises in Section 10.6.3 at the end of this chapter.

10.5 Dealing with time inconsistency

Imagine that you are at the grocery store on Friday. You would like to buy a pint of ice cream and are thinking about your possible consumption of ice cream on Saturday. Suppose that there are only three consumption levels: 0, $\frac{1}{2}$ pint and 1 pint. Your current ranking is as follows:

$$\tfrac{1}{2} \text{ pint on Saturday } \succ_{Friday} \text{ zero on Saturday } \succ_{Friday} 1 \text{ pint on Saturday.}$$

Thus, it seems that you should buy the ice cream and plan to eat half a pint on Saturday. However, suppose that you realize that, once you have ice cream at home on Saturday you will not be able to restrain yourself and will end up eating the entire tub of ice cream and be sick for the rest of the day, that is, you know that your preferences on Saturday will be

$$1 \text{ pint on Saturday } \succ_{Saturday} \tfrac{1}{2} \text{ pint on Saturday } \succ_{Saturday} \text{ zero on Saturday.}$$

Thus, you realize that, if you buy ice cream, then the end outcome will be that you will eat the entire carton of ice cream on Saturday, which – from Friday's point of view – is the worst outcome. Situations like these are referred to as situations where the agent *lacks self control*.

If we represent your preferences with a utility function that takes on values 0, 1 and 2, then we have

$$\begin{array}{l|l}
U_{Friday}(\tfrac{1}{2} \text{ pint on Saturday}) = 2 & U_{Saturday}(1 \text{ pint on Saturday}) = 2 \\
U_{Friday}(\text{zero on Saturday}) = 1 & U_{Saturday}(\tfrac{1}{2} \text{ pint on Saturday}) = 1 \\
U_{Friday}(1 \text{ pint on Saturday}) = 0 & U_{Saturday}(\text{zero on Saturday}) = 0
\end{array}$$

The above example can be represented as a tree, as shown in Figure 10.3. At the terminal nodes of the tree we write a vector of utilities for the final outcome, where the first number is the utility on Friday and the second number is the utility on Saturday.

The double edges represent the backward-induction reasoning. First you figure out that if you buy ice cream on Friday, then the decision of how much to eat will be made by "your Saturday self", who will prefer eating 1 pint to eating $\frac{1}{2}$ pint. Hence, on Friday you are effectively deciding between (1) buying ice cream and eating it all on Saturday and (2) not buying ice cream, thereby restricting your options on Saturday to only one: not eat ice cream. By not buying ice cream on Friday, you *commit* yourself to not eating ice cream on Saturday.

This example illustrates a common phenomenon whereby a decision maker who is aware of the fact that his intertemporal preferences are time-inconsistent might decide to restrict his own choices at a later date, by undertaking some form of commitment. The commitment must be such that it cannot be easily undone (otherwise it would not be a true commitment!). A situation similar to the one described above is the situation faced by a student who is going to the library to study for an exam and has to decide whether to take her laptop computer with her. Having the computer at hand will make it easier to study, but she fears that, later on, she will be tempted to waste her time on social media or browsing the internet. Several software applications are available to students who face this type of lack of self control.

10.5 Dealing with time inconsistency

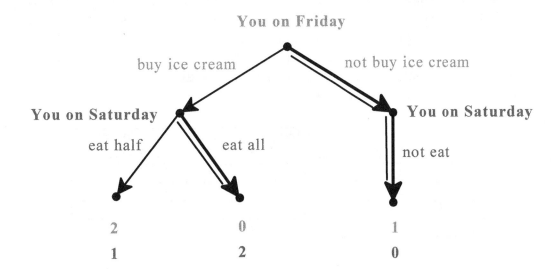

Figure 10.3: The ice cream decision problem

For example, *SelfControl* is a

> "free Mac application to help you avoid distracting websites. Just set a period of time to block for, add sites to your blacklist, and click 'Start'. Until that timer expires, you will be unable to access those sites – even if you restart your computer or delete the application".[8]

Similar programs are (1) *Focus*: "a Mac app to block distracting websites like Facebook and Reddit",[9] (2) *FocusWriter*: "a simple, distraction-free writing environment",[10] (3) *AntiSocial*: "a productivity application for Macs that turns off the social parts of the internet; when *Anti-Social* is running, you're locked away from hundreds of distracting social media sites, including Facebook, Twitter and other sites you specify",[11] (4) *StayFocusd*, which "blocks apps on iPhone and iPad, plus all browsers on Windows and Mac",[12] and more.

What if there is no possibility of commitment? What should a *DM* – who is aware of his time-inconsistent preferences – do in general? The best that one can do is to apply the method of backward induction, anticipating one's own future choices and acting accordingly in the present. We conclude this section by analyzing an example of this.

---

[8] https://selfcontrolapp.com/
[9] https://heyfocus.com/?utm_source=getconcentrating
[10] https://focuswriter.en.softonic.com/?ex=DSK-309.4
[11] https://itunes.apple.com/us/app/anti-social-block-social-media-content-from-websites/id1046835945?mt=8
[12] http://www.stayfocusd.com/

Suppose that you have a season pass to the theater, which entitles you to attend a play every Saturday for the next four weeks. It is now Friday of the first week and you have been told by your employer that you need to work one Saturday over the next four weeks (and thus you will have to miss the play on that Saturday). It is up to you to choose which Saturday. Let x be the outcome of attending a play and y be the outcome of working. Your possible plans are shown in Figure 10.4.

Plan	First Saturday	Second Saturday	Third Saturday	Fourth Saturday
A	y	x	x	x
B	x	y	x	x
C	x	x	y	x
D	x	x	x	y

Figure 10.4: The season pass example

Let us take a time period to be a week, with the current week being time 0. Assume that the instantaneous utilities are as follows: $u_t(y) = 0$, for every $t = 0, \ldots, 3$, and $u_0(x) = 4$, $u_1(x) = 6$, $u_2(x) = 7$, $u_3(x) = 13$ (for example, because the play tomorrow is a mediocre one, the one next week is a good one, the one in two weeks' time is a very good one and the one on the last week is the best of all). Then we can rewrite the table of Figure 10.4 in terms of utilities, as shown in Figure 10.5.

Choice	First Saturday	Second Saturday	Third Saturday	Fourth Saturday
A	0	6	7	13
B	4	0	7	13
C	4	6	0	13
D	4	6	7	0

Figure 10.5: The season pass example in terms of utilities

Suppose that your preferences can be represented by a hyperbolic-discounting utility function with $\beta = \frac{1}{2}$ and $\delta = \frac{9}{10}$. Let us consider two cases.

Case 1: You can commit (that is, make an irrevocable decision) today as to which Saturday you will work. What will you choose? Utilities at date 0 are as follows:

$$U_0(A) = 0 + 6\beta\delta + 7\beta\delta^2 + 13\beta\delta^3 = 10.274,$$

$$U_0(B) = 4 + 0\beta\delta + 7\beta\delta^2 + 13\beta\delta^3 = \boxed{11.573},$$

$$U_0(C) = 4 + 6\beta\delta + 0\beta\delta^2 + 13\beta\delta^3 = 11.439,$$

$$U_0(D) = 4 + 6\beta\delta + 7\beta\delta^2 + 0\beta\delta^3 = 9.535.$$

Thus, Option B gives the highest time-0 utility and you will commit to working on the second Saturday.

10.5 Dealing with time inconsistency

Case 2: You cannot commit today. Each Saturday you decide whether or not to go to work, if you have not already worked on a previous Saturday. Of course, if you do not show up at work on one of the first three Saturdays, then you will have no choice on the fourth Saturday: you will have to work on that day. You are fully aware of your preferences (hyperbolic discounting with the same β and δ every week). What will you do? Let us represent your decision problem using a tree and find the backward-induction solution. The tree is shown in Figure 10.6: the red numbers (at the top of each vector associated with a terminal node) were computed above, the blue numbers (in the middle of each vector) are the utilities from the point of view of Week 1 and the black numbers (at the bottom of each vector) are the utilities from the point of view of Week 2. The double edges show the backward-induction solution.

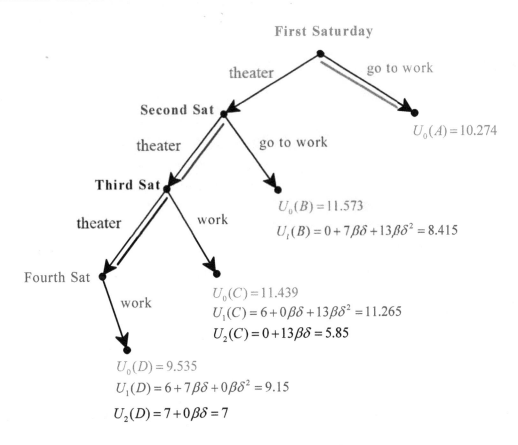

Figure 10.6: The decision tree for the season pass example

From the point of view of date 0, alternative B is the best: go to work on the second Saturday, which involves going to the theater at date 0. However, you anticipate that if you do so, then at every future date you will postpone working and end up working on the last Saturday, which – from the point of view of date 0 – is the worst alternative.[13] Hence, *you opt to go to work on the first Saturday in order to pre-empt your future procrastination.*

---

[13] On the third Saturday you will prefer going to the theater that day and to work the following Saturday (utility 7) to going to work on that day (utility 5.85); thus, you will go to the theater. Hence, on the second Saturday you will realize that your choice is between going to work that day (utility 8.415) or going to the theater that day and the following Saturday thus working on the last Saturday (utility 9.15) and you prefer the latter; thus, you will go to the theater.

Note that when you act in the way illustrated in the above examples, your present self is acting in a *paternalistic* way towards your future selves. Should your date-0 preferences have higher priority over your future preferences? Are you better off when you don't buy ice cream today to prevent your future self from binging? These are not easy questions to answer, but one argument for giving more weight to your date-0 preferences is that when you take a long-term point of view of your welfare, you are more detached and more objective in your assessment, while when you make decisions in the short term you are more short-sighted and susceptible to temptation.

> Test your understanding of the concepts introduced in this section, by going through the exercises in Section 10.6.4 at the end of this chapter.

10.6 Exercises

The solutions to the following exercises are given in Section 10.7 at the end of this chapter.

10.6.1 Exercises for Section 10.2: Present value and discounting

Exercise 10.1 A bond pays $10 one year from now, $15 two years from now, $20 three years from now and $25 four years from now. The yearly interest rate is 7%. What is the present value of the bond?

Exercise 10.2 Which of the following two options is better? (1) you get $100 today, (2) you wait three years and get $160 three years from now. The yearly rate of interest is 15%. Answer the question in two ways: (a) using the notion of present value and (b) using the notion of future value.

Exercise 10.3 You need to borrow $1,500 to lease a car for one year. You have two options: (1) apply for financing from the dealer, in which case you have to pay an application fee of $85 and you will be charged a yearly interest rate of 16%, or (2) borrow from a bank at a yearly interest rate of 21%. Which option should you choose?

Exercise 10.4 Congratulations: you won the lottery! Now you must collect the prize. You have two options: (1) get a one-time payment, today, of $11 Million, or (2) get six annual payments of $2 Million, with the first payment being collected today. The yearly interest rate is 4%. Based on present values, which option should you choose?

Exercise 10.5 You need to borrow $200 from a cousin.
(a) She agrees to lend you $200 but wants you to repay her $225 in **one** year. What is the yearly interest rate implicit in this offer?
(b) She agrees to lend you $200 but wants you to repay her $240 in **two** years. What is the yearly interest rate implicit in this offer?

10.6 Exercises

10.6.2 Exercises for Section 10.3: Exponential discounting

Exercise 10.6 Assume that preferences have an exponential discounting representation. For example, $U_0(z,t) = \delta^t u_t(z)$.

You have a free ticket to the movie theater. You can use it tonight to see a mediocre movie (call this alternative x) or you can use it next week to see a better movie (call this alternative y). Suppose that time periods denote weeks, $u_0(x) = 4$ and $u_1(y) = 7$. What should your time discount **rate** be for you to be indifferent, today, between the two options?

Exercise 10.7 Assume that preferences have an exponential discounting representation. Suppose that $u_{10}(x) = 12$. For $t = 10, 8, 6, 4, 2, 0$ and $\delta = 0.85$ calculate $U_t(x, 10)$ and draw a diagram showing these values (measure t on the horizontal axis and utility on the vertical axis).

Exercise 10.8 Assume that preferences have an exponential discounting representation. Your generous uncle gave you $800 on your birthday. You have the following options: (1) spend the $800 today, (2) put the $800 in a 3-year CD that pays interest at the rate of 5% per year, leave the money there for 3 years and spend the entire balance of your account at the end of the 3 years, (3) put the $800 in a 10-year CD that pays interest at the rate of 12% per year, leave the money there for 10 years and spend the entire balance of your account at the end of the 10 years. Suppose that your instantaneous utility function is the same at every date and is given by $u(\$m) = \frac{m}{2}$. Your time discount **rate** is 18%. Calculate today's utility for each of the three options.

10.6.3 Exercises for Section 10.4: Hyperbolic discounting

Exercise 10.9 Today is Thursday (= date 0) and you are thinking about the weekend. You really want to go to see a movie. Your favorite movie, *Ultimate Experience*, is coming out on Sunday. The other alternative is *Unlimited Boredom* which is showing on Saturday as well as Sunday. Thus, your options are: (1) stay at home (outcome x) on Saturday and go to see *Ultimate Experience* (outcome y) on Sunday, (2) stay at home (outcome x) on Saturday and go to see *Unlimited Boredom* (outcome z) on Sunday, (3) go to see *Unlimited Boredom* (outcome z) on Saturday and stay at home (outcome x) on Sunday. These are the only options, because you cannot afford to go to the movies both days. Time periods represent days, your instantaneous utility is the same every day, $u(x) = 1$, $u(z) = 5$, $u(y) = 7$. Your preferences are characterized by hyperbolic discounting with parameters $\beta = \frac{3}{4}$ and $\delta = \frac{4}{5}$.

(a) Calculate the utility of each option from the point of view of Thursday, Friday and Saturday.
(b) Are your preferences time consistent?

Exercise 10.10 Today you have to decide if and when to go to the gym. Plan A is to go to the gym tomorrow – with instantaneous utility of 0 –in which case you will feel energetic the next day – obtaining an instantaneous utility of 18. Plan B is to spend the day tomorrow watching TV – with instantaneous utility of 6 – but then you will feel tired and grumpy the next day – with instantaneous utility of 1. Your preferences are characterized by hyperbolic discounting with parameters $\beta = \frac{1}{6}$ and $\delta = \frac{6}{7}$.
  (a) Calculate the utility of the two plans from the point of view of today and of tomorrow.
  (b) Are your preferences time consistent?

10.6.4 Exercises for Section 10.5: Dealing with time inconsistency

Exercise 10.11 Bill is a recovering alcoholic. His friends are meeting at a bar at 8pm. It is now 7pm and he has to decide whether to meet his friends at the bar or drive to San Francisco to visit his cousin, whom he finds to be quite boring. At the moment, his preferences are as follows: his favorite outcome is for him to be with his friends without drinking any alcohol, his worst outcome is to (be with his friends and) drink alcohol and he ranks visiting his cousin strictly between those two outcomes. He thinks that if he goes to the bar then he will not be able to control himself and will order at least one alcoholic drink (probably several).
  (a) What would Bill do if he did not acknowledge his self-control problem?
  (b) Assume that Bill is aware of his self-control problem. Represent his decision problem as a tree and compute the backward-induction solution.

Exercise 10.12 You have a season ticket to the movie theater which entitles you to see a movie every Saturday for the next 3 weeks (this week and the following two weeks). It is now Friday of the first week and you have been asked by your parents to visit them one Saturday over the next three weeks (and thus you will have to miss the movie on that Saturday). You can choose which Saturday. Let x be the outcome of watching a movie and y the outcome of visiting with your parents.
  (a) Represent the possible choices you face as a table showing the sequence of outcomes for the next three Saturdays.

  For Parts (b)-(e) assume that a time period is a week, with the current week being time 0. Assume that the instantaneous utilities are as follows: $u_t(y) = 3$, for every $t \in \{0, 1, 2\}$, and $u_0(x) = 5$, $u_1(x) = 8$, $u_2(x) = 12$.
  (b) Represent again the possible choices you face as a table, but this time show the possible utility streams.

  For Parts (c)-(e) assume that your preferences can be represented by a hyperbolic-discounting utility function with $\beta = \frac{1}{3}$ and $\delta = \frac{4}{5}$.
  (c) Suppose that you have to make an irrevocable decision today as to which Saturday you will visit your parents. What will you choose?

10.6 Exercises

(d) Suppose that you don't have to commit now. Each Saturday you decide whether or not to go to see your parents, if you have not already done so on a previous Saturday. Of course, if you don't visit your parents on one of the first two Saturdays, then you will have no choice on the third Saturday: you will have to go and see them on that Saturday. You are fully aware of your preferences (hyperbolic discounting with the same β and δ every week). Represent your decision problem using a tree and find the backward-induction solution.

(e) Is there a difference between (c) and (d)?

Exercise 10.13 You have a season ticket to the movie theater which entitles you to see a movie every Saturday for the next 4 weeks. It is now Friday of the first week and you have been told by your employer that you need to work one Saturday over the next four weeks (and thus you will have to miss the movie on that Saturday). You can choose which Saturday. Let x be the outcome of watching a movie and y the outcome of working.

(a) Represent the possible choices you face as a table showing the sequence of outcomes for the next four Saturdays.

For Parts (b)-(e) assume that a time period is a week, with the current week being time 0. Assume that the instantaneous utilities are as follows: $u_t(y) = 0$, for every $t \in \{0, 1, 2, 3\}$, and $u_0(x) = 3$, $u_1(x) = 5$, $u_2(x) = 8$ and $u_3(x) = 13$ (for example, because the movie tomorrow is a mediocre one, the one next week is a good one, the one in two weeks' time is a very good one and the one on the last week is the best of all).

(b) Represent again the possible choices you face as a table, but this time show the possible utility streams.

For Parts (c)-(e) assume that your preferences can be represented by a hyperbolic-discounting utility function with $\beta = \frac{1}{2}$ and $\delta = \frac{9}{10}$.

(c) Suppose that you have to make an irrevocable decision today as to which Saturday you will work. What will you choose?

(d) Suppose that you don't have to commit now. Each Saturday you decide whether or not to go to work, if you have not already worked on a previous Saturday. Of course, if you don't show up at work on one of the first three Saturdays, then you will have no choice on the fourth Saturday: you will have to work on that day. You are fully aware of your preferences (hyperbolic discounting with the same β and δ every week). Represent your decision problem using a tree and find the backward-induction solution.

(e) Is there a difference between (c) and (d)?

10.7 Solutions to Exercises

Solution to Exercise 10.1. The present value of the bond is:

$$10\left(\frac{1}{1+0.07}\right) + 15\left(\frac{1}{1+0.07}\right)^2 + 20\left(\frac{1}{1+0.07}\right)^3 + 25\left(\frac{1}{1+0.07}\right)^4 = \$57.85.$$

$\square$

Solution to Exercise 10.2. (a) When the rate of interest is 15%, the present value of $160 available three years from now is $160\left(\frac{1}{1.15}\right)^3 = \$105.203$; on the other hand, the present value of $100 today is $100. Thus, it is better to wait and get $160 three years from now. (b) When the rate of interest is 15%, the future value, three years from now, of $100 available today is $100(1.15)^3 = \$152.10 < 160$, confirming that it is better to wait and get $160 three years from now. $\square$

Solution to Exercise 10.3. The cost of Option 1 is $(1,500)(0.16) + 85 = \$325$ while the cost of Option 2 is $(1,500)(0.21) = \$315$. Thus, you should choose Option 2. $\square$

Solution to Exercise 10.4. A naive calculation would be: $2 Million × 6 = $12 Million and thus Option 2 is better. However, one should compute the present value of Option 2, which is

$$2 \times 10^6 + \frac{2 \times 10^6}{1.04} + \frac{2 \times 10^6}{(1.04)^2} + \frac{2 \times 10^6}{(1.04)^3} + \frac{2 \times 10^6}{(1.04)^4} + \frac{2 \times 10^6}{(1.04)^5} = \$10,903,644.66.$$

Thus, in terms of present value, Option 1 is better. $\square$

Solution to Exercise 10.5.

(a) If you borrow $200 and have to repay $225, you are paying $25 in interest. So the interest rate is the solution to $200r = 25$, which is $\frac{25}{200} = 0.125 = 12.5\%$.

(b) If you borrow $200 at the rate of interest r then after two years the amount you need to repay is $200(1+r)^2$. Thus, you need to solve the equation $200(1+r)^2 = 240$. The solution is $r = 0.095 = 9.5\%$. $\square$

Solution to Exercise 10.6. It must be that $U_0(x,0) = U_0(y,1)$, that is, $\delta^0 u_0(x) = \delta u_1(y)$: $4 = \delta 7$. Hence, $\delta = \frac{4}{7}$. Since $\delta = \frac{1}{1+\rho}$, we must solve $\frac{1}{1+\rho} = \frac{4}{7}$. The answer is $\rho = \frac{3}{4} = 0.75$.

$\square$

10.7 Solutions to Exercises

Solution to Exercise 10.7. The utility at time t is given by $U_t(x, 10) = (12)(0.85)^{(10-t)}$. Thus, the values are:

Time t	0	2	4	6	8	10
Utility: $(12)(0.85)^{(10-t)}$	2.362	3.27	4.526	6.264	8.67	12

The diagram is shown in Figure 10.7. □

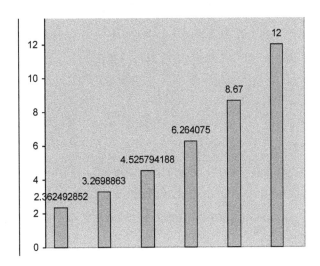

Figure 10.7: The diagram for Exercise 10.7

Solution to Exercise 10.8. First we have to figure out how much money you would have in your account under Options 2 and 3. Under Option 2, after 3 years you would have $m_3 = (800)(1.05)^3 = \$926.10$, while under Option 3 after 10 years you would have $m_{10} = (800)(1.12)^{10} = \$2,484.68$. Your time discount factor is $\delta = \frac{1}{1+0.18} = 0.8475$. Thus, utilities are as follows:

Option 1: $\delta^0 \left(\frac{m_0}{2}\right) = (0.8475)^0 \left(\frac{800}{2}\right) = 400$

Option 2: $\delta^3 \left(\frac{m_3}{2}\right) = (0.8475)^3 \left(\frac{926.10}{2}\right) = 281.87$

Option 3: $\delta^{10} \left(\frac{m_{10}}{2}\right) = (0.8475)^{10} \left(\frac{2,484.68}{2}\right) = 237.49$.

Thus, you are very impatient and will choose to spend the $800 now. □

Solution to Exercise 10.9. Let R = Thursday, F = Friday and S = Saturday. Then

(a) $U_R(Option\ 1) = \beta\delta^2 1 + \beta\delta^3 7 = \frac{3}{4}\left(\frac{4}{5}\right)^2 + \frac{3}{4}\left(\frac{4}{5}\right)^3 7 = 3.168.$
$U_R(Option\ 2) = \beta\delta^2 1 + \beta\delta^3 5 = \frac{3}{4}\left(\frac{4}{5}\right)^2 + \frac{3}{4}\left(\frac{4}{5}\right)^3 5 = 2.4.$
$U_R(Option\ 3) = \beta\delta^2 5 + \beta\delta^3 1 = \frac{3}{4}\left(\frac{4}{5}\right)^2 5 + \frac{3}{4}\left(\frac{4}{5}\right)^3 1 = 2.784.$
Thus, from the point of view of Thursday, Option 1 is the best.

$U_F(Option\ 1) = \beta\delta 1 + \beta\delta^2 7 = \frac{3}{4}\left(\frac{4}{5}\right) + \frac{3}{4}\left(\frac{4}{5}\right)^2 7 = 3.96.$
$U_F(Option\ 2) = \beta\delta 1 + \beta\delta^2 5 = \frac{3}{4}\left(\frac{4}{5}\right) + \frac{3}{4}\left(\frac{4}{5}\right)^2 5 = 3.$
$U_F(Option\ 3) = \beta\delta 5 + \beta\delta^2 1 = \frac{3}{4}\left(\frac{4}{5}\right) 5 + \frac{3}{4}\left(\frac{4}{5}\right)^2 1 = 3.48.$
Thus, also from the point of view of Friday, Option 1 is the best.

$U_S(Option\ 1) = 1 + \beta\delta 7 = 1 + \frac{3}{4}\left(\frac{4}{5}\right) 7 = 5.2.$
$U_S(Option\ 2) = 1 + \beta\delta 5 = 1 + \frac{3}{4}\left(\frac{4}{5}\right) 5 = 4.$
$U_S(Option\ 3) = 5 + \beta\delta 1 = 5 + \frac{3}{4}\left(\frac{4}{5}\right) = 5.6.$
Thus, from the point of view of Saturday, Option 3 is the best.

(b) No, because on Thursday you will plan to choose Option 1, on Friday you will renew your intention to choose Option 1, but on Saturday you will change your mind and choose Option 3. □

Solution to Exercise 10.10. Let today be date 0, tomorrow date 1 and the day after tomorrow date 2. The instantaneous utilities are

	Today (date 0)	Tomorrow (date 1)	Day after tomorrow (date 2)
Plan A		0	18
Plan B		6	1

(a) Utility at time 0:
$U_0(Plan\ A) = \beta\delta 0 + \beta\delta^2 18 = \frac{1}{6}\left(\frac{6}{7}\right) 0 + \frac{1}{6}\left(\frac{6}{7}\right)^2 18 = 2.204,$
$U_0(Plan\ B) = \beta\delta 6 + \beta\delta^2 1 = \frac{1}{6}\left(\frac{6}{7}\right) 6 + \frac{1}{6}\left(\frac{6}{7}\right)^2 1 = 0.98$

Utility at time 1:
$U_1(Plan\ A) = 0 + \beta\delta 18 = 0 + \frac{1}{6}\left(\frac{6}{7}\right) 18 = 2.571,$
$U_1(Plan\ B) = 6 + \beta\delta 1 = 6 + \frac{1}{6}\left(\frac{6}{7}\right) 1 = 6.143.$

Thus, at date 0 Plan A is viewed as better than Plan B, but at date 1 Plan B is viewed as better than Plan A.

(b) No, because today you decide to follow Plan A, but tomorrow you will switch to Plan B. □

10.7 Solutions to Exercises

Solution to Exercise 10.11.

(a) He will go to the bar, planning not to drink (but he will end up drinking and thus bringing about what at 7pm he considered to be the worst outcome).

(b) The tree is shown in Figure 10.8. The backward-induction solution is shown by the double edges. □

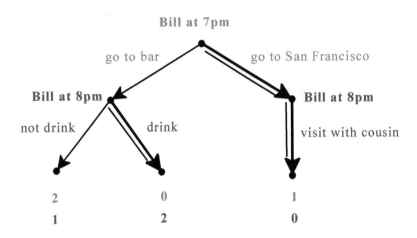

Figure 10.8: The tree for Exercise 10.11

Solution to Exercise 10.12.

(a)

Choice	1st Saturday	2nd Saturday	3rd Saturday
A	y	x	x
B	x	y	x
C	x	x	y

(b)

Choice	1st Saturday	2nd Saturday	3rd Saturday
A	3	8	12
B	5	3	12
C	5	8	3

(c) $U_0(A) = 3 + 8\beta\delta + 12\beta\delta^2 = 3 + 8\left(\frac{1}{3}\right)\left(\frac{4}{5}\right) + 12\left(\frac{1}{3}\right)\left(\frac{4}{5}\right)^2 = 7.69.$
$U_0(B) = 5 + 3\beta\delta + 12\beta\delta^2 = 5 + 3\left(\frac{1}{3}\right)\left(\frac{4}{5}\right) + 12\left(\frac{1}{3}\right)\left(\frac{4}{5}\right)^2 = \boxed{8.36}.$
$U_0(C) = 5 + 8\beta\delta + 3\beta\delta^2 = 5 + 8\left(\frac{1}{3}\right)\left(\frac{4}{5}\right) + 3\left(\frac{1}{3}\right)\left(\frac{4}{5}\right)^2 = 7.77.$

Thus, you will commit to visiting your parents on the second Saturday.

(d) The tree is shown in Figure 10.9. The backward-induction solution is shown by the double edges.

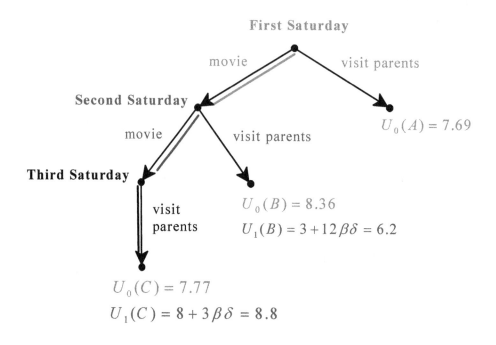

Figure 10.9: The tree for Exercise 10.12

(e) Yes: if you could commit you would visit your parents on the second Saturday, but when you are unable to commit you will end up visiting them on the last Saturday. □

Solution to Exercise 10.13.

(a)

Choice	1st Saturday	2nd Saturday	3rd Saturday	4th Saturday
A	y	x	x	x
B	x	y	x	x
C	x	x	y	x
D	x	x	x	y

(b)

Choice	1st Saturday	2nd Saturday	3rd Saturday	4th Saturday
A	0	5	8	13
B	3	0	8	13
C	3	5	0	13
D	3	5	8	0

(c) $U_0(A) = 0 + 5\beta\delta + 8\beta\delta^2 + 13\beta\delta^3 = 10.229$.
$U_0(B) = 3 + 0\beta\delta + 8\beta\delta^2 + 13\beta\delta^3 = \boxed{10.979}$.
$U_0(C) = 3 + 5\beta\delta + 0\beta\delta^2 + 13\beta\delta^3 = 9.989$.
$U_0(D) = 3 + 5\beta\delta + 8\beta\delta^2 + 0\beta\delta^3 = 8.49$.

Thus, you will commit to working on the second Saturday.

(d) The tree is is shown in Figure 10.10. The backward-induction solution is shown by the double edges.

(e) There is no difference: you will end up working on the second Saturday in both scenarios. □

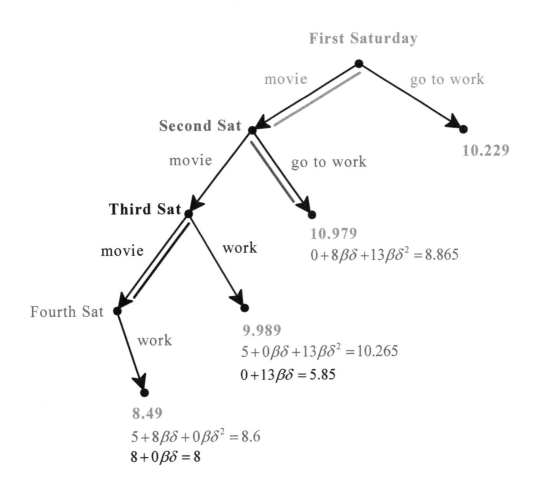

Figure 10.10: The tree for Exercise 10.13

IV Group Decision Making

11 Aggregation of Preferences 253
- 11.1 Social preference functions
- 11.2 Arrow's Impossibility Theorem
- 11.3 Illustration of the proof of Arrow's theorem
- 11.4 Application of Arrow's theorem to individual choice
- 11.5 Exercises
- 11.6 Solutions to Exercises

12 Misrepresentation of Preferences 285
- 12.1 Social choice functions
- 12.2 Strategic voting
- 12.3 The Gibbard-Satterthwaite theorem
- 12.4 Illustration of the proof of the Gibbard-Satterthwaite theorem
- 12.5 Exercises
- 12.6 Solutions to Exercises

11. Aggregation of Preferences

11.1 Social preference functions

Groups of individuals, or societies, often have to make decisions. Let X be the set of alternatives that society has to choose from. The elements of X could be alternative tax rates, alternative health insurance reforms, candidates in an election, etc. We shall assume that each individual in society has a complete and transitive ranking of the elements of X. The important issue that arises in a multi-person context is: *how to aggregate the possibly conflicting preferences of the individuals into a single ranking that can be viewed as "society's ranking"*. We shall denote the social ranking by $\succsim_S$ (the subscript 'S' stands for 'society'); thus, the interpretation of $x \succsim_S y$ is that – according to society as a whole – alternative x is at least as good as alternative y. As usual, $\succ_S$ will be used for strict preference ($x \succ_S y$ means that, from society's point of view, x is better than y) and $\sim_S$ for indifference ($x \sim_S y$ means that, from society's point of view, x is just as good as y).

In practice, there are a number of procedures that are commonly used to make collective decisions. The most popular one is the method of *majority voting*. As pointed out by the 18th century French scholar Nicolas de Condorcet,[1] majority voting can yield an intransitive social ranking: this is known as the *Condorcet paradox*.

---

[1] His full name was Marie Jean Antoine Nicolas de Caritat, Marquis of Condorcet (1743-1794).

For example, suppose that there are three voters: 1, 2 and 3. They have to choose a president among three candidates: A, B and C. Suppose that their preferences are as follows:

	1's ranking	2's ranking	3's ranking
best	A	C	B
	B	A	C
worst	C	B	A

Then

- In the choice between A and B, the majority (consisting of Individuals 1 and 2) prefers A to B. Thus, we conclude that (for the society consisting of these three individuals) A is better than B: $A \succ_S B$.

- In the choice between B and C, the majority (consisting of Individuals 1 and 3) prefers B to C. Thus, we conclude that (for the society consisting of these three individuals) B is better than C: $B \succ_S C$.

- In the choice between A and C, the majority (consisting of Individuals 2 and 3) prefers C to A. Thus, we conclude that (for the society consisting of these three individuals) C is better than A: $C \succ_S A$.

Thus, we have that $A \succ_S B$, $B \succ_S C$ and, in violation of transitivity, $C \succ_S A$.

Why is the lack of transitivity problematic? One reason is that a clever manipulator, by choosing the agenda, can bring about the outcome that he wants. For example, suppose that the agenda is set by Individual 3. She wants B to win, because it is her most preferred candidate. To achieve this result, she would first propose a vote between A and C; then the winner of the first vote (candidate C, supported by Individuals 2 and 3) would be put up against the remaining candidate (candidate B) and the final winner would be B (supported by Individuals 1 and 2).[2]

If the agenda were set by Individual 2, then she would first ask for a vote between A and B and then for a vote between the winner (candidate A) and C and the latter would be the final winner.

Similarly, Individual 1 would be able to get A to be the winner by choosing the agenda appropriately (first a vote between B and C and then a vote between the winner of the first vote and A).

In his Ph.D. thesis[3] the late Kenneth Arrow, joint winner (with John Hicks) of the Nobel Memorial Prize in Economics in 1972, addressed the question of how to construct a "good" or "reasonable" procedure for aggregating the preferences of a set of individuals into a group ranking.

The problem of aggregation of individual preferences is how to design a procedure that takes as input a list of rankings – one for each individual in the group – and produces as output a ranking to be interpreted as the group's ranking (or society's ranking). We call such a procedure a "social preference function", or SPF for short.

---

[2]This argument assumes that the voters cast their votes according to their true preferences, but – perhaps – one of them could gain by misrepresenting her preferences, that is, by voting according to a ranking that is different from her true ranking. This issue is studied in the next chapter.

[3]Published as a monograph: Kenneth Arrow, *Social Choice and Individual Values*, John Wiley & and Sons, 1951 (second edition published in 1963 by Yale University Press).

11.1 Social preference functions

Definition 11.1.1 Let $X = \{x_1, x_2, \ldots, x_m\}$ ($m \geq 2$) be a finite set of alternatives, $N = \{1, 2, \ldots, n\}$ ($n \geq 2$) a finite set of individuals, $\mathscr{R}$ the set of complete and transitive binary relations on X and Q the set of binary relations on X (thus, $\mathscr{R} \subseteq Q$).
Let $\mathscr{R}^n$ be the Cartesian product $\underbrace{\mathscr{R} \times \mathscr{R} \times \cdots \times \mathscr{R}}_{n \text{ times}}$ (thus an element of $\mathscr{R}^n$ is a list of complete and transitive preference relations on the set of alternatives X, one for each individual; we call an element of $\mathscr{R}^n$ a *profile of preferences*) and let S be a subset of $\mathscr{R}^n$. A *social preference function* (or *Arrovian social welfare function*) is a function $f : S \to Q$ that takes as input a profile of preferences for the individuals $(\succsim_1, \succsim_2, \ldots, \succsim_n) \in S \subseteq \mathscr{R}^n$ and produces as output a ranking $\succsim_S = f(\succsim_1, \succsim_2, \ldots, \succsim_n) \in Q$ for society.

For example, suppose that there are only two alternatives, A and B (thus, $X = \{A, B\}$ and $\mathscr{R} = \{A \succ B, A \sim B, B \succ A\}$), two voters ($N = \{1, 2\}$), $S = \mathscr{R}^2$ and the social ranking is constructed as follows: if at least one individual prefers alternative x to alternative y and the other individual considers x to be at least as good as y then x is declared to be better for society than y, otherwise society is said to be indifferent between x and y. Such a social preference function can be represented by the following table:

		Individual 2's ranking		
		$A \succ_2 B$	$A \sim_2 B$	$B \succ_2 A$
Individual	$A \succ_1 B$	$A \succ_S B$	$A \succ_S B$	$A \sim_S B$
1's	$A \sim_1 B$	$A \succ_S B$	$A \sim_S B$	$B \succ_S A$
ranking	$B \succ_1 A$	$A \sim_S B$	$B \succ_S A$	$B \succ_S A$

Alternatively, we can represent the above social preference function as a table where each column corresponds to a profile of rankings and below each profile the corresponding social ranking is recorded. This is shown in Figure 11.1.

Profile:	$A \succ_1 B$ $A \succ_2 B$	$A \succ_1 B$ $A \sim_2 B$	$A \succ_1 B$ $B \succ_2 A$	$A \sim_1 B$ $A \succ_2 B$	$A \sim_1 B$ $A \sim_2 B$	$A \sim_1 B$ $B \succ_2 A$	$B \succ_1 A$ $A \succ_2 B$	$B \succ_1 A$ $A \sim_2 B$	$B \succ_1 A$ $B \succ_2 A$
social ranking:	$A \succ_S B$	$A \succ_S B$	$A \sim_S B$	$A \succ_S B$	$A \sim_S B$	$B \succ_S A$	$A \sim_S B$	$B \succ_S A$	$B \succ_S A$

Figure 11.1: A social preference function with 2 alternatives and 2 individuals

As a second example, suppose that there are three alternatives A, B and C ($X = \{A,B,C\}$) and three individuals ($N = \{1,2,3\}$) and only strict rankings can be reported; thus, $S = \mathscr{P} \times \mathscr{P} \times \mathscr{P}$ where

$$\mathscr{P} = \{A \succ B \succ C,\ A \succ C \succ B,\ B \succ A \succ C,\ B \succ C \succ A,\ C \succ A \succ B,\ C \succ B \succ A\}$$

The preference function is defined as follows: for any two alternatives x and y, $x \succ_S y$ if and only if at least two individuals prefer x to y.[4] Since there are $6^3 = 216$ possible profiles of preferences, it is more laborious to represent the entire social preference function (one would need six tables, each with six rows and six columns);[5] however, we can illustrate it by listing a couple of entries:

$$\left.\begin{array}{l} \text{1's ranking:}\ C \succ_1 B \succ_1 A \\ \text{2's ranking:}\ B \succ_2 A \succ_2 C \\ \text{3's ranking:}\ A \succ_3 C \succ_3 B \end{array}\right\} \mapsto \text{social ranking: } B \succ_S A,\ A \succ_S C,\ C \succ_S B.$$

$$\left.\begin{array}{l} \text{1's ranking:}\ C \succ_1 B \succ_1 A \\ \text{2's ranking:}\ A \succ_2 B \succ_2 C \\ \text{3's ranking:}\ C \succ_3 A \succ_3 B \end{array}\right\} \mapsto \text{social ranking: } A \succ_S B,\ C \succ_S A,\ C \succ_S B.$$

It is clear that there are many possible social preference functions. Are they all "reasonable"? In principle, one could list them all and test each of them against some properties that are considered to be "reasonable" or "desirable". In practice, this is not feasible because of the large number of possibilities. However, it will be useful to provide an illustration for a simple case where the number of possibilities is small.

Consider again the case where there are only two alternatives, A and B (thus, $X = \{A,B\}$) and two voters ($N = \{1,2\}$), but restrict the set of rankings by ruling out indifference, that is, let $S = \{A \succ B, B \succ A\} \times \{A \succ B, B \succ A\}$ and $Q = \{A \succ B, B \succ A\}$.

Then there are 4 possible profiles of preferences for the two individuals and 16 possible preference functions, which are listed in the table below, where – as in Figure 11.1 – each column corresponds to a profile of rankings. Each row in the table represents a possible social preference function (SPF).

---

[4]Note that, since individuals are restricted to reporting strict preferences, for any two alternatives it will always be the case that at least two individuals will prefer one to the other.

[5]We will use such representations in the next chapter.

11.1 Social preference functions

profile → SPF ↓	$A \succ_1 B$ $A \succ_2 B$	$A \succ_1 B$ $B \succ_2 A$	$B \succ_1 A$ $A \succ_2 B$	$B \succ_1 A$ $B \succ_2 A$
SPF - 1	$A \succ_S B$	$A \succ_S B$	$A \succ_S B$	$A \succ_S B$
SPF - 2	$A \succ_S B$	$A \succ_S B$	$A \succ_S B$	$B \succ_S A$
SPF - 3	$A \succ_S B$	$A \succ_S B$	$B \succ_S A$	$A \succ_S B$
SPF - 4	$A \succ_S B$	$A \succ_S B$	$B \succ_S A$	$B \succ_S A$
SPF - 5	$A \succ_S B$	$B \succ_S A$	$A \succ_S B$	$A \succ_S B$
SPF - 6	$A \succ_S B$	$B \succ_S A$	$A \succ_S B$	$B \succ_S A$
SPF - 7	$A \succ_S B$	$B \succ_S A$	$B \succ_S A$	$A \succ_S B$
SPF - 8	$A \succ_S B$	$B \succ_S A$	$B \succ_S A$	$B \succ_S A$
SPF - 9	$B \succ_S A$	$A \succ_S B$	$A \succ_S B$	$A \succ_S B$
SPF - 10	$B \succ_S A$	$A \succ_S B$	$A \succ_S B$	$B \succ_S A$
SPF - 11	$B \succ_S A$	$A \succ_S B$	$B \succ_S A$	$A \succ_S B$
SPF - 12	$B \succ_S A$	$A \succ_S B$	$B \succ_S A$	$B \succ_S A$
SPF - 13	$B \succ_S A$	$B \succ_S A$	$A \succ_S B$	$A \succ_S B$
SPF - 14	$B \succ_S A$	$B \succ_S A$	$A \succ_S B$	$B \succ_S A$
SPF - 15	$B \succ_S A$	$B \succ_S A$	$B \succ_S A$	$A \succ_S B$
SPF - 16	$B \succ_S A$	$B \succ_S A$	$B \succ_S A$	$B \succ_S A$

(11.1)

In the next section we will consider several properties suggested by Arrow as an attempt to capture the notion of a "reasonable" SPF. Here we will give a preview of two of those properties.

The first property, called *Unanimity*, requires that if everybody in the group agrees that one alternative is better than another, then the social ranking should reflect this judgment. We can see in the above table that the bottom eight SPFs (SPF-9 to SPF-16) fail this property, because in the first column we have that both individuals consider A to be better than B ($A \succ_1 B$ and $A \succ_2 B$) and yet society judges B to be better than A ($B \succ_S A$).

By appealing to Unanimity we can also discard SPF-1, SPF-3, SPF-5 and SPF-7 because in the last column we have that both individuals consider B to be better than A ($B \succ_1 A$ and $B \succ_2 A$) and yet society judges A to be better than B ($A \succ_S B$). Hence, we can reduce our search for a "reasonable" SPF to the smaller table below:

profile → SPF ↓	$A \succ_1 B$ $A \succ_2 B$	$A \succ_1 B$ $B \succ_2 A$	$B \succ_1 A$ $A \succ_2 B$	$B \succ_1 A$ $B \succ_2 A$
SPF - 2	$A \succ_S B$	$A \succ_S B$	$A \succ_S B$	$B \succ_S A$
SPF - 4	$A \succ_S B$	$A \succ_S B$	$B \succ_S A$	$B \succ_S A$
SPF - 6	$A \succ_S B$	$B \succ_S A$	$A \succ_S B$	$B \succ_S A$
SPF - 8	$A \succ_S B$	$B \succ_S A$	$B \succ_S A$	$B \succ_S A$

In the reduced table, we can see that SPF-4 merely reproduces the ranking of Individual 1: in a sense, SPF-4 amounts to appointing Individual 1 as a "dictator". Similarly, SPF-6 merely reproduces the ranking of Individual 2, thus appointing Individual 2 as a "dictator".

A second property suggested by Arrow, called *Non-dictatorship*, aims at ruling this out. Thus, by appealing to Unanimity and Non-dictatorship, we can reduce the number of candidates for a "reasonable" SPF from sixteen to the two: SPF-2 and SPF-8, shown in the table below:

profile → SPF ↓	$A \succ_1 B$ $A \succ_2 B$	$A \succ_1 B$ $B \succ_2 A$	$B \succ_1 A$ $A \succ_2 B$	$B \succ_1 A$ $B \succ_2 A$
SPF - 2	$A \succ_S B$	$A \succ_S B$	$A \succ_S B$	$B \succ_S A$
SPF - 8	$A \succ_S B$	$B \succ_S A$	$B \succ_S A$	$B \succ_S A$

SPF-2 embodies the following rule: if both individuals agree in their ranking of the two alternatives, then reflect this common ranking in the social ranking; if there is disagreement, then declare A to be better than B for society.

SPF-8 embodies the following rule: if both individuals agree in their ranking of the two alternatives, then reflect this common ranking in the social ranking; if there is disagreement, then declare B to be better than A for society.

> Test your understanding of the concepts introduced in this section, by going through the exercises in Section 11.5.1 at the end of this chapter.

11.2 Arrow's Impossibility Theorem

As noted in the previous section, Arrow posed the following question: what properties should one impose on a social preference function in order to obtain a "reasonable" aggregation procedure? He listed some desirable properties, known as *Arrow's axioms*, and studied the implications of those properties.

The first axiom requires that there be no restrictions on what preferences each individual can *state* or *report* (except for the requirement that the reported preferences be "rational", in the sense that they satisfy completeness and transitivity). If, for some reason, some preferences were to be considered "inappropriate" or "unacceptable" they could always be ignored in forming the social ranking; but in terms of reporting preferences, anything should be allowed:

- **Axiom 1: Unrestricted Domain or Freedom of Expression.** The domain of the social preference function should be the entire set $\mathscr{R}^n$.

The second axiom requires that the social ranking satisfy the same "rationality" properties as the individual rankings: if $\succsim_S$ is the social ranking obtained by aggregating the reported rankings of the n individuals then $\succsim_S$ must be complete and transitive:

- **Axiom 2: Rationality.** The set of social rankings generated by the social preference function should be a subset of $\mathscr{R}$.

Thus, referring to Definition 11.1.1, if $f : S \to Q$ is the social preference function, then the Unrestricted Domain axiom requires that $S = \mathscr{R}^n$ and the Rationality axiom requires that $Q \subseteq \mathscr{R}$.

Note that the Rationality axiom in itself is sufficient to rule out majority voting as a "reasonable" method of aggregating preferences whenever there are three or more alternatives. Indeed, as we saw in Section 11.1, in such cases majority voting fails to guarantee transitivity of the social ranking.

11.2 Arrow's Impossibility Theorem

The aggregation of individual preferences into a preference ordering for the group is a difficult task because different individuals might have very different opinions on how to rank the alternatives under consideration. The aggregation rule must, somehow, resolve such potential conflicts. However, in the – perhaps rare – occasions where individuals agree, it seems straightforward to require that this agreement be reflected in the social ranking. This is what the third axiom postulates: if everybody strictly prefers x to y then society should also strictly prefer x to y:

- **Axiom 3: Unanimity or the Pareto Principle.** For any two alternatives $x, y \in X$, if $x \succ_i y$, for every $i = 1, 2, \ldots, n$, then $x \succ_S y$ (where $\succsim_S = f(\succsim_1, \succsim_2, \ldots, \succsim_n)$).

Note that the Unanimity axiom is a very weak requirement. Consider again the 3-person, 3-alternative example given in Section 11.1, reproduced below:

	1's ranking	2's ranking	3's ranking
best	A	C	B
	B	A	C
worst	C	B	A

If these are the reported preferences of the three individuals, then the Unanimity axiom imposes no restrictions at all, since, for any two alternatives, it is never the case that all three individuals rank them the same way (for example, for alternatives A and B we have that Individuals 1 and 2 strictly prefer A to B but Individual 3 has the opposite ranking: she prefers B to A). As a second example, suppose that the reported rankings are as follows:

	1's ranking	2's ranking	3's ranking
best	A	C	A
	B	A	C
worst	C	B	B

In this case the Unanimity axiom requires $A \succ_S B$, since every individual prefers A to B. It is silent concerning the ranking of B versus C, since there is disagreement among the individuals (2 and 3 rank C above B but 1 has the opposite ranking) and – for the same reason – it is silent concerning the ranking of A versus C. Finally, note that, if even just one individual is indifferent between alternatives x and y, then the Unanimity axiom is silent concerning the social ranking of x versus y.

Are there any social preference functions that satisfy the above three axioms? The answer is affirmative. For example, one could (1) allow each individual to report any complete and transitive ranking and (2) pick one individual and postulate that the social ranking should coincide with the ranking reported by that individual. Such an aggregation procedure, however, is hardly reasonable: it amounts to appointing one individual as a dictator and completely ignoring the preferences of all the other individuals. The fourth axiom explicitly rules this out.

- **Axiom 4: Non-dictatorship**. There is no individual i such that, for any two alternatives x and y, and for all profiles of preferences $(\succsim_1, \succsim_2, \ldots, \succsim_n)$, if $x \succ_i y$ then $x \succ_S y$ [where $\succsim_S = f(\succsim_1, \succsim_2, \ldots, \succsim_n)$].

  Equivalently, for every individual i there must be (at least) two alternatives x and y and a profile of preferences $(\succsim_1, \succsim_2, \ldots, \succsim_n)$ such that $x \succ_i y$ and $y \succsim_S x$ [where $\succsim_S = f(\succsim_1, \succsim_2, \ldots, \succsim_n)$].

The Non-dictatorship axiom does not allow a single individual to *always* have his/her *strict* preferences reflected in the social ranking.[6] Note that Non-dictatorship does not rule out the possibility of the social ranking mirroring the strict ranking of a particular individual *for some* alternatives:[7] it only rules out this being the case *for every pair of alternatives*.

Before stating the fifth, and last, axiom formally, we elucidate its content in an example. The axiom says that the social ranking of any two alternatives x and y should depend *only* on how the individuals rank x versus y and not on how other alternatives are ranked *vis a vis* x and y.

Let us illustrate this in a 2-person ($N = \{1, 2\}$), 3-alternative ($X = \{A, B, C\}$) context. Suppose that the social preference function under consideration yields the ranking $A \succ_S B$ when the stated rankings of the individuals are as follows:[8]

	individual 1	individual 2		
best	A	A, B		
	B		$\mapsto \quad A \succ_S B$	(11.2)
worst	C	C		

If we change the rankings of the two individuals without affecting the relative ranking of A and B (thus maintaining $A \succ_1 B$ and $A \sim_2 B$) then – according to the next axiom – it should still be true that $A \succ_S B$.

---

[6] It does allow for $x \sim_i y$ to coexist with $x \succ_S y$.

[7] For example, Non-dictatorship allows the SPF to consider two particular alternatives A and B to be exclusively under the control of one individual, say Individual 1, in the sense that the social ranking of A and B should coincide with the way in which A and B are ranked by Individual 1. For instance, it could be that A is the "state of the world" where Individual 1 is a member of a religious group and B is the state of the world where Individual 1 is not a member. Then having the social ranking reflect Individual 1's ranking of these two alternatives would amount to a guarantee of religious freedom to Individual 1.

[8] That is, $A \succ_1 B \succ_1 C$ and $A \sim_2 B \succ_2 C$.

11.2 Arrow's Impossibility Theorem

Thus, in each of the following 14 cases it must still be true that $A \succ_S B$:[9]

	1	2
best	A	A,B,C
	B	
worst	C	

	1	2
best	A	C
	B	
worst	C	A,B

	1	2
best	C	A,B
	A	
worst	B	C

	1	2
best	A,C	A,B
worst	B	C

	1	2
best	A	A,B
	C	
worst	B	C

	1	2
best	A	A,B
worst	B,C	C

	1	2
best	C	A,B,C
	A	
worst	B	

	1	2
best	A,C	A,B,C
worst	B	

	1	2
best	A	A,B,C
	C	
worst	B	

	1	2
best	A	A,B,C
worst	B,C	

	1	2
best	C	C
	A	
worst	B	A,B

	1	2
best	A,C	C
worst	B	A,B

	1	2
best	A	C
	C	
worst	B	A,B

	1	2
best	A	C
worst	B,C	A,B

- **Axiom 5: Independence of Irrelevant Alternatives.** Let x and y be two alternatives. Let $(\succsim_1, \succsim_2, \ldots, \succsim_n)$ and $(\succsim'_1, \succsim'_2, \ldots, \succsim'_n)$ be two profiles of individual rankings such that, for every $i = 1, 2, \ldots, n$, $x \succsim_i y$ if and only if $x \succsim'_i y$ (that is, the ranking of x and y is the same in $\succsim_i$ as in $\succsim'_i$, for every individual i). Then the ranking of x and y in the social ranking derived from $(\succsim_1, \succsim_2, \ldots, \succsim_n)$ must be the same as the ranking of x and y in the social ranking derived from $(\succsim'_1, \succsim'_2, \ldots, \succsim'_n)$. That is, if $\succsim_S = f(\succsim_1, \succsim_2, \ldots, \succsim_n)$ and $\succsim'_S = f(\succsim'_1, \succsim'_2, \ldots, \succsim'_n)$ then $x \succsim_S y$ if and only if $x \succsim'_S y$.

Clearly, if there are only two alternatives the Independence of Irrelevant Alternatives axiom is trivially satisfied. This axiom has bite only if there are at least three alternatives.

> (R) If there are only two alternatives (and any number of individuals) then the method of majority voting satisfies all of Arrow's axioms. The reader is asked to prove this in Exercise 11.6.

---

[9] The first two are obtained from (11.2) by keeping the preferences of Individual 1 fixed and changing the preferences of Individual 2 by changing the position of alternative C in the ranking (moving it to the same level as A and B or putting it above A and B). The next four are obtained by keeping the preferences of Individual 2 fixed and changing the preferences of Individual 1 by changing the position of alternative C in the ranking (above A, at the same level as A, between A and B, at the same level as B). Similarly for the remaining eight profiles.

The following theorem, known as *Arrow's impossibility theorem*, states that as soon as the number of alternatives exceeds 2, it is impossible to design an aggregation procedure that satisfies all of the five axioms given above.

> **Theorem 11.2.1** — **Arrow's Impossibility Theorem.** If the number of alternatives is at least three (that is, the cardinality of the set X is at least 3), then there is no social preference function that satisfies the five axioms listed above.

An equivalent formulation of Arrow's impossibility theorem is as follows: if f is a social preference function that satisfies any four of Arrow's axioms, then it must violate the remaining axiom. For example, since the method of majority voting satisfies Unrestricted Domain, Unanimity, Non-dictatorship and Independence of Irrelevant Alternatives, then it must violate Rationality (when the number of alternatives is at least 3): we saw an example of this in Section 11.1.

In Section 11.3 we illustrate the proof of Theorem 11.2.1 for the case of three alternatives and three voters.[10]

In the exercises for this section (see Section 11.5.2) several social preference functions are considered (e.g the Borda count) and the reader is asked to determine which of Arrow's axioms is satisfied and which is violated.

We conclude this section by considering a social preference function, known as the *Kemeny-Young method*, and analyzing it in terms of Arrow's axioms. The method works as follows. Fix a profile of individual rankings. For each pair of alternatives, x and y, we count:

1. the number of individuals for whom $x \succ y$; call this the score for $x \succ y$ and denote it by $\#(x \succ y)$,
2. the number of individuals for whom $x \sim y$; call this the score for $x \sim y$ and denote it by $\#(x \sim y)$, and
3. the number of individuals from whom $y \succ x$ (call this the score for $y \succ x$ and denote it by $\#(y \succ x)$.

Next we go through all the complete and transitive rankings of the set of alternatives and for each of them we compute a total score by adding up the scores of each pairwise ranking: for example, if there are three alternatives, A, B and C, then the score for the ranking $B \succ A \sim C$ is computed as $\#(B \succ A) + \#(B \succ C) + \#(A \sim C)$.

Finally, we select as social ranking the ranking with the highest score (if there are ties, we pick one of them). The idea of this method is to find the preference relation which is a "closest match" to the given profile of preferences.

For example, suppose that there are three alternatives: A, B and C and five voters. Their stated preferences are as follows:

	voter 1	voter 2	voter 3	voter 4	voter 5
best	A	B	B	C	B
	B	C	C	A	A
worst	C	A	A	B	C

---

[10]Relatively short proofs for the general case can be found in John Geanakoplos, "Three brief proofs of Arrow's impossibility theorem", *Economic Theory*, Vol. 26, 2005, pages 211-215 and Ning Neil Yu, "A one-shot proof of Arrow's impossibility theorem", *Economic Theory*, Vol. 50, 2012, pages 523-525.

11.2 Arrow's Impossibility Theorem

Then the scores are computed as follows:[11]

Ranking	Score
$A \succ B \succ C$	$\#(A \succ B) + \#(A \succ C) + \#(B \succ C) = 2 + 2 + 4 = 8$
$A \succ C \succ B$	$\#(A \succ C) + \#(A \succ B) + \#(C \succ B) = 2 + 2 + 1 = 5$
$B \succ A \succ C$	$\#(B \succ A) + \#(B \succ C) + \#(A \succ C) = 3 + 4 + 2 = 9$
$B \succ C \succ A$	$\#(B \succ C) + \#(B \succ A) + \#(C \succ A) = 4 + 3 + 3 = \boxed{10}$
$C \succ A \succ B$	$\#(C \succ A) + \#(C \succ B) + \#(A \succ B) = 3 + 1 + 2 = 6$
$C \succ B \succ A$	$\#(C \succ B) + \#(C \succ A) + \#(B \succ A) = 1 + 3 + 3 = 7$

Thus, the Kemeny-Young method selects, as social ranking, $B \succ_S C \succ_S A$, since it has the largest score (namely 10).

Let us now check which of Arrow's axioms is satisfied and which is violated by the Kemeny-Young procedure.

1. **Unrestricted domain**: this is satisfied by construction, since any complete and transitive ranking can be reported by the individuals.

2. **Rationality**: this is also satisfied by construction, since scores are only computed for complete and transitive rankings.

3. **Unanimity**: this is also satisfied. To see this, suppose that A and B are two alternatives such that $A \succ_i B$, for every individual $i = 1, 2, \ldots, n$. We need to show that $A \succ_S B$ where $\succsim_S$ is a ranking selected by the Kemeny-Young method. Suppose, by contradiction, that $B \succsim_S A$ and modify the ranking $\succsim_S$ by moving alternative A up in the social ranking to a position immediately above B but below any other alternative x such that $x \succ_S B$. For example, if the set of alternatives is $X = \{A, B, C, D, E, F\}$ and $\succsim_S$ is the ranking $E \succ_S B \sim_S D \succ_S A \sim_S F \succ_S C$, then the modified ranking would be as shown below:

	initial ranking:			modified ranking:	
	best	E		best	E
					A
		B, D			B, D
		A, F			F
	worst	C		worst	C

We want to show that the score of the modified ranking is higher than the score of $\succsim_S$ and thus $\succsim_S$ could not have been a ranking with maximum score. The only scores that change as a consequence of the modification are:

(1) The score for the pair (A, B). In the sum giving the total score for $\succsim_S$ there was either $\#(A \sim B)$ or $\#(B \succ A)$, which are both 0 (because of the hypothesis that $A \succ_i B$, for all $i = 1, 2, \ldots, n$) and now in the sum for the total score of the modified ranking there is $\#(A \succ B) = n$; thus, on this account, the total score increases by n;

---

[11] There is no need to consider rankings involving indifference since every pair (x, y) such that $x \sim y$ gets a score of zero and thus any such ranking would get a total score lower than one of the scores computed below.

(2) The scores for pairs of the type (A,x) where x is an alternative such that $B \succsim_S x \succsim_S A$ (that is, in the social ranking, x was above, or at the same level as, A and also not higher than B). In the sum giving the total score for $\succsim_S$ there was either $\#(x \sim A)$ or $\#(x \succ A)$ and now in the sum for the total score of the modified ranking there is $\#(A \succ x)$. Consider an arbitrary individual i who makes a positive contribution to $\#(x \sim A)$ or $\#(x \succ A)$, that is, an individual i such that either $x \sim_i A$ or $x \succ_i A$. Then this individual i contributed one point to the score for $x \sim_S A$ or for $x \succ_S A$ and that point is lost in the computation of the score of the modified ranking; however – by transitivity of $\succsim_i$ – for such an individual i it must be that $x \succ_i B$ because, by hypothesis, $x \succsim_i A$ and $A \succ_i B$ (the latter being true for every individual). Thus, such an individual i was not contributing to $\#(B \succ x)$ or $\#(B \sim x)$ in the computation of the score for $\succsim_S$ and is now contributing to $\#(x \succ B)$ in the modified ranking. Thus, one point lost and one gained on account of such an individual i. Hence, the net effect of modifying the ranking as explained above is an increase in the score of the ranking, implying that $\succsim_S$ could not have been a ranking with maximum score.

4. **Non-dictatorship**: this axiom is also satisfied. We need to show that there is no dictator. Consider an arbitrary individual; without loss of generality we can take it to be Individual 1 (otherwise we can just renumber the individuals). Fix two alternatives, say A and B, and a ranking for Individual 1 such that $A \succ_1 B$. For every other individual start with the same ranking as for Individual 1 but swap the positions of A and B. For example, if the set of alternatives is $X = \{A,B,C,D,E,F\}$ and the ranking of Individual 1 is $E \succ_1 A \succ_1 D \sim_1 F \succ_1 B \succ_1 C$ then the ranking of every other individual is as follows:

	1's ranking:			everybody else:	
best		E	best		E
		A			B
		D,F			D,F
		B			A
worst		C	worst		C

Then – if there are at least three individuals – the common ranking of the individuals other than 1 gets the highest score (and higher than any ranking that has $A \succ B$ in it), so that $B \succ_S A$, while – if there are exactly two individuals – then both the ranking of Individual 1 and the ranking of Individual 2 get the highest score (and the other rankings a lower score), so that the chosen social ranking *can* be the one of Individual 2, implying that $B \succ_S A$.

Since the Kemeny-Young method satisfies four of Arrow's five axioms, by Theorem 11.2.1 it must violate the remaining axiom, namely Independence of Irrelevant Alternatives. To see this, consider the following example, where there are three alternatives ($X = \{A,B,C\}$) and seven voters with the following stated preferences:

	1	2	3	4	5	6	7
best	A	A	A	B	B	C	C
	B	B	B	C	C	A	A
worst	C	C	C	A	A	B	B

11.2 Arrow's Impossibility Theorem

Then the scores are computed as follows:[12]

Ranking	Score
$A \succ B \succ C$	$\#(A \succ B) + \#(A \succ C) + \#(B \succ C) = 5 + 3 + 5 = \boxed{13}$
$A \succ C \succ B$	$\#(A \succ C) + \#(A \succ B) + \#(C \succ B) = 3 + 5 + 2 = 10$
$B \succ A \succ C$	$\#(B \succ A) + \#(B \succ C) + \#(A \succ C) = 2 + 5 + 3 = 10$
$B \succ C \succ A$	$\#(B \succ C) + \#(B \succ A) + \#(C \succ A) = 5 + 2 + 4 = 11$
$C \succ A \succ B$	$\#(C \succ A) + \#(C \succ B) + \#(A \succ B) = 4 + 2 + 5 = 11$
$C \succ B \succ A$	$\#(C \succ B) + \#(C \succ A) + \#(B \succ A) = 2 + 4 + 2 = 8$

Thus, the Kemeny-Young method selects, as social ranking, $\boxed{A \succ_S B \succ_S C}$. Now consider the following alternative profile of preferences, which differs from the previous one only in that the ranking of Voters 4 and 5 is $C \succ B \succ A$ instead of $B \succ C \succ A$ (we have highlighted the change with bold fonts).

	1	2	3	**4**	**5**	6	7
best	A	A	A	**C**	**C**	C	C
	B	B	B	**B**	**B**	A	A
worst	C	C	C	**A**	**A**	B	B

The scores for the new profile of preferences are computed as follows:

Ranking	Score
$A \succ B \succ C$	$\#(A \succ B) + \#(A \succ C) + \#(B \succ C) = 5 + 3 + 3 = 11$
$A \succ C \succ B$	$\#(A \succ C) + \#(A \succ B) + \#(C \succ B) = 3 + 5 + 4 = 12$
$B \succ A \succ C$	$\#(B \succ A) + \#(B \succ C) + \#(A \succ C) = 2 + 3 + 3 = 8$
$B \succ C \succ A$	$\#(B \succ C) + \#(B \succ A) + \#(C \succ A) = 3 + 2 + 4 = 9$
$C \succ A \succ B$	$\#(C \succ A) + \#(C \succ B) + \#(A \succ B) = 4 + 4 + 5 = \boxed{13}$
$C \succ B \succ A$	$\#(C \succ B) + \#(C \succ A) + \#(B \succ A) = 4 + 4 + 2 = 10$

Thus, in this case, the Kemeny-Young method selects, as social ranking, $\boxed{C \succ_S A \succ_S B}$. Note that *the ranking of A versus C has changed*: in the previous social ranking A was deemed to be better than C while in the new social ranking C is judged to be better than A. This is a violation of Independence of Irrelevant Alternatives since the ranking of A versus C has not changed in any of the individual rankings.

In the next section we illustrate the proof of Arrow's impossibility theorem in the special case where there are three alternatives and three individuals. The reader who is not interested in how one would go about proving this remarkable result can skip to Section 11.4 which points out a somewhat surprising application of Arrow's theorem to the case of individual decision making.

> Test your understanding of the concepts introduced in this section, by going through the exercises in Section 11.5.2 at the end of this chapter.

---

[12] There is no need to consider rankings involving indifference since every pair (x,y) such that $x \sim y$ gets a score of zero and thus any such ranking would get a total score lower than one of the scores computed below.

11.3 Illustration of the proof of Arrow's theorem

In this section we prove Arrow's impossibility theorem (Theorem 11.2.1) for the case where there are three alternatives, called A, B and C, and three individuals.

For each individual there are 13 possible complete and transitive rankings of the set $X = \{A, B, C\}$ and thus there are $13^3 = 2,197$ possible profiles of preferences. Thus, a Social Preference Function (SPF) that satisfies Unrestricted Domain and Rationality would associate with each of these 2,197 profiles one of the possible 13 complete and transitive rankings of $X = \{A, B, C\}$ (thus, there are $13^{2,197}$ possible SPF's!).

We can think of each SPF as a table consisting of 2,197 columns and two rows: in the first row we record a preference profile and in the second row the corresponding social ranking (similarly to what we did in Figure 11.1). For example, the following would be one column in such a table:

		voter 1	voter 2	voter 3
	best	A	C	A, C
profile of preferences:		C	A	
	worst	B	B	B

	best	A, B
social ranking:		
	worst	C

Note that a SPF that contains the above column violates Unanimity since the profile of preferences is such that everybody prefers A to B and yet society is indifferent between A and B (also, everybody prefers C to B and yet society ranks B above C).

Definition 11.3.1 Let P be a profile of preferences and let x and y be two alternatives.
1. We say that there is a *conflict on x over y in P* if one individual strictly prefers x to y while the other two individuals strictly prefer y to x.
2. We say that an individual is *decisive for x over y in P* if (a) that individual prefers x to y while the other two individuals prefer y to x and (b) in the social ranking associated with P, x is preferred to y (that is, society sides with the lone dissenter).

For example, in the following profile

	Voter 1	Voter 2	Voter 3
best	A	A	B
	B	B	C
worst	C	C	A

there is a conflict on B over A (Voter 3 prefers B to A while Voters 1 and 2 prefer A to B); furthermore, if it is the case that B is preferred to A in the corresponding social ranking, then Individual 3 is decisive for B over A.

11.3 Illustration of the proof of Arrow's theorem

Fix a social preference function f and assume that it satisfies all of Arrow's axioms. Through a series of three steps, outlined below, we will show that we reach a contradiction.

- Step 1: we show that in the presence of conflict over a pair of alternatives, society cannot be indifferent between these two alternatives.

- Step 2: we show that if society sides with the single dissenting individual in a given case of conflict over a pair of alternatives, then it must side with him all the time, thus making him a dictator.

- Step 3: it follows from the previous two steps that, in case of disagreement over a pair of alternatives, society must side with the majority. The final step is to show that the majority rule yields intransitivity of social preferences (the well-known Condorcet paradox: see Section 11.1).

We shall use the following notation: if P is a profile of preferences, then we denote the associated social ranking selected by the SPF f (that is, $f(P)$) by $\succsim_{S(P)}$.

STEP 1. Consider a profile of preferences P such that there is a conflict over a pair of alternatives. Without loss of generality, let this pair be (A, B) and let Individuals 1 and 2 prefer A to B, so that Individual 3 prefers B to A:

$$\begin{pmatrix} A \succ_1 B \\ A \succ_2 B \\ B \succ_3 A \end{pmatrix}. \tag{11.3}$$

Note that, by Independence of Irrelevant Alternatives, this information about how the individuals feel about A and B is sufficient to determine the social ranking of A and B for all profiles that contain (11.3). In this first step we show that it cannot be that society is indifferent between A and B in the social ranking associated with any profile of preferences that contains (11.3). Suppose, to the contrary, that there is a profile P that contains (11.3) and is such that, in the associated social ranking (denoted by $\succsim_{S(P)}$), A is deemed to be just as good as B:

$$A \sim_{S(P)} B. \tag{11.4}$$

Consider the following two profiles that satisfy (11.3):

	Profile I				Profile II		
	Voter 1	Voter 2	Voter 3		Voter 1	Voter 2	Voter 3
best	A	A	C	best	A	A	B
	C	C	B		B	B	C
worst	B	B	A	worst	C	C	A

- In Profile I everybody prefers C to B and thus, by Unanimity, in the social ranking associated with Profile I, it must be that C is preferred to B:

$$C \succ_{S(I)} B. \tag{11.5}$$

- By Independence of Irrelevant Alternatives and hypothesis (11.4), in the social ranking associated with Profile I society is indifferent between A and B:[13]

$$B \sim_{S(I)} A. \tag{11.6}$$

- By Rationality (in particular, transitivity of the social ranking associated with Profile I) it follows from (11.5) and (11.6) that

$$C \succ_{S(I)} A. \tag{11.7}$$

△ In Profile II everybody prefers B to C and thus, by Unanimity, in the social ranking associated with Profile II, it must be that B is preferred to C:

$$B \succ_{S(II)} C. \tag{11.8}$$

△ By Independence of Irrelevant Alternatives and hypothesis (11.4),[14]

$$A \sim_{S(II)} B. \tag{11.9}$$

△ By Rationality (in particular, transitivity of $\succsim_{S(II)}$), it follows from (11.9) and (11.8) that

$$A \succ_{S(II)} C. \tag{11.10}$$

△ Since, for every individual, the ranking of A and C is the same in Profile I and in Profile II, by Independence of Irrelevant Alternatives, it follows from (11.7) that

$$C \succ_{S(II)} A, \tag{11.11}$$

yielding a contradiction with (11.10).[15]

---

[13]Because, for each individual, the ranking of A and B is the same in P and in Profile I: they both satisfy (11.3).

[14]Again, because, for each individual, the ranking of A and B is the same in P and in Profile II: they both satisfy (11.3).

[15]Alternatively, by transitivity of $\succsim_{S(II)}$ one can infer from (11.9) and (11.8) that $A \succ_{S(II)} C$, contradicting (11.11).

11.3 Illustration of the proof of Arrow's theorem

Thus, since supposition (11.4) (namely that $A \sim_{S(P)} B$ for some profile of preferences P that contains (11.3)) leads to a contradiction, it must be that – in the social ranking associated with any profile of preferences P' that contains (11.3) – either $B \succ_{S(P')} A$ or $A \succ_{S(P')} B$.

STEP 2. Next we show that, in case of conflict over a pair of alternatives, society cannot side with the dissenting individual, otherwise that individual will be a dictator. We prove this through a number of lemmas.

Lemma 11.1 *If an individual is decisive for x over y in a particular profile P then he is decisive for x over y in any other profile where he strictly prefers x to y and the other two individuals strictly prefer y to x.*

Proof. This is an immediate consequence of Independence of Irrelevant Alternatives. ∎

Thus, by Lemma 11.1, one can simply state that 'individual i is decisive for x over y' without reference to a specific profile.[16]

Lemma 11.2 *If individual i is decisive for x over y then he is also decisive for x over z with $z \neq y$.*

Proof. Without loss of generality, we prove it for the case where

$$i = 1, \quad x = A, \quad y = B \quad \text{and} \quad z = C.$$

Assume that Individual 1 is decisive for A over B. Consider the profile P given below:

	Profile P		
	Voter 1	Voter 2	Voter 3
best	A	B	B
	B	C	C
worst	C	A	A

By hypothesis (namely, that Individual 1 is decisive for A over B),

$$A \succ_{S(P)} B$$

---

[16] Let P be a profile where Individual 1 is the only one who prefers A to B, that is, P contains

$$\begin{pmatrix} A \succ_1 B \\ B \succ_2 A \\ B \succ_3 A \end{pmatrix}. \tag{11.12}$$

Then there are $3^3 = 27$ profiles that contain (11.12): they are obtained by replacing, for each individual, one of the three squares shown below with alternative C:

Voter 1	Voter 2	Voter 3
□	□	□
A	B	B
□	□	□
B	A	A
□	□	□

and, by Unanimity,

$$B \succ_{S(P)} C$$

so that, by transitivity of $\succsim_{S(P)}$,

$$A \succ_{S(P)} C.$$

Thus, Individual 1 is decisive for A over C in profile P. Hence, by Lemma 11.1, Individual 1 is decisive for A over C in every profile that contains $\begin{pmatrix} A \succ_1 C \\ C \succ_2 A \\ C \succ_3 A \end{pmatrix}$. ∎

Lemma 11.3 *If individual i is decisive for x over y then he is also decisive for z over y with $z \neq x$.*

Proof. Without loss of generality, we prove it for the case where $i = 1, x = A, y = B$ and $z = C$. Assume that Individual 1 is decisive for A over B. Consider the profile P given below:

	Profile P		
	Voter 1	Voter 2	Voter 3
best	C	B	B
	A	C	C
worst	B	A	A

By hypothesis,

$$A \succ_{S(P)} B$$

and, by Unanimity,

$$C \succ_{S(P)} A$$

so that, by transitivity of $\succsim_{S(P)}$,

$$C \succ_{S(P)} B.$$

Thus, Individual 1 is decisive for C over B in profile P. Hence, by Lemma 11.1, Individual 1 is decisive for C over B in every profile that contains $\begin{pmatrix} C \succ_1 B \\ B \succ_2 C \\ B \succ_3 C \end{pmatrix}$. ∎

Lemma 11.4 *If individual i is decisive for x over y then he is also decisive for any alternative over any other different alternative.*

Proof. Without loss of generality, we prove it for the case where $i = 1, x = A, y = B$. Suppose that Individual 1 is decisive for A over B. We need to show that he is also decisive for the following: A over C, C over B, B over C, C over A and B over A.
   1. A over C: this follows from Lemma 11.2 (with $i = 1, x = A, y = B$ and $z = C$).
   2. C over B: this follows from Lemma 11.3 (with $i = 1, x = A, y = B$ and $z = C$).

11.3 Illustration of the proof of Arrow's theorem

3. B over C: by Point 1, Individual 1 is decisive for A over C; thus, by Lemma 11.3 (with $i = 1, x = A, y = C$ and $z = B$), 1 is decisive for B over C.
4. C over A: by Point 2, Individual 1 is decisive for C over B; thus, by Lemma 11.2 (with $i = 1, x = C, y = B$ and $z = A$), 1 is decisive for C over A.
5. B over A: by Point 3, Individual 1 is decisive for B over C; thus, by Lemma 11.2 (with $i = 1, x = B, y = C$ and $z = A$), 1 is decisive for B over A. ∎

Lemma 11.5 *If individual i is decisive for x over y then, for every profile P that contains $x \succ_i y$, $x \succ_{S(P)} y$.*

Proof. Without loss of generality, we prove it for the case where $i = 1, x = A, y = B$. The hypothesis is that Individual 1 is decisive for A over B. By Lemma 11.4, Individual 1 is also decisive for A over C. Consider the following profile P:

	Profile P		
	Voter 1	Voter 2	Voter 3
best	A	C	C
	C	A	B
worst	B	B	A

Since 1 is decisive for A over C,

$$A \succ_{S(P)} C.$$

By Unanimity,

$$C \succ_{S(P)} B.$$

Thus, by transitivity of $\succsim_{S(P)}$,

$$A \succ_{S(P)} B.$$

By Independence of Irrelevant Alternatives, $A \succ_{S(P')} B$ for any other profile P' that contains $\begin{pmatrix} A \succ_1 B \\ A \succ_2 B \\ B \succ_3 A \end{pmatrix}$. By swapping the ranking of Individuals 2 and 3 in P, an analogous argument shows that $A \succ_{S(P'')} B$ for any other profile P'' that contains $\begin{pmatrix} A \succ_1 B \\ B \succ_2 A \\ A \succ_3 B \end{pmatrix}$. Finally, if a profile contains $A \succ_i B$ for every individual i, then in the corresponding social ranking A is strictly better than B by Unanimity. Thus, we have covered every possible case. ∎

Corollary 11.3.1 *If there is a profile of preferences P where there is a conflict (that is, there are two alternatives x and y and individual i strictly prefers x to y, whereas the other two individuals strictly prefer y to x) and the associated social ranking sides with individual i (that is, $x \succ_{S(P)} y$) then individual i is a dictator.*

Proof. If there is a profile of preferences P where there is a conflict and the associated social ranking sides with the dissenting individual, call him i, then, by Lemma 11.4, i is decisive for every pair of alternatives. Thus, by Lemma 11.5, for any two alternatives x and y, if P is a profile that contains $x \succ_i y$ then in the associated social ranking x is strictly preferred to y (that is, $x \succ_{S(P)} y$). This is precisely the definition of individual i being a dictator. ∎

STEP 3. By Step 1 if there is a conflict over a pair of alternatives, then society cannot be indifferent between the two alternatives, that is, society has to side either with the lone dissenting individual or with the majority.

By Step 2, if society sides with the lone dissenting individual, then that individual must be a dictator. Thus, if the SPF satisfies Non-dictatorship, whenever there is a conflict society must side with the majority. But then, because of the Condorcet paradox, the SPF cannot satisfy transitivity, that is, it must fail Rationality. The Condorcet paradox was illustrated in Section 11.1 and is reproduced below. Consider the following profile of preferences:

	Voter 1	Voter 2	Voter 3
best	A	C	B
	B	A	C
worst	C	B	A

Profile P

Then

- In the choice between A and B, the majority (consisting of Individuals 1 and 2) prefers A to B. Thus, since society must side with the majority, it must be that $A \succ_{S(P)} B$.
- In the choice between B and C, the majority (consisting of Individuals 1 and 3) prefers B to C. Thus, since society must side with the majority, it must be that $B \succ_{S(P)} C$.
- In the choice between A and C, the majority (consisting of Individuals 2 and 3) prefers C to A. Thus, since society must side with the majority, it must be that $C \succ_{S(P)} A$.

Thus, we have that $A \succ_{S(P)} B$, $B \succ_{S(P)} C$ and – in violation of transitivity – $C \succ_{S(P)} A$.

This concludes the proof of Arrow's theorem for the case of three individuals and three alternatives. The proof for the general case is not much different. Instead of referring to a single individual as being decisive one starts with a group of individuals being decisive and then one shows that if a (non-empty) group T is decisive,[17] then there is a single individual in T who is decisive. Having established this, one can then essentially repeat the three-step proof given above.

> Test your understanding of the concepts introduced in this section, by going through the exercises in Section 11.5.3 at the end of this chapter.

---

[17] Note that, for every pair of alternatives x and y, there must be a non-empty group who is decisive for x over y: indeed the group N consisting of all the individuals satisfies the definition of decisiveness.

11.4 Application of Arrow's theorem to individual choice

Although Arrow's theorem was conceived within the context of group decision making, it also has an interesting application within the setting of individual decision making.

We often evaluate alternatives along different dimensions. Consider the following example: Jane is relocating because of her job and is looking to buy a house in the new location. She has seen two houses that are offered at the same price. House A is rather far from the workplace but is in very good condition and requires very little remodeling. House B is very close to her new place of work but is in very poor condition and requires substantial remodeling. This is illustrated in Figure 11.2, where on the horizontal axis we measure the amount of remodeling required – the less the better – and on the vertical axis we measure the house's distance from the workplace – the less the better.

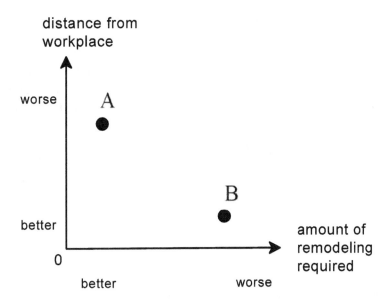

Figure 11.2: Two houses ranked in terms of two dimensions

It is clear that along the "distance dimension", denoted by d, house B is better than house A ($B \succ_d A$), while along the "remodeling dimension", denoted by r, house A is better than house B ($A \succ_r B$). Thus, in order to decide which house to buy, Jane will need to somehow resolve this conflict.

Let us now look at a three-attribute example. John is considering buying a new car. He has narrowed down his choice to three models, which he ranks as follows in terms of three attributes (price, speed and fuel efficiency):

		Attribute		
		Price	Speed	Fuel efficiency
Model	A	Best	Worst	Middle
	B	Middle	Best	Worst
	C	Worst	Middle	Best

Suppose that John decides to rank model x above model y if and only if the former is better than the latter in terms of at least two attributes.

Then his ranking will be as follows: $A \succ B$ (because A is better than B in terms of price and fuel efficiency), $B \succ C$ (because B dominates C in terms of price and speed) and $C \succ A$ (because C is better than A in terms of speed and fuel efficiency).

Thus, his ranking violates transitivity (and he can be subjected to a money pump: see Chapter 1). Of course, we are familiar with this example because it is nothing more than Condorcet's paradox.

In general we can think of each attribute as a "voter" and of the individual's overall ranking as the "social ranking", that is, we can think of multi-attribute situations as a problem of aggregation of preferences.

Suppose that there there are at least three alternatives and an individual is able to come up with a complete and transitive ranking of the alternatives in terms of each of two or more attributes and aims to "extract" a ranking of the set of alternatives by devising a method that satisfies the following properties:

1. For each attribute, no complete and transitive ranking of the alternatives should be ruled out in principle.

2. The overall ranking should be complete and transitive.

3. If an alternative x is better than another alternative y in terms of each attribute then x should be better than y in the overall ranking.

4. No single attribute should be a "dictator" in the sense that, for every pair of alternatives x and y, x being better than y in terms of that attribute is sufficient for x to be ranked above y in the overall ranking.

5. In the overall ranking, the ranking of any two alternatives x and y should be based only on how these two alternatives are ranked according to each attribute.

Then, by Arrow's theorem, it is impossible to find such a method.

> Test your understanding of the concepts introduced in this section, by going through the exercises in Section 11.5.4 at the end of this chapter.

11.5 Exercises

The solutions to the following exercises are given in Section 11.6 at the end of this chapter.

11.5.1 Exercises for Section 11.1: Social preference functions

Exercise 11.1 Consider the following voting procedure, called the *Borda count*. Each person states a strict ranking (that is, no indifference is allowed) of the m alternatives and the committee chair proceeds as follows. For each voter's ranking, the chair assigns m points to the alternative ranked first, $m-1$ points to the alternative ranked second, and so on. Then, for each alternative, the chair adds up all the points and ranks the alternatives based on the total points received. This procedure thus extracts a social ranking from a profile of individual rankings.

(a) Consider the following rankings of three alternatives, called a, b and c, by three individuals. What is the social ranking obtained with the Borda count?

	Voter 1	Voter 2	Voter 3
best	a	b	c
	b	a	b
worst	c	c	a

(b) Consider now the following ranking. What is the social ranking obtained with the Borda count?

	Voter 1	Voter 2	Voter 3
best	a	c	b
	b	a	c
worst	c	b	a

Exercise 11.2 There are four candidates for one position. The candidates are identified by the first letter of their last name: a, b, c and x. There are seven voters, with the following preferences (most preferred at the top and least preferred at the bottom).

Voter:	1	2	3	4	5	6	7
best	x	a	b	x	a	b	x
	c	x	a	c	x	a	c
	b	c	x	b	c	x	b
worst	a	b	c	a	b	c	a

Suppose that the Borda count is used and voters report their preferences truthfully.
(a) What is the social ranking? Who wins the election? If voting takes place over the four candidates and then, **after the election**, candidate x is disqualified, who is the chosen candidate according to the social ranking?
(b) Suppose that, **just before the vote**, candidate x drops out (e.g. because he is disqualified). What is the new social ranking, given that voting is only over candidates a, b and c? Who wins the election?

Exercise 11.3 As shown in Section 11.1, the majority rule does not always yield a transitive social ranking. In this exercise you are asked to show that there are other problems with the majority rule. Consider the method of *majority voting with a pre-determined agenda*: it is established in advance that a series of votes will be taken, each vote will concern two alternatives and the winner of one vote will be put up against another alternative for the next vote, etc., until a final choice is made. The sequence in which votes will be taken is pre-determined; for example, first there will be a vote to choose between a and b and then there will be a vote to choose between the winner of the first vote and c, and so on.

(a) Give an example with three voters and four alternatives where this procedure will end up selecting an alternative y as the final choice despite the fact that there is another alternative x *that everybody prefers to y*.

(b) So far we have assumed that individuals vote according to their true preferences. Now consider the situation where there are three voters and three alternatives: a, b and c and the agenda is such that the first vote is between a and b and the second vote is between the winner of the first vote and c. Construct an example where (that is, specify a possible profile of preferences such that) one voter can gain by "lying", that is, by voting according to a ranking which is not her true ranking.

11.5.2 Exercises for Section 11.2: Arrow's impossibility theorem

Exercise 11.4 Consider again the Borda count (explained in Exercise 11.1).

(a) Which of Arrow's axioms does the Borda count satisfy?

(b) Which of Arrow's axioms does the Borda count violate? Show by means of an example that the property you claim to be violated is indeed violated.

Exercise 11.5 Consider the following social preference function, which could be named "Reverse Dictatorship". First of all, each individual is allowed to state any complete and transitive ranking of the alternatives.
Secondly, for any two alternatives x and y, (1) if $x \succ_1 y$ then $y \succ_S x$ and (2) if $x \sim_1 y$ then $x \succsim_S y$ if and only if $x \succsim_2 y$ (thus the social ranking is determined exclusively by the rankings of Individuals 1 and 2).

(a) Illustrate this aggregation procedure for the case of two alternative ($X = \{A, B\}$) and two individuals ($N = \{1, 2\}$), using a table.

(b) Now consider the general case of any number of alternatives (greater than or equal to 2) and any number of individuals (greater than or equal to 2). For each of Arrow's axioms state whether this procedure satisfies or violates the axiom and provide enough details to support your claim.

11.5 Exercises

Exercise 11.6 In this exercise you are asked to show that the majority rule satisfies all of Arrow's axioms when there are only two alternatives. First, let us define (a version of) the majority rule.
Majority rule: (1) $x \succ_S y$ if and only if the number of individuals who prefer x to y is greater than the number of individuals who prefer y to x and (2) $x \sim_S y$ if and only if the number of individuals who prefer x to y is equal to the number of individuals who prefer y to x (note that it is possible for these two numbers to be equal to zero, which is the case when everybody is indifferent between x and y).
Prove that the majority rule defined above satisfies all of Arrow's axioms when the set of alternatives is $X = \{A, B\}$.

Exercise 11.7 In Section 11.1 we considered the case where there are only two alternatives, A and B (thus, $X = \{A, B\}$) and two voters ($N = \{1, 2\}$) and restricted the set of rankings by ruling out indifference, that is, $S = \{A \succ B, B \succ A\} \times \{A \succ B, B \succ A\}$ and $Q = \{A \succ B, B \succ A\}$. We showed that in this case there are 16 possible social preference functions, which are listed in (11.1). By appealing to Unanimity and Non-dictatorship we were able to narrow down the list to the two SPFs shown below:

profile →	$A \succ_1 B$	$A \succ_1 B$	$B \succ_1 A$	$B \succ_1 A$
SPF ↓	$A \succ_2 B$	$B \succ_2 A$	$A \succ_2 B$	$B \succ_2 A$
SPF - 2	$A \succ_S B$	$A \succ_S B$	$A \succ_S B$	$B \succ_S A$
SPF - 8	$A \succ_S B$	$B \succ_S A$	$B \succ_S A$	$B \succ_S A$

Show that these two SPFs satisfy Arrow's axioms (except for, of course, Unrestricted Domain).

Exercise 11.8 There are three alternatives: A, B and C and five voters. Their stated preferences are as follows:

	Voter 1	Voter 2	Voter 3	Voter 4	Voter 5
best	A	B	B	C	C
	B	C	C	A	A
worst	C	A	A	B	B

Use the Kemeny-Young method (explained in Section 11.2) to determine the associated social ranking. [Note: you can restrict attention to strict rankings.]

11.5.3 Exercises for Section 11.3: Illustration of the proof of Arrow's theorem

Exercise 11.9 Let the set of alternatives be $X = \{A, B, C\}$.
(a) List all the complete and transitive rankings of the elements of X.
(b) If there are 4 voters, how many profiles of preferences are there if we require every individual ranking to be complete and transitive?
(c) If there are 2 individuals, how many social preference functions are there that satisfy Unrestricted Domain and Rationality?

11.5.4 Exercises for Section 11.4: Application of Arrow's theorem to individual choice

Exercise 11.10 Dan wants to come up with a ranking of three items, call them A, B and C. He wants to buy the one that ends up being ranked highest. There are three attributes that he can use to rank each alternative. He decides to use the following method.

First of all, for each attribute he classifies each item as 'very good' (V), 'good' (G) or 'mediocre' (M).

Then he assigns 3 points for a judgment of V, 2 points for a judgment of G and 1 point for a judgment of M.

Finally, he adds up the points scored by each item and ranks the items according to the total number of points received.

Which of Arrow's axioms (restated as explained in Section 11.5.4) does this method satisfy and which does it violate?

11.6 Solutions to Exercises

Solution to Exercise 11.1.

(a) Alternative a gets $3 + 2 + 1 = 6$ points, b gets $2 + 3 + 2 = 7$ points and c gets $1 + 1 + 3 = 5$ points. Thus, the social ranking is

$$\begin{array}{ll} \text{best} & b \\ & a \\ \text{worst} & c \end{array}$$

(b) Each alternative gets 6 points. Thus, the social ranking is: society is indifferent among all three alternatives. □

Solution to Exercise 11.2. Recall that the preferences of the seven voters are as follows:

Voter:	1	2	3	4	5	6	7
best	x	a	b	x	a	b	x
	c	x	a	c	x	a	c
	b	c	x	b	c	x	b
worst	a	b	c	a	b	c	a

(a) With the Borda count (and sincere reporting) x gets $4 + 3 + 2 + 4 + 3 + 2 + 4 = 22$ points, a gets $1 + 4 + 3 + 1 + 4 + 3 + 1 = 17$, b gets $2 + 1 + 4 + 2 + 1 + 4 + 2 = 16$ and c gets $3 + 2 + 1 + 3 + 2 + 1 + 3 = 15$. Thus, the social ranking is

$$\begin{array}{ll} \text{best} & x \\ & a \\ & b \\ \text{worst} & c \end{array}$$

and the winner is x. If, after the election, x is disqualified and drops out then the next best candidate will be chosen, that is candidate a.

(b) Eliminating x from the above profile we have:

Voter:	1	2	3	4	5	6	7
best	c	a	b	c	a	b	c
	b	c	a	b	c	a	b
worst	a	b	c	a	b	c	a

and using the Borda count with this profile we have that a gets $1+3+2+1+3+2+1 = 13$ points, b gets $2+1+3+2+1+3+2 = 14$ points and c gets $3+2+1+3+2+1+3 = 15$ points. Thus, the social ranking becomes

best   c
          b
worst a

that is, a complete reversal of the previous one! The winner is now c, who was the lowest ranked candidate before! □

Solution to Exercise 11.3.

(a) Here is an example with three voters and four alternatives: a, b, x and y. The voters' preferences are as follows:

Voter:	1	2	3
best	x	a	b
	y	x	a
	b	y	x
worst	a	b	y

The agenda is as follows: the first vote is between a and x, the second vote is between the winner of the first vote and b, the third vote is between the winner of the second vote and y. Then the winner of the first vote is a, the winner of the vote between a and b is b and, finally, the winner of the vote between b and y is y. Thus, the selected alternative is y. However, *all three voters strictly prefer x to y*!

(b) Let there be three voters and three alternatives: a, b and c and suppose that the agenda is to choose first between a and b and then the winner is put up against c. Let the voters' preferences be as follows:

	1's ranking	2's ranking	3's ranking
best	a	b	c
	b	c	a
worst	c	a	b

If everybody votes sincerely, then in the vote between a and b, the winner is a and in the final vote between a and c the winner is c, which is Voter 1's worst outcome. If 1 voted as if her true preferences were $b \succ_1 a \succ_1 c$, then she will vote for b in the first round, so that (if everybody else votes sincerely) the winner is b and then in the final vote between b and c, the winner is b, whom Voter 1 prefers to c (according to her *true* preferences $a \succ_1 b \succ_1 c$). □

Solution to Exercise 11.4.
  (a) The Borda count satisfies Rationality, Non-dictatorship and Unanimity.
  (b) The Borda count violates Unrestricted Domain (also called Freedom of Expression) because it does not allow expression of indifference between two or more alternatives. The Borda count also violates Independence of Irrelevant Alternatives. To see this, consider the following profile of preferences:

	1's ranking	2's ranking	3's ranking
best	a	b	c
	b	c	a
worst	c	a	b

The Borda count assigns 6 points to each alternative and thus the social ranking is $a \sim_S b \sim_S c$; note that, in particular, $\boxed{a \sim_S b}$. Consider now the following profile of preferences, which does not differ from the previous one in terms of how the three individuals rank a versus b:

	1's ranking	2's ranking	3's ranking
best	a	b	a
	b	c	c
worst	c	a	b

In this profile the Borda count assigns 7 points to a, 6 points to b and 5 points to c, so that the associated social ranking is

best	a
	b
worst	c

so that, in particular, $\boxed{a \succ_S b}$ yielding a violation of Independence of Irrelevant Alternatives.[18] □

Solution to Exercise 11.5.
  (a) The table is as follows:

		Individual 2's ranking		
		$A \succ_2 B$	$A \sim_2 B$	$B \succ_2 A$
Individual 1's ranking	$A \succ_1 B$	$B \succ_S A$	$B \succ_S A$	$B \succ_S A$
	$A \sim_1 B$	$A \succ_S B$	$A \sim_S B$	$B \succ_S A$
	$B \succ_1 A$	$A \succ_S B$	$A \succ_S B$	$A \succ_S B$

---

[18] Since, for each individual, the ranking of a and b is the same in the two profiles (namely, $a \succ_1 b$, $b \succ_2 a$, and $a \succ_3 b$), Independence of Irrelevant Alternatives requires that the social ranking of a and b be the same in the two profiles.

11.6 Solutions to Exercises

(b) The Unrestricted Domain axiom is satisfied by construction (each individual is allowed to state any complete and transitive ranking.

The Unanimity axiom fails: suppose that $x \succ_i y$, for all $i \in N$; then, in particular, $x \succ_1 y$ and thus we have that $y \succ_S x$.

The Independence of Irrelevant Alternatives axiom is satisfied: the ranking of any two alternatives is only based on how individuals 1 and 2 rank them and nothing else.

The Non-dictatorship axiom is satisfied: individual 1 is clearly not a dictator and individual 2 is not a dictator either because in the case where $x \succ_2 y$ and $x \succ_1 y$ we have that $y \succ_S x$.

The Rationality axiom requires some thinking. Clearly the social ranking is complete, because for any two alternatives x and y, the rule yields a social ranking of them (if $x \succ_1 y$ then $y \succ_S x$, if $y \succ_1 x$ then $x \succ_S y$ and if $x \sim_1 y$ then the social ranking of x and y mirrors the ranking of Individual 2).

The issue is whether the social ranking is transitive. The answer is affirmative and we prove this by contradiction. Suppose that transitivity fails, that is, suppose there are three alternatives x, y and z such that

- $x \succsim_S y$ (which implies that $y \succsim_1 x$),
- $y \succsim_S z$ (which implies that $y \succsim_1 z$)
- and yet $z \succ_S x$.

Let us think about why it is the case that $z \succ_S x$. There are two possibilities.

CASE 1: $z \succ_S x$ because

$$x \succ_1 z. \tag{11.13}$$

From $y \succsim_1 x$ (implied by the hypothesis that $x \succsim_S y$) and (11.13) we get, by transitivity of 1's ranking, that $y \succ_1 z$, but this requires $z \succ_S y$, contradicting our hypothesis that $y \succsim_S z$. Thus, this case is ruled out.

CASE 2: $z \succ_S x$ because

$$x \sim_1 z \text{ and } z \succ_2 x. \tag{11.14}$$

It cannot be that $y \succ_1 x$ because, together with $x \sim_1 z$ it would yield (by transitivity of 1's ranking) that $y \succ_1 z$, from which it would follow that $z \succ_S y$, contradicting your hypothesis that $y \succsim_S z$. Thus, since $y \succsim_1 x$ (implied by the hypothesis that $x \succsim_S y$), it must be that $y \sim_1 x$, so that (by transitivity of 1's ranking) $x \sim_1 y \sim_1 z$ and thus the ranking of any two of these three alternatives mirrors the ranking of Individual 2. Since Individual 2's ranking is transitive we have reached a contradiction. Thus, we conclude that the Rationality axiom is indeed satisfied.

To sum up: the social preference function under consideration satisfies all of Arrow's axioms, except Unanimity. □

Solution to Exercise 11.6.
1. Unrestricted Domain is satisfied, because the rule allows for every possible individual ranking ($A \succ B, A \sim B$ and $B \succ A$).
2. Rationality is also satisfied: transitivity is trivially true when there are only two alternatives and completeness is satisfied because one of $A \succ_S B$, $A \sim_S B$ and $B \succ_S A$ is always true.
3. Unanimity is clearly satisfied because when all the individuals prefer x to y the number of individuals who prefer x to y is n and the number of individuals who prefer y to x is 0 and thus $x \succ_S y$.
4. Non-dictatorship is satisfied because, for every pair of alternatives x and y and for every individual, there is a profile where she prefers x to y and everybody else prefers y to x, in which case either $y \succ_S x$, if $n \geq 3$, or $x \sim_S y$, if $n = 2$.
5. Independence of Irrelevant Alternatives, like transitivity, is trivially true when there are only two alternatives. □

Solution to Exercise 11.7.
1. Rationality is clearly satisfied (as remarked in the previous exercise, transitivity is trivially satisfied when there are only two alternatives).
2. Unanimity is also clearly satisfied: it only requires $A \succ_S B$ in the first column and $B \succ_S A$ in the fourth column.
3. Non-dictatorship is also satisfied. In SPF-2 Individual 1 is not a dictator because of column 3 ($B \succ_1 A$ but $A \succ_S B$) and Individual 2 is not a dictator because of column 2 ($B \succ_2 A$ but $A \succ_S B$). In SPF-8 Individual 1 is not a dictator because of column 2 and Individual 2 is not a dictator because of column 3.
4. As remarked in the previous exercise, Independence of Irrelevant Alternatives is trivially satisfied when there are only two alternatives. □

Solution to Exercise 11.8. The stated preferences are:

	voter 1	voter 2	voter 3	voter 4	voter 5
best	A	B	B	C	C
	B	C	C	A	A
worst	C	A	A	B	B

The scores are computed as follows:

Ranking	Score
$A \succ B \succ C$	$\#(A \succ B) + \#(A \succ C) + \#(B \succ C) = 3 + 1 + 3 = 7$
$A \succ C \succ B$	$\#(A \succ C) + \#(A \succ B) + \#(C \succ B) = 1 + 3 + 2 = 6$
$B \succ A \succ C$	$\#(B \succ A) + \#(B \succ C) + \#(A \succ C) = 2 + 3 + 1 = 6$
$B \succ C \succ A$	$\#(B \succ C) + \#(B \succ A) + \#(C \succ A) = 3 + 2 + 4 = \boxed{9}$
$C \succ A \succ B$	$\#(C \succ A) + \#(C \succ B) + \#(A \succ B) = 4 + 2 + 3 = \boxed{9}$
$C \succ B \succ A$	$\#(C \succ B) + \#(C \succ A) + \#(B \succ A) = 2 + 4 + 2 = 8$

Thus, the Kemeny-Young method selects either $B \succ C \succ A$ or $C \succ A \succ B$ as social ranking. □

11.6 Solutions to Exercises

Solution to Exercise 11.9.

(a) There are 13 such rankings:

(1) $A \sim B \sim C$, (2) $A \sim B \succ C$, (3) $A \sim C \succ B$, (4) $B \sim C \succ A$,
(5) $A \succ B \sim C$, (6) $B \succ A \sim C$, (7) $C \succ A \sim B$, (8) $A \succ B \succ C$,
(9) $A \succ C \succ B$, (10) $B \succ A \succ C$, (11) $B \succ C \succ A$, (12) $C \succ A \succ B$,
(13) $C \succ B \succ A$.

(b) We have to specify one of 13 possible rankings for each individual, thus the total number of profiles is $13^4 = 28{,}561$.

(c) With 2 individuals the number of profiles of preferences is $13^2 = 169$. For each of these we have to pick one ranking out of the 13 listed in Part (a), thus the total number of SPFs is $13^{169} = 18{,}048 \times 10^{184}$ (greater than 18 followed by 187 zeros)! □

Solution to Exercise 11.10. This is essentially the Borda count (see Exercise 11.5.1) applied to this context. It satisfies all of Arrow's axioms except for Independence of Irrelevant Alternatives.[19] To see this, consider the following classification:

	Attribute 1	Attribute 2	Attribute 3
Very good	A	C	B
Good	B	A	C
Mediocre	C	B	A

Then each alternative gets $3+2+1=6$ points and thus the derived ranking is $A \sim B \sim C$. Now consider the following alternative ranking which preserves the ordinal ranking of A and B in terms of each attribute:

	Attribute 1	Attribute 2	Attribute 3
Very good	A, C	A, C	B, C
Good	B	B	A
Mediocre			

Then A gets $3+3+2=8$ points, B gets $2+2+3=7$ points and C gets $3+3+3=9$ points. Thus, the associated ranking is $C \succ A \succ B$. Hence, the ranking of A and B has changed from $A \sim B$ to $A \succ B$, despite the fact that the ordinal ranking A and B in terms of each attribute has not changed: a violation of Independence of Irrelevant Alternatives. □

---

[19] Contrary to Exercise 11.5.4, Unrestricted Domain *is* satisfied, because the stated rule does not require a strict ranking in terms of individual attributes: for example, all three items can be classified as V in terms of one attribute.

12. Misrepresentation of Preferences

12.1 Social choice functions

Arrow's theorem says that it is not possible to extract from a profile of individual preferences a preference ranking for society with a procedure that satisfies five desirable properties: Unrestricted Domain, Rationality, Unanimity, Non-dictatorship and Independence of Irrelevant Alternatives. Perhaps Arrow's approach is too demanding, in that it requires that a ranking of the entire set of alternatives be obtained for society. After all, if the purpose of voting procedures is to arrive at some choice among the alternatives, then we can dispense with a complete ranking and just focus on the final choice. Thus, we could look for a simpler object that extracts from a profile of individual preferences one alternative, to be thought of as *society's choice*. Such an object is called a Social Choice Function (SCF).

Definition 12.1.1 Let $X = \{x_1, x_2, \ldots, x_m\}$ ($m \geq 2$) be a finite set of alternatives, $N = \{1, 2, \ldots, n\}$ ($n \geq 2$) a finite set of individuals, $\mathscr{R}$ the set of complete and transitive binary relations on X, $\mathscr{R}^n$ the cartesian product $\underbrace{\mathscr{R} \times \mathscr{R} \times \cdots \times \mathscr{R}}_{n \text{ times}}$ (thus an element of $\mathscr{R}^n$ is a list of complete and transitive preference relations on the set of alternatives X, one for each individual; we call an element of $\mathscr{R}^n$ a *profile of preferences*) and let S be a subset of $\mathscr{R}^n$. A *social choice function* is a function $f: S \to X$ that takes as input a profile of preferences for the individuals $(\succsim_1, \succsim_2, \ldots, \succsim_n) \in S$ and produces as output an alternative $f(\succsim_1, \succsim_2, \ldots, \succsim_n) \in X$ to be thought of as "society's choice".

For example, suppose that there are only two alternatives, a and b (thus $X = \{a, b\}$), only strict rankings can be reported (that is, $S = \{a \succ b, b \succ a\} \times \{a \succ b, b \succ a\}$), and two voters ($N = \{1, 2\}$). Then, in order to construct a SCF we need to replace each □ in the following table with either an a or a b:

Chapter 12. Misrepresentation of Preferences

		Individual 2's ranking	
		$a \succ_2 b$	$b \succ_2 a$
Individual 1's	$a \succ_1 b$	☐	☐
ranking	$b \succ_1 a$	☐	☐

Thus, there are $2^4 = 16$ possible SCFs, which are listed below:

(SCF-1)

		2	
		$a \succ_2 b$	$b \succ_2 a$
1	$a \succ_1 b$	a	a
	$b \succ_1 a$	a	a

(SCF-2)

		2	
		$a \succ_2 b$	$b \succ_2 a$
1	$a \succ_1 b$	a	a
	$b \succ_1 a$	a	b

(SCF-3)

		2	
		$a \succ_2 b$	$b \succ_2 a$
1	$a \succ_1 b$	a	a
	$b \succ_1 a$	b	a

(SCF-4)

		2	
		$a \succ_2 b$	$b \succ_2 a$
1	$a \succ_1 b$	a	b
	$b \succ_1 a$	a	a

(SCF-5)

		2	
		$a \succ_2 b$	$b \succ_2 a$
1	$a \succ_1 b$	b	a
	$b \succ_1 a$	a	a

(SCF-6)

		2	
		$a \succ_2 b$	$b \succ_2 a$
1	$a \succ_1 b$	a	a
	$b \succ_1 a$	b	b

(SCF-7)

		2	
		$a \succ_2 b$	$b \succ_2 a$
1	$a \succ_1 b$	a	b
	$b \succ_1 a$	a	b

(SCF-8)

		2	
		$a \succ_2 b$	$b \succ_2 a$
1	$a \succ_1 b$	a	b
	$b \succ_1 a$	b	a

(SCF-9)

		2	
		$a \succ_2 b$	$b \succ_2 a$
1	$a \succ_1 b$	b	a
	$b \succ_1 a$	a	b

(SCF-10)

		2	
		$a \succ_2 b$	$b \succ_2 a$
1	$a \succ_1 b$	b	a
	$b \succ_1 a$	b	a

(SCF-11)

		2	
		$a \succ_2 b$	$b \succ_2 a$
1	$a \succ_1 b$	b	b
	$b \succ_1 a$	a	a

(SCF-12)

		2	
		$a \succ_2 b$	$b \succ_2 a$
1	$a \succ_1 b$	a	b
	$b \succ_1 a$	b	b

(SCF-13)

		2	
		$a \succ_2 b$	$b \succ_2 a$
1	$a \succ_1 b$	b	a
	$b \succ_1 a$	b	b

(SCF-14)

		2	
		$a \succ_2 b$	$b \succ_2 a$
1	$a \succ_1 b$	b	b
	$b \succ_1 a$	a	b

(SCF-15)

		2	
		$a \succ_2 b$	$b \succ_2 a$
1	$a \succ_1 b$	b	b
	$b \succ_1 a$	b	a

(SCF-16)

		2	
		$a \succ_2 b$	$b \succ_2 a$
1	$a \succ_1 b$	b	b
	$b \succ_1 a$	b	b

12.1 Social choice functions

Which of these SCFs should one reject on the basis of some general "reasonable" requirements?

First requirement: **Unanimity**. If all the individuals list alternative x at the top of their reported rankings then x should be chosen. In the above example this requirement amounts to insisting that the main diagonal be as follows: $\begin{matrix} a \\ & b \end{matrix}$.

By appealing to Unanimity we can thus reject SCF-1, SCF-3, SCF-4, SCF-5, SCF-8, SCF-9, SCF-10, SCF-11, SCF-13, SCF-14, SCF-15 and SCF-16. Thus, we are left with the following four SCFs:

(SCF-2)
$$\begin{array}{c|cc} & \multicolumn{2}{c}{2} \\ & a \succ_2 b & b \succ_2 a \\ \hline 1 \begin{array}{c} a \succ_1 b \\ b \succ_1 a \end{array} & \begin{array}{c} a \\ a \end{array} & \begin{array}{c} a \\ b \end{array} \end{array}$$

(SCF-6)
$$\begin{array}{c|cc} & \multicolumn{2}{c}{2} \\ & a \succ_2 b & b \succ_2 a \\ \hline 1 \begin{array}{c} a \succ_1 b \\ b \succ_1 a \end{array} & \begin{array}{c} a \\ b \end{array} & \begin{array}{c} a \\ b \end{array} \end{array}$$

(SCF-7)
$$\begin{array}{c|cc} & \multicolumn{2}{c}{2} \\ & a \succ_2 b & b \succ_2 a \\ \hline 1 \begin{array}{c} a \succ_1 b \\ b \succ_1 a \end{array} & \begin{array}{c} a \\ a \end{array} & \begin{array}{c} b \\ b \end{array} \end{array}$$

(SCF-12)
$$\begin{array}{c|cc} & \multicolumn{2}{c}{2} \\ & a \succ_2 b & b \succ_2 a \\ \hline 1 \begin{array}{c} a \succ_1 b \\ b \succ_1 a \end{array} & \begin{array}{c} a \\ b \end{array} & \begin{array}{c} b \\ b \end{array} \end{array}$$

Second requirement: **Non-dictatorship**. There should not be a "dictator", that is, an individual whose top alternative is always chosen. In the above example there should not be an individual who is such that if he reports $a \succ b$ then a is chosen and if he reports $b \succ a$ then b is chosen.

On the basis of Non-dictatorship we must thus reject SCF-6 (where Individual 1 is a dictator) and SCF-7 (where Individual 2 is a dictator).

Hence, we are left two SCFs:

(SCF-2)
$$\begin{array}{c|cc} & \multicolumn{2}{c}{2} \\ & a \succ_2 b & b \succ_2 a \\ \hline 1 \begin{array}{c} a \succ_1 b \\ b \succ_1 a \end{array} & \begin{array}{c} a \\ a \end{array} & \begin{array}{c} a \\ b \end{array} \end{array}$$

(SCF-12)
$$\begin{array}{c|cc} & \multicolumn{2}{c}{2} \\ & a \succ_2 b & b \succ_2 a \\ \hline 1 \begin{array}{c} a \succ_1 b \\ b \succ_1 a \end{array} & \begin{array}{c} a \\ b \end{array} & \begin{array}{c} b \\ b \end{array} \end{array}$$

Can these two remaining SCFs be considered "reasonable" or "good"? Are there any other requirements that one should impose?

One issue that we have not addressed so far is the issue of misrepresentation of preferences. We have implicitly assumed up to now that each individual, when asked to report her ranking of the alternatives, will do so sincerely, that is, she will not report a ranking that is different from her true ranking. Is this an issue one should worry about? In the next section we will go through a number of popular SCFs and show that they all provide incentives for individuals to lie in reporting their preferences.

> Test your understanding of the concepts introduced in this section, by going through the exercises in Section 12.5.1 at the end of this chapter.

12.2 Strategic voting

We shall illustrate the issue of strategic voting, or misrepresentation of preferences, in several popular voting methods which can be viewed as social choice functions.

Plurality voting with a default alternative. We illustrate this procedure for the case of three alternatives: $X = \{a,b,c\}$ and three voters: $N = \{1,2,3\}$. We assume that each voter can only report a strict ranking of the alternatives (that is, indifference is not allowed). Thus – as we saw in the previous chapter – there are six possible rankings that an individual can choose from when deciding what to report: $a \succ b \succ c$, $a \succ c \succ b$, $b \succ a \succ c$, $b \succ c \succ a$, $c \succ a \succ b$, $c \succ b \succ a$. To simplify the notation, we shall write them as abc, acb, bac, bca, cab, cba, that is, we read xyz as $x \succ y \succ z$. We take a to be the designated default alternative and the voting procedure is as follows:
- If two or more individuals list alternative b at the top of their ranking, then b is chosen,
- if two or more individuals list alternative c at the top of their ranking, then c is chosen,
- otherwise, the default alternative a is chosen (thus, a is chosen when two or more individuals list it at the top of their ranking or when there is complete disagreement, in the sense that one individual lists a at the top, another lists b at the top and the third lists c at the top).

How can we represent this voting procedure or SCF? We need six tables: each table labeled with one possible reported ranking of Individual 3; each table has six rows: each row labeled with one possible reported ranking of Individual 1, and six columns: each column labeled with one possible reported ranking of Individual 2. Inside each cell of each table we write the alternative chosen by the procedure described above. This is shown in Figure 12.1.

Let us first check if this SCF satisfies Unanimity and Non-dictatorship. Unanimity requires that when an alternative is listed at the top of each reported ranking then it should be chosen, that is, it requires the following, which is highlighted in Figure 12.2:
1. in the two tables at the top (corresponding to the cases where Voter 3 reports abc or acb) there should be an a in the following cells: (row 1, column 1), (row 1, column 2), (row 2, column 1) and (row 2, column 2) [these are the cases where every voter ranks a at the top],
2. in the two tables in the middle (corresponding to the cases where Voter 3 reports bac or bca) there should be a b in the following cells: (row 3, column 3), (row 3, column 4), (row 4, column 3) and (row 4, column 4) [these are the cases where every voter ranks b at the top],
3. in the two tables at the bottom (corresponding to the cases where Voter 3 reports cab or cba) there should be a c in the following cells: (row 5, column 5), (row 5, column 6), (row 6, column 5) and (row 6, column 6) [these are the cases where every voter ranks c at the top].

Thus, Unanimity only restricts the values in four cells in each table as shown in Figure 12.2.

Non-dictatorship is also satisfied, since for each individual there is at least one situation where she lists an alternative, say x, at the top and yet that alternative is not chosen because the other two individuals list a different alternative, say y, at the top.

12.2 Strategic voting

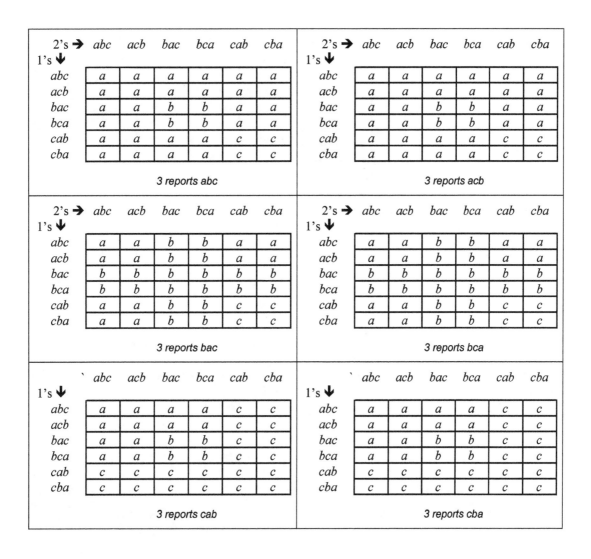

Figure 12.1: Plurality voting with a as the default alternative

Chapter 12. Misrepresentation of Preferences

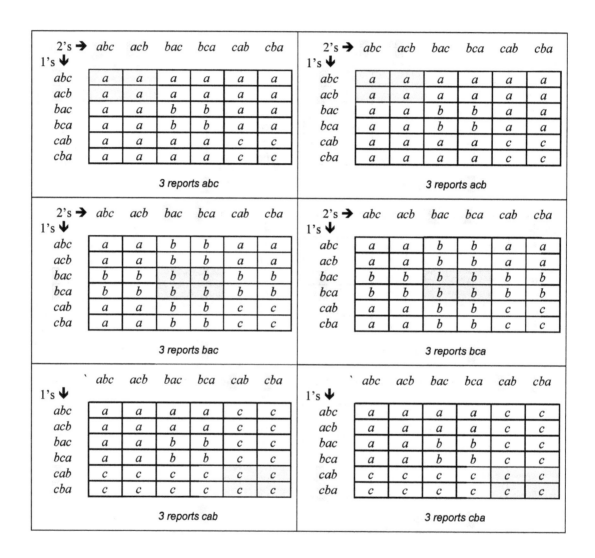

Figure 12.2: The highlights show the restrictions imposed by Unanimity

12.2 Strategic voting

It remains to verify if it is the case that no individual can ever gain by lying about her preferences, that is, by reporting a ranking that is not her true ranking. We call this requirement *Non-manipulability* or *Strategy-proofness*. Unfortunately, this requirement is violated in this voting procedure. To see this, focus on the first table in Figure 12.1, corresponding to the case where Individual 3 reports the ranking *abc*. This table is reproduced in Figure 12.3. Consider the sixth column, corresponding to the case where Individual 2 reports the ranking *cba*. Suppose that the true ranking of Individual 1 is *bca* (4th row); if she reports her preferences truthfully, that is, if she reports *bca* (recall that this means $b \succ_1 c \succ_1 a$) then the chosen alternative is a,[1] which is the worst, according to her true preferences; if, on the other hand, she lies and reports the false ranking *cab* then the chosen alternative is c, which – according to her true ranking – is better than a (in her true ranking, namely *bca*, *c* is the middle-ranked alternative while a is the worst).

2's →	abc	acb	bac	bca	cab	cba
abc	a	a	a	a	a	a
acb	a	a	a	a	a	a
bac	a	a	b	b	a	a
bca (true ranking)	a	a	b	b	a	a
cab (reported ranking)	a	a	a	a	c	c
cba	a	a	a	a	c	c

3 reports abc

Figure 12.3: The top-left table in Figure 12.2

The Condorcet method with a default alternative. The Condorcet method selects that alternative – called the *Condorcet winner* – that would win a majority vote in all the pairwise comparisons with each of the other alternatives; if such an alternative does not exist, then a pre-determined default alternative is selected. As we did with plurality voting, we illustrate this procedure for the case of three alternatives: $X = \{a,b,c\}$ and three voters: $N = \{1,2,3\}$, assuming that each voter can only report a strict ranking of the alternatives. As before, we denote the ranking $x \succ y \succ z$ by *xyz*. We take a to be the designated default alternative. Let us first see what alternative the Condorcet method would select in a couple of situations. If the reported rankings are as follows:

	Voter 1	Voter 2	Voter 3
best	c	b	a
	b	a	b
worst	a	c	c

then b is the Condorcet winner: a majority (consisting of Voters 1 and 2) prefers b ro a and a majority (consisting of Voters 2 and 3) prefers b to c. Thus, b is selected. On the other

---

[1] Because there is complete disagreement: Voter 1 lists b at the top, Voter 2 lists c at the top and Voter 3 lists a at the top; hence, the default alternative, namely a, is chosen.

hand, if the reported rankings are:

	Voter 1	Voter 2	Voter 3
best	a	c	b
	b	a	c
worst	c	b	a

then there is no Condorcet winner: a beats b but is beaten by c, b beats c but is beaten by a and c beats a but is beaten by b (indeed, the majority rule yields a cycle: a majority prefers a to b, a majority prefers b to c and a majority prefers c to a). Thus, since there is no Condorcet winner, the default alternative a is chosen.

As we did with plurality voting, we can represent this SCF by means of six tables, each with six rows and six columns, as shown in Figure 12.4. The reader might want to try to construct the tables before looking at Figure 12.4.

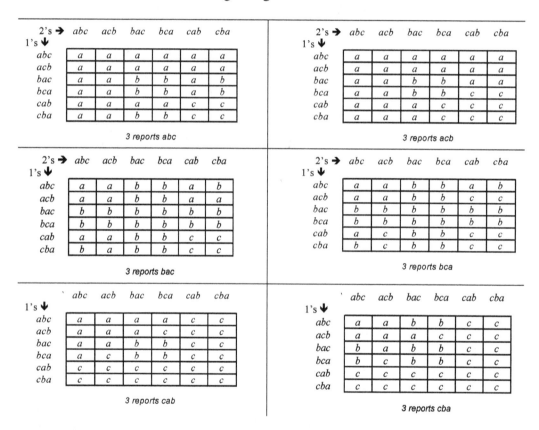

Figure 12.4: The Condorcet method with a as the default alternative

Note that this is a different SCF from the one shown in Figure 12.1. For example, the entry in the first table, row 6 and column 3 (corresponding to reported rankings cba for Voter 1, bac for Voter 2 and abc for Voter 3) is a for plurality voting (the default alternative since no two voters rank the same alternative at the top), but b for the Condorcet method (b is the Condorcet winner).

It is straightforward to verify that the SCF shown in Figure 12.4 satisfies Unanimity and Non-dictatorship (see Exercise 12.6). On the other hand, it fails to satisfy Non-manipulability. To see this, suppose that Voter 2's true ranking is bca and consider the first table, row 5 and column 4, corresponding to the case where Voter 1 reports cab, Voter 2

12.2 Strategic voting

reports *bca* (thus, a truthful report) and Voter 3 reports *abc*. Then the chosen alternative is *a*, which is the worst in Voter 2's true ranking. If Voter 2 were to misrepresent his preferences by reporting *cab*, then the chosen alternative would be *c*, which – according to his true ranking *bca* – is better than *a*.

The Borda count. The Borda count is the following SCF. Each voter states a strict ranking (that is, no indifference is allowed) of the m alternatives. For each voter's ranking, m points are assigned to the alternative ranked first, $m-1$ points to the alternative ranked second, and so on, up to 1 point for the worst alternative. Then, for each alternative, all the points are added up and the alternative with the largest score is chosen. A tie-breaking rule must be specified in case two or more alternatives receive the largest score.

Like the previous two SCFs, the Borda count satisfies Unanimity and Non-dictatorship but fails to satisfy Non-manipulability. For example, suppose that there are five alternatives: $X = \{a,b,c,d,e\}$ and five voters: $N = \{1,2,3,4,5\}$. Suppose that Voter 1's true ranking is:

	Voter 1's true ranking
best	a
	c
	d
	b
worst	e

(12.1)

Suppose also that Voter 1 expects the other voters to report the following rankings:

	Voter 2	Voter 3	Voter 4	Voter 5
best	b	b	c	a
	c	c	d	b
	e	a	a	e
	d	e	e	d
worst	a	d	b	c

If Voter 1 reports her true ranking, then we get the following profile of rankings:

	Voter 1	Voter 2	Voter 3	Voter 4	Voter 5	score
best	a	b	b	c	a	5
	c	c	c	d	b	4
	d	e	a	a	e	3
	b	d	e	e	d	2
worst	e	a	d	b	c	1

Applying the Borda count we get the following scores, so that **alternative c is chosen**.

$$a: 5+1+3+3+5 = 17$$
$$b: 2+5+5+1+4 = 17$$
$$c: 4+4+4+5+1 = \boxed{18}$$
$$d: 3+2+1+4+2 = 12$$
$$e: 1+3+2+2+3 = 11$$

If, instead of her true ranking (12.1), Voter 1 were to report the following ranking:

$$
\begin{array}{ll}
\text{best} & a \\
& e \\
& d \\
& c \\
\text{worst} & b
\end{array}
$$

then we would get the following profile of rankings:

	Voter 1	Voter 2	Voter 3	Voter 4	Voter 5	score
best	a	b	b	c	a	5
	e	c	c	d	b	4
	d	e	a	a	e	3
	c	d	e	e	d	2
worst	b	a	d	b	c	1

Applying the Borda count we get the following scores:

$$
\begin{array}{l}
a: 5+1+3+3+5 = \boxed{17} \\
b: 1+5+5+1+4 = 16 \\
c: 2+4+4+5+1 = 16 \\
d: 3+2+1+4+2 = 12 \\
e: 4+3+2+2+3 = 14
\end{array}
$$

so that **alternative a would be chosen**, which – according to her true ranking (12.1) – Voter 1 prefers to c. Hence, Voter 1 has an incentive to misrepresent her preferences.

Note that manipulability of a SCF does not mean that for *every* individual there is a situation where that individual can bring about a better outcome by misrepresenting her preferences. A SCF is manipulable as long as there is *at least one* individual who can bring about a better outcome by reporting a ranking which is different from her true ranking in *at least one* situation.

For example, consider the following SCF. There are three alternatives: $X = \{a,b,c\}$ and three voters: $N = \{1,2,3\}$. Each voter reports a strict ranking of the alternatives. Voter 1 is given privileged status in that her top-ranked alternative is assigned 1.5 points (and the other two alternatives 0 points), while for each of the other two voters his top-ranked alternative is assigned 1 point (and the other two alternatives 0 points). The alternative with the largest number of points is selected. This SCF is shown in Figure 12.5 on the next page.

12.2 Strategic voting

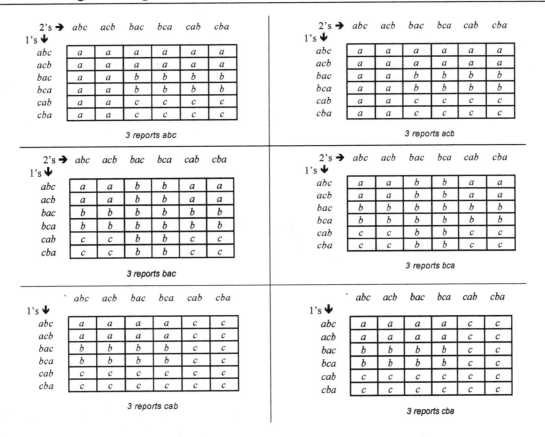

Figure 12.5: Majority voting with a slight advantage given to Voter 1

The privileged status of Voter 1 has an impact only when there is complete disagreement, as is the case, for example, in the first table, row 3, column 5, corresponding to the case where Voter 1 reports *bac*, Voter 2 reports *cab* and Voter 3 reports *abc*. In this case *b* gets 1.5 points, *c* gets 1 point and *a* gets 1 point, so that *b* – the top alternative in Voter 1's reported ranking – is selected. In this SCF *there is no situation where Voter 1 can benefit from misreporting her preferences*. To see this, suppose that the top-ranked alternative in Voter 1's *true* ranking is x. One of two scenarios must occur:

1. Voters 2 and 3 report the same alternative, call it y, at the top of their ranking (it might be that $y = x$ or might it be be that $y \neq x$). In this case alternative y is chosen and it will be chosen no matter what ranking Voter 1 reports (y already gets 2 points and Voter 1's report either adds 1.5 points to y or assigns 1.5 points to an alternative different from y). Thus, in this scenario, telling the truth and lying produce the same outcome; in particular, lying cannot be better than truthful reporting.

2. Voters 2 and 3 report different alternatives at the top of their rankings. In this case if Voter 1 reports truthfully, the chosen alternative will be x (either there is complete disagreement and x gets 1.5 points, while the other two alternatives get 1 point each, or one of Voters 2 and 3 has x at the top, in which case x gets 2.5 points). If Voter 1 lies then the alternative at the top of her reported ranking is chosen (same reasoning: either it is chosen because there is complete disagreement or it is chosen because Voter 1 forms a majority with one of the other two voters). Thus, if the alternative at the top of her reported ranking is not x, then Voter 1 is worse off by lying.

On the other hand, for both Voter 2 and Voter 3 there are situations where they gain by misrepresenting their preferences. We shall show this for Voter 2 and let the reader show that Voter 3 can gain by misrepresentation (Exercise 12.7). For Voter 2, consider the situation represented by the first table (Voter 3 reports *abc*) and row 6 (Voter 1 reports *cba*) and suppose that Voter 2's true ranking is *bac* (column 3). If Voter 2 reports truthfully, then the selected alternative is *c*, which is the worst from his point of view; if, on the other hand, Voter 3 reports *abc*, then the selected alternative is *a*, which – according to Voter 2's true ranking *bac* – is better than *c*.

> Test your understanding of the concepts introduced in this section, by going through the exercises in Section 12.5.2 at the end of this chapter.

12.3 The Gibbard-Satterthwaite theorem

The Gibbard-Satterthwaite theorem is a result published independently by philosopher Allan Gibbard in 1973[2] and economist Mark Satterthwaite in 1975.[3]

As for the case of Arrow's theorem, the objective is to determine if there are Social Choice Functions (see Definition 12.1.1) that satisfy some "reasonable" properties, which we will call *axioms*, as we did in the previous chapter.

We assume that the domain of the Social Choice Function (SCF) is the set of profiles of **strict rankings** of the set of alternatives X (that is, indifference is ruled out). Let $\mathscr{P}$ denote the set of strict rankings of the elements of X. Then the domain of the SCF is taken to be $\mathscr{P}^n = \underbrace{\mathscr{P} \times \cdots \times \mathscr{P}}_{n \text{ times}}$. Thus, individuals are not allowed to report indifference between any two alternatives, but – subject to this restriction – any strict ranking can be reported. Hence, this is a limited form of the property of Unrestricted Domain considered in the previous chapter. The axioms that we consider are the following:

- **Axiom 1: Unanimity**. If alternative x is the top-ranked alternative in the reported ranking of every individual, then it should be chosen by society: if, for every individual i, $x \succ_i y$ for every alternative $y \neq x$ then $f(\succ_1, \ldots, \succ_n) = x$.

- **Axiom 2: Non-dictatorship**. There is no individual i whose top alternative – in her reported ranking – is always chosen. Formally, this can be stated as follows: for every individual $i \in N$, there is a profile of reported preferences $(\succ_1, \ldots, \succ_n)$ such that if $f(\succ_1, \ldots, \succ_n) = x \in X$ then x is not at the top of $\succ_i$ (that is, there exists a $y \in X$ such that $y \neq x$ and $y \succ_i x$).

---

[2] Allan Gibbard, "Manipulation of voting schemes: a general result", *Econometrica*, 1973, Vol. 41 (4), pages 587-601.

[3] Mark Satterthwaite, "Strategy-proofness and Arrow's conditions: existence and correspondence theorems for voting procedures and social welfare functions", *Journal of Economic Theory*, 1975, Vol. 10 (2), pages 187-217.

12.3 The Gibbard-Satterthwaite theorem

- **Axiom 3: Non-manipulability or Strategy-proofness.** There is no situation where some individual can gain by reporting a ranking different from her true ranking. Formally, this can be stated as follows. Fix an arbitrary individual $i \in N$ and an arbitrary profile $(\succ_1, \ldots, \succ_{i-1}, \succ_i, \succ_{i+1}, \ldots, \succ_n) \in \mathscr{P}^n$ and let $f(\succ_1, \ldots, \succ_{i-1}, \succ_i, \succ_{i+1}, \ldots, \succ_n) = x \in X$. Then there is no $\succ_i' \in \mathscr{P}$ such that $f(\succ_1, \ldots, \succ_{i-1}, \succ_i', \succ_{i+1}, \ldots, \succ_n) \succ_i x$ (think of $\succ_i$ as the true ranking of individual i and $\succ_i'$ as a possible lie).

The following theorem provides an "impossibility result" similar to Arrow's impossibility theorem.

> **Theorem 12.3.1** [Gibbard-Satterthwaite theorem] If the set of alternatives X contains at least three elements, there is no Social Choice Function $f : \mathscr{P}^n \to X$ that satisfies Unanimity, Non-dictatorship and Non-manipulability.

An alternative way of stating the above theorem is as follows: if a SCF satisfies Unanimity and one of the other two axioms then it fails to satisfy the third axiom (for example, if a SCF satisfies Unanimity and Non-dictatorship then it violates Non-manipulability).[4]

In the next section we illustrate the logic of the proof of Theorem 12.3.1 by focusing on the simple case of three alternatives and two voters.[5]

> Test your understanding of the concepts introduced in this section, by going through the exercises in Section 12.5.3 at the end of this chapter.

---

[4]Sometimes the Gibbard-Satterthwaite theorem is stated with the premise 'if the range of the SCF contains at least three alternatives ...', but this clause is implied by the assumptions that the set X contains at least three elements and that the SCF satisfies Unanimity.

[5]A relatively simple proof for the general case can be found in Jean-Pierre Benoit, "The Gibbard-Satterthwaite theorem: a simple proof", *Economics Letters*, Vol. 69, 2000, pages 319-322. See also the references therein for alternative proofs.

12.4 Illustration of the proof of the Gibbard-Satterthwaite theorem

In this section we prove the Gibbard-Satterthwaite theorem (Theorem 12.3.1) for the case where there are three alternatives, called x, y and z, and two individuals ($N = \{1,2\}$). There are six possible strict rankings of the set $X = \{x,y,z\}$ and thus any SCF can be represented as a table with six rows and six columns. We will show that any SCF that satisfies Unanimity and Non-manipulability must violate Non-dictatorship. Fix a SCF that satisfies Unanimity. Then the blocks on the main diagonal must be filled as shown in Figure 12.6 (Unanimity forces the values of 12 out of 36 entries; as usual, xyz means $x \succ y \succ z$ and similarly for the other rankings).

		Voter 2					
		1 xyz	2 xzy	3 yxz	4 yzx	5 zxy	6 zyx
Voter 1	A xyz	x	x				
	B xzy	x	x				
	C yxz			y	y		
	D yzx			y	y		
	E zxy					z	z
	F zyx					z	z

Figure 12.6: The requirement of Unanimity

Now consider the highlighted cell A4 in Figure 12.6. By Non-manipulability there cannot be a z there otherwise Voter 1, with true preferences xyz (row A), would gain by lying and reporting yxz (row C) when Voter 2 reports yzx (column 4). Thus, in cell A4 there must be either an x or a y. *The strategy of the proof is to show that if there is an x in cell A4 then Voter 1 must be a dictator, while if there is a y in cell A4 then Voter 2 must be a dictator.* We will only prove the first part, that is, that if there is an x in cell A4 then Voter 1 must be a dictator.

Suppose that there is an x in cell A4. Then there must be an x also in cell B4 (the cell marked with a ① in Figure 12.7) otherwise Voter 1, with true preferences xzy (row B), would gain by reporting xyz (row A) when Voter 2 reports yzx (column 4). Now, from Voter 2's point of view, there must be an x in all the boxes marked with a ② otherwise Voter 2, with true preferences yzx (column 4), would gain by "moving" either left or right to get the "non-x" which she prefers to x. Thus, the top two rows are entirely made of x's.

Now consider the highlighted cell C6 in Figure 12.7. There cannot be a z there because Voter 1, with true preferences yxz (row C), would gain by reporting xzy (row B) when Voter 2 reports zyx (column 6); furthermore, there cannot be an x in cell C6 because Voter 2, with true preferences zyx (column 6), would gain by reporting yzx (column 4) when Voter 1 reports yxz (row C). Thus, **there must be a y in cell C6**. It follows that there must be a y also in cell D6 below, otherwise Voter 1, with true preferences yzx (row D), would gain by reporting yxz (row C) when Voter 2 reports zyx (column 6). Thus, we have reached the configuration shown in Figure 12.8.

12.4 Illustration of the proof of the Gibbard-Satterthwaite theorem

		Voter 2					
		1 *xyz*	2 *xzy*	3 *yxz*	4 *yzx*	5 *zxy*	6 *zyx*
A	*xyz*	*x*	*x*	② *x*	(not z) **x**	② *x*	② *x*
B	*xzy*	*x*	*x*	② *x*	① *x*	② *x*	② *x*
C	*yxz*			*y*	*y*		
D	*yzx*			*y*	*y*		
E	*zxy*					*z*	*z*
F	*zyx*					*z*	*z*

Figure 12.7: Inferences from the presence of *x* in cell A4

		Voter 2					
		1 *xyz*	2 *xzy*	3 *yxz*	4 *yzx*	5 *zxy*	6 *zyx*
A	*xyz*	*x*	*x*	*x*	*x*	*x*	*x*
B	*xzy*	*x*	*x*	*x*	*x*	*x*	*x*
C	*yxz*			*y*	*y*	①	*y*
D	*yzx*			*y*	*y*	not *x* ① not *z* ②	*y*
E	*zxy*					*z*	*z*
F	*zyx*					*z*	*z*

Figure 12.8: Further inferences

Now consider the highlighted cell D5: there cannot be a z there otherwise Voter 2, with true preferences zyx (column 6), would gain by reporting zxy (column 5) when Voter 1 reports yzx (row D) and there cannot be an x, otherwise Voter 1, with true preferences yzx (row D), would gain by reporting zxy (row E) when Voter 2 reports zxy (column 5). Hence, **there must be a y in cell D5**. Then there must be a y also in cell C5 otherwise Voter 1 with true preferences yxz (row C) would gain by reporting yzx (row D) when Voter 2 reports zxy (column 5). Thus, we have reached the configuration shown in Figure 12.9.

		Voter 2					
		1 xyz	2 xzy	3 yxz	4 yzx	5 zxy	6 zyx
A	xyz	x	x	x	x	x	x
B	xzy	x	x	x	x	x	x
C	yxz	②	②	y	y	y	y
D	yzx	②	②	y	y	y	y
E	zxy					z	z
F	zyx					z	z

Figure 12.9: Updated configuration

Now there must be a y in the remaining cells of rows C and D (marked with a ② in Figure 12.9) because otherwise Voter 2 with true preferences zxy (column 5) would gain by reporting either xyz (column 1) or xzy (column 2) when Voter 1 reports a ranking corresponding to either row C or row D. Thus, we have shown that rows C and D consist entirely of y's.

Now consider cell E4 in Figure 12.10: there cannot be a y there because Voter 1, with true preferences zxy (row E), would gain by reporting xyz (row A) in the situation represented by column 4 and there cannot be an x because Voter 2, with true preferences yzx (column 4), would gain by reporting zxy (column 5) in the situation represented by row E.

Thus, **there must be a z in cell E4**. Then there must be a z also in cell F4 below otherwise Voter 1, with true preferences zyx (row F), would gain by reporting zxy (row E) in the situation represented by column 4.

Now in the highlighted cells F1, F2 and F3 there cannot be an x because Voter 1, with true preferences zyx (row F), would gain by reporting yzx (row D) and there cannot be a y because Voter 2, with true preferences yzx (column 4), would gain by reporting the ranking corresponding to either column 1 or column 2 or column 3 in the situation represented by row F. Thus, **there must be a z in F1, F2 and F3**. This implies that there must be a z in the remaining cells too because Voter 1, with true preferences zxy (row E) would gain by reporting zyx (row F).

12.5 Exercises

		Voter 2					
		1 xyz	2 xzy	3 yxz	4 yzx	5 zxy	6 zyx
V o t e r 1	A xyz	x	x	x	x	x	x
	B xzy	x	x	x	x	x	x
	C yxz	y	y	y	y	y	y
	D yzx	y	y	y	y	y	y
	E zxy				not x not y	z	z
	F zyx	not x ① not y ②	not x ① not y ②	not x ① not y ②	(z)	z	z

Figure 12.10: The last steps

Hence, we have shown that the SCF must have all x's in rows A and B, all y's in rows C and D and all z's in rows E and F, making Voter 1 a Dictator (in rows A and B her reported top alternative is x and it is chosen no matter what Voter 2 reports, in rows C and D her reported top alternative is y and it is chosen no matter what Voter 2 reports and in rows E and F her reported top alternative is z and it is chosen no matter what Voter 2 reports).

The proof that if there had been a y in cell $A4$, then Voter 2 would have been a Dictator is similar and we will omit it.

12.5 Exercises

The solutions to the following exercises are given in Section 12.6 at the end of this chapter.

12.5.1 Exercises for Section 12.1: Social choice functions

Exercise 12.1 Suppose that there are three alternatives: $X = \{a,b,c\}$ and two voters: $N = \{1,2\}$ and consider SCFs that only allow the reporting of strict rankings so that each individual must report one of the following:

$$a \succ b \succ c,\ a \succ c \succ b,\ b \succ a \succ c,\ b \succ c \succ a,\ c \succ a \succ b,\ c \succ b \succ a.$$

To simplify the notation, write them as abc, acb, bac, bca, cab, cba. In this case we can represent a SCF by means of a table with six rows (each row labeled with one ranking for Individual 1) and six columns (each column labeled with one ranking for Individual 2).

(a) How many SCFs are there?

(b) Fill in the table as much as you can by using only the Unanimity principle.

(c) How many SCFs that satisfy the Unanimity principle are there?

(d) Show the SCF that corresponds to the case where Individual 2 is a dictator.

Exercise 12.2 Consider again the case where there are three alternatives: $X = \{a,b,c\}$ and two voters: $N = \{1,2\}$ and only strict rankings can be reported. Consider the SCF shown in Figure 12.11.

(a) Does this SCF satisfy Unanimity?

(b) Show that this SCF satisfies Non-dictatorship.

1's ranking ↓ \ 2's ranking →	abc	acb	bac	bca	cab	cba
abc	a	a	a	b	c	a
acb	a	a	b	a	a	c
bac	b	a	b	b	b	c
bca	a	b	b	b	c	b
cab	a	c	c	b	c	c
cba	c	a	b	c	c	c

Figure 12.11: An SCF when $X = \{a,b,c\}$ and $N = \{1,2\}$

12.5.2 Exercises for Section 12.2: Strategic voting

Exercise 12.3 In Section 12.1 we considered the case of two alternatives and two voters, with only strict rankings being allowed. We saw that in this case there are 16 possible SCFs, but by appealing to Unanimity and Non-dictatorship, one can reduce the number to the two SCFs shown below:

(SCF-2)

		2	
		$a \succ_2 b$	$b \succ_2 a$
1	$a \succ_1 b$	a	a
	$b \succ_1 a$	a	b

(SCF-12)

		2	
		$a \succ_2 b$	$b \succ_2 a$
1	$a \succ_1 b$	a	b
	$b \succ_1 a$	b	b

(a) For SCF-2 show that neither individual can ever gain by misrepresenting his/her preferences. Give enough details in your argument.

(b) For SCF-12 show that neither individual can ever gain by misrepresenting his/her preferences. Give enough details in your argument.

12.5 Exercises

Exercise 12.4 Consider the SCF of Exercise 12.2, which is reproduced in Figure 12.12.

(a) Show that there is at least one situation where Individual 1 can gain by misrepresenting her preferences.

(b) Show that there is at least one situation where Individual 2 can gain by misrepresenting his preferences.

2's ranking →	abc	acb	bac	bca	cab	cba
1's ranking ↓						
abc	a	a	a	b	c	a
acb	a	a	b	a	a	c
bac	b	a	b	b	b	c
bca	a	b	b	b	c	b
cab	a	c	c	b	c	c
cba	c	a	b	c	c	c

Figure 12.12: An SCF when $X = \{a,b,c\}$ and $N = \{1,2\}$

Exercise 12.5 Consider the Borda count explained in Section 12.2, with the following tie-breaking rule: if two or more alternatives get the highest score, then the alternative that comes first in alphabetical order is chosen. Suppose that there are three alternatives: $X = \{a,b,c\}$ and three voters: $N = \{1,2,3\}$. Voter 1's true ranking is:

	Voter 1's true ranking
best	a
	b
worst	c

(12.2)

Suppose that Voter 1 expects the other two voters to report the following rankings:

	Voter 2	Voter 3
best	c	c
	b	b
worst	a	a

(a) What alternative will be chosen if Voter 1 reports her true ranking (12.2)?

(b) Show that, by misrepresenting her preferences, Voter 1 can obtain a better alternative than the one found in Part (a).

Chapter 12. Misrepresentation of Preferences

Exercise 12.6 Consider the SCF shown in Figure 12.13 (the Condorcet method with a default alternative, previously shown in Figure 12.4), where there are three voters and three alternatives.

(a) Show that it satisfies the Unanimity principle.
(b) Show it satisfies the Non-dictatorship principle.

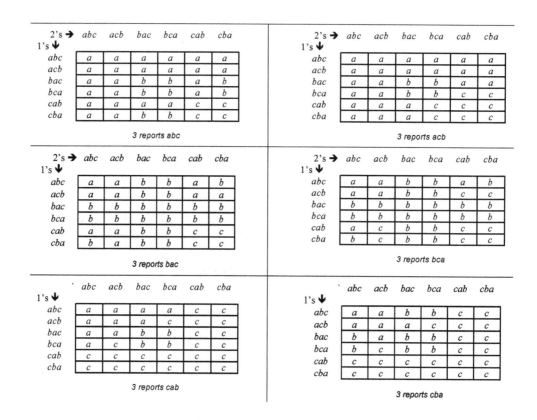

Figure 12.13: The Condorcet method with a as the default alternative

Exercise 12.7 Consider the SCF shown in Figure 12.14 (majority voting with a slight advantage given to Voter 1), which reproduces Figure 12.5.
Show that there is at least one situation where Voter 3 can benefit from misrepresenting his preferences.

Exercise 12.8 Consider again the SCF shown in Figure 12.14 (which reproduces Figure 12.5). At the end of Section 12.2 we showed that there is no situation where Voter 1 (the one who has a slight advantage in that her top alternative is assigned 1.5 points instead of 1 point) can gain by misrepresenting her preferences.
Suppose now that (perhaps as a result of previous discussions) it is common knowledge among the three voters that Voter 1's true ranking is acb (that is, $a \succ_1 c \succ_1 b$). Hence, it is reasonable to assume that Voter 1 will report her ranking truthfully (she cannot gain by lying) and, indeed, it is common knowledge between Voters 2 and 3 that they expect Voter 1 to report acb.

12.5 Exercises

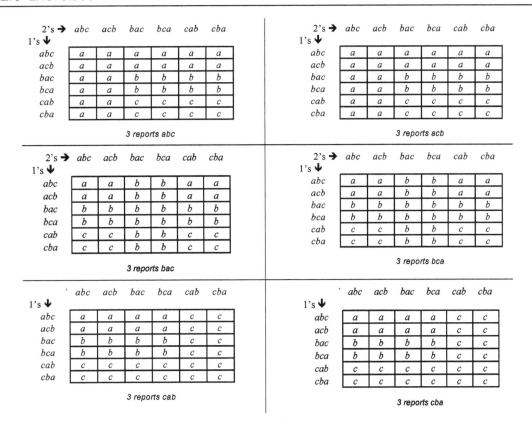

Figure 12.14: Majority voting with a slight advantage given to Voter 1

By postulating that Voter 1 reports *acb*, we can reduce the SCF of Figure 12.14 to an SCF with only two voters: Voter 2 and Voter 3.

(a) Draw a table that represents the reduced SCF. For example, this table should show that if Voter 2 reports *bca* and Voter 3 reports *cba*, then the chosen alternative is *a* (it gets 1.5 points from Voter 1's report, while each of *b* and *c* get only 1 point each).

(b) In the reduced SCF, can Voter 2 ever gain from misrepresenting his preferences?

(c) In the reduced SCF, can Voter 3 ever gain from misrepresenting his preferences?

(d) Suppose that Voter 3's true ranking is *bac*. Can Voter 3 gain by reporting a different ranking?

(e) Suppose that Voter 2 knows that Voter 3's true ranking is *bac* and expects her to report truthfully. Suppose also that Voter 2's true ranking is *cba*. What ranking should Voter 2 report?

12.5.3 Exercises for Section 12.3: The Gibbard-Satterthwaite theorem

Exercise 12.9 Consider the two SCFs of Exercise 12.3 (SCF-2 and SCF-12), reproduced below:

$$
\text{(SCF-2)}\quad
\begin{array}{c|cc}
 & \multicolumn{2}{c}{2} \\
 & a \succ_2 b & b \succ_2 a \\
\hline
1\;\; a \succ_1 b & a & a \\
\;\; b \succ_1 a & a & b \\
\end{array}
\qquad
\text{(SCF-12)}\quad
\begin{array}{c|cc}
 & \multicolumn{2}{c}{2} \\
 & a \succ_2 b & b \succ_2 a \\
\hline
1\;\; a \succ_1 b & a & b \\
\;\; b \succ_1 a & b & b \\
\end{array}
$$

In Section 12.1 they were shown to satisfy Unanimity and Non-dictatorship and in Exercise 12.3 they were shown to satisfy Non-manipulability.

Explain why these two SCFs do not constitute a counterexample to the Gibbard-Satterthwaite theorem (Theorem 12.3.1).

Exercise 12.10 There are five alternatives ($X = \{a,b,c,d,e\}$) and fourteen voters ($N = \{1,2,\ldots,14\}$). Consider the following SCF: each voter submits a strict ranking of the alternatives and there are no restrictions on what strict ranking can be submitted. Then the procedure is as follows:

1. if Individuals 1-5 all rank the same alternative at the top, then that alternative is chosen, otherwise
2. if Individuals 6-10 all rank the same alternative at the top, then that alternative is chosen, otherwise
3. if there is a Condorcet winner in the reported rankings of Individuals 11-13 (the definition of Condorcet winner was explained in Section 12.2) then that alternative is chosen, otherwise
4. the top-ranked alternative of individual 14 is chosen.

Does this SCF satisfy Non-manipulability?

12.6 Solutions to Exercises

Solution to Exercise 12.1.

(a) The table has 36 cells that need to be filled, each with one of a, b or c. Thus, there are $3^{36} = 1.5009 \times 10^{17}$, that is, more than 150,000 trillions (recall that a trillion is 10^{12} or a million million) SCFs!

(b) The Unanimity principle restricts only the values in 12 of the 36 cells, as shown in Figure 12.15 below.

(c) In Figure 12.15 there are 24 remaining cells to be filled in (each with one of a, b or c) and thus there are $3^{24} = 282.43 \times 10^9$ (that is, more than 282 billions) SCFs that satisfy the Unanimity principle!

(d) The case where Individual 2 is a dictator corresponds to the SCF shown in Figure 12.16 below. □

2's → 1's ↓	abc	acb	bac	bca	cab	cba
abc	a	a				
acb	a	a				
bac			b	b		
bca			b	b		
cab					c	c
cba					c	c

Figure 12.15: The restrictions imposed by the Unanimity principle

2's → 1's ↓	abc	acb	bac	bca	cab	cba
abc	a	a	b	b	c	c
acb	a	a	b	b	c	c
bac	a	a	b	b	c	c
bca	a	a	b	b	c	c
cab	a	a	b	b	c	c
cba	a	a	b	b	c	c

Figure 12.16: Individual 2 is a dictator

Chapter 12. Misrepresentation of Preferences

Solution to Exercise 12.2.

(a) Yes, this SCF satisfies Unanimity: when both individuals rank alternative x at the top, x is chosen by society (the main diagonal consists of a block of four a's, a block of four b's and a block of four c's, fulfilling the requirement shown in Figure 12.15).

(b) This SCF also satisfies Non-dictatorship. In Figure 12.17 we have highlighted two cells to show this.

For Individual 1, consider the cell in row 4 and column 1: her ranking is bca, thus her top-ranked alternative is b, and yet the chosen alternative (when Individual 2 reports the ranking abc) is a, not b.

For Individual 2, consider the cell in row 1 and column 6: his ranking is cba, thus his top-ranked alternative is c, and yet the chosen alternative (when Individual 1 reports the ranking abc) is a, not c. (Of course, other cells could have been used to make the same point.) □

1's ranking ↓ \ 2's ranking →	abc	acb	bac	bca	cab	cba
abc	a	a	a	b	c	a
acb	a	a	b	a	a	c
bac	b	a	b	b	b	c
bca	a	b	b	b	c	b
cab	a	c	c	b	c	c
cba	c	a	b	c	c	c

Figure 12.17: Neither individual is a dictator

12.6 Solutions to Exercises

Solution to Exercise 12.3.

(a) SCF-2. Individual 1 cannot gain by misrepresenting her preferences: *if her true ranking is $a \succ_1 b$* then by reporting truthfully she gets her top alternative a and by misrepresenting she might get a or b; *if her true ranking is $b \succ_1 a$* and she reports truthfully, then there are two possibilities:

(1) Individual 2 reports $a \succ_2 b$, in which case the outcome is a, and would still be a if Individual 1 lied, and

(2) Individual 2 reports $b \succ_2 a$, in which case if Individual 1 reports truthfully then she gets her top alternative b, while if she lies then she get her worst alternative, namely a.

Individual 2 cannot gain by misrepresenting his preferences: *if his true ranking is $a \succ_2 b$* then by reporting truthfully he gets his top alternative a and by misrepresenting he might get a or b; *if his true ranking is $b \succ_2 a$* and he reports truthfully, then there are two possibilities:

(1) Individual 1 reports $a \succ_1 b$, in which case the outcome is a, and would still be a if Individual 2 lied, and

(2) Individual 1 reports $b \succ_1 a$, in which case if Individual 2 reports truthfully then he gets his top alternative b, while if he lies then he gets his worst alternative, namely a.

(b) SCF-12. Individual 1 cannot gain by misrepresenting her preferences: *if her true ranking is $b \succ_1 a$* then by reporting truthfully she gets her top alternative b and by misrepresenting she might get a or b; *if her true ranking is $a \succ_1 b$* and she reports truthfully, then there are two possibilities:

(1) Individual 2 reports $b \succ_2 a$, in which case the outcome is b, and would still be b if Individual 1 lied, and

(2) Individual 2 reports $a \succ_2 b$, in which case if Individual 1 reports truthfully then she gets her top alternative a, while if she lies she get her worst alternative, namely b.

Individual 2 cannot gain by misrepresenting his preferences: *if his true ranking is $b \succ_2 a$* then by reporting truthfully he gets his top alternative b and by misrepresenting he might get a or b; *if his true ranking is $a \succ_2 b$* and he reports truthfully, then there are two possibilities:

(1) Individual 1 reports $b \succ_1 a$, in which case the outcome is b, and would still be b if Individual 2 lied, and

(2) Individual 1 reports $a \succ_1 b$, in which case if Individual 2 reports truthfully then he gets his top alternative a, while if he lies he gets his worst alternative, namely b. □

Solution to Exercise 12.4.

(a) There are several situations where Individual 1 can gain by lying. For example, suppose that her true ranking is *bca* (row 4) and Individual 2 reports *abc* (column 1). Then, by reporting truthfully, Individual 1 brings about outcome *a*, which is her worst outcome, but by lying and reporting *bac* she obtains her most preferred outcome, namely *b*.

(b) There are several situations where Individual 2 can gain by lying. For example, suppose that his true ranking is *abc* (column 1) and Individual 1 reports *bac* (row 3). Then, by reporting truthfully, Individual 2 brings about outcome *b*, which is his middle-ranked outcome, but by lying and reporting *acb* he obtains his most preferred outcome, namely *a*. □

Solution to Exercise 12.5.

(a) If Voter 1 reports her true ranking then we get the following profile:

	Voter 1	Voter 2	Voter 3	score
best	a	c	c	3
	b	b	b	2
worst	c	a	a	1

The scores computed according to the Borda rule are:

$a: 3+1+1 = 5$
$b: 2+2+2 = 6$
$c: 1+3+3 = \boxed{7}$

so that alternative *c* is chosen (Voter 1's worst).

(b) If instead of her true ranking Voter 1 reports the following ranking:

best   *b*
         a
worst *c*

then the profile of reported rankings is

	Voter 1	Voter 2	Voter 3	score
best	b	c	c	3
	a	b	b	2
worst	c	a	a	1

The scores computed according to the Borda rule are:

$a: 2+1+1 = 4$
$b: 3+2+2 = 7$
$c: 1+3+3 = 7$

The largest score is 7 and is shared by both *b* and *c*. According to the tie-breaking rule, in case of ties the alternative that comes first in alphabetical order is chosen. Thus, the chosen alternative *b*, which Voter 1 (according to her true ranking $a \succ_1 b \succ_1 c$) prefers to *c*. Thus, Voter 1 gains by lying and reporting a ranking which is different from her true ranking. □

12.6 Solutions to Exercises

Solution to Exercise 12.6.

(a) Unanimity requires the following:

(1) in the two tables at the top (corresponding to the cases where Voter 3 reports *abc* or *acb*) there should be an *a* in the following cells: (row 1, column 1), (row 1, column 2), (row 2, column 1) and (row 2, column 2) [these are the cases where every voter ranks *a* at the top],

(2) in the two tables in the middle (corresponding to the cases where Voter 3 reports *bac* or *bca*) there should be a *b* in the following cells: (row 3, column 3), (row 3, column 4), (row 4, column 3) and (row 4, column 4) [these are the cases where every voter ranks *b* at the top],

(3) in the two tables at the bottom (corresponding to the cases where Voter 3 reports *cab* or *cba*) there should be a *c* in the following cells: (row 5, column 5), (row 5, column 6), (row 6, column 5) and (row 6, column 6) [these are the cases where every voter ranks *c* at the top].

The SCF shown in Figure 12.13 indeed satisfies these constraints.

(b) To see that Voter 1 is not a dictator, consider the first table (Voter 3 reports *abc*), row 4 (Voter 1 reports *bca*) and column 1 (Voter 2 reports *abc*): *b* is at the top of Voter 1's reported ranking and yet the chosen alternative is *a*.

To see that Voter 2 is not a dictator, consider the first table (Voter 3 reports *abc*), row 1 (Voter 1 reports *abc*) and column 4 (Voter 2 reports *bca*): *b* is at the top of Voter 2's reported ranking and yet the chosen alternative is *a*.

Finally, to see that Voter 3 is not a dictator, consider the first table (Voter 3 reports *abc*), row 6 (Voter 1 reports *cba*) and column 4 (Voter 2 reports *bca*): *a* is at the top of Voter 3's reported ranking and yet the chosen alternative is *b*. □

Solution to Exercise 12.7. Consider the situation where Voter 1 reports the ranking *cab* (row 5 of any table) and Voter 2 reports *bca* (column 4 of any table).
Suppose that Voter 3's true ranking is *abc* (first table).
If Voter 3 reports truthfully, then the selected alternative is *c*, which is the worst from his point of view; if, on the other hand, Voter 3 reports *bac* (the second table in the first column of tables), then the selected alternative is *b*, which – according to Voter 3's true ranking *abc* – is better than *c*. □

Solution to Exercise 12.8.

(a) The reduced SCF is shown in Figure 12.18 below.

(b) Yes, there are situations where Voter 2 can gain by misrepresenting his preferences. For example, if his true ranking is *cba* (row 6) and he expects Voter 3 to report *bac* (column 3), then by reporting truthfully he brings about his worst outcome, namely *a*, while by lying and reporting *bca* (row 4) he brings about outcome *b* which he prefers to *a*.

(c) Yes, there are situations where Voter 3 can gain by misrepresenting her preferences. For example, if her true ranking is *cba* (column 6) and she expects Voter 2 to report *bac* (row 3), then by reporting truthfully she brings about her worst outcome, namely *a*, while by lying and reporting *bca* (column 4) she brings about outcome *b* which she prefers to *a*.

(d) If Voter 3's true ranking is *bac*, then there is no situation where she can gain by misrepresenting her preferences:

(1) if Voter 2 reports *abc* or *acb*, then the outcome is *a* no matter what Voter 3 reports,

(2) if Voter 2 reports *bac* or *bca*, then, by reporting truthfully, Voter 3 gets her best outcome, namely *b*,

(3) if Voter 2 reports *cab* or *cba*, then, by reporting truthfully, Voter 3 gets outcome *a* and by lying she gets either *a* or her worst outcome, namely *c*.

(e) If Voter 2's true ranking is *cba* and he expects Voter 3 to report *bac*, then he should lie and report either *bac* or *bca* (and thus bring about outcome *b* which he prefers to *a*, which is the outcome he would get if he reported truthfully). □

2's ↓ \ 3's →	abc	acb	bac	bca	cab	cba
abc	a	a	a	a	a	a
acb	a	a	a	a	a	a
bac	a	a	b	b	a	a
bca	a	a	b	b	a	a
cab	a	a	a	a	c	c
cba	a	a	a	a	c	c

Assuming that Voter 1 reports acb

Figure 12.18: The reduced SCF from Figure 12.5

Solution to Exercise 12.9. They do not constitute a counterexample to the Gibbard-Satterthwaite theorem because the set of alternatives contains only two elements. The Gibbard-Satterthwaite theorem is based on the premise that there are at least three alternatives. □

Solution to Exercise 12.10. This SCF fails to satisfy Non-manipulability. One can try to show this by identifying a situation where some individual can gain by misrepresenting her preferences, but a quicker proof is by invoking the Gibbard-Satterthwaite theorem. All we need to do is show that this SCF satisfies Unanimity and Non-dictatorship, so that – by the Gibbard-Satterthwaite theorem – it must violate Non-manipulability.

That Unanimity is satisfied is obvious: if all the individuals list the same alternative x at the top, then – in particular – the first five individuals list x at the top and thus x is chosen. That the SCF satisfies Non-dictatorship is also straightforward: (1) for any of the first five individuals, if she reports x at the top, but at least one of the other first five does not and all of individuals 6-10 report $y \neq x$ at the top, then y is chosen ; (2) for any of Individuals 6-14, if he reports x at the top but the first five individuals all report $y \neq x$ at the top, then y is chosen. □

V Biases in Decision Making

13 Biases in Decision Making 315
    13.1   Introduction
    13.2   Incomplete preferences and manipulation of choice
    13.3   Gains versus losses
    13.4   Framing
    13.5   The confirmation bias
    13.6   The psychology of decision making

Index 327

13. Biases in Decision Making

13.1 Introduction

This book has been concerned with rational decision making. In this chapter we give an overview of some common departures from rationality, which are often called "biases in decision making". This is a topic that deserves a book-length treatment in itself. Indeed, it is the object of a relatively new field within economics, called *behavioral economics*. The importance of behavioral economics has been underscored by the award of the Nobel Memorial Prize in Economic Sciences to Daniel Kahneman in 2002 "for having integrated insights from psychological research into economic science, especially concerning human judgment and decision-making under uncertainty" and to Richard Thaler in 2017 "for his contributions to behavioral economics: by exploring the consequences of limited rationality, social preferences, and lack of self-control, he has shown how these human traits systematically affect individual decisions as well as market outcomes". There are several recent books on behavioral economics and the reader is referred to them for an in-depth analysis.[1]

In the following sections we will link to various topics discussed in earlier chapters and highlight some deviations from the principles of rationality discussed there.

---

[1] The following is only a partial list.
Dan Ariely, *Predictably irrational: the hidden forces that shape our decisions*, 2010, Harper Perennial.
Edward Cartwright, *Behavioral economics*, 2014, Routledge.
Sanjit Dhami, *The foundations of behavioral economic analysis*, 2017, Oxford University Press.
Daniel Kahneman, *Thinking, fast and slow*, 2013, Farrar, Straus and Giroux.
George Loewenstein and Matthew Rabin, *Advances in behavioral economics*, 2003, Princeton University Press.
Richard Thaler, *Misbehaving: the making of behavioral economics*, 2015, W. W. Norton & Company.
Nick Wilkinson and Matthias Klaes, *An introduction to behavioral economics*, 2nd edition, 2012, Palgrave Macmillan.
A useful resource is also the following website: https://www.behavioraleconomics.com/

13.2 Incomplete preferences and manipulation of choice

In Chapter 2 we began by considering decision making in situations of certainty and identified a first requirement of rationality, namely the ability to rank any two possible outcomes (completeness) and transitivity of such a ranking. In Section 3 of Chapter 2 we explained the reasons why transitivity of preferences is deemed to be a requirement of rationality. We also mentioned one reason why preferences may fail to be complete: when alternatives are described in terms of several attributes, it may be straightforward to rank them in terms of each attribute but it may be difficult to "aggregate" those attribute-based rankings; indeed, in Section 4 of Chapter 11 we saw that this difficulty can be viewed as an implication of Arrow's Impossibility Theorem.

Let us consider an example of multi-attribute alternatives: Erin, being tired of spending 75 minutes commuting to work every day, is looking to buy a house closer to her place of work. She has seen two houses: House A is better in terms of size but worse in terms of commuting time, while House B is worse in terms of size but better in terms of commuting time. The two houses are represented in Figure 13.1 as points in a two-attribute diagram. Each axis represents an attribute, which gets better as one moves away from the origin: one attribute is the size of the house (the larger the square footage the better) and the other is saving in commuting time relative to the current time of 75 minutes (the greater the amount of time saved the better).

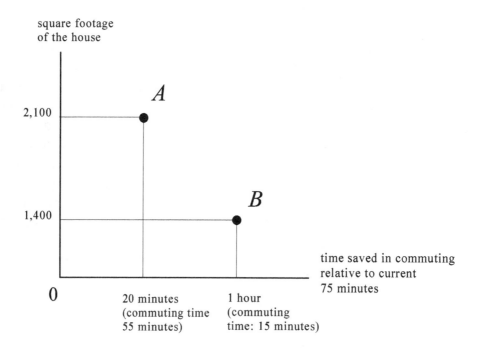

Figure 13.1: Two houses described in terms of two attributes

Suppose that Erin is unable to come up with a ranking of these two houses, that is, her preferences fail to be complete. It has been shown that in such situations people are susceptible to manipulation. For example, if you are a real estate agent and you want to induce Erin to buy House A (e.g. because you will get a larger commission), then what you could do is show her a third house which is worse than A in both dimensions, call this house $A\downarrow$. House $A\downarrow$ is shown in Figure 13.2. Erin will notice that A is unambiguously better than $A\downarrow$ and is likely to then take the extra step of ranking A also above B and thus end up choosing A.[2]

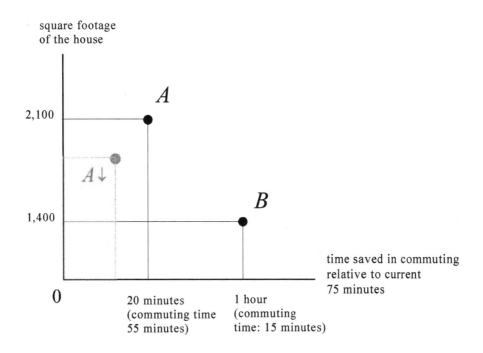

Figure 13.2: A third house, $A\downarrow$, which is inferior to A

In Chapter 1 of his book *Predictably irrational*, Dan Ariely gives several examples of this phenomenon. In an interesting experiment, Ariely and his co-authors presented several women with the photographs of two handsome men, call them A and B, and asked with whom they would want to go on a date. More or less 50% chose A and the other 50% chose B. They then presented another group of women with the photographs of *three* men: the same two as before, A and B, plus a less attractive version of A, call him $A\downarrow$, obtained by "photoshopping" the original photo of A, creating a distorted nose, a less symmetric face, etc. Of the second group of women, 75% chose A and only 25% chose B! A similar result was obtained by presenting yet another group of women with a different triple of photographs: the same two as before, A and B, plus a less attractive version of B, call it $B\downarrow$: about 75% chose B and 25% chose A. The trend turned out to be the same, whether the choosers were women (looking at photographs of men) or men (looking at at photographs of women) and whether the prospective dates were handsome or not. As long as there was a worse version of one of the two, the better version was more likely to be chosen.

When preferences are incomplete the use of a third choice as a *decoy* can often be used to manipulate choice.

---

[2]Note that, while House $A\downarrow$ is worse than House A in both dimensions, it is better than House B in one dimension (size) but worse in the other (commuting time).

13.3 Gains versus losses

In Chapter 5 we introduced Expected Utility Theory and discussed the notion of attitude to risk within the context of money lotteries. Recall that a person is said to be risk averse if she prefers the expected value (with probability 1, that is, for sure) of a money lottery to the lottery, and risk loving if she has the opposite ranking. It has been amply documented that many people tend to be risk-averse when dealing with potential gains and risk-loving when dealing with potential losses. For example, if given a choice between receiving $50 for sure – call this lottery A – and tossing a fair coin and receiving $100 if the outcome is Heads and nothing if the outcome is Tails – call this lottery B – many people will prefer the former to the latter, thus displaying risk-aversion:

$$A = \begin{pmatrix} \$50 \\ 1 \end{pmatrix} \succ B = \begin{pmatrix} \$100 & \$0 \\ \frac{1}{2} & \frac{1}{2} \end{pmatrix}.$$

On the other hand, the same people when presented with a choice between *losing* $50 for sure – call this lottery A' – and tossing a coin and losing $100 if the outcome is Heads and nothing if the outcome is Tails – call this lottery B' – they will choose the latter, thus displaying risk-loving:

$$B' = \begin{pmatrix} -\$100 & -\$0 \\ \frac{1}{2} & \frac{1}{2} \end{pmatrix} \succ A' = \begin{pmatrix} -\$50 \\ 1 \end{pmatrix}.$$

Kahneman and Tversky[3] suggested that the reason for this tendency is rooted in an affective bias: "the aggravation that one experiences in losing a sum of money appears to be greater than the pleasure associated with gaining the same amount". This phenomenon is often referred to as *loss aversion*.

Is this different risk attitude towards potential gains and potential losses rational? The answer, of course, depends on what we mean by "rational". If we take Expected Utility Theory as capturing the notion of rationality when dealing with uncertainty (that is, when choosing among lotteries) then the answer is a qualified Yes: it is possible for a person with von Neumann-Morgenstern preferences to have the preferences indicated above for a pair of choices (A versus B and A' versus B') but *not systematically*.

Consider, for example, an individual who has an initial wealth of $100, satisfies the axioms of Expected Utility and, when offered a choice between lottery $A = \begin{pmatrix} \$50 \\ 1 \end{pmatrix}$ and lottery $B = \begin{pmatrix} \$100 & \$0 \\ \frac{1}{2} & \frac{1}{2} \end{pmatrix}$, states that she prefers A to B ($A \succ B$). Could she also prefer B' to A' ($B' \succ A'$), where $A' = \begin{pmatrix} -\$50 \\ 1 \end{pmatrix}$ and $B' = \begin{pmatrix} -\$100 & -\$0 \\ \frac{1}{2} & \frac{1}{2} \end{pmatrix}$? Given that her initial wealth is $100, the above lotteries can be re-written in terms of final wealth levels as follows:

$$A = \begin{pmatrix} \$150 \\ 1 \end{pmatrix}, B = \begin{pmatrix} \$200 & \$100 \\ \frac{1}{2} & \frac{1}{2} \end{pmatrix}, A' = \begin{pmatrix} \$50 \\ 1 \end{pmatrix} \text{ and } B' = \begin{pmatrix} \$0 & \$100 \\ \frac{1}{2} & \frac{1}{2} \end{pmatrix}$$

---

[3] Daniel Kahneman and Amos Tversky, Prospect theory: An analysis of decision under risk, *Econometrica*, 1979, Vol. 47, pages 263-291.

13.3 Gains versus losses

Let U be this individual's normalized von Neumann-Morgenstern utility function on the set of wealth levels $\{\$0, \$50, \$100, \$150, \$200\}$. Assuming that she prefers more wealth to less,

$$\begin{array}{cc} \text{outcome} & U \\ \$200 & 1 \\ \$150 & a \\ \$100 & b \\ \$50 & c \\ \$0 & 0 \end{array} \quad \text{with} \quad 0 < c < b < a < 1. \tag{13.1}$$

Since she prefers $A = \begin{pmatrix} \$150 \\ 1 \end{pmatrix}$ to $B = \begin{pmatrix} \$200 & \$100 \\ \frac{1}{2} & \frac{1}{2} \end{pmatrix}$, $U(\$150) = a > \frac{1}{2}U(\$200) + \frac{1}{2}U(\$100) = \frac{1}{2}(1+b)$, that is,

$$2a > 1 + b. \tag{13.2}$$

If she also prefers $B' = \begin{pmatrix} \$0 & \$100 \\ \frac{1}{2} & \frac{1}{2} \end{pmatrix}$ to $A' = \begin{pmatrix} \$50 \\ 1 \end{pmatrix}$, then $\frac{1}{2}U(\$0) + \frac{1}{2}U(\$100) = \frac{1}{2}b > U(\$50) = c$, that is:

$$b > 2c. \tag{13.3}$$

Inequalities (13.2) and (13.3) are compatible with each other. For example, the following values satisfy both inequalities: $a = 0.8$, $b = 0.4$ and $c = 0.1$. Hence, it is possible for an individual with von Neumann-Morgenstern preferences to display risk aversion towards a potential gain and risk loving towards a symmetric loss. However, this *cannot happen at every wealth level*. To see this, consider the same individual whose utility function (13.1) satisfies inequalities (13.2) and (13.3), but with a different initial wealth than before, say $\$200$.[4] Then the prospect of losing $\$50$ for sure corresponds to the wealth lottery $A'' = \begin{pmatrix} \$150 \\ 1 \end{pmatrix}$ while the prospect of losing $\$100$ with probability $\frac{1}{2}$ and nothing with probability $\frac{1}{2}$ corresponds to the wealth lottery $B'' = \begin{pmatrix} \$100 & \$200 \\ \frac{1}{2} & \frac{1}{2} \end{pmatrix}$ and risk loving towards these potential losses requires that $B'' \succ A''$, that is, $\frac{1}{2}U(\$100) + \frac{1}{2}U(\$200) = \frac{1}{2}b + \frac{1}{2}1 > U(\$150) = a$, that is,

$$2a < 1 + b \tag{13.4}$$

but (13.4) contradicts (13.2).

---

[4]We could add outcomes $\$250$ and $\$300$ and assign to them utility d and e respectively, with $1 < d < e$, but it is not necessary for the argument below.

As noted by Kahneman and Tversky (*Econometrica*, 1979, p. 277), people tend to evaluate options in terms of changes in wealth or welfare, rather than final states. They observe that this is

> "[...] compatible with basic principles of perception and judgment. Our perceptual apparatus is attuned to the evaluation of changes or differences rather than to the evaluation of absolute magnitudes. When we respond to attributes such as brightness, loudness, or temperature, the past and present context of experience defines an adaptation level, or reference point, and stimuli are perceived in relation to this reference point. Thus, an object at a given temperature may be experienced as hot or cold to the touch depending on the temperature to which one has adapted. The same principle applies to non-sensory attributes such as health, prestige, and wealth."

People who are consistently (that is, at every initial level of wealth) risk-averse towards gains and risk-loving towards losses cannot satisfy the axioms of expected utility. If those axioms capture the notion of rationality, then those people are irrational.

13.4 Framing

Consider the situation described in Figure 13.3. Which option would you choose?

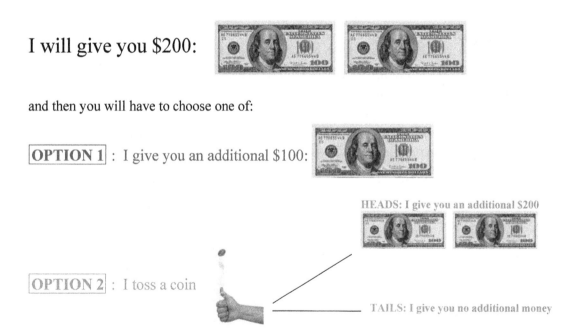

Figure 13.3: A choice between two money lotteries

13.4 Framing

Now consider the situation described in Figure 13.4. Which option would you choose?

I will give you $400:

and then you will have to choose one of:

OPTION 1 : **You pay a tax of $100**.

OPTION 2 : I toss a coin

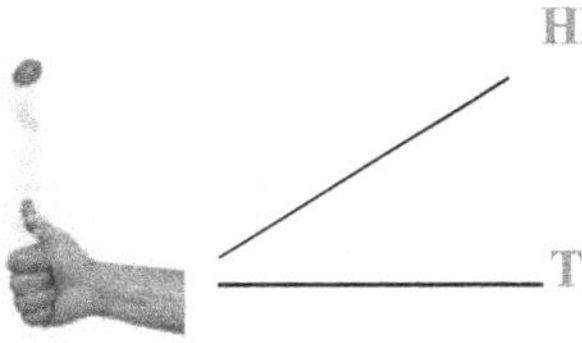

HEADS: You pay no tax

TAILS: You pay a tax of $200

Figure 13.4: Another choice between two money lotteries

In experiments many people stated that in the situation described in Figure 13.3 they would choose Option 1, while in the situation described in Figure 13.4 they would choose Option 2. Such a response can be seen as a reflection of the phenomenon described in the previous section, namely the different risk attitude towards potential gains and towards potential losses: the situation described in Figure 13.3 has to do with potential gains and the risk-averse response is to choose Option 1, while the situation described in Figure 13.4 has to do with potential losses and the risk-loving response is to choose Option 2.

However, in this case we have a more fundamental violation of rationality than in the case described in the previous section, because *there is no difference between the two situations described in Figures 13.3 and 13.4!* Let W be your initial wealth. In the situation described in Figure 13.3, Option 1 leaves you with a final wealth of $\$(W+300)$ and the same is true of Option 1 in the situation described in Figure 13.4! Similarly, in the situation described in Figure 13.3, Option 2 corresponds to the money lottery (in terms of final wealth) $\begin{pmatrix} \$(W+400) & \$(W+200) \\ \frac{1}{2} & \frac{1}{2} \end{pmatrix}$ and the same is true of Option 2 in the situation described in Figure 13.4! Thus, in both situations you are asked to choose between $\$(W+300)$ for sure and the lottery $\begin{pmatrix} \$(W+400) & \$(W+200) \\ \frac{1}{2} & \frac{1}{2} \end{pmatrix}$.

People who choose Option 1 in one case and Option 2 in the other fall victim to the *framing effect*. Framing is the phenomenon by which people rank the *same* two alternatives differently, depending on how the alternatives are presented or described to them.

As documented by Kahneman and Tversky[5], even well-educated people fall easily prey to framing. They presented a group of doctors and public health officials with what has become known as the "Asian disease problem":

> Imagine that the United States is preparing for the outbreak of an unusual Asian disease, which is expected to kill 600 people. Two alternative programs to combat the disease have been proposed. Assume that the exact scientific estimates of the consequences of the programs are as follows:
>
> - If Program A is adopted, 200 people will be saved.
> - If Program B is adopted, there is a one-third probability that 600 people will be saved and a two-thirds probability that no people will be saved.

Of the respondents, 72% chose Program A while the remaining 28% chose Program B.

A second group was presented with the following description:

> Imagine that the United States is preparing for the outbreak of an unusual Asian disease, which is expected to kill 600 people. Two alternative programs to combat the disease have been proposed. Assume that the exact scientific estimates of the consequences of the programs are as follows:
>
> - If Program A is adopted, 400 people will die.
> - If Program B is adopted, there is a one-third probability that nobody will die and a two-thirds probability that 600 people will die.

In this case the percentages were reversed: the great majority of respondents chose Program B.

As in the previous example, there is no difference between Program A in the first description and Program A in the second description: when the total number of potential victims is 600, "200 people will be saved" is the same outcome as "400 people will die"; similarly, Program B is the same in both descriptions: it corresponds to the lottery $\left(\begin{array}{cc} \text{no deaths} & \text{600 deaths} \\ \frac{1}{3} & \frac{2}{3} \end{array} \right)$. What explains the different response to the two descriptions is that the first is framed in terms of gains (lives saved) and the risk-averse response is to choose Program A, while the second description is framed in terms of losses and the risk-loving response is to choose Program B.

---

[5] Amos Tversky and Daniel Kahneman, The framing of decisions and the psychology of choice, *Science*, 1981, Vol. 211, pages 453-458.

13.5 The confirmation bias

In Chapter 8 we discussed the notion of information and how to rationally revise one's beliefs in response to new information. In Chapter 9 we addressed the issues of how to assign a value to potential information and when it is worth acquiring costly information. Sometimes the issue is not whether or not to acquire information, but what information to acquire: what potential item of information is most useful? The principles discussed in Chapter 8 can be of help in answering this question.

In the late 1980s researchers presented a group of physicians with hypothetical diagnostic situations involving alternative items of information that could be acquired.[6] The subjects were told something along the following lines:

> You are facing a patient who could be suffering from one of two diseases, A and B, which are equally likely in the general population. The two diseases require very different treatments. For both diseases the two main symptoms are fever and a skin rash. It so happens that your patient has both symptoms. You remember a piece of information, namely that 66% of the patients with Disease A have fever and 34% do not. There are three additional pieces of information that you could be looking up:
>
> (I) information about the proportion of people with Disease B who have fever,
> (II) the proportion of people with Disease A who have a skin rash,
> (III) the proportion of people with Disease B who have a skin rash.
>
> It is an emergency situation and you only have time to look up one of the three. Which one would you choose, if any?

Let us see how one would approach this problem using the tools discussed in Chapter 8.

Since the patient has both F (fever) and R (rash) you should try to determine $P(A|F\&R)$. By Bayes' theorem,

$$P(A|F\&R) = \frac{P(F\&R|A)P(A)}{P(F\&R|A)P(A) + P(F\&R|B)P(B)}$$

Since the prior (the base rate) is

$$P(A) = P(B) = 0.5,$$

this reduces to

$$P(A|F\&R) = \frac{P(F\&R|A)}{P(F\&R|A) + P(F\&R|B)}.$$

Thus, one would need to know the proportions of people with Diseases A and B who have both fever and rash. Unfortunately, the only information we are given is the percentage of

---

[6] F.M. Wolf, L.D. Gruppen and J.E. Billi, Differential diagnosis and the competing-hypotheses heuristic. A practical approach to judgment under uncertainty and Bayesian probability, *Journal of the American Medical Association*, 1985, Vol. 253, pages 2858-2862. We follow the account given in J. Frank Yates, *Judgment and decision making*, 1990, Prentice Hall, page 177.

people with Disease A who have fever, that is, $P(F|A) = 0.66$. We do not even have the potential to learn $P(F\&R|A)$ and $P(F\&R|B)$: neither of these two pieces of information is listed above as a possibility. Then the best course of action is to take advantage of the information one does have, namely that $P(F|A) = 0.66$. Using Bayes' rule again we have that

$$P(A|F) = \frac{P(F|A)P(A)}{P(F|A)P(A) + P(F|B)P(B)} = \frac{(0.66)(0.5)}{(0.66)(0.5) + P(F|B)0.5} = \frac{0.66}{0.66 + P(F|B)}.$$

Thus, the information that one should seek out is item (I) in the list given above, namely $P(F|B)$: the proportion of patients with Disease B who have fever. If $P(F|B) < 0.66$ then one would judge Disease A to be more likely than Disease B and if $P(F|B) > 0.66$ then one would diagnose Disease B.[7]

In the experiment, most physicians opted for item (II) in the above list: the proportion of people with Disease A who have a skin rash ($P(A|R)$). The rationale for this is that when one sees that the patient has fever and that 66% of patients with Disease A have fever, one hypothesizes that the patient has Disease A. Given that hypothesis, one forms the expectation that item (II) would reveal that a high percentage of Disease A victims have a skin rash. The request for item (II) from the above list represents an instance of *positive testing*, whereby a person seeks information that is expected to be consistent with one's current hypothesis. Item (II), however, is not useful in this example. Suppose that you discover that, say, 75% of Disease A victims have rashes. Would this affect how sure you are that you were correct in your hypothesis that the patient has Disease A? If you are like many people, you will become even more convinced that you were right. However, since you know nothing about the commonness of either fever or rash among Disease B victims, your newly acquired information about rash does not help you differentiate between the two diseases.

What we have described above is an instance of the so-called *confirmation bias*, which is the tendency to search for information that confirms one's prior beliefs. As Kahneman observes,[8]

> "Contrary to the rules of philosophers of science, who advise testing hypotheses by trying to refute them, people (and scientists, quite often) seek data that are likely to be compatible with the beliefs they currently hold."

---

[7]If $P(F|B) < 0.66$ then $P(A|F) > \frac{1}{2}$ and thus $P(B|F) < \frac{1}{2}$. Similarly, if $P(F|B) > 0.66$ then $P(A|F) < \frac{1}{2}$ and thus $P(B|F) > \frac{1}{2}$. Item (II) on the list is $P(A|R)$ and item (III) is $P(B|R)$; neither of these two can be usefully combined with the information at hand, namely the value of $P(A|F)$.

[8]Daniel Kahneman, *Thinking, fast and slow*, 2013, page 66.

13.6 The psychology of decision making

We conclude this chapter by mentioning other common cognitive biases and decision-making biases, without going into the details. The interested reader is referred to the references listed in Footnote 1 as well as to overviews given in TED talks by Dan Ariely[9], Dan Gilbert[10], Daniel Kahneman[11] and others.[12] For a comprehensive list of systematic biases in judgment and decision making see https://en.wikipedia.org/wiki/List_of_cognitive_biases. Examples of items on this list are the following:

- The *anchoring bias* is the tendency to be influenced by a (often irrelevant) piece of information – the "anchor"– received before a judgment is formed or a decision is made.[13]

- The *status quo bias* arises when the current state of affairs (or *status quo*) is taken as a reference point and any change from that baseline is perceived as a loss. We tend to want things to remain the way they are, even if we did not originally make the choice(s) that led to the *status quo*.[14]

- The *endowment effect* is the tendency to overvalue an object merely because one owns it. People are commonly willing to pay less to obtain a good than they are willing to accept as payment for selling the good.[15]

An excellent discussion of the psychology of decision making is provided by Dan Gilbert in his book *Stumbling on happiness* (2007, Vintage).

---

[9] https://www.ted.com/search?q=dan+arieli
[10] https://www.ted.com/search?q=dan+gilbert
[11] https://www.ted.com/search?q=daniel+kahneman
[12] https://www.ted.com/search?q=behavioral+economics
[13] See, for example, Amos Tversky and Daniel Kahneman, Judgment under uncertainty: heuristics and biases, *Science*, 1974, Vol. 185, pages 1124-1131.
[14] See, for example, Samuelson, W. and Zeckhauser, R., Status quo bias in decision making. *Journal of Risk and Uncertainty*, 1988, Vol.1, pages 7-59.
[15] An early laboratory demonstration of the endowment effect was offered by Jack Knetsch and J.A Sinden, Willingness to pay and compensation demanded: experimental evidence of an unexpected disparity in measures of value, *Quarterly Journal of Economics*, 1984, Vol. 99, pages 507-521. The participants in this study were endowed with either a lottery ticket or $2. Some time later, each subject was offered an opportunity to trade the lottery ticket for the money, or vice versa. Very few subjects chose to switch. See also Richard Thaler, Toward a positive theory of consumer choice, *Journal of Economic Behavior and Organization*, 1980, pages 39-60.

Index

Symbols

(β, δ) model 232

A

act 28
    strictly dominant 30
    weakly dominant 31
affine transformation 79
aggregation of preferences 253
Allais paradox 86
Ariely, Dan 317
Arrovian social welfare function 255
Arrow's impossibility theorem . . 258, 262
Arrow, Kenneth 254
attitude to risk
    aversion 183
    neutrality 48, 179
auction
    first price 32
    second price 33

B

backward induction 50, 104
basic outcome 73
Bayes' formula 137, 139, 140
Bayes' rule 137, 139, 140
behavioral economics 315
belief 157
    AGM revision function 162
    probabilistic revision 163
    revision 157, 160
    updating 157
binary relation 16
Borda count 293

C

choice
    framing 320
    manipulation 22, 316
conditional probability 136
Condorcet method 291
Condorcet paradox 253
confirmation bias 323

D

decision problem 28
decision tree 43, 101
dictator 259, 287
discount factor 223
discount rate 223
discounting 222
    exponential 225

E

Ellsberg paradox 88
expected utility 75
expected value 48

F

framing 320
freedom of expression 258

G

gain 318
Gibbard, Alan 296
Gibbard-Satterthwaite theorem 297

H

Hurwicz index 109

I

impatience 222
independence 130, 137
    irrelevant alternatives 261
index of pessimism 110
information 155, 173
    imperfect 186
    partition 156
    perfect 156, 179, 183
    set 156
    sources 197
    value 179, 183
interest rate 223
irrelevant alternatives 261

K

Kahneman, Daniel 315
Kemeny-Young method 264

    hyperbolic 232
distribution 129
    joint 130
    marginal 130
dominance 29, 30
    strict 29, 30
    weak 30, 31

L

LexiMin 35
loss 318
loss aversion 318
lottery
    compound 81
    money 48
    simple 73

M

majority voting 253
manipulation of choice 22, 316
MaxiMin 34
MinMaxRegret 36, 105
money lottery 48
money pump 22

N

natural frequencies 132
non-dictatorship 260, 287, 296
non-manipulability 291, 297
normalized utility function 78

P

Pareto principle 259
partition 156
plausibility order 161
preference
    aggregation 253
preference relation 16
    indifference 17
    strict preference 17
preferences
    completeness 17, 81
    transitivity 17, 81
present bias 235
present value 222
probability 129
    conditional 136
    distribution 129
    independence 130, 137
    joint 130
    marginal 130

measure 129
sample space 129
psychology 325

R

rate
dicsount 223
interest 223
rational choice 20
rationality 258
regret 36, 105
revision 157, 160
risk
aversion 183
neutrality 179

S

Satterthwaite, Mark 296
set
complement 128
De Morgan's Laws 128
disjoint 128
intersection 128
subset 127
union 128
Simpson's paradox 142
social choice function 285
social preference function 255
state 27
strategic voting 288
strategy-proofness 291, 297
strict dominance 29
strictly dominant 30

T

Thaler, Richard 315
time consistency 229
time inconsistency 233, 236
tree 43

U

unanimity 259, 287, 296
unrestricted domain 258
updating 157

utility
discounted 227
exponential 227
utility function 18
normalized 78
ordinal 18
von Neumann-Morgenstern ... 75
utility maximization 21

V

von Neumann-Morgenstern
ranking 74
utility function 75
voting
Borda count 293
Condorcet method 291
default alternative .. 288, 291
plurality 288
strategic 288

W

weak dominance 30
weakly dominant 31

CPSIA information can be obtained
at www.ICGtesting.com
Printed in the USA
LVHW100107300819
629482LV00013B/186/P